# A Sesquicentennial History of Iowa State University

# Tradition and Transformation

# A Sesquicentennial History of Iowa State University
# Tradition and Transformation

*Editors*
Dorothy Schwieder
Gretchen Van Houten

*Authors*
John R. Anderson
J. L. Anderson
Jenny Barker Devine
Amy Bix
Peter Butler
Charles M. Dobbs
David Hamilton
Gregory L. Geoffroy
Tom Kroeschell
Pamela Riney-Kehrberg
Dorothy Schwieder

Published on the occasion of
Iowa State University's
anniversary of its charter date on March 22, 1858.

Iowa State University Press

Dorothy Schwieder, volume editor, was a member of the Iowa State University history faculty from 1966 to 2000. She has written or coauthored seven books on Iowa history, the most recent being *Iowa: The Middle Land* (Iowa State University Press, 1996).

Gretchen Van Houten, executive editor, has worked in the publishing industry from the early eighties in various capacities from proofreader to editorial director, including as director at Iowa State University Press.

Iowa State University Library/Special Collections Department supplied source material for many of the vignettes.

Iowa State University Press is an imprint of:
Blackwell Publishing Professional
2121 State Avenue, Ames, Iowa 50014, USA

Orders:      1-800-862-6657
Office:      1-515-292-0140
Fax:         1-515-292-3348
Web site:    www.blackwellprofessional.com

Blackwell Publishing Ltd
9600 Garsington Road, Oxford OX4 2DQ, UK
Tel.: +44 (0)1865 776868

Blackwell Publishing Asia
550 Swanston Street, Carlton, Victoria 3053, Australia
Tel.: +61 (0)3 8359 1011

Authorization to photocopy items for internal or personal use, or the internal or personal use of specific clients, is granted by Blackwell Publishing, provided that the base fee is paid directly to the Copyright Clearance Center, 222 Rosewood Drive, Danvers, MA 01923. For those organizations that have been granted a photocopy license by CCC, a separate system of payments has been arranged. The fee codes for users of the Transactional Reporting Service are ISBN-13: 978-0-8138-1651-7/2007 $.10.

First edition, 2007

Library of Congress Cataloging-in-Publication Data

A sesquicentennial history of Iowa State University: tradition and
transformation/editors, Dorothy Schwieder with Gretchen Van Houten;
authors, John R. Anderson...[et al.].
    p. cm.
  Includes bibliographical references and index.
  ISBN-13: 978-0-8138-1651-7 (alk. paper)
  ISBN-10: 0-8138-1651-3 (alk. paper)
  1. Iowa State University—History.  I. Schwieder, Dorothy, 1933- II. Van Houten,
Gretchen. III. Anderson, John R.
  LD2547.S47 2007
  378.777'546—dc22
                         2006023697

The last digit is the print number: 9 8 7 6 5 4 3 2 1

# Contents

# Contributors

## Editors

**Dorothy Schwieder,** Volume Editor. University Professor Emerita of History, Iowa State University

Volume editor Dorothy Schwieder was a member of the Iowa State University history faculty from 1966 to 2000, during which time she taught the History of Iowa course almost every semester. Dr. Schwieder taught in-service Iowa history courses to area public schools teachers and has presented hundreds of talks on Iowa history to groups throughout the state. She served on the board for the State Historical Society of Iowa for eighteen years and on the Humanities Iowa Speakers Bureau for fifteen. She has written or coauthored seven books on Iowa history, the most recent being *Iowa: The Middle Land* (Iowa State University Press, 1996).

**Gretchen Van Houten,** Executive Editor

Editorial consultant Gretchen Van Houten has worked in the publishing industry from 1982 through 2006 in various capacities from proofreader to editorial director. She was the last director at Iowa State University Press before it was sold to Blackwell Science, now Blackwell Publishing, Inc. She stayed on at Blackwell as editorial director, overseeing a successful transition to commercial publishing, and eventually became senior publisher for the agriculture list. In her years at Iowa State Press, Ms. Van Houten worked in a developmental role with authors on numerous books about Iowa, many of them histories aimed at a general readership.

## Contributors

**John R. Anderson** is Assistant to the President for Communications at Iowa State University. He has been employed by Iowa State since 1980 in communications and administrative positions.

**J. L. Anderson** holds a Ph.D. in Agricultural History and Rural Studies from Iowa State University. His dissertation is a study of the ways farmers used technology in the post-World War II period to remake their fields and farmsteads. In August 2006 he joined the History Department of the University of West Georgia as an Assistant Professor.

**Jenny Barker Devine** is a Ph.D. Candidate in the Agricultural History and Rural Studies program at Iowa State University. She is the author of *A Century of Brotherhood: 100 Years of Sigma Alpha Epsilon at Iowa State University* (Ames: Sigma Alpha Epsilon, McMillan Publishing, 2005).

**Amy Bix** is Associate Professor of History at Iowa State University and a faculty member of Iowa State's Program in the History of Technology and Science. Her book *Inventing Ourselves Out of Jobs? America's Debate over Technological Unemployment, 1929–1981* was published by Johns Hopkins University Press in 2000. She is currently finishing a book entitled *Engineering Education for American Women: An Intellectual, Institutional, and Social History.*

**Peter Butler** is a lecturer in the Department of Landscape Architecture at Iowa State University. He holds a Bachelor of Arts degree in English–Creative Writing from the University of Wisconsin–Madison, a Bachelor of Landscape Architecture degree from Iowa State University, and a Master of Landscape Architecture degree from Iowa State University. He teaches beginning and upper-level Landscape Architecture design studios.

**Charles M. Dobbs** is a Professor of History at Iowa State University. He earned his B.A. from the University of Connecticut and his M.A. and Ph.D. from Indiana University, all in history. He is the author of *The Unwanted Symbol* (1981) and *The United States and East Asia Since 1945* (1990). He recently finished *Triangles, Symbols, and Constraints: The United States, the Soviet Union, and the People's Republic of China, 1963–1969* and is currently working on *Trade and Security: The United States and East Asia, 1961–1969.*

**David Hamilton** is Associate Professor of History at the University of Kentucky (Lexington). He earned his B.S. at Iowa State in 1976 and his Ph.D. at the University of Iowa in 1985. He has written *From New Day to New Deal: American Farm Policy from Hoover to Roosevelt, 1928–1933* (1991). His wife, Cynthia Parks Hamilton, is also an Iowa State graduate (1976) and the daughter of W. Robert Parks.

**Gregory Geoffroy** is the fourteenth President of Iowa State University (inaugurated July 1, 2001). He also holds the rank of Professor of Chemistry. He previously served as Senior Vice President for Academic Affairs and Provost at the University of Maryland and as a faculty member and administrator at the Pennsylvania State University. He earned a B.S. from the University of Louisville and a Ph.D. in chemistry from the California Institute of Technology.

**Tom Kroeschell** is Associate Athletics Director for Media Relations at Iowa State University. He has worked as a Cyclone athletic publicist since 1985.

**Pamela Riney-Kehrberg** is Professor of History and Director of the Program in Agricultural History and Rural Studies. She is author and editor of three books, *Rooted In Dust* (1994), *Waiting on the Bounty* (1999), and *Childhood on the Farm* (2005).

# Preface and Acknowledgments

In 1942, Earle Dudley Ross published his long-awaited history of Iowa State College, covering its first eighty years. Ross's history describes the early struggles of "the college on the prairie," its important land-grant mission, the heavy emphasis on agricultural courses and research, and the gradual expansion of other curricula. While Ross's book, *The History of Iowa State College*, has stood the test of time, more than a half century has elapsed since its first printing.

In 2008, Iowa State University celebrates its 150th anniversary. In planning for that celebration, the university's Sesquicentennial Committee chose as its major project the preparation of a current history of the university. Their plan was to build on Earle Ross's earlier history rather than duplicate it. Accordingly, this book is designed to accomplish two goals: to emphasize the history of Iowa State University from 1940 to 2000 and at the same time to provide readers with historical context by sketching out in very broad strokes the school's earlier development from 1869 to 1940.

The second major decision concerned the content itself. A Book Advisory Committee was formed to help with the difficult work of determining content and method of organization. Faced with time and space limitations, the editors and the committee decided to produce an anthology, each chapter dealing with an important part of Iowa State's history and each written by a different expert. The resulting ten chapters are divided into two parts: part 1, composed of four chapters, first provides a brief look at the major developments in the school's first eighty years. The remaining three chapters of part 1 present a chronological approach to the period since 1940, highlighting the school's presidential administrations. The six chapters in part 2 examine Iowa State's history since 1940 from a different perspective, that of major topics such as athletics and student life. By combining the chronological and topical approaches, this study provides for a more encompassing look at the past as well as a more interesting one. Regrettably, given the tremendous growth in all areas of the school's history during the past sixty years, not all deserving topics could be included, particularly the development of major departments and programs.

Part 1 begins with a summary chapter of Iowa State's first eighty years. In "Foundations of the People's College: The Early Years of Iowa State," Pamela Riney-Kehrberg, ISU Professor of History, writes about the reasons for the creation of the college and the needs to which the college responded in its early years. Throughout, Professor Kehrberg places emphasis on the state's political, economic, and cultural forces that helped to shape the college and its student body through the school's often difficult years of development and depression. Professor Kehrberg's chapter provides an indispensable background and springboard for understanding the ever-increasingly varied and numerous developments that followed.

The remaining three chapters in part 1 provide readers with a view of the school's development primarily from the perspectives of five of Iowa State's presidents: Charles E. Friley, James H. Hilton, W. Robert Parks, Gordon P. Eaton, and Martin Jischke. In chapter 2, "Iowa State at Mid-Century: The Friley and Hilton Years," ISU History Professor Emerita Dorothy Schwieder details the school's development during the Friley and Hilton eras, the years from 1940 to 1965. Friley presided over the school during the desperate years of the Great Depression and World War II, which were followed by explosive enrollments after the war. Iowa State's myriad contributions to the war effort are described, along with the changes brought by the enrollment of veterans. In 1953, Hilton became the tenth president of Iowa State, the only alumnus to hold that position. The Hilton years were marked by economic difficulty throughout the state but almost continual growth in enrollment and significant campus expansion. In 1959, Iowa State College became, fittingly, Iowa State University. Hilton's dream of an Iowa State Center was initiated during his presidency. While the Friley and Hilton years were seemingly slower paced and less dynamic than the hectic days of the mid-sixties, the policies initiated in both administrations laid the groundwork for the innovative and far-reaching changes that followed.

David Hamilton, Associate Professor of History at the University of Kentucky, provides a personal and scholarly look at W. Robert Parks's twenty-one-year tenure as president of Iowa State. In "Science with Humanity: The Parks Years," Hamilton writes about Parks's background, leadership style, and aspirations for the university. He places the Parks years in the broader context of the sometimes violent protests of the Vietnam era, important political events, and Parks's continual but sometimes unsuccessful efforts to implement his program of "The New Humanism." Hamilton discusses pressures for change at the university, tensions regarding faculty matters, and, more generally, the suspicion and the mistrust that developed toward public institutions during the 1960s and 1970s. Given Parks's long tenure and the many changes in students' social values as well as pressing external political and economic change, the Parks years were a crucial period.

Charles M. Dobbs, Professor of History at Iowa State, completes the trilogy of chapters addressing presidential administrations. The title of Dobbs's chapter, "Strategic Focus and Accountability: The Eaton-Jischke Years," is particularly descriptive of the years from 1986 to 2000. Dobbs points out that Eaton reasserted the school's basic mission of science and technology, focusing on practical research that brought money into the university. Eaton initiated the largest fund-raising effort up to that time and by 1990 vowed to make Iowa State the nation's top land-grant university. President Jischke continued many of Eaton's programs but also made a strong effort to connect the university to the people of Iowa, initiating visits by Iowa State faculty and staff to all parts of the state. Both Eaton and Jischke faced periods of economic difficulty, which made it essential to secure more money through major fund-raising campaigns and from other outside sources. As Dobbs makes clear, the programs advanced by Eaton and Jischke were not always popular with ISU faculty.

The chapters in part 2 take a different approach. Institutions of higher learning exist because of the students who attend and the faculty who educate them; everyone lives and works, moreover, within a common setting, the campus itself. The first of these chapters, "Loyal and Forever True: Student Life at Iowa State University," is written by Jenny Barker Devine, ISU history graduate student. Barker Devine provides a detailed and engaging view of the many generations of students who matriculated here. She emphasizes student activities during World War II, the new activities and organizations that emerged after the war, and the social changes of the 1960s. Student life changed dramatically in the 1960s and 1970s, changes reflected in students' social activities, organizational life, and involvement in activities such as the civil rights movement and the Vietnam War protests. As Barker Devine points out, student life continued to change in major ways in the 1980s and 1990s.

Rounding out the coverage of student life is the chapter "Athletics at Iowa State University, " written by Tom Kroeschell, ISU Associate Athletics Director, Media Relations. Kroeschell provides a comprehensive view of changes in athletic programs, tracing their history from the days of Pop Warner in the late 1800s through the roaring twenties, the Great Depression, up to the present. He covers the rise of women's athletics and the creation of the Big 12 Conference. Kroeschell writes about team activities as well as the feats of outstanding athletes and the personalities of the various coaches at ISU. He not only surveys a wide array of topics that highlight sport activities but also details outstanding occurrences such as the tragic plane crash that killed members of the women's cross-country track team.

Amy Bix, ISU Associate Professor of History, has contributed the chapter entitled "Iowa State Faculty: The People and the Disciplines." Professor Bix highlights the ways in which the composition of the faculty has changed since the 1940s, the diversification of faculty in terms of gender and race, and the ever-increasing professionalization of faculty. Like the student body, faculty have responded both to internal and external influences, particularly the political issues of the 1960s, and the need for greater diversity among both faculty and students. Bix traces out the changes in faculty governance and the faculty's relationship to both students and administrators.

While most chapters deal with campus personnel or programs, J. L. Anderson, University of West Georgia History Department, writes about Iowa State's outreach programs. Anderson writes in "The People's University: Iowa State Cooperative Extension and Outreach" that perhaps the most defining characteristic of the school's land-grant status is ISU's Cooperative Extension, which through the years has tied the campus to every part of the state. Anderson traces the development of Extension from the early days of the Corn Trains to the present statewide programs serving both rural and urban populations. Anderson includes discussion of other outreach programs including WOI-TV and Radio.

The most commonly shared experience of all ISU students and faculty is the campus itself; students, faculty members, even visitors to the ISU campus retain a strong sense of its buildings, its landscaping, in essence, its beauty. In chapter 9,

"The Practical and the Picturesque: The Iowa State Campus," Peter Butler, lecturer in Landscape Architecture, writes about Iowa State as "place." Butler discusses the many stages of development from the original siting of the college to the philosophy of ISU's presidents and includes the many influences operating on the actual architectural plans for campus buildings. He discusses Iowa State's many pieces of public art as well as the artists who created them.

The final chapter deals with the way in which university programs and university graduates have affected the state, the nation, and the world. John R. Anderson, Assistant to the President for Communications at ISU, writes about a broad range of topics such as establishment of the Ames Laboratory, the Center for Agricultural and Rural Development (CARD), and, more recently, the development of the World Food Conference. Anderson documents the struggle for recognition of ISU's role in developing the computer. His chapter is appropriately entitled "Impacts of Iowa State University: Its National and International Presence and Its Enduring Legacies." Anderson writes also about legacies on campus, particularly the impact of the first artist-in-residence, Christian Petersen. Anderson highlights the lives of outstanding Iowa Staters including faculty member J. V. Atanasoff and Frank Spedding as well as ISC athlete Jack Trice.

While the present history covers events through the administration of Martin Jischke, it seems fitting that this history should conclude with a look beyond the present. Iowa State President Gregory L. Geoffroy gives us an "Afterword: Poised the Future" in which he briefly discusses Iowa State today and his view of the school's future.

One final word about content: In an effort to enhance the personal side of the story, we have designed a format that includes short vignettes, primarily biographical sketches of former students, staff, and faculty. These pieces are placed between chapters. Here readers will find student remembrances of the 1940s, social activities of the 1950s, descriptions of extracurricular activities in the 1980s, and faculty reflections on changes in curriculum and student life. The Iowa State experience has been meaningful to tens of thousands of people who once worked and studied here. All persons, no doubt, have different remembrances of their college years—their special professors, their favorite classes, and meaningful friendships. We hope at least a few of these fond memories will be rekindled through the history and personal stories we tell here.

Several editorial decisions should also be mentioned. While the editors and the Book Advisory Committee clearly planned to emphasize ISU history from 1940 on, we also realized that Ross's book, written in the 1930s, had little, if any, coverage on subjects such as student life, athletics, and the physical development of the campus. It seemed fitting then to include the early history of select topics as well as post-1940 coverage. At the same time, to provide uniformity of chapter content, the decision was made to end the history in 2000. It should also be noted that to cover their topics most effectively, some authors have written about similar events but in different contexts, thus resulting in some duplication of material. Finally, a word about variations in institutional titles. Before 1959, when Iowa State College became Iowa State University, several name changes occurred. Originally known as Iowa State Agricultural College and Farm, the name was changed to Iowa State College of Agriculture and Mechanic Arts in 1882. However, college personnel were never consistent in their use of formal titles, also using the names Iowa Agricultural College or Iowa State College. Given these inconsistencies, the authors have used names most common during their research periods.

The acknowledgments for this project are many. To Paul Lasley and Roger Baer, we express our thanks for their initiation of this project as well as their continued support and confidence that the project could be completed. To Paul especially, a thank you for tenacious pursuit of personnel to get the project under way. To the Sesquicentennial Committee—Tanya Zanish-Belcher, Donald Beitz, Dianne Bystrom, Cynthia Jeffrey, Mary West Greenlee, Doug Kenealy, Steven Martin, Pamela Riney-Kehrberg, Steffen Schmidt, Ann Thompson, Joan Bowles, Carole Custer, Carol Gieseke, Marc Harding, John McCarroll, Patricia Miller, Mark Settle, Ann Wilson, Laura Bestler-Wilcox, Cory Hanson, Robert Harvey, Ed Lewis, Keith Whigham, and Jerry Klonglan—thank you all for your strong conviction that this up-to-date history of Iowa State should be the central focus of the Sesquicentennial celebration.

The Book Advisory Committee members—Andrej Plakans, Pamela Riney-Kehrberg, Charles Dobbs, and Tanya Zanish-Belcher, all of Iowa State, and Tom Morain, Director of Community Outreach at Graceland University—deserve special praise for their willingness to help shape this project from beginning to end and to be involved in each stage of production. They deserve much credit for the completion of the project.

A special thanks to our history graduate student, Jenny Barker Devine, for her willingness to undertake any task, always with good humor, and always resulting in work of the highest quality. Jenny's extensive knowledge of the archival holdings proved especially valuable.

The Special Collections Department of the Parks Library provided extraordinary assistance to everyone on the project. Director Tanya Zanish-Belcher offered support and assistance within the Archives and served as a source of archival expertise on both the Sesquicentennial and Book Advisory Committees. Our special thanks to Becky Jordan for typing many pages of student oral histories. Special Collections is a virtual treasure trove for all aspects of university history and the use of its resources has been indispensable to this history project.

We also wish to thank Warren Madden, ISU's Vice President for Business and Finance, and Tahira Hira, Assistant to the President for External Relations and Executive Administration and Professor of Human Development and Family Studies, for their unceasing efforts to complete all arrangements, both financial and contractual, for the publishing of the manuscript.

Our thanks go also to ISU President Gregory Geoffroy for his overall support of the project and for his willingness to approve financial support for the creation of the book.

Dorothy Schwieder, Volume Editor
Gretchen Van Houten, Executive Editor

# Some Historical Highlights

1858, March 22—Bill signed by Iowa Governor Ralph P. Lowe to establish State Agricultural College and Model Farm.

1861—Iowa State's first buildings, farmhouse, and cattle barn completed by local builders.

1862, September 11—Iowa first state to accept provisions of Morrill Act, designed to fund educational facilities in agriculture and mechanic arts.

1868—Adonijah Welch appointed as first President.

1869—First class of 173 students—136 men and 37 women—arrive on campus.

1870—Nation's first off-campus Extension programs, farmers' institutes, conducted by college farm superintendent.

1872—Iowa State graduates its first class of 26 students—24 men and 2 women.

1873—Students begin publishing *The Aurora*, Iowa State's first student newspaper.

1877—Iowa State awards its first Master of Science degree to J.C. Arthur, a student in botany, who goes on to become an expert on rust fungi.

1878—Alumni Association founded.

1879—College of Veterinary Medicine founded, first at a land-grant institution.

1888—Iowa State completes its Agricultural Experiment Station (Hatch Act, 1887).

1890—Morrill Hall completed, providing space for a library, chapel, museum, and recitation rooms.

1893—Class of 1894 publishes first edition of *The Bomb*, the Iowa State yearbook.

1894—George Washington Carver becomes Iowa State's first African American graduate.

1895—"Cyclone" designation earned following football upset against Northwestern.

1899—Campanile completed and installed with carillon of ten bells.

1899—Cardinal and gold chosen as official Iowa State colors.

1901—President Beardshear and family become first occupants of the Knoll.

1902—Fire destroys south wing of Old Main, causing housing crisis for students.

1904—Students found Cardinal Guild, later to become Government of Student Body.

1904—First Engineering Experiment Station in the nation established at Iowa State.

1906—Beardshear Hall completed to replace Old Main as central building on campus.

1912—First Homecoming celebration.

1916—LaVerne Noyes (Class of 1872) donates $10,000 for landscaping campus and constructing a lake.

1922—First VEISHEA held to celebrate accomplishments of the five colleges.

1928—Memorial Union completed at cost of nearly $1 million.

1934—Christian Petersen becomes Iowa State's first Artist-in-Residence.

1935—Swans Lancelot and Elaine presented to ISC by VEISHEA Central Committee.

1939—Friley Hall completed as men's dormitory to accommodate 1,420 students.

1939, October—Prototype of digital computer completed and demonstrated (later called the Atanasoff-Berry Computer).

1946—First Christmas Tree Lighting ceremony.

1947—U.S. Atomic Energy Commission locates major research facilities in Ames (Ames Laboratory).

1950—WOI-TV goes on the air on channel 4.

1954—Iowa State adopts Cy as official mascot.

1957—Creation of Center for Agricultural and Rural Development (CARD) furthers Iowa State's entry into world community.

1958—Iowa State celebrates its centennial.

1959, July 4—Iowa State College becomes Iowa State University of Science and Technology.

1966—University Extension formed from Cooperative Extension, Engineering Extension Service, the Center for Industrial Research and Service (CIRAS), and the Agriculture Short Course Office.

1968—Alumni and friends found the Order of the Knoll.

1969—C.Y. Stephens Auditorium, first building of Iowa State Center, completed.

1970—Black Cultural Center opens for African American students.

1975—Schemann Building dedicated, officially completing Iowa State Center.

1976—ISU hosts World Food Conference as its contribution to nation's bicentennial.

1981—Sloss House opens as a women's center.

1985—Institute for Physical Research and Technology (IPRT) created to secure federal funding for research in the physical sciences.

1986—Creation of ISU Research Park and ISIS (small business incubator).

1987-89—First ISU long-range strategic plan conceived and announced.

1988—Football stadium renamed in honor of Jack Trice, Iowa State's first African American football player.

1992—Carrie Chapman Catt Center for Women in Politics established.

1993—Sale of university-owned WOI-TV to Citadel Communications.

1994—Two-millionth volume added to library.

1994—Students publish last edition of *The Bomb*.

1995—Formation of Big 12 Conference from old Big Eight and former Southwest conferences.

2001—Beginning of fund-raising for restoration of Morrill Hall.

# Part I

# Vignettes

## Carrie Chapman Catt: A National Heroine

In 1877, a young farm woman from Floyd County enrolled at Iowa State Agricultural College and Model Farm. Carrie Lane, later to become Carrie Chapman Catt, would graduate three years later, and within two decades would be nationally recognized for her work promoting woman's suffrage. In 1920, the suffragists would succeed when the Nineteenth Amendment to the U.S. Constitution was ratified, granting women everywhere in the country the right to vote.

Carrie Lane arrived at Iowa State when the school was in its infancy. Classes had started less than a decade earlier and Carrie was the only female in a class of seventeen. Apparently she had looked at other schools but decided that Iowa State offered the best financial bargain. Like many students, Carrie worked to help pay her college expenses. She started washing dishes at nine cents per hour and also worked as a maid in a dormitory. At the end of her freshman year, she became the assistant librarian at ten cents an hour, and during her senior year, she was named as the library's first assistant.

As a young college student, Carrie displayed the same leadership qualities, tenacious nature, and political convictions that would distinguish her later career. Her most well-known accomplishment at Iowa State, the formation of a women's course in military training, underscores those traits. Carrie had heard the school commandant talk about the value of compulsory military exercise for men. Believing that the same exercise would benefit women, Carrie led a delegation of females to call on the instructor. Although somewhat amused at the request, he consented to drill the women but explained that he could not supply them with either uniforms or guns. He suggested they try "the local broom factory for implements of the regulation length." The women provided their own blue percale uniforms. The result was Company G (G for girls), which proudly marched around campus with their broomsticks. In another event that foreshadowed her future career, Carrie, as a member of the Crescent Literary Society, became the first woman to give an oration before a debating society at Iowa State, winning a debate on the subject of woman's suffrage.

Carrie graduated in 1880 at the top of her class and took a job as principal of Mason City High School. There she met her first husband, Leo Chapman, a local newspaper editor. Carrie was soon writing a column for the paper, entitled "Woman's World." While in Mason City, Carrie conducted a door-to-door survey asking women about their views on the issue of woman's

*(continued)*

suffrage. Later Catt insisted that she or her associates had visited every home in Mason City. The women's responses were overwhelmingly in favor of woman's suffrage. Catt would use that data again and again to counter the anti-suffragists' argument that women didn't really want the vote.

Following Leo Chapman's death, Carrie spent much of her time lecturing and organizing the suffrage campaign. In 1895, Carrie became involved in the major suffrage organization, the National American Woman Suffrage Association. She was elected president of the NAWSA in 1900. Earlier Carrie had married a fellow Iowa Stater, George Catt, and in 1904, she resigned her presidency of NAWSA because of her husband's poor health.

In 1915, suffragists convinced Catt to once again take the NAWSA presidency. Known as a superb organizer and an excellent speaker, Catt revitalized the group and set about campaigning for an amendment to the U.S. Constitution. Catt soon came up with a strategy that dominated the campaign from 1916 until 1920. She called it "the Winning Plan." The plan called for concerted action at both the state and federal levels. By 1916, eleven states had granted full suffrage to women; some states like Iowa had granted women the vote in specific elections. In states where the full vote had been secured, suffragists worked to convince their state legislators to send resolutions to the U.S. Congress, urging a national suffrage amendment. In the remaining states, women were to continue pushing state legislatures to pass suffrage amendments to their state constitutions. A major goal of the Winning Plan was to have close coordination between women working at both levels of government. After many frustrating disappointments, the suffragists would finally succeed. The U.S. House of Representatives passed the suffrage amendment in 1918, but the women would have to wait until 1919 for the U.S. Senate to do the same. That year, the Senate amendment carried, but just barely. Ratification by the necessary thirty-six states took place quickly, and on August 26, 1920, the struggle for woman's suffrage was over. Finally, everywhere in the country, women had full suffrage rights.

During her later years, Catt continued her reform work and received numerous honors for her many contributions to American society. In 1920, she helped organize the League of Women Voters based on the idea that political education is necessary for a well-functioning democracy. A short time later, Catt founded the National Committee on the Cause and Cure of War. In 1932, she received the Merit Award, bestowed by the Chicago Chapter of the ISC Alumni Association, one of the highest honors given by the college. Catt died in 1947. In 1995, ISU officials renamed Botany Hall Carrie Chapman Catt Hall, in Catt's honor. Officials also created the Plaza of Heroines whereby other women could be honored by having a brick inscribed with their name and placed in the plaza of Catt Hall.

Dorothy Schwieder

# "A Very Curious Little Contraption": Getting to and from Campus in the Early Years

From Iowa State's earliest days, the students and faculty have relied on the city of Ames for commerce and culture. Yet during the 1870s and 1880s, Ames was a separate town located three miles from the Iowa State campus. In 1873, when J. E. Cobbey arrived as a student, he walked from the depot in Ames through miles of "pastures and fields" to Old Main.

After 1874, the students' primary means of travel was the College Bus, a horse-drawn vehicle that made two or three daily trips between the campus and Ames. The bus lumbered over what is now Lincoln Way, then an "unpleasant and often difficult" road marred by frequent floods, mud, and deep ruts left by heavy wagon wheels. Nonetheless, Anna Dean, who graduated in 1892, recalled the excitement of riding on the bus at the start of each term and reuniting with all of her friends in front of Old Main.

By the end of the nineteenth century, this system was no longer adequate for the new "sophisticated" student. During the 1890s, Iowa State experienced tremendous growth, and these years saw the construction of modern facilities in Morrill Hall, Margaret Hall, and Botany Hall (now Catt Hall). It was within this progressive spirit, in August 1890, an editorial in the *Iowa State Student* favored the construction of a modern and efficient rail line into Ames. A rapid transit line, the editorial stated, would not only foster good relations between the city and the college but would transform Ames into "one of the most enthusiastic college towns in the west."

In January 1891, the Board of Trustees made a formal agreement with the Ames Street Railway Company for the construction of a railroad extending from central campus to downtown Ames. Only eight months later, in August 1892, the "Dinkey," a small, smoke-billowing steam engine pulling two or sometimes three passenger cars, made its first run from the campus depot, the Hub, located south of the newly constructed Morrill Hall. The tiny train quickly proved popular with students and faculty. For five cents per ride, they could easily go into town for shopping, concerts, and visiting "in just a few moments, and with just as much comfort on cold, wet days, as on warm, sunny ones." In November 1892, although enrollment stood at just 519, the *Aurora*, a student newspaper, reported that the Dinkey carried more than one thousand passengers within one twenty-four-hour period.

In general, the students and faculty of Iowa State held the tiny railroad in high regard. When Fredrica Shattuck arrived in the fall of 1907 as a professor of speech, she found the Dinkey to be "a very curious little contraption," like

(continued)

nothing she had ever seen before. Like the old College Bus, however, the Dinkey had its problems. Snow and flooding frequently interrupted regular service, as did occasional derailments and repairs to the tracks. Smoke and soot from the locomotives polluted the grounds, while the Board of Trustees worried that sparks from the smokestacks could set the campus ablaze.

Editorials often appeared in the *Iowa State Student* complaining of poor service, faulty equipment, and the potential for accidents. In March 1904, the editor of the *Iowa State Student* described the two Dinkey locomotives as "the most wonderful relics of antiquity" and the passenger cars as worth little more than "junk carriers."

In September 1907, after only sixteen years of service, the Dinkey made its final run through campus. The year before, in 1906, the Board of Trustees voted to replace the tiny steam engine with a cleaner, more efficient electric trolley operated by the Fort Dodge, Des Moines, and Southern Railway. After it began operation in the fall of 1907, the "Interurban," as the electric trolley was known, was considered a great improvement over the Dinkey. Yet it was not immune from scathing editorials in the *Iowa State Student*. Students complained that the slow-moving, overcrowded trolley rarely ran on time, often leaving passengers to wait for hours in "the raw, cold northwest wind."

Such complaints were not simply the grumblings of discontent students. In April 1909, Iowa State President Albert Boyton Storms wrote a lengthy letter to the president of the Fort Dodge, Des Moines, and Southern Railway complaining of poor, irregular service, especially during peak hours. He wrote that such faults were unacceptable, especially when the faculty, staff, and students "depend on this service for reaching their classes and laboratories."

During the 1920s, the Interurban faced increasing competition from a bus service between Ames and the campus, as well as increased automobile ownership. The town was growing rapidly, and no longer seemed so far away from Iowa State. As early as 1921, the Fort Dodge, Des Moines, and Southern Railway reported a sharp decline in the number of passengers. The trend continued throughout the decade, until 1930, when the Interurban service was discontinued and the tracks removed from campus.

Jenny Barker Devine

# Jack Trice: Once Forgotten, Always Remembered

Jack Trice was born the son of Green and Anna Trice in 1902 in Hiram, Ohio. Trice attended East Tech High School in Cleveland, where he was a star athlete. When his football coach, Sam Willaman, was named head coach at Iowa State, Trice and several other athletes followed him west. Trice majored in animal husbandry and his goal was to settle in the South after his graduation and help the black farmers of that area. He was a studious young man, and despite his participation in intercollegiate athletics, Trice managed to pass forty-five college credits with a 90 percent average. Because there were no athletic scholarships granted in those days, he worked odd jobs to finance his education and support his wife and mother.

On the gridiron, Trice was a stellar performer in the line. He played on the freshman team in 1922, and the following year was considered by many to be all-conference caliber. But the promising career ended abruptly. Trice played in the season-opener, a 14–6 win over Simpson on September 29 in Ames. He traveled to Minneapolis the following weekend for an October 6 showdown at Minnesota. Iowa State was playing a strong defensive game that day and trailed by only four points, 14–10, at the half. It was during intermission that Trice began to acknowledge a sore left shoulder, but nevertheless, he returned to action in the second half. Midway through the third quarter, the Minnesota team ran a play off left tackle. Trice immediately saw that he wouldn't be able to reach the ball carrier, so he threw himself in front of the Minnesota interference in a roll block. He was toppled over on his back and trampled on.

Trice wanted to continue playing but never returned to the game. According to newspaper accounts, the crowd chanted, "We're sorry Ames, we're sorry." Doctors at a Minneapolis hospital allowed Trice to return to Ames with the team, which lost the game 20–17. Trice rode back on a Pullman coach. He rested his body on a straw mattress and was immediately taken to the university hospital upon his arrival in Ames. His condition worsened as he developed respiratory problems Sunday afternoon.

At 3 P.M. on Monday, October 8, 1923, Jack Trice died of hemorrhaged lungs and internal bleeding throughout the abdomen. The following Tuesday, classes were postponed and a funeral service was held before four thousand students and faculty members on the central grounds of campus.

A letter written by Jack Trice to himself on the eve of the Minnesota game was read at the University memorial service at the Campanile.

(*continued*)

"My thoughts just before the first real college game of my life: The honor of my race, family and self is at stake. Everyone is expecting me to do big things. I will. My whole body and soul are to be thrown recklessly about the field. Every time the ball is snapped, I will be trying to do more than my part. Fight low, with your eyes open and toward the play. Watch out for crossbucks and reverse end runs. Be on your toes every minute if you expect to make good. Jack"

A memorial scholarship was created, and a memorial to Trice is located in the Jacobson Athletic Building's Gary Thompson Hall of Honor. A statue in his honor was unveiled in 1984 and was moved to the east side of the Jacobson Athletic Building in 1997, greeting visitors entering Jack Trice Stadium.

Tom Kroeschell

*Chapter 1*

# Foundations of the People's College: The Early Years of Iowa State

## Pamela Riney-Kehrberg

The story of Iowa State's first seventy-five years is largely a story of an institution defining and refining itself. Founded as the state's college of agricultural and mechanic arts, Iowa State broadened its emphasis and expanded its offerings as the years went by. The institution seriously considered its motto, "Science with Practice," and developed innovative laboratory programs in many disciplines, offering students a unique opportunity to apply their knowledge in "real world" settings. Students also worked to define their institution, founding organizations and traditions that extend even to the present day. Iowa State was an early pioneer in coeducation, and female students have played a central role in the development of the school. After weathering the hard times of World War I and the Great Depression, the college was prepared to take on the challenges of World War II.

Iowa State was an idea long before it was an educational institution. Residents began to develop educational institutions even before Iowa achieved statehood, and the universities began to take shape well before the public school system had been fully established. Founded in 1858 by an act of the state legislature as the Iowa State Agricultural College and Model Farm (later to become Iowa State College, and then Iowa State University), the college was intended to provide a practical education in agriculture and the mechanic arts to the residents of the state. According to the act, education at the institution was to be "forever free" to state residents. The passage of the law, however, did not guarantee that an agricultural college would be created. The state had yet to acquire a site for the institution or to raise all of the funds necessary to build the institution. Legislators always assumed that the federal government would provide at least some of the funds necessary for the creation of the college, in 1858 presenting Congress with a request for a donation of 50,000 acres of land, to be used to establish agricultural schools in the state.[1]

On July 2, 1862, Congress passed the act that would make the state's educational dreams possible. The Land Grant College Act, also known as the Morrill Act, provided to the states the means of establishing agricultural and mechanical colleges. Each state received 30,000 acres for each senator and representative that the state had in 1860. Proceeds from the sale of the land would provide the financial foundation for a school of the agricultural and mechanic arts. The Morrill Act specified, however, that schools founded under the act were not to be narrow in focus but to provide other "scientific and classical studies" as well. The primary condition for the grant of the land was that the colleges would proceed to develop a school within five years and would use none of the funds for "purchase, erection, preservation, or repair of any building or buildings." Iowa was the first state to accept the terms of the act. Under the Morrill Act, the State of Iowa received 203,309 acres of land, the proceeds from which would help to build Iowa State College.[2]

After many delays and much legal wrangling, Iowa State Agricultural College opened its doors to students on March 17, 1869. The freshman class included ninety-three students, seventy-seven men and sixteen women. The college also had a preparatory department for students who needed additional tutoring prior to entrance, which included eighty students, fifty-nine men and twenty-one women.[3] In order to be admitted, students were required to pass at least 75 percent of the entrance examination, which included questions in grammar, spelling, geography, arithmetic, and algebra. In 1871, a sample examination included such questions as "Name and define all the parts of speech"; "Through what waters does one sail going from New Orleans to Hong Kong and return, going around the world? What winds favor him? Near what lands does he pass?"; and "State the processes of getting the nearest common divisor, and the least common multiple of algebraic quantities, with examples." Admission came with expectations about student behavior as well. The administration assumed that students, male or female, would be individuals of character and sound morals. As President Adonijah Welch remarked in his second annual report, "The Iowa State Agricultural College is in no sense a reform school. Its province is to instruct and encourage those who are earnest seekers for higher education and not to reform those who are idle and morally perverse. . . . The State and national bounty must not be wasted on thoughtless boys and girls who do not appreciate it, will not profit by it, and parents are earnestly advised not to send children here, who have proved unmanageable at home."[4] Only the academically and morally sound young person would be welcome at Iowa State.

Once a student gained admission, he or she would usually come to live on campus, although some day students would commute from their families' homes in Ames. In its first years, student life at the college was rugged indeed. Ames itself was a new creation, with only 650 residents. The college site, just to the west of Ames, was remote and isolated. An early observer of the school site suggested that the students had been "banished, remote from civilization and its attendant temptations, to study nature in its native wildness . . . almost as wild as when Noah's Ark floated over a world of water." Old Main comprised the whole of the college's instructional buildings, and it served as housing for most of the faculty and students as well as classroom space. John Boyd Hungerford, a student in the 1870s, recalled that life in Old Main was academically and socially rewarding but "fraught with difficulties." The school's rules required students to arrive on campus with their own bed tick, but they were provided sheets, pillows, pillowcases, and the clean straw to fill their ticks. In addition, the college furnished students' rooms with "two straight backed chairs, a wardrobe, study table, washbowl and pitcher and waste receptacle." Students were only occasionally felled by diseases common to frontier living such as malaria, typhoid, and ptomaine poisoning. Most of the college's students would not have found this too spartan an environment, since they generally came from fairly modest backgrounds and farm or blue-collar families.[5]

The cost of attending Iowa State was relatively modest as well. The college estimated costs for students in 1870–1871 of $123 to $149 for the academic year and also estimated that students could earn $50 of that sum while employed on campus. Before 1880, the entire four-year course was only $760. One of the requirements of all students was that they complete several hours of manual labor per week as a condition of their acceptance to the school. This paid employment helped to defray expenses. For young people who had generally lived on farms and worked for their parents as part of their daily routine, the manual labor requirement probably would have been less onerous than their chores at home. This would remain a part of student life until 1884, being eliminated, at least in part, because some students were more interested in making money than pursuing their studies. The Iowa State calendar accommodated the economic needs of students as well by providing a very long winter break, coinciding with the winter term of Iowa's rural schools. As a result, many students spent their winter vacations working as country schoolteachers, thereby earning a large proportion of their costs for the year.[6] The latter years of the nineteenth century were not easy ones for family farmers, and many students bore the costs of their own educations. The relatively modest cost of the college degree meant that a fairly broad range of students were able to take advantage of ISC's offerings.

Iowa State began as a "people's college," open to young men and women with a wide variety of economic backgrounds. Many of them were like young Henry C. Taylor, who grew up in Van Buren County. Raised on his father's farm, he learned all of the lessons necessary to operate a farm of his own. When he was a teenager, however, his progressive father offered him a choice: land to farm or the funds to attend college. He began college at Iowa State in 1891. Although he offered to use his education to help run the family farming operation, his father insisted that he follow a different path. He said, "You are well prepared for far more important work, and there are plenty of people to run farms." Although Iowa State prepared many young people to return to agriculture, better educated and able to manage their land, many, like Henry C. Taylor, chose to pursue other opportunities made possible by an ISC education. His choice was to return to teach at ISC and pursue a career in agricultural economics. Ultimately, he would become the head of the Department of Agriculture's Bureau of Agricultural Economics.[7] In fact, the path that Taylor took was an often-heard criticism of ISC: that it took farm boys and girls away from the land and sent them on to other fields of endeavor.

In addition to its beginning as a people's college, one of the chief features of the new college was that it was a coeducational institution. As early as 1864, the state legislature was planning for the education of both men and women. Before the

*President Adonijah Welch, first president of Iowa State Agricultural College, served from 1868 to 1883. (Used by permission of Iowa State University Library/Special Collections Department)*

college opened, legislators established moral safeguards that would make the institution a wholesome place for females. No alcohol would be sold within two miles of the college, and alcohol and tobacco use by students would be prohibited. In 1882 the administration banned dancing on college grounds because it was "injurious to the progress of the student" and "not a proper amusement for young people." They also likely believed that dancing would bring male and female students into far too close contact. Coeducation required that a high level of propriety be preserved.

Iowa State was one of the very first coeducational land-grant institutions in the United States and the institution's first president, Adonijah M. Welch, emphasized its importance in his inaugural address. In fact, two-thirds of his address was devoted to the topic of coeducation and he advocated for full and fair education for Iowa's young women. As he said in his inaugural address:

Can she not see and hear, and smell and taste? Does she not apprehend and analyze, abstract and imagine, classify, generalize, judge and reason? Does she not experience all the countless shades and undulations of feeling? And are her desires and energies of will less numerous or less powerful than yours, my ancient friend?

*Mary Welch, wife of President Adonijah Welch, was a strong advocate of education for women. (Used by permission of Iowa State University Library/Special Collections Department)*

In Welch's view, if not the view of the average American of the day, educating women was as natural and as necessary as educating men.

As a result of the emphasis on coeducation, Iowa State would be a national leader in the development of domestic economy as a course of study for women, second only to Kansas State Agricultural College. Mary Welch collaborated with her husband to create opportunities for women's education. Although not completely in place until the late 1880s, Iowa State had a domestic economy department as early as 1875. Students listened to lectures on "Drainage," "Water Supply," "Care of Health," "Sewing and Mending," and other related topics, all intended to provide young women the latest information in household management. At Iowa State, young women could learn to be scientific farm wives, but the Welches also hoped that they would be prepared to earn "an honorable support" and make a living for themselves in suitable and respectable employment. As new careers opened for women, they would take advantage of the domestic economy curriculum to become educators, extension workers, and journalists.[8]

Although a leader in women's education, the point of coeducation at Iowa State was decidedly not to promote absolute equality in men's and women's studies. Men and women met in many classrooms, but women did not have the same courses of study open to them as men, and were not encouraged to participate in the same college activities. For example, although all students took the same basic core courses in English, mathematics, history, the natural sciences, and literature, women then went into a separate "ladies' course" in domestic economy. They focused on such topics as chemistry for the household and botany for the garden. Interestingly, Mary Welch also taught a course called Managing the Help, indicating that she and other administrators imagined that students would be running relatively affluent farm and city households, rather than the more modest homes from which many of the institution's students came.[9] In addition to restricted opportunities for education, the college would also maintain separate and special rules for the protection of young women well into the twentieth century. Although developed by the women themselves, and approved by the faculty, they were rules that even strict parents would approve, including early hours for "lights out," limited hours for male callers, and required chaperones for social events. Women were allowed to attend only college-sanctioned social events.[10]

Coeducation, as originally planned and executed at Iowa State, was intended to fit young women for a separate place in the adult world rather than for the same roles as their male peers. Many young women, however, saw the possibilities of their education beyond its application to home economics. A number of early ISC graduates parlayed their domestic science degrees into other opportunities. Hattie Raybourne, class of 1873, worked in a number of offices in the State Capitol, including being an assistant in the land office. Alice Whited, valedictorian in 1879, served as a county auditor, eventually becoming state auditor. Sallie Stalker, 1873, and Kate N. Tupper, 1875, both studied medicine. A number of graduates became women homesteaders, establishing their own midwestern and western farms.[11]

In their campus activities, too, women were known to subvert administrators' intentions for their ladylike education and behavior. The Morrill Act of 1862 demanded that all men participate in military training. In 1878, Iowa State's women began to demand military drill. Carrie Chapman Catt, suffragist and political activist, was active in the move to establish military drill for women. Catt and others like her wished to participate in this activity and persuaded the faculty to set aside separate space for their drill. Women at Iowa State engaged in military drill from 1879 through the 1890s. In fact, in 1893, they joined the men's battalions in a trip to the Columbian Exposition, also known as the Chicago World's Fair, as a part of the Iowa delegation. Although the crowd was shocked by the sight of so many young women engaged in military drill, the women marched out of an exhibition to a "storm of hand-clapping."[12] In spite of coeducation's limits, Iowa State offered young women a number of experiences that they otherwise never would have had.

President Welch announced also that equal education was available not just for women but for the individual of "any race who has reached the years of discretion." This, too, was a revolutionary idea in the late nineteenth century.[13] The persistence of that philosophy allowed for a very fortunate occurrence—George Washington Carver's 1891 enrollment in the institution. It was not, however, an easy transition for Carver. On his arrival, boys shouted names at him, and the only living space he could find was a room in an old office. The dining hall manager would not serve him any place other than the basement. A friend from Indianola,

*Suffragist and women's rights advocate Carrie Chapman Catt argued for women's military drill while a student at Iowa State College. This group of women is participating in military drill posed in front of Old Main, circa 1894. Old Main was the most important college building from ISC's opening in 1868 until its destruction by fire in 1902. It sat on the site of the present-day Beardshear Hall. (Used by permission of Iowa State University Library/Special Collections Department)*

Mrs. W. A. Liston, came to campus and helped him overcome some of his social problems. He worked his way through college doing manual labor on campus, making and selling hominy, and working as a masseur for the football team. He focused on botany and horticulture and was known as the "green thumb boy" for his abilities with plants. Because of his skill, the faculty asked him to continue with postgraduate studies and appointed him to the faculty in botany. Upon completion of his degree, he accepted a position at the Tuskegee Institute. By the time of his death in 1943, he had become one of the nation's best-known living scientists, concerned with improving southern agriculture for the benefit of all.[14]

Unfortunately, the practical problems that Carver faced in finding accommodations would not be resolved any time soon. Although not written anywhere, Iowa State had an unofficial policy that barred students of color from living with white students. In 1910, President Raymond Pearson wrote, "Negro students are entirely welcome at this institution; they have no discourtesy shown them by fellow students or others. It is not always easy for a Negro student to find rooming and boarding accommodations except where there are enough to room and board together, as is the case with Filipinos and with students of other nationalities." African Americans were to find room and board with each other, not with white students. In 1919, in response to this problem, Archie and Nancy Martin, an African American couple who had moved to Ames from Georgia, opened a rooming house for African American students at 218 Lincoln Way. Because of lobbying on the part of Archie Martin, it gradually became easier for African American students to find lodging, but they would not be allowed into the dormitories until after World War II.[15]

As the institution became more established, there was a good deal of discussion—and disagreement—about exactly what kind of school Iowa State should be. In 1884 the state legislature broadened the college's mission by asking that more liberal arts be taught. Enrollment in the agricultural course declined, causing the college to drop the scientific agriculture program. Predictably, in a farm state this caused a legislative uproar, leading to the 1891 creation of an agricultural short course, and then the creation of a four-year course in agriculture. Iowa State was the first school in the country to offer a course in agricultural engineering. The school's agricultural mission, however, extended well beyond the classroom into the barns and fields of the state's farms. In 1898 the institution added what were called the Farm and Home Excursions, which brought both male and female visitors from throughout the state to see what was being done at Iowa State College. This would become the very popular Farm and Home Week, which gave farm couples the opportunity to visit and learn about the latest developments in agriculture and domestic science as well as the institution and its programs.

By the early years of the twentieth century, Iowa State was developing a more formal extension program, which would take practical and scientific information to the citizens of Iowa, particularly in the area of corn production. The passage of the Hatch Act by Congress in 1887 provided federal funding for agricultural extension programs, and Iowa State established its own agricultural experiment station as a result. Federal money was extremely important to the fledgling institution since the agricultural economy often faltered, and state funding was always tight. Perry Greeley Holden, head of the Agronomy Department and an organizer of extension programs, believed that every Iowan was "a pupil or a student" of the institution, and should have the benefit of the knowledge generated in Ames. He quite literally took agricultural education on the road, organizing the Seed Corn Gospel Train. The train was a traveling exhibit, where farmers could learn how to select and test seed corn and learn other important facts about corn cultivation. The organization of agricultural short courses in various locations around the state led to the further education of thousands of Iowans. Recognizing the potential for such programs, the General Assembly passed the Extension Act of 1906, providing for extension work in Iowa eight years before Congress passed the Smith-Lever Act, extending extension work throughout the nation. Iowa State continued to be both a general college and a purveyor of agricultural knowledge to the farmers of the state.[16]

Over time, the curriculum became more elaborate, and embraced a wider and wider variety of subjects. At first simply divided into curricula in agriculture and mechanic arts, new programs evolved as needed. As always, administrators at Iowa State had to consider state needs in revising and developing the school's program. From a very early date, the state legislature mandated that there be no unnecessary duplication of courses between the agricultural college, teacher's college, and state university. Economic depressions in the 1870s and 1890s encouraged state legislators to think of education programs in the most economical ways. Duplication of efforts between institutions would only mean wasting precious state dollars.

Mindful of the economic constraints within which the state operated, college administrators added new offerings with care. Horticulture, because of its relationship to agriculture, was an early addition to the curriculum. Veterinary science was also a natural, and in 1879 became a course of study. Engineering evolved from a single course of study to a number of specialized courses before the turn of the century. The social sciences received increasing attention, with the creation of courses in agricultural economics and rural sociology. The basic sciences remained very much the essential course of study for most students, with the liberal arts receiving relatively little attention until after 1900. English, modern languages, and history had a very small place in the curriculum, although elocution was a primary component of the curriculum as well as student life in the form of debates and literary societies. William Wynn, a professor in the early years, complained that upon arrival at Iowa State College, he became professor of "English Literature, Latin, History, Rhetoric, Grammar, Moral Science, Agricultural Theology, and everything else of a literary character that my Atlas-like shoulders were able to bear. Indeed on the first morning of my arrival Dr. Welch introduced me to the whole body of students, as one who would be responsible for the entire literary side of the curriculum, and for the chapel services on the Sabbath Day."[17] A broadened curriculum and a more consistently specialized faculty would come with time.

This uncertainty over exactly what the institution should be resulted in troubles for various university presidents. President Welch's 1883 departure from the presidency was hastened by his own poor health and the concerns of those who wanted to see a greater emphasis on vocational training. He was followed by Seaman Knapp, serving from 1883 to 1884, who was appointed in order to steer the college more consistently toward the pursuit of agricultural education. Knapp returned to work in agriculture, and was followed by Leigh Smith John Hunt, whose experience was largely as a school administrator. Although he was not as directly involved in quarrels over the focus of the college, he was perceived as being a poor match for a state agricultural college, often setting out from campus in a fancy coach with a footman in livery. His term was an academic mismatch, resulting in the resignation of professors and a strike by the senior class. William Chamberlain, a peacemaker, followed, but he too ran afoul of state politics. An Ohioan, he persistently aggravated the Iowa farmers he addressed with references to his home state. Again, there was student unrest, and President Chamberlain departed. These administrators faced a persistent problem: how to satisfy their various and generally disagreeing constituencies. Farmers and agricultural interests in

*President William Beardshear, who served from 1891 until his death in 1902, was one of the institution's most popular presidents. (Used by permission of Iowa State University Library/Special Collections Department)*

the state often had somewhat different ideas about education at Iowa State College than the faculty, the legislature, and, sometimes, the students. Administrators were often caught in the crossfire between the different factions attempting to define the institution and its purposes. It is perhaps unsurprising that ISC had four different presidents, and five different acting presidents, in between its founding and 1890.

In the next decade, President W. M. Beardshear struggled with the legislature over the issue of institutional funding. Although he did not blame the depression of the 1890s for ISC's woes, it is clear that the faltering economy placed constraints on the institution. In the 1898–1899 biennial report Beardshear wrote, "As a college we have suffered by waiting four years without adequate appropriations for buildings and equipment. . . . In order for Iowa to do her share and to be true to her own youth, prompt action and liberal provision must be made for the Iowa State College."[18] In the years just before World War I, state support for the institution did indeed grow and residents became increasingly committed to the institution. In 1916, a county newspaper columnist wrote, "The Iowa State College at Ames comes the nearest to being a college for the people of any school in the state. . . . It is a school for boys and girls and for men and women of any age."[19]

In various forms of outreach, faculty at Iowa State attempted to bring together their interests and the needs of the residents. From its creation, both the legislature and the college community saw service to the state as an important part of ISC's mission. One early venture of Iowa State College, the development of a state highway commission, was an important marriage of academic and state interests. At the turn of the century Iowa had few hard-surfaced roads, and research undertaken at the college indicated that improved roads might improve the economic and social conditions of the state's farmers. While some legislators wanted to create a separate roads department, debates in the General Assembly indicated that no such department would be forthcoming without greater public education about the issue. Given a perennially tight agricultural economy, the state's residents would have to be convinced that the benefits of improved roads would be worth the costs.

The college was the logical institution to undertake the task. Charles F. Curtiss, dean of agriculture, and Anson Marston, dean of engineering, spearheaded the college's effort. The General Assembly voted to make Iowa State College the "Highway Commission for Iowa," and made an initial two-year grant of $7,000 for the purpose. The General Assembly directed the college to develop a plan for highway construction throughout the state, conduct demonstrations of highway construction, provide information and instruction to county officials on construction and maintenance of roadways, and report to the governor the results of this work. The Iowa Highway Commission prepared a manual for highway officers, conducted surveys pertinent to roadwork, and organized road construction and maintenance. Professor S. W. Beyer conducted experiments on road materials. The college actively lobbied for "good roads," meaning hard-surfaced roads, throughout the state. Although over time the state highway commission would become less intimately tied to the college administration, it would continue to be housed on campus for a number of years, and research done at Iowa State would continue to inform its activities.[20]

The development of the college as a social space accompanied its development as an academic institution. Life at ISC was not all work and no play. In the early days of the college, if students were to have a social life, they would have to create it themselves. A good distance separated the new college from Ames, and in bad weather (which was most of the late fall, winter, and spring) the dirt roads connecting the two were all but impassable. The college also encouraged students, especially women, to entertain themselves within the bounds of the campus. Many students belonged to campus literary societies, which hosted essay and speech contests as well as debates. Speech contests, in fact, were the first intercollegiate competitions on campus until the arrival of intercollegiate athletics in the 1890s. Students also developed professional organizations, a glee club, and a college band. Intramural sports were encouraged, and basketball was one of the first women's sports on campus. In the early days, the college actively discouraged organized athletics, since administrators believed students could better use their time in manual labor and military drill. Students, however, persisted in their athletic interests and formed a baseball team early in the life of the college.[21]

Intercollegiate athletics arrived at Iowa State in the 1890s. In 1892 the Iowa

Inter-Collegiate Base Ball Association was formed with Iowa State, Drake University, Iowa College at Grinnell, and the State University of Iowa as members. In the same year, football came to Iowa State on a rather informal basis. It would not be until 1895, and the arrival of Glenn S. "Pop" Warner as coach, that football practices and games were held on anything resembling a normal schedule. In 1895, the Iowa State team received its nickname, the "Cyclones," from a *Chicago Tribune* columnist describing Iowa State's decisive 36–0 win over Northwestern University. Concerns about the balance between athletics and academics appeared early. After various national athletic scandals, the faculty in March of 1894 resolved that all athlete scholars should be enrolled students carrying at least fifteen hours per semester, and that their performance in the previous semester should be "creditable." Additionally, they asked that student athletes be provided a clean bill of health by the college physician. Only years later would such requirements become a part of national standards.[22]

Sororities and fraternities got off to a slow start at Iowa State, not because of any opposition from the faculty but because of opposition from student groups. The student newspaper, the *Aurora*, led the attack on fraternities as undemocratic secret organizations. Even so, in 1875, the Omega chapter of Delta Tau Delta became the first fraternity on campus. The first sorority, the Iowa Gamma of Pi Beta Phi, organized in 1877. Student discord over the fraternities and sororities resulted in a riot in May of 1888. Following the riot, the faculty decided to deny the use of college buildings to fraternities and sororities. In 1891, President Beardshear officially banned ISC students from joining fraternities and sororities. It should be noted, however, that the action against fraternities and sororities did not seem to diminish President Beardshear's popularity appreciably. He lifted the ban on dancing, in place since 1882, and also lifted the ban on students taking part in social activities off campus. He was a very popular president, and under his administration both enrollment and state support for education grew. After Beardshear's untimely death in 1902, fraternities and sororities would again appear, as a result of an acute housing shortage on campus. In 1905, President Storms allowed fraternities and sororities to establish chapters. In the 1920s, concerns about student conduct would lead to the appointment of a faculty advisor for each fraternity, and periodic conferences with the administration. The sororities already employed house mothers, and combined with the conduct regulations already in place for women students, the administration believed no further regulation was necessary.[23]

Time and circumstances altered the balance between work and play on the ISC campus. World War I demanded action on the part of students and faculty. When the United States went to war in the spring of 1917, all able-bodied male students increased their efforts at drill. The institution required all of them to drill from 11:00 to 12:15, and most participated in another afternoon drill period from 4:00 to 6:00. Many of the male faculty also participated. Women students channeled their energies into Red Cross activities and applied themselves to the problem of conserving food and fiber. Daily chapel was a casualty of the war with students far

St. Patricks Day ISC.

*In 1915, students engaged in a St. Patrick's Day blanket toss outside of Beardshear Hall. (Used by permission of Iowa State University Library/Special Collections Department)*

too busy for required daily devotions. In the spring of 1917, five hundred students left campus early, two hundred to join the military and three hundred for war employment. A number of faculty members, too, left for service; one of those was the college's president. President Raymond Pearson, a dairyman and educator, went to Washington as an assistant secretary of agriculture for the duration of the conflict. The faculty agreed with his decision to go, and his desire to return, and Dean Edgar W. Stanton stood in for him until the war's end. Other departures for the duration included the Ames Ambulance Unit, made up of thirty-six students from the college. After training at Camp Crane, Allentown, Pennsylvania, they served on the Italian-Austrian front.[24]

Life on campus, meanwhile, adapted to the needs of a nation at war. Drill continued as ever. Students organized relief drives and raised funds for the war effort. They even reorganized their extracurricular activities to accommodate the changes caused by war. The lack of students available to run the *Green Gander*, the male-run campus humor magazine, led women to found their own publication, the *Emerald Goose*. The campus also became home to training programs for soldiers. In April of 1918, five hundred soldiers came to ISU to train to be auto mechanics, blacksmiths, and machinists. Although completely separate from the college's academic program, it operated under the direction of Professor W. H. Meeker of Mechanical Engineering. Later in the war, students enlisted into a cadet reserve corps, which combined a strenuous program of military training with ongoing academic work. Faculty members turned their research efforts to the problems of wartime. The engineering faculty worked on various military problems such as communications, camp construction, and conservation. Those in home economics worked on practical problems in food, clothing, and health. Faculty in the natural sciences concentrated on food production for wartime use.[25]

All of this would be disrupted by the fall 1918 arrival on campus of the Spanish influenza epidemic. This particularly deadly strain of the flu killed 500,000 Americans, far more than had died in the course of World War I. Campus was placed under a three-month quarantine, and there were as many as 1,250 students infected at one time. Eight female students who violated the quarantine were placed under house arrest. All available campus facilities were pressed into service, with sick students taking up residence in the college hospital, the gymnasium, a church basement, and any available space in Campustown. The epidemic resulted in fifty-one deaths among young men involved in training activities on campus.[26] While the campus battled the Spanish flu, the war came to a close.

In the end, roughly 6,000 students, alumni, and faculty served during World War I. Of those 6,000, 118 died. Their loss was honored in the construction of Memorial Union as a living monument to the sacrifices of World War I. Students began the fund drive in the years immediately following the war, and enough had been raised by 1927 to begin construction. Memorial Union opened in September of 1928. The names of those who died in World War I can be found in the Gold Star Hall, along with the names of those lost in World War II, Korea, and Vietnam.[27]

At the war's end, more students than ever enrolled at ISC. By 1920, there were 4,479 students on campus, and more than 2,000 enrolled in summer school and short courses. Not surprisingly, these were years of construction on campus, with the Armory, library, hospital, physics, and home economics buildings coming into being. In addition to new buildings, new disciplines emerged. Increased interest in the social sciences led to the development of instruction in economics, and changes in other social science and humanities departments. Graduate education also received an increased emphasis, with enrollment in the Graduate College climbing from only 123 in 1919–1920 to 669 in 1939–1940. By the end of the 1920s, ISC had the largest graduate enrollment of any of the land-grant institutions in the United States.[28] These changes encouraged Raymond Hughes, president from 1927 to 1936, to push for greater systematization and organization on campus. New programs included counseling and guidance for students, as well as a freshman orientation program. Based on the idea of the Soviet Union's five-year plans, he asked for special efforts in long-range planning. For the Twenty-Year Program Survey, each department and administrative unit inventoried its accomplishments and forecast its future.[29]

Student life took on a different character than it had during the earnest days of World War I. Historian and ISC history professor Earle Ross has suggested that the students of the 1920s were "all too little concerned with the past—indifferent to its struggles and contemptuous of its triumphs. . . . The jazz age, with flapper and sheik flouting conventions and affecting ultra-sophistication, made its impress on the land grant as on other colleges." Articles from the *Green Gander*, which returned with the men after the war, would suggest that the students of the 1920s,

*Members of the Student Army Training Corps stood sentry on the Squaw Creek Bridge during the 1918 flu epidemic. (Used by permission of Iowa State University Library/Special Collections Department)*

like students in most times, were apt to flaunt convention and make light of their studies. A snippet from the November 1921 issue illustrated these attitudes: "When I was a kid I thought that—College professors knew everything. College students studied every night till 12 o'clock. Men never smoked at college. College students never copied examinations." A mocking article suggested that the dean of women had an impossible task, since "college co-eds refuse to take life seriously and a Dean of Women has no easy time," and the students at ISC were proceeding in a "mad race down the incline of social ruin." The writer alluded to vast numbers of

*A May 1924 illustration from the Green Gander illustrates some amusing student attitudes of the day. (Used by permission of Iowa State University Library/Special Collections Department)*

students necking in the quiet recesses of the quad, carousing at picnics, and enjoying unchaperoned fraternity and sorority parties. This is perhaps why the authors of the student handbook felt it necessary to remind students, first and foremost, to "STUDY. THAT IS YOUR BUSINESS WHILE IN COLLEGE." In spite of the mocking tone of the *Green Gander*, all was not parties, necking, and general misbehav-

*This Mechanical Engineering float won first prize in the 1923 VEISHEA parade. (Used by permission of Iowa State University Library/Special Collections Department)*

ior. More serious entertainments also had their place. Political speakers and debates gathered large audiences, and a number of student religious organizations had their origins in the 1920s.[30]

A notable student-led innovation of the 1920s was the creation of VEISHEA. For many years, the various colleges had held their own annual celebrations. Home Economics celebrated annually with "May Day." The engineers had their own event on St. Patrick's Day, and Agriculture hosted an annual Agriculture Carnival. In 1922, students brought together the best elements of all of these events and created VEISHEA, the name of which stood for ISC's divisions at that time: Veterinary, Engineering, Industrial Science, Home Economics, and Agriculture. That first VEISHEA included a parade, with two miles of floats and bands, several dances, plays, a carnival, a riding exhibition, a baseball game against the University of Nebraska, and a "sham battle" the ROTC staged around Lake LaVerne. Acclaimed as a success, it became an annual event organized by students for the benefit of the campus community. It also became a showcase for the students and their accomplishments. The 1930 student handbook commented, "Veishea is one of the big events of the year and is considered one of the most desirable times for the parents and friends of students to visit them and the college."[31]

In the new century, Iowa State became known for developing innovative academic programs, many of which brought together the latest research with labora-

*This agriculturally themed float was featured in the 1923 VEISHEA parade. (Used by permission of Iowa State University Library/Special Collections Department)*

tory experiences illustrating its practical application. The Home Economics Department joined fifty others all across the United States in instituting a home management house program, essentially a laboratory experience in home economics. The Smith-Hughes Act, which provided federal matching funds for home economics education, made the program possible. Beginning in 1918, seniors in Home Economics were required to live for two, and then later six, weeks in a home management house, where they would practice all of the skills necessary for maintaining as wives and mothers an efficient and modern home. Those who planned for careers in education and extension would also learn the use of the latest in household appliances, and know how to demonstrate them to others. Home management house residents made the soft furnishings for the home, planned and prepared meals, and developed budgets, among other tasks. As in the case of Mary Welch's course in "managing the help," they were often working in conditions that were far more luxurious than those from which they came, or to which they might go after graduation. Iowa State prided itself in providing its students with the opportunity to use the most up-to-date home appliances.

After 1924, students in the home management houses also served as surrogate mothers to babies that Iowa State obtained from social service agencies in Des Moines. The first two babies were Gretchen and Sonny, who arrived on campus at sixteen and thirteen months. The goal of bringing them to campus was to give young women as realistic a home management experience as possible, and to provide a scientifically managed, superior quality home to youngsters who had been living in orphanages and boarding homes. The young women applied their skills in child development, nutrition, and sewing to the babies' needs. When they became too old to remain on campus, the babies would either return to their mothers in Des Moines or would be adopted, many by families in Ames. Gretchen, for example, returned to her mother, while Sonny, whose mother was dying of tuberculosis, found an adoptive family. As these babies left, others like Betty and Charles came to take their place. The program would continue until the late 1950s, when changing attitudes about child development and changing circumstances of college women would make the home management house system obsolete. Many of the young women involved in the program remembered it as their best educational experience at Iowa State College.[32]

Home Economics was not the only program making use of the best of laboratory facilities. In Engineering, the college's motto of "Science with Practice" prevailed, and students combined a theoretical knowledge of the subjects necessary to engineering with their own intensive laboratory experiences. A look at the 1920–1921 college catalog shows that the Mechanical Engineering students of the 1920s took many courses with which students today would be familiar: Dynamics of Engineering, Mechanics of Materials, Hydraulics, and Thermodynamics. Scientific theory, however, came with a great deal of practice in laboratory facilities and shops on campus. In addition to their theoretical topics, students had required courses in which they were expected to get their hands dirty. Students could enroll in Power Engineering, in which they learned the operation and maintenance of steam and gas engines, steam boilers, pumps, and other machinery. The department offered a course in Forge Work, where students learned forging and welding iron, and forging, dressing, hardening, and tempering steel tools. Foundry Work was also a possibility, as was Sheet Metal Work and Pipe Fitting. Engineering students learned to make machines, not just understand the theory behind them, and gained practical experience outside of the lecture hall. The department believed that by combining theoretical knowledge with "the experience and judgment gained in practical work," students would be able to move into positions of responsibility, understanding their work from the ground up.[33]

Another notable marriage of "Science with Practice" came in the area of statistics. Beginning in 1924, George W. Snedecor of the Mathematics Department organized seminars for agricultural researchers, to help them apply the latest in statistical methods to problems in field research. To facilitate these seminars, Snedecor had computational machines brought to campus, an early use of business machines for the analysis of research data. In 1933, he organized the Statistical Laboratory, the first of its kind in the United States. The same year, Snedecor would become the Station Statistician of the Iowa Agricultural Experiment Station. In his hands, statistics were not an abstraction, but a tool available to scientists, particularly in biology and agriculture, for the improvement of animals and crops.[34] As in the case of the Home Economics and Mechanical Engineering programs, Snedecor's vision of his role as an educator and researcher integrated theory and practice.

These educational developments came, in many ways, in the face of adversity. The Great Depression hit the state of Iowa hard. It could be argued, in fact, that the Depression came to Iowa in the 1920s, rather than the 1930s. As a farm state, Iowa keenly felt the collapse of agricultural prices in the aftermath of World War I. As prices fell by almost 50 percent, farmers who had expanded their operations during the war found that they could not pay off their loans in the postwar period. Prices would fall even further with the onset of the Great Depression. Highly dependent upon the farm economy and farmers, city dwellers suffered too. Predictably, the effect on Iowa State College was not a positive one. Both enrollment and state support fell. By 1934 enrollment had fallen approximately 25 percent. In response to diminishing state revenues, the state appropriation fell by more than 25 percent. The university attempted to keep regular faculty members on staff, but those on less regular appointments lost their jobs. Vacancies went unfilled. Deep salary cuts were necessary to keep the college afloat.[35]

Students, too, felt the pinch of Depression economics. Many parents of college students had a hard time providing food, clothing, and shelter for those still at home, and could not help children who were away at school with their expenses. In order to pay tuition, many students had previously relied on off-campus employment. In those years, jobs were few and far between. Businesses closed, and those still open scaled back their work forces. Finding off-campus employment became extremely difficult. The college's own emergency loan funds for students were soon exhausted. The school, in response, developed cooperative dormitories, where students did their own cleaning and cooking in order to decrease costs. Students also rented their books, instead of buying them. The college did what it could to provide loans and temporary employment to students in need of additional aid. Also important to students was employment through the New Deal's National Youth Administration, a program that was the precursor to today's work-study program. Students worked in various positions across campus and earned a minimum wage. The intention was to keep them in school and out of the unemployment lines. Jobs for graduates were hard to come by, and everyone benefited from keeping students in school as long as possible.[36]

The Depression also highlighted the importance of Iowa State's contribution to agricultural knowledge. President Franklin D. Roosevelt chose Henry A. Wallace, a 1910 graduate, as secretary of agriculture. Wallace recruited a number of fellow ISC graduates to join the department, placing a serious drain on the college's staff, particularly in agricultural economics. In an era when agriculture was under serious stress, specialists such as those at Iowa State were in particular demand for government work.[37]

Iowa State had a special relationship with another New Deal program, the Public Works of Art Project (PWAP). Famed Iowa artist Grant Wood administered the state's program, and Iowa State became home to the two most significant works of art created in the state by the PWAP. In 1933 and 1934, Grant Wood personally designed and supervised the painting of a large set of murals for the college library entitled *When Tillage Begins, Other Arts Follow*. The piece, the largest of Grant Wood's murals, illustrated the breaking of the prairie, as well as depicting the major branches of knowledge taught at Iowa State: the agricultural arts, home economics, and engineering. The second major piece of artwork sponsored by the PWAP was sculptor Christian Petersen's fountain and sculptures produced for the dairy industry building. What began as a simple desire for a fountain became in addition a complex mural following milk production from the cow through various stages of processing. The project was such a success that in 1935

*This panel, depicting modern milking methods, is a part of Christian Petersen's Dairy Industry Building sculpture. (Used by permission of Iowa State University Library/Special Collections Department)*

the college asked Petersen to join the university staff, where he taught applied art to the young women in the Home Economics Department. He was the first artist-in-residence at an American university.[38]

That does not mean, however, that ISC received only positive comment during the Depression. Veterinarians at Iowa State were in the forefront of the fight against bovine tuberculosis. Because of the threat that it posed to anyone drinking milk, by the end of the 1920s the state had made testing mandatory. Although it did improve public health, farmers with diseased herds faced the loss of cattle with only the promise of partial reimbursement from the state and federal governments. In good times the losses might pinch, but in hard times they could be devastating. Rumors began to spread that ISC veterinarians were condemning healthy cattle and selling them to meat packers. Irate farmers hung veterinarians in effigy and smashed their cars. Iowa State Extension personnel and professors were accused of "preparing [the farmer] to accept 'the lowly position of peasant,'" and told to "Try to run a farm of your own." They were forced to ask for protection from the National Guard. In the end, the veterinarians escaped from public wrath unharmed, but the experience was discouraging. Experts from ISC were close at hand and easy to blame when the problems of the Great Depression threatened the livelihoods of Iowa's farmers.[39]

As World War II loomed on the horizon, Iowa State College approached eighty years of development and change. What began as the idea of progressive state legislators had become the state's college of agricultural and mechanic arts, providing students a balance of academic and technical training. Beginning with a freshman class of fewer than a hundred students, the institution had grown by leaps and bounds. During the 1940–1941 academic year, 7,262 students enrolled as undergraduate and graduate students, and another 18,553 attended short courses. Despite drastic fluctuations in the state's fortunes, the college persisted in providing an education to Iowa's youth as well as its farmers. It was the home of innovative programs, many of which combined the latest in theory with the latest in practice. The numbers of graduates and faculty who during one national crisis or another had been called to service in Washington were a testament to the importance of the work being done at Iowa State College. The college faced the future with a solid record of achievement but also with a number of issues to be resolved, such as how to define the ongoing emphasis of the college and how to manage the growth and development of the institution. The state could justifiably be proud of Iowa State College, which had become an educational leader and innovator.[40]

# Vignettes

## A V-12 Experience

Galen Jackson remembers that the V-12 program, the Navy's effort in World War II to train future officers, changed his life. Growing up in Rock Rapids, Jackson was a freshman at the University of Nebraska when the V-12 program was initiated at Iowa State. At the insistence of a fraternity brother who was applying for the program, Jackson also applied. He recalled the experience as rigorous, but it provided him with opportunities he would not have had otherwise.

Jackson related that the V-12 exam featured several pages of multiple choice questions that took about an hour to complete; those who scored in the top 10 percent of the exam were accepted into the program. Two weeks later, much to Jackson's surprise, he received notification of his acceptance. Navy officials ordered him to proceed to Iowa State, where he was assigned to Birch Hall, formerly a women's dormitory. Along with other students, he ate his meals in Birch, and in the evening, sometimes listened to an all-Navy jazz band that played in the dormitory parlor.

Along with his classes, Jackson participated in several college activities. His schedule fulfilled the military planners' intent that the V-12 program would emulate the normal pattern of college life. He also became sports editor for the student newspaper, which, much to his delight, allowed him to attend all the varsity football and basketball games. Far more important, his association with the student paper led to his introduction to a lovely VEISHEA queen candidate, Pat Stow, who later became his wife. For Jackson and other V-12 trainees, the college atmosphere extended to athletics, as during Jackson's last term at Iowa State he played varsity baseball.

After completing V-12 training at ISC, Jackson went to Cornell University for a ninety-day midshipman course. He then opted to serve on a subchaser class PC ship. He served aboard PC475, which had formerly been commanded by band leader Vaughn Monroe. Jackson returned to private life following his Navy service, but like many veterans, his military contacts continued to be important after the war. For a time, he worked for Wagner Electric Company in upper New York state, a firm where former Commander A. F. Duernberger, the organizer of the ISC Naval Training School, was also employed. Later Jackson returned to his hometown of Rock Rapids, where he became a partner in an engineering consulting business with a former V-12 classmate.

Dorothy Schwieder

# Letters from Home

For the hundreds of Iowa State students and alumni who entered the military in World War II, ties to home and other familiar places were vitally important. Once in uniform, college friends stayed in touch with one another and many looked forward to hearing news about Iowa State. Students also stayed in touch with former professors. During the war, Professor I. E. Melhus, head of the Botany Department, corresponded with a number of his former students. A collection of letters in Special Collections at the ISU Library reveal the friendships between Melhus and Botany students and Melhus's interest in the students' military experience, their personal lives, and in their postwar plans.

The military men and women wrote Melhus about their training, their impressions of military installations, and occasionally about their impressions of foreign countries; some wrote with gratitude about the help and support that Melhus had given them while in school; occasionally soldiers and sailors commented about the nature of the war and their hope that it would soon end. One former student sent Melhus a Christmas card with a snapshot of the soldier's five and one-half month old daughter. The letters reveal a strong bond between Melhus and his former students, a bond that undoubtedly helped alleviate the homesickness of former students and also continued their ties to Iowa State.

The letters indicate as well the many diverse military activities of former Iowa State students. In August 1944, Bryce Wadley wrote that he was still in the Army Veterinary Service and that it appeared he would not be sent overseas. He added, "From now until Christmas we will be very busy inspecting the Thanksgiving and Christmas turkeys for the Army." Many letters ended with good wishes for Melhus's wife and family. At the end of the war, Melhus received a printed form, "Greetings from Tokyo," from Navy lieutenant Al Rubin. Rubin wrote on the form, "I remember when we were back in the States, the theme song was, 'Good-bye Momma I'm Off to Yokohama' . . . well surprisingly enough, we are at last in the heart of Japan much sooner than anyone of us ever anticipated." Rubin was on one of the first transports to arrive in Tokyo Bay following Japan's surrender. At least one letter was from a female student, Rosemary Smith, stationed at the Air Force Technical School, Chanute Field, Illinois, where she served as an instrument flying instructor. Smith inquired about work at the department's experiment farms and the work of other professors. She wrote, "Have you taken on any more girls? It is surely a wonderful opportunity for any girls who are properly qualified."

The letters also included academic topics. Surprisingly, some former students continued to work on their master's theses while in the service. Other students wrote about their observations of plants and trees in foreign places. Al Rubin wrote Melhus often, and frequently commented about the plants and trees he observed in other places. In June 1944, Rubin wrote about his observations regarding fruits and vegetables in Panama. Rubin had met a plant pathologist in the Canal Zone who was conducting experiments on sugar cane and rubber, which Rubin viewed as quite successful. Rubin also commented on "a most interesting tree imported from India in 1907 but never permitted to be planted until 1924," because of the prejudice of Panamanians. He did not elaborate. In what appeared to be almost an after-thought, Rubin wrote that he recently married the "the most charming girl who possesses all the traits I ever hoped to find in a wife."

Through the war years, the many letters written by Melhus's former students to their Iowa State professor clearly indicate the military men and women's warm feelings toward Iowa State, but even more clearly, the affection and gratitude they felt toward the Botany professor who cared so much about them.

Dorothy Schwieder

# Work during the War Years

A popular refrain at Iowa State has been, "I'm working my way through college." In every decade since the school's founding, students have worked both on and off campus to pay their college expenses. Jobs have varied, as well as hours worked, but employment has been a necessity for a large number of students. Katy Bell Seidel and Harris Seidel attended Iowa State during World War II and both remember the many different jobs they held while in school.

Katy graduated from Burnside High School, where she heard about Iowa State through her home economics teacher, an ISC graduate. After attending a junior college, Katy enrolled at Iowa State in fall quarter 1942; she graduated in December 1944, majoring, as did most young women then, in home economics education. Out-of-state tuition was $41 for one year while the total cost of Katy's college education was $2,000. For part of her time at ISC, Katy lived in one of the co-op dorms, Freeman and Barton. Students living there could reduce their college expenses by working one hour per day. They prepared meals, served them in the dining halls, and cleaned up the kitchens afterward. Each dorm served three meals a day. Co-op students also cleaned the dorm hallways; first floor cleaning included the parlor. Katy and Harris both recall that the evening meal was a sit-down dinner and students were expected to dress accordingly and to follow proper etiquette. Songfests sometimes followed the evening meals.

Katy also had a variety of other jobs during her college years. She worked in Ames one summer, living in the Roger Williams House, the student center for First Baptist Church; she worked there seven hours a week. During the regular academic year, she cleaned a faculty member's apartment weekly, worked at the Roger Williams House, and sometimes helped with college registration. She often worked forty hours a week in addition to carrying a regular college course load.

Born on a North Dakota farm, Harris first attended a California community college before coming to Iowa State. Before enrolling, he had not visited the campus, but a community college instructor had urged him to attend Iowa State because it was an excellent engineering school. He arrived in November 1942 and graduated in October 1944 with a degree in civil engineering. Harris worked in three different women's dorms under Elsie Guthrie, starting in Birch and then later working in Oak and Elm. He started at the very bottom in the kitchen on pots and pans, advanced to running the dishwasher, and eventually became a substitute waiter; he then worked his way up to head waiter for which he wore a special white jacket. Harris believed he "had the best job in the world." His work hours were limited to meal times, and the pay consisted of three good meals a day.

Harris also remembers that he held a variety of other jobs both on and off campus. He set pins in the Memorial Union Bowling Alley and worked at the ISC Seed Laboratory, testing seed germination. One summer he worked for a local farmer, driving a tractor cultivating corn.

For Katy, the best college experience was living in a home management house where home economics students experienced homemaking firsthand. That experience included caring for a six-month-old baby as well as preparing food and performing other household duties. For Harris, it was being allowed to enroll late after arriving in Ames on November 16, 1942, more than halfway through fall quarter. He recalls, "I was very lucky to have Professor Jack Dodds take up my cause with the Admissions Office and arrange for me to enroll in his surveying course. I was able to do all the work, complete the course, and enroll full-time for the winter quarter."

Dorothy Schwieder

*Chapter 2*

# Iowa State at Mid-Century: The Friley and Hilton Years

Dorothy Schwieder

The years of the mid-twentieth century—1940–1965—were a time of tumult and transition at Iowa State. In this twenty-five-year period, the school moved from being an inwardly focused college devoted to serving its students and meeting the state's agricultural and industrial needs to becoming a university gaining steadily in worldwide outreach and recognition. During this time Iowa State contributed to a global war, coped with postwar demands and pressures, survived a 1950s national recession, and expanded both on and off campus. By 1965, Iowa State had strengthened its programs in the social sciences and humanities, attracted hundreds of international students to campus, and earned an outstanding reputation in its core fields of science and technology.

This period of trial, change, and expansion was guided by two strong presidents. While both Charles E. Friley and James H. Hilton were sons of the South, they differed significantly in their public persona and personal style. President Friley—formal, concise, and businesslike in manner—never wavered in his insistence that the college produce well-educated students who were also moral, well-rounded citizens for the world. He shepherded Iowa State during the final years of the Great Depression, and then through all of World War II: the initial buildup and mobilization, the war effort itself, and the enormous postwar expansion of higher education that followed on the heels of the GI Bill. Following Friley's retirement in 1953, his successor, James H. Hilton, brought a more casual, informal tone to the school. His friendly manner and self-deprecating humor won many friends throughout the state. His ability to work well with the Iowa General Assembly, moreover, eventually paid dividends in the form of increased state appropriations. Hilton presided over the school during a time of considerable expansion in faculty, physical facilities, and international programs, particularly in the last five years of his administration. Iowa State, in fact, grew more rapidly during the Hilton years than at any time previously. He envisioned the creation of the Iowa State University Center—a concert hall, a small theater, a coliseum, and a meeting center—one of his greatest legacies. By 1965, it was clear that Iowa State bore the indelible imprint of both men and their solid, steady, yet often inspired leadership.

Charles E. Friley's time at Iowa State began in 1932 when he arrived on campus to serve as dean of the Division of Industrial Science. A native of Louisiana, and the son of a college president, he spent his early academic career in Texas. He graduated from Sam Houston Teachers' College in 1909 and taught several years in the Texas public schools before earning a bachelor of science degree from the Agricultural and Mechanical College of Texas (now Texas A&M University). Friley continued his education, earning an M.A. from Columbia University. He also conducted research in educational administration at Columbia University and the University of Chicago, teaching courses in college administration at the latter school. Before leaving for Iowa, Friley served as dean of the School of Arts and Sciences at Texas A&M.[1]

Once at Iowa State, Friley rose rapidly through the administrative ranks. When Herman Knapp retired as vice president in 1935, Friley was named as his replacement. A year later, Iowa State officials tapped Friley to take over as acting president due to the illness of President Raymond M. Hughes. In March 1936, following Hughes's resignation, college officials inaugurated the forty-nine-year-old Friley as Iowa State College's ninth president.[2]

Without question Friley's educational attainments and experiences made him well qualified for the presidency of Iowa State, particularly given his academic work in college administration. Not surprisingly, contemporaries responded positively to Friley's many qualifications. Earle Ross, an Iowa State faculty member at the time and author of *The History of Iowa State College*, believed the new president possessed an understanding and a vision of both the technical field and the social mission of the land-grant school that made him well suited for the presidency. Louis M. Thompson, longtime associate dean of agriculture, was another Friley contemporary. Thompson knew Friley at Texas A&M when Thompson was an undergraduate there and later as a faculty member at Iowa State. Thompson recalled that Friley, a tall man, carried himself as a proud person and had a formal, reserved nature. Thompson added that Friley did not interact much with people outside the college. The former associate dean of agriculture had high praise for Friley's integrity and administrative and teaching abilities and as a person who took faculty views into consideration when making major decisions. In keeping with Thompson's view, the *Des Moines Tribune* later described Friley as "businesslike . . . efficient, precise, perhaps a little austere."[3]

Like Ross and Thompson, Iowa State's student body also responded enthusiastically to Friley's presidency. From 1936 to the early 1940s, the student yearbook, the *Bomb*, offered informal views of Friley's administration as well as his personal interests. Editors wrote that Friley's southern accent and ready smile had won him many friends on campus. Two years into Friley's administration, the *Bomb* editors observed that although the president "is imposing and formal in his executive role, he is a very charming and informal host." In 1940, *Bomb* editors wrote that Friley enjoyed relaxing at the piano keyboard and especially enjoyed playing Chopin; the president, they related, read prodigiously, preferring history books, but also kept up on educational trends.[4]

For President Friley, the first five years of his administration were difficult ones, but by 1940, Iowa State had passed a crucial milestone: it had weathered the almost decade-long Depression of the thirties. And while the campus undoubtedly showed signs of benign neglect, given the long Depression, for President Friley

*Charles E. Friley at the time of his inauguration as president of Iowa State College. Friley served as president from 1936 to 1953. (Used by permission of Iowa State University Library/Special Collections Department)*

and for the roughly 6,500 undergraduate students enrolled in the fall term, the future must have looked bright. Traditionally, the school, with its heavy emphasis on science and technology, attracted considerably more male students than females. In 1940, that pattern continued as approximately 1,800 students were enrolled in home economics undergraduate classes and roughly 4,500 students were enrolled in the undergraduate courses in agriculture, engineering, and science as well as in veterinary medicine.[5] Women traditionally majored in home economics subjects such as child development, food and nutrition, home economics education, and textiles and clothing while males typically majored in one of the eight areas in engineering or in agricultural or science courses such as botany, chemistry, and physics.

At the same time, Iowa's economic fortunes were slowly rebounding and the college would share in that recovery. Along with increased enrollment, limited construction was taking place on campus. The women's gymnasium was constructed in 1940 at a cost of $223,625. Previously, women's physical education was housed in Margaret Hall, but that building was destroyed by fire in 1938. The Collegiate Press Building was also constructed in 1940 at a cost of $40,000, and the Library Storage Building was constructed at a cost of $11,472.[6] Although not explicitly stated in any of Friley's speeches, faculty morale was, no doubt, at a low ebb because of low salaries and faculty and budget reductions during the thirties. In 1940, ISC's total budget was $3.8 million.

Like earlier Iowa State presidents, Friley held a conventional view of the school's core mission. Iowa State College had been founded as an agricultural institution, with emphasis on science and technology, and it had not strayed far from its roots since its opening in 1869. The land-grant mission remained the core of the college's existence; this mission, in turn, rested on strong science departments and the divisions (later colleges) of Agriculture, Engineering, Veterinary Medicine, and Home Economics. Students could takes courses in the humanities and social sciences, but administrative officials made clear that these departments existed to provide service rather than to be major entities in their own right. Cooperative Extension was another vital part of the school's land-grant mission.

Throughout his seventeen-year administration, President Friley frequently expressed his educational views. Perhaps the most basic was his conviction that the school must accomplish two things with all students: help them acquire knowledge in their special fields, and help them acquire the characteristics of an educated individual. He defined the latter as "the ability to think and speak clearly, [have an] objective approach to the solution of problems, an adequate concept of values, and [an] appreciation of the implications of personal integrity, worthy home membership and responsible citizenship." Some years later, an ISC press release described Dr. Friley as a president who "has become best known for his insistence that technically trained individuals must first of all be good citizens with a broad understanding of the cultural, moral and spiritual values of living."[7] Friley's frequently emphasized themes reached back into the nineteenth century, when the teaching of proper morality vied in importance with proper learning. Although not a native midwesterner, Friley had a philosophy of education that marched lockstep with those who were.

While Friley's initial years as president were dominated by Depression-era concerns, he had only a brief respite before his administration faced an even greater challenge. In September 1941, with America's involvement in World War II clearly on the horizon, Dr. Friley expressed concern about campus mobilization, yet hoped that the war would have minimum impact on the college's regular programs.[8] That concern became real when Japan bombed Pearl Harbor and the mobilization of campus students and faculty quickly got under way. Before long, Iowa State College took on the appearance of a campus where wartime concerns shared equal billing with those of traditional learning. In fact, by mid-1942, the school motto might have been "Iowa State has gone to war."

About a month after Pearl Harbor, President Friley created the Student Defense Council (later the Student War Council), composed of seventeen students and several faculty advisers. The president asked the council to work closely with the administration in coordinating students' efforts in defense work. Virtually all students were expected to be involved with some aspect of defense work. The 1943 *Bomb* reported that the council met each Saturday noon in the Memorial Union. Later in the year, the council established a war chest to raise money for worthy organizations. Members solicited donations from campus organizations and also supported fund-raisers, including dances, Campus Varieties (a campus talent show), and a bas-

*Four Iowa State coeds taking part in ambulance training during World War II. The women learned vehicle maintenance, including changing tires and oil and checking fan belts and spark plugs. (Used by permission of Iowa State University Library/Special Collections Department)*

ketball game. Officials soon enlarged the Student War Council to nineteen members, all presidents of major campus organizations. By this time, the War Chest Fund had grown to $1,400.[9]

The 1943 student yearbook featured a war theme throughout, leaving no doubt that wartime concerns and needs dominated campus life. Included were short articles featuring the activities of countless campus organizations as well as those of faculty and students. One feature described special training in ambulance driving for ISC coeds who "donning overalls and gas masks as part of their training . . . have been graduated from six sections of Ambulance Driving." Held one evening each week for two hours, the classes covered emergency situations such as changing tires and oil, checking fan belts and spark plugs, greasing cars, and blacking out headlights. The training sessions also included talks by experienced ambulance drivers as well as actual nighttime driving experience. Students received certificates after twenty hours of work. Dr. A. R. Lauer supervised the activities under the sponsorship of the Student War Council.[10]

Even in the midst of a global war, however, troublesome local issues still surfaced. In the early forties, a highly acclaimed Iowa State economics professor,

Theodore W. Schultz, authored a paper in which he favorably compared the taste of a new soybean-based spread (commonly known as oleomargarine) with that of butter. Schultz also served as head of the Economics and Sociology Department. In a state with strong dairy interests—well represented in the General Assembly—a paper that seemingly endorsed the use of oleomargarine was simply unacceptable. College officials were soon bombarded with unhappy comments from irate dairy farmers and unhappy legislators. These groups apparently exerted sufficient pressure on President Friley that he agreed to a recommendation for a "revised study" of the oleo versus butter issue. To Schultz, Friley's action was a denial of academic freedom; Schultz resigned from Iowa State in 1943 and took a position at the University of Chicago. Iowa State administrators may have had some regrets over their actions, however, as Schultz went on to win a Nobel Prize for his work in economics.[11]

While the oleomargarine controversy did not go away, it was soon overshadowed by continued wartime issues, particularly the presence of hundreds of naval trainees on campus. While Iowa State was home to numerous training programs, naval activity clearly dominated. The initial naval trainees, 200 in total, had arrived in June 1942; this represented the first program at Iowa State in the specialized training of men for active duty. In 1943, the *Bomb* reported that 3,100 Navy men were enrolled in electrical and diesel training courses, noting that sailors were a familiar sight on campus and throughout the town. The Navy men attended classes all day with liberty to leave campus on Saturday and Sunday. In an unusual aspect of the training facilities, officials converted several dorm floors in Hughes and Friley Halls into areas resembling a ship's quarters so sailors would become more comfortable in that environment. The *Bomb* reported, "There are no doors on the rooms, double and triple decker bunks are used and, according to Navy regulation, clothing and gear are kept in ship shape and in the smallest space possible in the ship's quarters."[12]

Iowa State ultimately became home to four major naval training programs: the Electrical School, the Diesel School, the Bakers' and Cooks' School, and the V-12 Navy College Training Program. The Electrical School courses were conducted the same as college courses, meeting daily for sixteen weeks. The Diesel program lasted eight weeks and prepared men for service on submarines, PT boats, submarine chasers, and auxiliary craft and for amphibian service. Students in the Bakers' and Cooks' School assisted in preparation of food for other naval trainees who ate in the Memorial Union. The dining room in newly constructed Friley Hall served as mess hall for 750 naval trainees, officers, and other navy personnel. An additional naval training program, the Amphibious Fireman's School, was short-lived as it was started in August 1944 and was discontinued three months later.[13]

The V-12 Program brought the largest number of military men to Iowa State's campus. This initiative was designed to provide the U.S. Navy with properly trained officer candidates for combat duty. Officials who designed the program believed that it provided necessary educational fundamentals, particularly mathematics and physics, for future officers. The top naval commanders emphasized that the V-12 Program was a college program and naval officials hoped that the typical pattern of college life would be followed. Accordingly, college faculties selected academic courses for all V-12 students as well as administering the exams; academic credit was given for the courses. Faculty members were to keep academic standards high and inform naval authorities if they believed students should be dropped from the program. Upon graduation, the V-12 students, referred to as NROTC trainees, were commissioned. The men then went to midshipmen's schools and on to operational or other training before joining the fleet. Smaller numbers of naval trainees transferred to flight training, supply corps schools, and medical, dental, or theological schools for advanced training before assignment to other fields.[14]

For the most part, Navy programs and the ISC curriculum seemed to blend fairly well. In one case, however, specific Navy rules did not quite jibe with college practices. All Navy training programs included physical fitness training, and in general, college officials were able to provide the additional programs. In fact, by 1943, the men's Physical Education Department had adjusted its curriculum to train the Navy men, and planned to give the V-12 men six hours of physical training each week. There was only one hitch: naval medical officers objected to the practice of trainees having to run from the locker room under the east bleachers [Clyde Williams Field], where they dressed, to the Men's Gymnasium for their workout; the men returned to the locker room at the end of the exercise period. This arrangement necessitated "a minute or so in the outer air." Responding to the medical officer's concerns, Dean of the Engineering Division T. R. Agg suggested that adjustments could be made, but added, "It happens that the civilian students here at the College have been following this practice for years with no observable ill effects."[15] To Dean Agg, an Iowan born and bred, "a minute or so in the outer air" was bracing and beneficial.

Space, however, was a more serious concern. As military training programs got under way, student housing became a major problem on the ISC campus. In 1943, the *Bomb* reported that the most important responsibility of the Dormitory Council was the "mass moving of dormitory women into fraternity homes to make room for incoming service men." During certain phases of the war years, military training demands necessitated frequent moves by traditional students.[16]

While naval training programs and other wartime demands created extra responsibilities for all divisions within the college, Engineering bore the greatest burden. The naval electrical and diesel training programs were handled there, at times with 3,100 enrollees. The newly created Curtiss-Wright Cadette program, which enrolled ninety-seven women, was also a part of the division. As the 1943 yearbook pointed out, these programs when combined with the needs of traditional engineering students produced "a grave strain on both the staff and the equipment of the division." The *Bomb* also noted that the division graduated forty civilian pilots every two months, as well as teaching twelve-week short courses designed for war industry service. The division taught courses in the new field of radar aircraft warning systems as well.[17]

The Curtiss-Wright program for women marked the greatest change in Iowa State's traditional engineering program, as for the first time, female students were invited to take engineering courses. As a school administrator noted in 1943, engineering had always been considered strictly a man's profession; before World

*In 1943, plane manufacturer Curtiss-Wright set up an engineering program for women at Iowa State. Three ISC engineering cadettes are shown receiving instruction regarding an aircraft engine. (Used by permission of Iowa State University Library/Special Collections Department)*

War II, very few women were trained as engineers anywhere in the country. That view would begin to change when the Curtiss-Wright Aircraft Manufacturing Company proposed to train young women in aeronautical engineering. Curtiss-Wright officials had experienced a shortage of engineers due to the military draft, and they believed that females could serve ably in that capacity. The aviation company realized that a typical four-year program would simply take too long, given wartime needs; the cadette program, therefore, would focus on those courses needed to perform specific aeronautical tasks. Government officials and Curtiss-Wright then selected seven colleges and universities around the nation, including Iowa State, to take part in the cadette program; government officials also contacted personnel at other colleges and universities in an attempt to locate female college students qualified to enter the program, particularly young women who had taken physics and math courses. In total, officials selected 711 students to enter the cadette program.[18]

In February 1943, ninety-seven young women, including seven from Iowa, moved into the top three floors of the Memorial Union and began their cadette training at Iowa State. Curtiss-Wright agreed to cover the cost of the women's room, board, and tuition and to pay a ten-dollar weekly stipend to each. One former ISC cadette, Jean Nickerson Patterson, remembered that the women "were relatively isolated," but all got along well together. Their courses included aircraft drafting, engineering mechanics, mathematics courses including a review of algebra and introduction to trigonometry, and "enough calculus to apply to any problems that will be needed on the job." The program emphasized aircraft design and the construction process and also included classes in oxygen acetylene welding, soldering, brazing, and arc welding.[19] The women spent forty hours each week in class.

At the end of the ten-month program, ISC officials realized the program had succeeded far beyond their expectations. The planners originally believed that only 50 percent of the women would finish the program, and only 25 percent would join the workforce. But by December 1943, 90 percent of the ISC cadettes had completed the program and 75 percent went into the workforce. Many ISC graduates went to St. Louis to work in the Curtiss-Wright production facilities; their salary was $135 per month.[20] This nontraditional program of training young women in the engineering field was deemed a major success, not only at ISC but at the other colleges and universities as well. And, while many women left the workforce during the postwar years, it seems likely that the Curtiss-Wright Cadette program played some part in helping to break down future barriers for aspiring female engineers.

While the college's military training and special engineering programs provided the most obvious signs of a nation at war, all college divisions were caught up in wartime programs. The Home Economics Division emphasized "self sufficiency in the home" along with the most practical and efficient methods for aiding the war effort. Topics included home gardening, canning, the remaking of clothing, and learning first aid techniques. Within the division, faculty in all departments developed programs to help Iowa families cope with wartime restrictions and shortages. Textiles and Clothing faculty taught women how to extend the life of clothing; faculty in Food and Nutrition, given the restrictions imposed by food rationing, developed programs on planning and preparing appetizing and nutritious diets; and faculty in Home Management offered assistance in extending the life of home equipment.[21] Home Economics faculty worked hand in hand with home demonstration Extension agents who carried the information to families throughout the state.

The Home Economics Division also addressed an additional wartime need: the training of nursery school teachers. Throughout the country as married women with children went to work outside the home, often in defense plants, the need for child care facilities skyrocketed. Some women could rely on family members for child care, but others needed day care facilities. In 1942, the federal government acknowledged that its day care facilities were woefully inadequate but vowed to remedy the program quickly. Iowa State College responded to that need by shortening the program for child development majors from eight to seven quarters. The major also included a course in the organization of wartime nursery schools.[22]

Other departments tackled major problems and also developed new programs.

The Economics Department concentrated on helping solve the problem of farm labor shortages, while the library faculty presented a program on WOI Radio called *The Challenge to Democracy,* in which they reviewed books related to the war. In addition to presenting an abundance of wartime programming, radio station WOI promoted the sale of war bonds.[23]

By 1943, accelerated programs and night courses had become the norm at Iowa State. Beginning in June of that year, the Division of Veterinary Medicine added a summer term so they could offer courses year-round instead of during the traditional three quarters schedule. That change allowed new freshmen to begin in the summer quarter of 1943 and then complete a four-year degree in three years. To accommodate additional courses and programs, evening classes were started. Not only did this boost the number of courses that could be taught, but it also helped alleviate the shortage of classrooms during daytime hours. The 1943 school yearbook explained that evening classes were no longer an oddity but an accepted part of campus life.[24]

Students themselves continued to contribute time and energy to wartime programs like promoting the sale of war bonds and conducting scrap metal drives. They also forfeited favorite activities. In 1943, students decided to forego corsages for school dances and instead use the money to buy war stamps and bonds. Such dances were described as "Stamp Corsage Dances." In 1945, VEISHEA was celebrated for one day only in an effort to conserve resources. School dances continued but were fewer in number than before. And consistent with changes elsewhere, as more men went into the military, female students took over offices and responsibilities formerly performed by males.[25]

Even with myriad changes and adjustments, however, some aspects of campus life remained the same. One tradition—having a celebrity select "*Bomb* beauties"—continued. In 1942, well-known movie star Ronald Reagan, a former announcer for WHO Radio in Des Moines, picked Iowa State's loveliest coeds to adorn the pages of the school yearbook. When the yearbook was published that year, *Bomb* staffers worked with the library personnel to send copies to ISC alumni serving in the military.[26]

While most of Iowa State's wartime programs were highly visible, one program—the most highly acclaimed war contribution—was not. This was a secret program that produced uranium for the Manhattan Project, which created the atomic bomb. Early in the war, scientists working on development of the bomb faced a shortage of high-quality purified uranium. Two scientists at Iowa State, Harley Wilhelm and William Keller, decided to try to produce the material. The two men "took a small iron pipe with a cap and sealed it at the bottom. They lined the container with magnesium oxide and poured in calcium and uranium tetrafluoride. They hooked up a Champion spark plug to spark an intense heating process." Wilhelm later explained, "We opened it up and we had two ounces of nice pure uranium metal."[27] Wilhelm quickly notified Frank Spedding, head of the ISC Chemistry Department and an expert in rare metals; Spedding, in turn, contacted Arthur Compton at the University of Chicago, a scientist and supervisor of one major area of research that came to be known as the Manhattan Project.

Soon a group of scientists at Iowa State was involved in a project that Spedding

*Side view of campus building known as Little Ankeny. Iowa State scientists carried out uranium production here in World War II. (Used by permission of Iowa State University Library/Special Collections Department)*

described as "solving many of the metallurgical problems" involved with the Manhattan Project. The highly secretive work was done in a former women's gym on the ISC campus, known as Little Ankeny; the nickname seemed appropriate since nearby Ankeny was home to a large munitions factory. Iowa State officials estimated that the Ames group produced about two million pounds of high-quality uranium during the war years. Subsequently, this wartime research program led to the establishment of the Ames Laboratory at ISU.[28]

In an interview some years after the war, Professor Spedding related a humorous incident that happened during this intense, demanding period. He explained that the ISC project produced a green dust that filtered out of the wooden women's gym building and collected on the ground; workmen deposited the dust in the college dump. Before long, personnel feared that someone might analyze a sample of the material and figure out what was actually occurring in Little Ankeny. Officials decided that the dust and the ground around it should be collected and shipped east for disposal. Spedding related, "This meant that we had to pack up hundreds of barrels of material and ship it. We sometimes accused the east that they wanted good Iowa soil when we had to take that nice black dirt away from the building." Before long, there was a shortage of shipping containers. When Dr. Keller suggested that whiskey barrels might work, he dictated to his secretary that he wanted a thousand barrels from Hiram Walker's distillery. The order read that ISC wanted an actual thousand barrels of whiskey. Alarmed at the order, the college purchasing agent contacted Dr. Spedding, inquiring, "Do you really need this whiskey through the college? Can't you get it some other way?" The matter was eventually straightened out, and the scientists got the empty barrels but avoided a potential scandal, as drinking alcoholic beverages on campus was clearly illegal at the time.[29]

On October 12, 1945, the Iowa State scientists would be honored for their extraordinary contribution to the war effort. For their uranium production program, the college would receive one of the nation's highest awards, the United States Army-Navy Production Award for Excellence. Presiding at the Iowa State award ceremony, Colonel K. D. Nichols explained that the Iowa State scientists' approach not only produced uranium more cheaply than before but also produced a material with greater purity and at a rate previously unobtainable. The method was adopted for use in other metal-producing plants. Officials at Iowa State and elsewhere in the state had reason to be tremendously proud of the accomplishment: the college had won not one award, but a total of five. Colonel Nichols pointed out that four stars decorated the official "E Flag," and the flag itself represented "six months of excellence of production and research." Major General Leslie R. Groves, director of the entire atomic bomb project, presented the award.[30]

The contributions of the Ames scientists to the production of uranium stand as an extraordinary contribution to the war effort, but thoughtful Americans greeted the onset of the nuclear age with mixed emotions, as did President Friley. What did the future hold now that this potentially cataclysmic energy force had been unleashed? In his convocation address just a month after the dropping of the bombs on Japan, Friley spoke eloquently but with guarded optimism about the future of the nuclear age. He noted in his typical erudite manner that "science has revealed to us the ultimate earthly power . . . [and] we have become as gods, with new and almost infinite power for good and evil." He believed that the country was now at the "threshold of an era in which mankind, having unlocked the door to this staggering secret of nature, may be able to fashion a world of peace, happiness and prosperity . . . or with hellish ingenuity he may fabricate weapons to destroy himself."[31]

Among those who sacrificed for the war effort, however, one group stands out above the rest. In the main entry to the ISU Memorial Union—known as the Gold Star Hall—338 names are chiseled in stone under the simple heading "World War II." These are the men, some graduates and some whose education was disrupted by war, who made the ultimate sacrifice for their country. Included are the names of two brothers, Glen and Wayne Cunningham. The brothers had a special association with Iowa State and the community of Ames. They had grown up in Ames, where their father, Ray Cunningham, served for many years as a popular director of the campus YMCA. Lt. Glen R. Cunningham was stabbed to death in a hospital by a mental patient on May 10, 1943; Lt. Wayne E. Cunningham, a P-38 fighter pilot, was killed in action in the Philippines on April 25, 1945, only a few months before the war ended. In the recesses of Special Collections in the ISU Library, a file holds a poignant reminder of the Cunningham family's terrible loss. A faded pamphlet entitled *In Loving Memory,* published on May 27, 1945, includes the pictures of the two handsome, smiling young men dressed in their military uniforms. For the Cunningham family and hundreds of others, memories of those sacrifices would last a lifetime.[32]

At war's end, difficult decisions lay ahead for the school. In his convocation address in September 1945, President Friley acknowledged the extraordinary contributions of everyone at Iowa State to the war effort. But he quickly added that peacetime status would mark another period in the history of the college containing major challenges. Friley envisioned an expansion of the campus physical plant and a rapidly growing Cooperative Extension Service. He noted that freshmen enrollment was up 65 percent but the staff was depleted from wartime needs. He issued a call for an efficiency of operations characterized by better use of classrooms and laboratories, a constant survey of course offerings to prevent an unnecessarily large number of classes, and the need to eliminate obsolete or unnecessary course content. He believed that counseling for the student body would be needed as well.[33]

Veterans began to enroll at ISC soon after the war ended. Wayne Moore, longtime ISU vice president for business and finance, arrived back on campus in the summer of 1945, following his military service. An Iowa State staff member told Moore that probably "a few more students would be showing up" and asked Moore to be available to advise them. His pay was 50 cents an hour.[34] Instead of a few students, the college experienced a deluge of thousands of returning veterans. Officials were so overwhelmed, in fact, that classes started three days late in the fall of 1946. As a stopgap measure, administrators set up a freshman engineering program at Camp Dodge near Des Moines. The program ended the following year. Veterans continued to enroll and by 1948, the school's total enrollment was over ten thousand. Iowa State officials had originally anticipated the heaviest enrollment of veterans in 1947 and 1948. In preparation for that increase, college officials established new intensive short courses in agriculture and engineering, ranging in length from three months to two years.[35] Housing needs for married veterans as well as for traditional students also ranked high among administrative concerns.

The main impetus for the dramatic enrollment increase was the GI Bill of Rights—formally known as the Servicemen's Readjustment Act of 1944. The legislation provided veterans with tuition, books, fees, and a monthly subsistence allowance. Veterans were free to select their own schools while the educational institutions were free to accept or reject the applicants. Officials viewed these two conditions as major reasons for the program's success. Both educators and government officials, however, consistently underestimated the number of veterans who would take advantage of the program. In the fall of 1946, over one million veterans enrolled, almost doubling the total number of college students nationwide. According to one historian, "the GI Bill was the most ambitious venture in mass higher education that had ever been attempted by any society."[36]

*Following World War II, Iowa State officials created housing for returning veterans and their families. Above is a view of Pammel Court. (Used by permission of Iowa State University Library/Special Collections Department)*

In the three years following the end of the war, Iowa State officials created several types of married student housing. The first was Pammel Court, named after L. H. Pammel, longtime head of the Botany Department at ISC and an internationally known scholar. Pammel Court began to take shape in 1945 when one hundred "drab government trailers," each seven by twenty-two feet, were moved to the north end of campus, south of the Chicago and North Western railroad tracks (now Union Pacific). The *Iowa State Daily* later wrote about life in the trailers: "from the kitchen it was one step to the living room, two steps to the baby's bedroom, one step to the door, and no steps to the closet. A couch on one end of the trailer opened into a bed." Families paid rents ranging from $22.50 to $25 per month, but the trailers had no plumbing and water was carried from public taps.[37]

During the next two years, several additions were made to Pammel Court. Shortly after the trailers arrived, fifty prefabricated houses were assembled; students described these as "luxury apartments" in comparison to the original trailers. The next addition consisted of fifty Quonset huts shipped by the Federal Public Housing Administration from Tacoma, Washington. The largest addition to Pammel, the Boom Town project, started in July 1946. The project included the erection of 317 army tropical Quonsets and barracks that had been modernized. When a large number of returning veterans and their wives arrived in the fall of 1946, fortunately Pammel Court housing projects were already under way. At the height of its development, Pammel Court included 152 trailers, 100 Quonset apartments, 70 prefabricated houses, 734 barrack apartments, and 50 private

*Returning World War II veterans register for classes in State Gym. The GI Bill made it possible for thousands of veterans to attend Iowa State. (Used by permission of Iowa State University Library/Special Collections Department)*

trailer lots. By January 1951, the demand for veterans' housing was easing and college officials began allowing nonveterans to move into Pammel.[38]

Returning veterans and their families rarely had much money for nonessentials, but through assistance from the college and their own organizational initiatives, they did manage to enjoy some social events. In May 1947, the college social bureau held a May Daze for Marrieds, to give married couples a weekend of fun and relaxation. The three-day event included a dog show, diaper derby (the winner was the father who could change his child's diaper the fastest), a tiny tot parade, a dance with "hard luck" costumes, and an old-time vaudeville show. By 1949, Pammel residents had developed the Share the Sitter Plan, where parents exchanged babysitting, thus avoiding the hiring of sitters. At times when there were too few sitters to go around, "a 'walker' would go from trailer to trailer checking the children every twenty minutes."[39]

Barely had veterans' housing needs been addressed, however, when President Friley faced another challenge. Maintaining good relations with college alumni was a crucial matter, and in March 1947, the relationship between the college alumni association and Friley had apparently become frayed. The Iowa State Alumni Association president, Claude Coykendall of Ames, had contacted the

State Board of Education (later, the Board of Regents) with complaints about administrative procedures at Iowa State specifically related to President Friley. Coykendall made clear that the Alumni Association had not asked for the president's resignation but rather for an investigation into the complaints. More specifically, Coykendall charged that "Friley's methods have caused some faculty members to leave the institution and have hindered efforts to obtain replacements." Apparently one faculty member involved, Carl J. Drake, former head of the Zoology Department, had been shifted to a research status by Friley. The *Des Moines Register* reported that Professor Drake had gone to court to fight the change but had lost. The *Register* quoted another source that the quality of Iowa State "has been deteriorating [under Friley] and it does not occupy the position it once did." The same source noted that some faculty members had left ISC because they believed they had been treated poorly.[40]

The State Board of Education hurriedly set up a subcommittee to look into the allegations. One week later, the Board gave a full endorsement to Friley, issuing the following statement: "The Board has carefully considered this information and examined into conditions at Iowa State college. It has the utmost confidence in President Friley and the administration of Iowa State college. It considers President Friley to be one of the most distinguished land grant college presidents in the United States."[41]

While the board's total endorsement of Friley marked the end of the public airing of charges, the view persisted on campus that Friley was dictatorial. In his biography of President W. Robert Parks, Robert Underhill relates an exchange between President Parks and Home Economics Dean Helen LeBaron in which Parks stated that some "good people thought Friley was pretty dictatorial, [and] arbitrary." LeBaron responded, "Was he ever!" She related her first budget hearing with Friley in which he told her, "Look, Helen, all you do is write in the names of your people on a piece of paper, and I'll write in the salaries." To another longtime Iowa State administrator, Friley's administrative style was to keep a close watch on all aspects of college life. Wayne Moore, who began his ISU career under Friley, noted that the president ran Iowa State single-handedly. As a result Friley knew every name in the budget and personally approved every salary change. Moore viewed Friley as a highly capable administrator who was a product of his generation in terms of his administrative style.[42]

During the last five years of Friley's presidency, new construction and remodeling projects were increasingly apparent on campus, but in 1950, a new type of expansion took place. On February 21, WOI-TV went on the air. Iowa State College had the distinction of starting the first licensed educationally owned and operated television station in the nation. A year later, in a review of Friley's accomplishments, the ISC Information Service noted that Friley "was one of the nation's first educators to see the great potential value of television as an education medium." Five years earlier, Friley had appointed a college committee to study the educational and technical possibilities of television.[43] WOI-TV quickly became a valuable teaching tool, a training facility for students, and an important means of broadcasting off-campus educational programs.

In March 1953, Charles E. Friley's seventeen-year tenure as president of ISC came to an end. The school had a mandatory retirement age of sixty-five for its president, and reaching that, Friley was obligated to relinquish his presidency. During his administration, Iowa State had grown from a college of 5,788 undergraduate students to a total enrollment of 7,800. At the peak of the veterans' enrollment, that number reached about 10,000. Throughout his administration, Friley appreciated the significance of past policies, but seemed always to be looking ahead, anticipating future problems and future opportunities. There were few aspects of the college that Friley did not personally manage and few policies at Iowa State that did not bear a strong imprint of his tenure.[44] The man who always had time to talk with students, yet who seemed businesslike, formal, and "perhaps a little austere," was stepping down.[45]

The man who replaced Charles Friley as Iowa State's president, James H. Hilton, was also a southerner by birth. Hilton grew up on a farm near Hickory, North Carolina; he attended North Carolina State College for one year and then transferred to Iowa State in 1923, where he majored in animal husbandry. Hilton had selected Iowa State because he felt the school had a better program in livestock production than did North Carolina. Hilton's early ties to Iowa State were further strengthened when he worked for three years as a Greene County Extension agent. Hilton then earned an M.S. from the University of Wisconsin and joined the Purdue University staff in 1939; six years later, he was awarded the D.Sc. degree at Purdue. He returned to North Carolina State as head of animal husbandry and three years later officials there named him dean of agriculture. In 1953, Hilton became Iowa State's tenth president.[46]

While both Dr. Friley and President Hilton claimed a southern heritage, their public demeanors differed significantly. The reserved, decorous administration of Dr. Friley gave way to a more relaxed, casual regime of President Hilton. In the January 1953 issue of the ISC *Alumnus Magazine*, the headline read, "Jim Is Coming Back." The informality inherent in the use of the president's nickname, Jim, apparently set the tone for the new administration. With Hilton, in fact, there seemed to be a strong sense of the familiar, perhaps because of his earlier associations with Iowa State. In the *Alumnus* article, Rex Conn, the farm editor of the Cedar Rapids *Gazette,* lauded Hilton for his highly successful work at North Carolina State. Conn described Hilton's methods there as "simple, direct, and effective." Conn believed that North Carolina State had identified Hilton for the chancellory of the college and that the University of Illinois sought him as dean of agriculture. In other words, Conn suggested, Iowans had scored a real coup. Another publication pointed out that Iowans could identify with Hilton because he had done manual labor—taking care of the college dairy herd, building silos, and constructing sheep-dipping vats—to pay for his college expenses; then, through hard work, he had risen above his humble beginning to achieve both academic and administrative success.[47]

Even Hilton's first contact regarding the ISC presidency was informal, and undoubtedly, regarded as a plus by most Iowans. Vincent B. Hamilton had known "Jimmy" Hilton when the two were undergraduates at Iowa State. Some thirty

*This photograph of James H. Hilton was taken shortly before he became Iowa State's tenth president in 1953. Hilton had received an undergraduate degree from Iowa State in the mid-1920s. (Used by permission of Iowa State University Library/Special Collections Department)*

years later, Hamilton served on the Board of Regents and chaired the Regents' Faculty and Personnel Committee. In a later interview, Hamilton recalled that following Dr. Friley's retirement, the regents had a list of about 250 names of prospective presidential candidates, including Hilton's. Hamilton believed that Hilton would make an excellent president, so while on a trip to Tennessee with his wife, Hamilton decided to make a side trip to visit James Hilton in North Carolina. Staying in a motel in Tennessee, Vincent wanted to write Hilton about getting together. The motel room had no writing paper and Hamilton didn't have a fountain pen. So he wrote on a two-cent postcard, in pencil, asking Hilton if he was interested in the ISC presidency. Apparently Hilton's secretary thought the card was a joke but passed it along to Hilton anyway. Hilton and his wife, Lois, met the Hamiltons at Gatlinburg, Tennessee, to discuss the position. Soon after that meeting, Hilton was hired as ISC's president. Reflecting on Hilton's accomplishments at Iowa State, Hamilton observed, "I'm delighted to have been a little part of that picture."[48]

Hilton's varied experiences at North Carolina State obviously influenced his approach to the Iowa State presidency, but his earlier experience in Cooperative Extension should also be considered. A county Extension agent at a time when Extension was the primary source of information for Iowa farmers, Hilton's

Extension work included developing skills in leadership, organization, communications, and, last but not least, salesmanship. County agents, after all, were expected to convince farmers to adopt new methods of farming and farm management. And, basic to all responsibilities, a county agent must get to know his clientele. Louis Thompson, who knew Hilton well, believed he came to Iowa State with a sense of mission to develop the school into a larger, more widely known educational institution and that Hilton drew successfully on his Extension experience to accomplish those goals. More specifically, Thompson believed that Hilton's strong commitment to maintaining good contacts with school alumni and cultivating ties with individual state legislators stemmed from his experience as a county agent. Moreover, given the large number of farmers in Iowa in the 1950s, Hilton also had a solid base of support throughout the state.

Hilton had hardly settled into his new position when it became clear that events outside the college would have a major impact on the school. By 1953, Iowa's economy was facing serious problems. Iowa agriculture, the state's major industry, had prospered during World War II, but by 1953, state officials were increasingly aware of an economic downturn in the agricultural sector. In their publication *The Iowa Basebook for Agricultural Adjustment,* agricultural economists at Iowa State noted that the farm problem was taking shape with "surpluses, lower farm prices, lower farm incomes, higher farm costs." The economists expressed amazement over the fact that while the general economy seemed to be doing well, the farm economy was not. In other words, agriculture seemed to be out of adjustment with the rest of the economy. Frequent drought throughout Iowa added further to the farm difficulties.[49]

For several years, Hilton expressed considerable concern over the state's economic difficulties. Obviously for many institutions of higher learning, such as ISC, farm distress meant fewer taxes collected, and, therefore, lower state appropriations. In an address to the staff in the fall of 1953, Hilton, in his usual direct manner, confronted the problem head-on. He stated, "we are now operating on an entirely new and restricted budgetary system. . . . This presents a difficult situation for all of us." He forewarned the faculty that they would be called upon to teach heavier loads than before, and there would be less money for supplies and instructional materials. At the same time, Hilton assured the faculty that he and his staff would do all they could to help carry on the work of the college.[50] That same candor remained evident in Hilton's speeches the following year.[51]

During the mid-fifties, other college officials were also seeking solutions to the state's perplexing economic problems. Cooperative Extension personnel did some real soul-searching as to how to help farm families improve profits and make farm living more attractive. Extension responded with the Farm and Home Development Program to help farm families do long-range social and economic planning. Another change was to accelerate programs helping farm people better understand issues such as tariffs and foreign trade, given Iowans' increasing involvement in international trade. Also mid-decade, Iowa State officials established the Center for Agriculture and Rural Development (CARD). Earl O. Heady, later to become the first Charles F. Curtiss Distinguished Professor in Agriculture, instigated the center. Like earlier ISC economists, Heady and his staff were concerned about problems with agricultural adjustment; the center was to assist the state's agriculture sector by finding new ways to utilize Iowa's farm products and to research marketing and processing problems.[52]

In spite of the state's economic problems, early in his presidency Hilton outlined plans for what would become one of his major legacies, the Iowa State University Center. Hilton had conceived the plans for the center either shortly after he arrived or perhaps even before becoming president. Vincent Hamilton recalled that when Hilton first arrived on campus, the Hiltons and Hamiltons spent a weekend together. Hamilton related that Hilton "drove me around and pointed out that there wasn't a single place on this campus to have graduation that was really accommodating." Hamilton remembered that when he was in school, "we had graduation in the gymnasium and the English sparrows were in there, too." Later, graduation was held in the Armory. "You couldn't hear very well unless you were in the front four or five [rows]."[53] At the staff convocation in his second year, Hilton envisioned the center to include an auditorium, a little theater, a coliseum, and a space to house other activities such as radio and television. He believed the center should be built east of the women's dormitories and north of Lincoln Way. He concluded, "[T]that is one of my dreams for the future. It probably will take years to complete it. You may think I am unrealistic, a dreamer, a visionary or just plain crazy. But I may say to you that I have already been called all those things and some other things, too, about this project, and if any of you feel that I should be discouraged in this venture you should think up some other terms—because I am quite determined about this Center."[54] While there were undoubtedly skeptics and naysayers, Hilton was true to his word. Believing the center should be built by private funds—without any state funding—he initiated a major fund-raising campaign. That campaign laid the basis for what later became the Iowa State University Foundation. Construction would get under way in the 1960s; the four-structure complex was completed in 1975.[55]

For the remainder of the 1950s, Hilton's speeches to the staff made it abundantly clear that the state continued to experience hard times. In the fall of 1955, Hilton pointed out that student enrollments were increasing, but state appropriations were not. In terms of capital improvements, Hilton lamented "this is a sad, sad story," as the college had requested $4,343,000 for capital improvements for the biennium and the state legislature had appropriated only $1,674,000. Expressing concern for increased enrollment and the subsequent problems of adequate student housing and classroom and laboratory space, Hilton explained that the college either had to have more space or restrict enrollment. But he added, "I can think of no greater tragedy than for Iowa State College to finish the first century of existence by saying to some of the youth of this state we are sorry we cannot admit you because there is no room for you."[56]

Even with budget shortfalls, however, Iowa State did respond to increased student housing needs. Hawthorne Court, a ninety-six-unit housing area for married students, was added to Pammel Court in 1956. Two dormitories, Westgate in 1955 and Linden Hall in 1957, were constructed for female students and Helser Hall, a residence for male students, was completed in 1957.[57]

That same year, President Hilton confronted a very different issue: changing the name of Iowa State College to Iowa State University. He presented the issue to the ISC staff in September 1957, asking for faculty input into the matter. At the time, Hilton himself was not convinced that the name change was necessary, but according to Robert Underhill, sentiment had been growing for the name change for over a decade, as it was obvious that ISC with its graduate programs was a university in "everything but name." In the next two years, ISC faculty committees researched the possible consequences of the change along with a committee that studied the actual cost of education for all three state schools. Moreover, in 1958, W. Robert Parks was named dean of instruction at ISC and Parks, along with the college deans, felt strongly that the name change was necessary. At the same time, a major opponent to the change was Virgil Hancher, president of the State University of Iowa. Hancher saw each of the three state schools as having a distinct purpose and felt strongly about retaining that distinction. In fact, Hancher had earlier proposed consolidating Iowa's three institutions of higher learning into one university system, such as officials had done in North Carolina and California. The change would have turned the State University of Iowa into the flagship institution with Iowa State Teachers College and Iowa State College being satellites of the Iowa City school.[58]

Early in 1959 the regents requested that Presidents Hilton, Hancher, and J. W. Maucker of Iowa State Teachers College meet to determine a plan for future development of the three institutions. Clearly a part of this request was the need for each institution to clarify the nature and extent of its liberal arts offerings. Records of these meetings indicate that President Hilton had to walk something of a tightrope in stating Iowa State's need for courses in the humanities and social sciences while always de-emphasizing their importance in relationship to the school's basic mission—science and technology. Even with his own faculty, Hilton had to walk a rather fine line in supporting the need for majors in areas of the non-scientific and technical fields, sometimes adding the qualifier that the majors in the social sciences and humanities would be intended to "complement and support the central scientific and technological purposes of our institution."[59]

By March 1959, the issue of Iowa State's name change continued to strain relations between Presidents Hancher and Hilton. In that month, President Hancher had sent a memorandum to the Board of Regents regarding the liberal arts programs at the three state schools. Hilton believed that Hancher had misrepresented ISC's curriculum, purpose, and functions, and had failed to recognize ISC as a "broadly based Land-Grant institution."[60] Hilton further criticized Hancher's memorandum for repeatedly indicating that the liberal arts were "SUI's own exclusive province." Moreover, Hilton disagreed with Hancher's contention "that strong departments and major programs [at the three state schools] in these areas . . . would involve duplication, competition, and waste, and lead to mediocrity in teaching and scholarship."[61]

Later in the year, the state legislature and the Board of Regents would support the name change from Iowa State College to Iowa State University. At the same time, Iowa State changed the name of its divisions to colleges. Hilton had little comment about the name change, but he did allude to the difficult process as "an interesting and nerve-racking battle." He added, "Suffice to say, I am glad that task is over, and we will not have to go through this again. I am sure that the change in name was worth the struggle."[62]

While budget shortfalls, faculty matters, and name changes dominated the administration's schedule, student activities were also of vital interest. When asked what student social events were important in the mid-fifties, then ISC student Jim Wiggins replied, "panty raids, panty raids, panty raids." The fad of male students attempting to invade women's dormitories to steal their underwear was nationwide in the mid-fifties. Wiggins remembered that while male students instigated the raids, they were usually "cheered on" by coeds leaning out dormitory windows, waving their unmentionables. Regarded as frivolous by some students and administrators, this behavior was also viewed as potentially dangerous, given the possibility of student injuries. By spring 1956, the panty raid phenomenon was in full swing on college campuses. At Iowa State, on May 24, a group of students, estimated from seven hundred to a thousand, had congregated near Barton Hall, a women's dormitory. The students had begun assembling on campus at around 10:30 P.M. but apparently had made only one attempt to enter the dormitory. Members of the Cardinal Guild (the student government association), assisted by college athletes, then appeared and blocked the male students' entry into the dorm. Although the would-be raiders brought along a ladder, common sense prevailed when the athletes simply stood on the ladder to prevent its use. For a time, the students closed Highway 30, a transcontinental highway, through Campustown. Finally, by 1:30 A.M. student leaders had convinced the crowd to go home.[63]

Iowa State's administrators reacted with dispatch in an attempt to ward off any future raids. The May 24 event, described by the *Des Moines Register* as a "near riot," was taken seriously. Administrators took disciplinary action against twenty-three students: ten were suspended, ten were placed on probation, and three were reprimanded. The matter attracted considerable press coverage throughout the state and did not escape the attention of the Board of Regents, who took the matter up at their June meeting.[64]

Not all students agreed with the administration's quick action. The *Iowa State Daily Student* accused the administration of grandstanding because some legislators were scheduled to visit campus a few days later. A newspaper editorial complained that the suspended students were given only eighteen hours to leave campus. One student complained that he had only two hours to "prepare a defense."[65] Another newspaper reported that students were circulating petitions on campus requesting that the suspensions be reconsidered. It is not clear if all suspensions held, but it is clear that Iowa State's administrators wanted no more panty raids.

In 1959, Iowa State would again be in the limelight but this time in a more positive way. On September 23, 1959, the university attracted national attention when Soviet Premier Nikita Khrushchev visited the campus. The visit came as part of Khrushchev's twelve-day national tour. The previous day the Soviet delegation had visited the home of Iowa farmer and seed corn producer Roswell Garst in Coon Rapids. Garst had issued the invitation to visit Iowa. The Russians then traveled by motorcade to the ISU campus. Their arrival was not without a few suspenseful moments for as the motorcade drove down Osborn Drive, "four men clad in identical trenchcoats, pulled-down fedoras, and dark glasses suddenly stepped into the

*Soviet Premier Nikita Khrushchev and his wife, Nina, visit with ISU students in the Household Equipment Laboratory in MacKay Hall. Dean Helen LeBaron and Iowa State President James Hilton stand behind Khrushchev. U.S. Ambassador to the United Nations Henry Cabot Lodge is to the right of Hilton. The Khrushchevs' ISU visit was part of a twelve-day tour through the United States in September 1959. (Used by permission of Iowa State University Library/Special Collections Department)*

street. Carrying violin cases, they marched toward the car with the Russian leader." Four security men quickly appeared and "firmly" moved the students back into the crowd. As Robert Underhill pointed out, the event was a prank by "fun-loving college students," but in later years, such an intrusion would have been viewed much more seriously.[66]

Once on campus, President Hilton greeted the Soviet delegation at the front of MacKay Hall, the home economics building. Inside, Dean Helen LeBaron greeted the visitors. In response to hearing that home economics courses prepared American women for marriage, Khrushchev commented, "In Russia, we don't have such schools. We learned such things from our mothers." Nina Khrushchev accompanied her husband on the home economics tour and according to one account, "showed great interest in a display of cooking utensils." Khrushchev's visit was obviously a major campus event, and as he emerged from MacKay Hall, hundreds of spectators waved to him, shouting, "Hi, Nikki." Before leaving campus, President Hilton presented the Soviet premier with a history of Iowa State.[67]

*President James Hilton and Home Economics Dean Helen LeBaron entertain students from Baroda University (Baroda, India) at the Knoll. The Knoll is the president's home and is located on campus. (Used by permission of Iowa State University Library/Special Collections Department)*

That same year, internationalism of another kind would involve Iowa State faculty. International programs had been a part of Iowa State for several decades, but in the late 1950s, those programs took on greater importance. According to Hilton, in fact, after 1950, over a hundred ISC staff members had served on foreign assignments and had worked on technical assistance programs in forty-five different countries; moreover, over 1,700 visitors from seventy-six different countries had visited the campus to observe the work of administrators and faculty. But in 1959, a new type of international program started taking shape as school officials began exploring the development of a five-year cooperative relationship between Iowa State and Baroda University in India. Baroda had been founded ten years earlier and desired to upgrade its postgraduate training and research in home economics so it could eventually offer the M.A. and Ph.D. Iowa State's College of Home Economics was invited to work with Baroda officials to accomplish those goals. In 1960, the Ford Foundation awarded a grant of $525,000 for a three-year program of postgraduate training and research in Home Science at Baroda.[68]

By the end of the fifties, several additional international issues were of concern to President Hilton and other Iowa State officials. In 1957, the Soviet Union launched several satellites known as Sputnik; American efforts to do the same were unsuccessful. The Soviet's success with Sputnik caused some real soul-searching regarding the American educational system. While Soviet students studied science and math, American educators and government officials acknowledged that American students received far less training in those areas. Congress soon passed the National Defense Education Act in 1958 to provide fellowships, grants, and loans to encourage young Americans to study science, mathematics, and foreign languages. President Hilton referred to the Soviet successes in his 1960 convocation speech when he stated that the country's "whole educational system [is] under attack." He noted that "as a result of this public clamor, plus a genuine desire on the part of those engaged in education, improvements are being made. Standards are being raised. Some so-called educational frills are going by the boards. Honors programs are being established for the especially gifted students."[69]

In 1961, the resignation of Provost James Jensen to take the presidency at Oregon State University provided an opportunity for administrative reorganization that spoke to the new demands for science courses and scientific research. According to Robert Underhill, Jensen's resignation gave Hilton the opportunity to break up "the multitudinous duties" of the provost and distribute these duties between two newly named vice presidents. J. Boyd Page, the new vice president of research, was specifically charged with maintaining contact between the university and various federal agencies including the National Science Foundation, the National Aeronautics and Space Administration, the Department of Health, Education, and Welfare, and the National Institutes of Health; Page retained his position as dean of the graduate college. W. Robert Parks, who came to Iowa State in 1958 as dean of instruction, was named vice president for academic affairs. The naming of two vice presidents allowed Hilton in the later years of his presidency to spend more and more time with the Board of Regents, alumni, and state government officials. For Parks, the promotion to vice president of academic affairs provided further evidence that he was favored by Hilton to be the next ISU president.[70]

The beginning of the 1960s brought additional changes to Iowa State, but not of the same magnitude as elsewhere. The decade of the 1950s had been a relatively quiet time on college campuses as students were portrayed as passive, silent, and career oriented. That would change dramatically, as in the sixties, students' war protests and general unrest seemed everywhere. Eventually Iowa State students would demonstrate against the Vietnam War, but in comparison with other schools, even the University of Iowa, the ISU protest would be muted. And, for Hilton, that protest lay in the future. During the remainder of his presidency, problems continued to surface, but seemed more a continuation of previous issues than new or unusual challenges.

In his convocation speech in September 1961, Hilton raised the issue of ever-increasing student enrollments. In pre–World War II days, low enrollments had been a problem, but no longer. More and more Iowa students were attending college. Apparently the university expected a great increase in 1963, but Hilton observed that the vanguard of the increase had arrived in September 1961. The increase was so great, in fact, that at one point Hilton suggested limiting student enrollment. And, as the president pointed out, with more students enrolling, there were the corresponding problems of inadequate physical facilities and shortages of well-trained teachers.[71]

But while high enrollments called for additional resources, it seemed the problem had come at a fortuitous time. In the late fifties, the Iowa economy was clearly rebounding. Most importantly, the agricultural sector was recovering from the recession of the fifties. These changes would bode well for state appropriations for institutions of higher learning, including Iowa State. In his faculty convocation two years later, Hilton took note of that fact: "I have never seen any legislature more genuinely interested in higher education than the 1963 Iowa General Assembly. I do not wish to imply that this was true of every single member, but it was true of most of them, and particularly of the leadership in both the House and Senate. They proved this in a very tangible way in their support of the three institutions." Very likely, the president's good relations with the legislature were a factor in the increased appropriations.[72] Louis Thompson, in fact, recalled that Hilton knew many legislators individually and worked diligently to cultivate ties with them; moreover, he knew their particular leanings on legislation important to Iowa State.

On one occasion when Hilton feared a particular university appropriation would not pass, he knew which key legislator opposed the bill. The legislator's son attended Iowa State and Thompson served as his advisor; Thompson also knew the student's father. Hilton requested that Thompson contact the legislator on behalf of the university, which Thompson did. And the bill passed.[73] One more time it seemed that Hilton's Extension background came into play: know your constituency well.

While campus construction and remodeling projects would move forward at a fairly rapid rate after 1960, almost from the beginning of Hilton's administration, expansion had been evident. In 1959 and 1960, campus improvements included an addition of one hundred units to Hawthorne Court. The administration also made curricula changes including new majors in English, speech, modern foreign language, and physical education for women as well as the creation of a new Department of Nuclear Engineering and a graduate program in aeronautical engineering. Officials had set up a new university computer system as well.[74] It was after 1960, however, with an improved Iowa economy, that campus construction projects would multiply. In 1962, Hilton explained that the total expenditures for buildings then under construction as well as buildings to be started during the year was $17.5 million. New construction and remodeling projects continued throughout the 1960s.[75]

A year before Hilton's retirement, he and Virgil Hancher would have one more public confrontation. Although the state's economy had improved by the early sixties, state officials continued to voice interest in economizing measures for the state's schools of higher learning. In early 1964, Governor Harold Hughes requested that the Board of Regents examine the possibility of combining the Extension services operated separately by each of the three state-supported schools. Hughes believed that the ISU Extension Service was "too heavily geared to agriculture and should concentrate more on non-farm subject matter." Hughes added, "there is a growing need for expanded extension services in such areas as public school problems, taxation, and industrial and community development." Perhaps no issue would strike closer to the heart of Iowa State's land-grant mission than a change in the status of Cooperative Extension. Extension had been an integral part of Iowa State since the early 1900s, and ISU Cooperative Extension had long been viewed as a model by other state Extension agencies. Cooperative Extension, moreover, brought in considerable state and federal funds to the university. For President Hilton, a former county Extension agent and a strong backer of ISU Extension, a major change in that program must have seemed unthinkable.[76]

Responding to Hughes's comments, President Hancher suggested that the University of Iowa "be given authority to run extension services" at Iowa, Iowa State University, and State College of Iowa (now University of Northern Iowa). At the same time, Hancher repeated an earlier suggestion: that the state adopt a "one university system" by combining the three state schools under the control of one university president.[77] Within a short time, Governor Hughes apparently retreated from his earlier suggestion of combining Extension services, and although the Board of Regents may have discussed the issue, no action was taken. Cooperative Extension would remain safely within the Iowa State fold. Since Presidents Hilton and Hancher retired shortly thereafter, the Extension consolidation issue marked the end of their public disagreements.

In the fall of 1964, in his last convocation speech, Hilton noted the many campus improvements during the previous year, the continued high enrollments, and, he added with a note of exasperation, the increasing parking problem: "Lord have mercy on our souls! What a problem this is! No matter how many additional parking spaces are provided each year they are filled and there is a clamor for more." At the same time, the president demonstrated one reason that Iowans felt a kinship with Jim Hilton: he revisited some of the amusing incidents from his twelve-year presidency, including a students' riot when told they could not have Monday off following the football win over Missouri, and the panty raid in which students were suspended. For Iowa Staters, Hilton's ability to laugh at himself was another of his endearing traits.[78]

In his final convocation, the man Iowa State had so enthusiastically welcomed back in 1953 made clear his enduring affection for that institution. He noted that the past eleven years had been "rough, tough, exciting, glorious years" but on June 30, 1965, he would be ready to step down. He added, "I will always love you for making these past eleven years the happiest years of my life. Although I will give up the responsibilities of president next June, I hope to spend the rest of my life working for Iowa State."[79]

In the middle two and one-half decades of the twentieth century—from 1940 to 1965—Iowa State University had gone through a rapid and far-reaching transition. First and foremost, the school had been transformed from a college to a university, not only in name but also in size, breadth, outreach, and reputation. Officials had transformed the school from a college with a major focus on science, agriculture, home economics, and veterinary medicine to a more broadly based institution with a growing presence around the world. No longer were the humanities and social sciences only appendages. While they remained small in comparison to the older curriculums, by 1965, they were expanding areas deserving of recognition.

Two men had guided this transition. Although Charles Friley and James Hilton differed in temperament and public persona, they were equally committed to their school's development and continued excellence. President Friley took office in 1936, a year when Iowans were still reeling from the Great Depression. The greatest challenge of Friley's career, however, was presiding over a school caught up in the needs of a global war. Once the war ended, his administration had to contend with increased enrollments, the housing needs of married students, and the need to expand various curriculums. The man with a southern accent and formal demeanor retired after seventeen years of dealing with desperate measures brought on by depression and war.

James Hilton became ISU's tenth president in 1953. From the beginning, Hilton seemed to be a man of the people, and a man of much personal warmth.[80] While not facing a worldwide depression or a global war, Hilton, nevertheless, faced pressing issues throughout his presidency, including problems created by greatly expanding enrollments, an almost continual need for more faculty, and an increase in the size of the physical campus. The *Des Moines Register* pointed out at the time of Hilton's death in 1982 that he had guided the school through its major growth years, had worked to create programs in the humanities, and was the major force behind the development of the Iowa State University Center. More specifically the *Register* noted that during the Hilton years, enrollment rose from 7,800 to more than 12,400 students and the value of the physical plant increased from $28 million to $71 million.[81]

Presidents Friley and Hilton were also part of what would soon be a lost tradition at American universities: longtime administrators who saw their lives intertwined and almost inseparable from the schools over which they presided. Both men had served the school and the state in different ways before becoming president, and, therefore, had some previous knowledge of the school and of the state. For both men, there was no moving on until retirement. For Friley, there was the deeply held conviction that education should shape the total person, in moral and ethical ways, not just educate the student for a profession. Friley, in fact, would be the last Iowa State president to emphasize explicitly Iowa State's role in the development of students' character. During his tenure, Hilton envisioned a university that aspired to excellence and to serve the world through its academic programs and international programs; moreover, he clearly envisioned a university with first-class facilities that came to be embodied in the Iowa State Center.

Finally, the history of Iowa State in the mid-twentieth century is the story of an institution that responded well to both external and internal challenges, often with inadequate resources. It was an institution, moreover, that never wavered in its intent to provide a strong, solid education for its young people, and, at the same time, to produce good citizens for the world. Throughout these mid-century years, the institution remained focused on carrying out its mission as Iowa's land-grant school and, as the following chapters demonstrate, insisting that the mission continue to be central to the school's identity. By 1965, when W. Robert Parks assumed the ISU presidency, the university was on the cusp of far greater change and challenges; the foundation for the future, however, had been carefully laid throughout the middle years of the twentieth century.

# Vignettes

## Keeping House: Home Management Houses at Iowa State College

The first time that Frances Worth Prueitt tasted pizza, she was a student at Iowa State College, majoring in home economics. During the late 1940s, Prueitt lived with several other senior women in a home management house, a campus facility designed to teach women the hands-on art of homemaking. In their six-week stay, Prueitt and the other women learned, under the guidance of a housemother, to use the most modern home equipment, including refrigerators and electric stoves. They studied the latest methods in cooking, shopping, sewing, cleaning, entertaining, and even infant care. The recipe for pizza, however, came from an unlikely source: one of the women who lived in the house happened to be dating a man who had served in Italy during the Second World War, and he brought the recipe home as a souvenir.

Beginning in the 1870s, as part of its land-grant mission, Iowa State College admitted women into its home economics programs in order to produce scientifically trained housewives. Throughout the late 1800s, women took courses such as Home Nursing and Garden Biology, that applied chemistry, biology, and other natural sciences to daily household tasks. For most of the female students who grew up on farms or in rural communities, these courses were the first time they used new technologies like sewing machines, running water, and electric appliances.

In 1918, Catherine MacKay, the dean of home economics, wanted the female students to gain greater practical experience before graduation. Though many women applied their home economics degrees to careers in food service, social work, journalism, business, art, education, and science, the majority of women planned to marry and raise families. In order to prepare the women for family life, Iowa State joined several other colleges across the nation in establishing home management houses. When the first students moved in, they spent two weeks learning the latest methods for budgeting, preparing meals, cleaning, doing laundry, and entertaining. They also left their mark on the house by designing small accent furnishings like draperies and napkins.

Beginning in 1924, the students' stay increased to six weeks in order to provide a more thorough experience. That year, Home Economics Dean Anna Richardson received permission to secure infants from state agencies, and thereby give the home management houses a real "family atmosphere." The first two infants, Gretchen and Sonny, arrived in the spring of 1924 and

*(continued)*

**69**

initiated a thirty-year practice of hands-on child care for the women of Iowa State. In addition to household chores, women in the home management houses learned to keep strict feeding and play schedules, discipline the children, make infant clothing, and create baby-friendly rooms.

The students often became strongly attached to the infants. They created baby books for each of them, and when the babies were adopted by families at the end of their stay, the student "mothers" wrote heartfelt letters wishing them well. In 1932, when two-year-old "Baby Janice" left Iowa State to live with her adoptive family, one letter written by the students said, "We hope that we have contributed some small part toward her development for she greatly enlarged our experience."

Though there was some concern that the babies had too many mothers and no fathers, male faculty and students often visited the home management houses to observe the women and make social calls. During the Second World War, for example, several women's boyfriends came for dinner, then donned aprons and washed the dishes. Men involved with the naval training programs liked to stop by, play with and take pictures of the infants, then treat the women to ice cream.

In addition to the babies, most students found the entertainment and social activities to be a highly memorable part of their stay in the houses. Even during the 1930s, when few had money to spare, residents hosted formal dinners, luncheons, and teas. Not all of the social events occurred seamlessly, however, and occasionally required creative solutions. In 1935, for example, when one student prepared purple gravy that should have been brown, the students decided to serve dinner by candlelight in order to cover up the "unappetizing color."

By the late 1950s and early 1960s, the home management program was no longer a relevant experience for many college women. Though most women still hoped to marry and raise a family, fewer women actually majored in home economics, while new technologies significantly eased housework. At the same time, students in this time period demanded greater freedoms and more time to work, socialize, and study. In 1958, due to ethical concerns, high expenses, and the introduction of foster homes, Iowa State ended its infant care program. Yet for the more than three thousand women who lived in home management houses over fifty years, learning to "keep house" proved to be a memorable and lifelong experience.

Jenny Barker Devine

# "So You're Pinned":
# Dating and Marriage After World War II

Students who entered Iowa State after 1945 had grown up during the uncertainty of the Great Depression and experienced the ravages of war. For the first time in nearly two decades, economic prosperity and new opportunities allowed young people to pursue their dreams. Students often wished to earn a degree, find a steady job, start a family, and settle down into a comfortable, predictable life. After 1945, and throughout the 1950s, couples across the country tended to marry younger and have more children than their parents and grandparents, giving rise to a "baby boom." Marriage and family became a central part of student life. Even jokes in the campus humor magazine, *Green Gander,* reflected students' preoccupation with marriage, sex, and childrearing. In the spring of 1951, a blurb in the *Green Gander* defined matrimony as "an institution of learning in which a man loses his bachelor's degree and his wife acquires a master's."

As these trends took hold on college campuses across the country, courtship and dating rituals also changed. When young couples began dating, they were more likely to seek long-term commitments rather than fun nights out with a variety of different people, as their parents had. It was not unusual to move quickly from casual "Coke Dates" and dances at the Memorial Union to a "steady" relationship. The tradition of getting "pinned," when a man gave his fraternity pin to his sweetheart, grew in importance during this period because it signified a new level of commitment between dating and marriage. A 1953 poll of Iowa State students revealed that the majority of students believed that to be pinned signified that a couple was "engaged to be engaged." Getting pinned was not to be done haphazardly, however; and in order to assist students (and parents) in understanding this new trend, articles outlining rigid courtship rituals, as well as an engagement column, appeared frequently in campus publications. One 1953 article in the *Iowa Agriculturalist* entitled "So You're Pinned" stated that the junior year was the best time to be pinned because it allowed the couple enough time to "actually know whether the pin-mate was the right spouse."

Articles also instructed students on proper customs to announce their commitments. A man typically passed cigars and arranged for the men of his residence hall or fraternity to serenade the woman. Once a woman became either pinned or engaged, she anonymously announced a "Candle Passing," where the women of her dormitory or sorority gathered in a circle and passed a single candle. After the candle had been passed around three times, the

*(continued)*

woman throwing the party blew it out and made her announcement. This was usually followed by a "5-Pound Party," which involved the distribution of chocolates among friends. Two pounds of chocolates signified that a woman was pinned, while five pounds signified that she was engaged. The custom required the man to purchase the chocolates that his sweetheart gave out to her friends.

During the 1950s, these 5-Pound Parties, though done in the past, became more elaborate affairs with decorative themes and lively entertainment. Most importantly, these parties represented a key transition in the life of coeds and became an essential part of the college woman's experience. Even women who did not become engaged by the time of graduation could throw a "Lemon Party," when, instead of chocolate candy, they gave boxes of lemon drops to their girlfriends.

Jenny Barker Devine

# "The Queen of Our College": Margaret Sloss, DVM

In 1938, newspapers across Iowa announced that Margaret Sloss had just become the first woman to earn a Doctor of Veterinary Medicine at Iowa State College. The newspaper reporters marveled at the "tall, blue-eyed athletic woman," who was "clad in her white laboratory coat." At that time, it was almost unheard of for women to earn a veterinary degree. Between 1880 and 1937, the College of Veterinary Medicine had graduated 930 men, but no women. And across the country, only twenty-seven women could "tack 'DVM' to their names." When asked about her accomplishment, however, Sloss simply remarked, "It's really nothing at all."

Margaret Wragg Sloss spent most of her life on the Iowa State campus, and throughout her career, she challenged many of the barriers facing professional women. Born in 1901 in Cedar Rapids, Sloss (nicknamed "Toot" at a young age) moved to Ames when she was just nine years old. Her father, Thomas Sloss, was hired as the superintendent of buildings, grounds, and construction for Iowa State College. He moved his family into a small house on the east side of campus, now known as the Sloss House and the current home of the Iowa State Women's Center. Sloss grew up there in the midst of scientists, laboratories, and classrooms. She became interested in veterinary medicine at a young age, and later recalled playing as a child at the newly constructed animal hospital near the family home.

"The veterinary hospital was the first building my father had anything to do with constructing," she said. "And one of my favorite people then was Old Dad Gray, caretaker at the clinic. He was a tolerant old fellow and I used to tag him for hours. He even let me ride along on calls occasionally."

After graduating from Ames High, she enrolled at Iowa State, where she participated in the theater and excelled in sports, earning letters in field hockey, basketball, and tennis. She maintained her enthusiasm for Cyclone athletics for the rest of her life and could often be found at sporting events, cheering for Iowa State.

In 1923, Sloss earned her BS from Iowa State College, and became the first woman hired as a technician in veterinary pathology. She soon left for medical school in Iowa City, where she was successful but not professionally fulfilled. Sloss later recalled that she had little intention of breaking barriers, because she was simply following her interests. She merely went on the assumption that she was "medically and scientifically minded and would rather be in veterinary medicine than in human medicine." So after one year of medical

*(continued)*

school, Sloss returned to her job at Iowa State as a laboratory technician, where the dean of veterinary medicine, Charles Stange, encouraged her to pursue a career in veterinary medicine and to share her talents with others through teaching. Sloss earned an MS in 1932, then shortly thereafter began work on a DVM.

In 1941, Sloss became an instructor of veterinary medicine at Iowa State and was eventually promoted through the ranks to full professorship in 1965. Through her writings, Sloss was widely recognized by veterinary professionals across the nation and the world. In 1948, she coauthored a book entitled *Veterinary Clinical Parasitology* with Dr. Edward A. Benbrook, and edited subsequent editions. Today, this book remains widely known by her name and, in its seventh edition, continues to be a best seller in its field.

Sloss also took a keen interest in promoting women in the veterinary profession, and in 1947, helped to establish the Women's Veterinary Medical Association. In 1950, she started an extremely popular ten-week laboratory course for the wives of veterinary students to familiarize them with microscopes, laboratory techniques, and procedures used by veterinarians in their practices. In doing this, she hoped that the students' wives would take a greater interest in their husbands' prospective careers.

She rarely spoke of her own experiences with discrimination, however, and was often quoted as saying, "I've never had any trouble. If you don't look for it, you don't find it. I tend to my knitting and expect others to tend to theirs. The people who really count are for you. I'm not a suffragette, but I do believe women have some real built-in abilities that men lack."

Throughout her career, Sloss received many honors and awards. In 1940, the Women's Centennial Congress honored her for breaking into a career previously closed to women, and in 1959, she received the Iowa State Faculty Citation. Yet perhaps none of her awards demonstrated the extent of her success and influence as did the hundreds of cards and letters that poured in for her retirement in 1972. Former student Dennis J. Carr reflected the spirit of many of the letters when he wrote, "Many uncut diamonds passed through the veterinary school and graduated as jewels of veterinarians due to a considerable amount of polishing by faculty members like yourself."

Likewise, George Christensen, a former dean of veterinary medicine, and then the vice president for academic affairs, wrote to thank Sloss for her "many kindnesses, counsel, and cheerful comments during the years in which we have known each other." He went on to write, "I am truly honored to be listed among your many friends. Margaret Sloss is more than a teacher to her many students and more than a colleague to countless faculty members."

The thousands of students who studied under her tutelage took comfort in her openness and patience and rarely forgot the lessons they learned in Dr. Sloss's laboratory, especially if the lessons included one of her quiet, gentle "scoldings." Though highly successful personally and professionally, Sloss remained a genuine, even humble individual. In 1978, she remarked, "I've been interviewed so many times—I really find it hard to believe people find my past so interesting." Sloss died on December 11, 1979, and is interred in the Iowa State University Cemetery.

Jenny Barker Devine

*Chapter 3*

# Science with Humanity: The Parks Years

## David Hamilton

In the history of Iowa State University, no president served longer than W. Robert Parks, who became the university's eleventh president in 1965. He entered the presidency hoping to build and expand on Iowa State's established fields of strength in order to establish a more broad-based university. He also believed that higher education needed to regain a fuller appreciation for humanistic learning, and he called on Iowa State to accept what he called a "new humanism" in teaching and research throughout the university. When he stepped down twenty-one years later in 1986, Iowa State had undergone an explosion in enrollments and a massive rebuilding of the campus. The university had endured the turmoil that engulfed most college campuses from 1965 to 1975 and also the strains caused by inflation and recession. The university had undergone more changes than at any time since it first began holding classes in 1869. These twenty-one years were a difficult time and a creative time that saw the blending of the old and the new to create a very different Iowa State. Some of these changes were intended and some were brought about by the upheavals and transformations occurring throughout American society after 1965.[1]

Iowa State in 1965 was a university with 12,450 students and about 1,300 faculty. Its annual budget was $46 million and tuition for the year was $495. Nearly four-fifths of the roughly 11,000 undergraduate students were from Iowa and most of the rest from nearby Minnesota, Illinois, and South Dakota. Nearly all of these students lived either in a fraternity or a sorority or one of the Iowa State dormitories, where the rigid rules and restrictions of in loco parentis were firmly applied. Woe be to a student who came in after hours. The women's and men's dorms were strictly separated and the women's dorms watched over by matronly supervisors. Slide rules accompanied a goodly portion of the students to class. Female students usually wore blouses and skirts; male students sported short hair and often wore jackets and ties to class. In the classroom, they were taught by an even more formally dressed faculty. Because Iowa State's most heavily enrolled fields were the then male-dominated disciplines of engineering, agriculture, and the sciences, 60 percent or more of its students were young men. There were women students in all of Iowa State's six colleges, but they were disproportionately enrolled

*Viewed from the front of Beardshear Hall, students in the mid-1960s walk between Beardshear Hall and Curtiss Hall on central campus. (Used by permission of Iowa State University Library/Special Collections Department)*

in home economics and in the departments that would be reorganized into the College of Education in 1968. The football team occasionally won a game.[2]

It is often true of good colleges and universities that the students are part of a family lineage of alumni, and this was certainly the case at Iowa State. Many of the students in 1965 were the sons or daughters of men and women who had gone to Iowa State before them, and in not a few cases their parents had met at Iowa State. The university had experienced steady changes since the 1930s and 1940s, but even with new buildings and new dormitories, most of these alums would have had little difficulty finding their way about the campus in 1965. VEISHEA was still a rite of spring, and while the Kingston Trio had taken the place of groups such as Harry Cool and his Orchestra as the VEISHEA band, the open houses, the parade, and the VEISHEA queen were traditions that linked one generation of Iowa Staters to another.[3]

Iowa State in 1965, however, was on the brink of major changes. These changes were shaped, initially, by the great sense of optimism and hope that prevailed in the United States during the early and mid-1960s. The economy was growing, incomes were rising, and opportunities seemed, if not boundless, certainly widely available. In addition, there was a deeply shared sense that the United States had developed new ways of achieving and sustaining social progress and of addressing social ills. The nation had acted to dismantle the South's system of segregation and Lyndon Johnson had begun a "War on Poverty" that would help produce a "Great Society." The nation's universities, meanwhile, were attracting more students, and their administrators and their faculties were eager to generate the knowledge and expertise needed to address the problems of a modern society. There was a widely held faith that scientists and engineers would produce ever-greater technological marvels that would in turn create more productive businesses and farms. Social scientists would apply new knowledge to social problems in order to attack poverty and social inequities. Elementary and secondary teachers would make use of modern methods to better prepare their students for modern life. There were problems, to be sure, but they seemed to be problems that could be studied, managed, and resolved.[4]

This sense of optimism pervaded America's burgeoning colleges and universities, and on the campuses across the nation, faculty members, administrators, and students saw post–World War II universities as institutions vital to the future of America. Clark Kerr, the influential chancellor of the University of California, had dubbed the large, modern university the "multiversity" because of its multiple functions and its expanding role in addressing multiple needs. These institutions, he said, were "knowledge factories" that were generating the expertise necessary for modern life. To Kerr and other university presidents, it was essential that the nation's larger public universities continue to grow and expand in order to meet the needs of a changing world. Iowa State's new president believed that Iowa State should join with the nation's other leading universities to meet these needs.[5]

W. Robert Parks had grown up in rural Tennessee as the youngest of seven children. His father had been a rural mail carrier, but two older brothers had worked their way through graduate school to earn doctorate degrees, and he followed their path. He went first to Berea College, a small college in Kentucky that drew its students from Appalachia and the surrounding region. After Berea, he did graduate work at the University of Kentucky and the University of Wisconsin. From Wisconsin he moved to the staff of the Bureau of Agricultural Economics of the Department of Agriculture and then to the Navy, where he was a junior officer during World War II. Parks arrived in Ames in 1948 and began teaching popular courses on government-agriculture relations and American political theory. With colleagues such as Paul Sharp and Norman Graebner, two historians then at the beginning of distinguished careers, he became part of a small but outstanding group of teachers in what was then the single Department of History, Government, and Philosophy. Because his own research focused on the politics of agriculture and the challenges of administering national agricultural policies, he developed

*Former Iowa State President James H. Hilton, standing, and newly appointed President W. Robert Parks at the time of the presidential transition in 1965. Hilton served as president from 1953 to 1965. Parks had earlier been a political science professor, dean of instruction, and vice president for academic affairs at Iowa State. (Courtesy of David Hamilton)*

close ties to the faculty in agricultural economics and the other agricultural fields. Parks left Iowa State in 1956 for the University of Wisconsin, but he returned two years later when Iowa State President James H. Hilton created the position of dean of instruction as a means of making him part of the Iowa State administration. In 1961, he became the university's vice president for academic affairs, and when Hilton retired in 1965 Parks enjoyed widespread faculty support to become Iowa State's next president.[6]

A tall, lanky man with dark hair and a long face, Parks was much liked for his friendly nature, gentle humor, unflappable nature, and absolute sense of fairness. He was a reserved, dignified man who detested any display of pretension—intellectual or otherwise. He had come of age during the Great Depression and World War II when America's public institutions at all levels had responded to unprecedented crises, and he drew from this experience a deep faith in the ability of the public sector to create a fairer, more secure, more decent society. The institution he most cherished was the university and particularly the public land-grant university. Berea, Kentucky, and Wisconsin had allowed him to move out of the limited rural world he had known as a youth, and he believed that access to higher education was a fundamental feature of a democratic society.

Parks knew that Iowa State in 1965 was both a distinguished university and a limited university. Its colleges of Agriculture and Veterinary Medicine were outstanding; its Engineering school was highly regarded; and departments such as Physics, Chemistry, and Statistics had well-deserved national reputations. The federal government's Ames Lab, then a part of the Atomic Energy Commission, gave the science departments additional stature and financial support. Its Extension system reached out to several hundred thousand rural and small-town Iowans in a variety of ways. The institution had moved well beyond the kind of technical training in farm operations that had once characterized the land-grant colleges (and had earned them the derisive "Moo U." nickname). There were other strong parts of the university as well, but Iowa State's strengths were narrowly focused. The university library illustrated the strengths and weaknesses of Iowa State. The building was cramped and badly outdated, and while the scientific collections were superb, missing from the holdings in the humanities were basic works of literature. It was a library well suited for work on Mendel but certainly not Milton.[7]

Parks began his presidency determined to reshape Iowa State. He was not consumed with personal ambition. (In later years, many universities would inquire if he might consider taking on another presidency. He always politely declined.) About Iowa State, however, he was deeply ambitious. The university could not remain static; in its own tradition and in the tradition of the land-grant universities, it had to evolve and change in order to meet the needs of the people of Iowa and of the nation. Hence, one ambition, as he stated in his first address to the faculty, was to make Iowa State a "truly broad-based university" with a more extensive undergraduate curriculum, a wider array of graduate programs, and new research pursuits. Parks made clear a second ambition in his 1966 inaugural address when he appealed for what he called a "new humanism." The modern world, he argued, was a scientific world and science had produced unprecedented levels of abundance, convenience, and leisure. But science and technology by themselves could be dehumanizing. They could function in conflicting ways to sustain and enrich life and to diminish and even destroy it. Their full potential as a "liberalizing and liberating force" could be realized only if they were integrated with humanistic learning. Hence he sought to dedicate Iowa State to "the goal of bringing all of our disciplines in the sciences and humanities together into a new educational unity, achieved through a broad concern for the human and humane." He called on the faculty to reach beyond specialized disciplinary knowledge to build a unified community of scholars and teachers. This challenge, he believed, should undergird Iowa State's future development.[8]

This was no small vision of what Iowa State might become. At a university formally known as "Iowa State University of Science and Technology," he was calling for the creation of an enlarged and expanded university and for a university dedicated to liberal education. This fusion of scientific and humanistic learning reflected Parks's own intellectual commitment to the ideas of the philosopher John Dewey and the educational theorist Alfred North Whitehead, as well as his reactions to the horrors of atomic warfare and the darker possibilities of technological development. He shared much of the optimism of Clark Kerr and other university presidents about what their institutions might achieve, but he did not share the

*ISU President W. Robert Parks and other ISU administrators gathered on the steps of Beardshear Hall in the late 1960s. From left, Wayne Moore, George Christensen, Parks, J. Boyd Page, Wilbur Layton, Arthur Gowan, and Carl Hamilton. (Courtesy of David Hamilton)*

rather smug self-assurance that science and technology alone could solve all problems. Science was now too important to be left only to scientists.

Unstated but implicit in Parks's vision of Iowa State were two assumptions. One was that universities must be marked by openness for free inquiry and debate. A second was that as much as possible they must be autonomous institutions in order to protect academic freedom in classrooms, in the pursuit of scholarly research, and in the many activities of a university beyond the classroom and laboratory. With autonomy, however, came responsibility. University presidents, he realized, faced the difficult balancing act of encouraging open inquiry while also ensuring that debate was carried out in ways that opened rather than closed minds.

The changes he envisioned for Iowa State, Parks realized, would have to come gradually and be accepted and approved by both the faculty and the regents. One of his first steps was to bring together a group of senior administrators who were to work with him for all or most of his tenure as Iowa State's president. This group included George Christensen, the dean of veterinary medicine who became vice president for academic affairs; Daniel Zaffarano, the chairman of the Physics Department who became dean of the graduate school and vice president for research; Wayne Moore, who was the vice president for business and administration; and Carl Hamilton, the vice president for information and development. When Hamilton retired, Wayne Moore took over as head of development and public relations and his outstanding associate Warren Madden became the vice president for business and administration. Collectively, these men were much like Parks himself—unpretentious, unflappable, and selflessly dedicated to the university. In the two decades that they led Iowa State, they formed an exceptionally strong group of administrators who worked quietly and steadily to broaden Iowa State's teaching and research mission.[9]

Outside of his immediate circle of vice presidents, one person was vitally involved in the Parks presidency and that was his wife, Ellen Sorge Parks. They had met in graduate school at Madison, where she became the first woman to earn a doctorate in political science at the University of Wisconsin. A voracious reader with a wide-ranging intellect and an intense interest in contemporary politics, Ellen Parks shared her husband's lifelong commitment to Iowa State and to the city of Ames. For twenty-one years as the university's first lady, she made the Knoll not an isolated private residence but a scene of a staggering number of faculty and student receptions, alumni events, and fund-raising affairs, and she presided over these functions with grace and charm and a fierce pride in the university.

Parks's quest to broaden and redefine Iowa State's mission benefited from the state of Iowa's prosperity during the late 1950s and the first part of the 1960s. Iowa did not enjoy the economic boom that spurred university growth in some states, but the farm economy was marked by stable and rising profits and so was the state's manufacturing base and its service-oriented businesses, such as the insurance companies and banking institutions centered in Des Moines. The state's relative prosperity made institutional change easier, but there were still serious obstacles with which to contend. One of these was the uneasy relationship between Iowa State and the University of Iowa. During the late 1950s and early 1960s, relations had become especially strained. Iowa saw itself as the state's only comprehensive university and usually resisted Iowa State's efforts to redefine and broaden its institutional mission. It had tried to stop Iowa State from offering an undergraduate degree in English, lobbied the state legislature to prevent legislation that would authorize Iowa State to change its name from Iowa State College to Iowa State University (the state of Iowa, its lobbyist argued, had one university and needed only one university), waged a furious effort to deny Iowa State membership in the prestigious American Association of Universities, and steadfastly refused to play Iowa State in football. More importantly, it could generally count on preferential support from the Board of Regents when it came to divvying up the state's higher education budget and to allocating funds for building projects. An unofficial rule of thumb was a two-to-one ratio for capital spending in Iowa's favor.[10]

Parks knew that the existing budgetary rules would stymie any hopes for an expanded Iowa State, and he knew that if every new degree program and every request for a new building were to face University of Iowa opposition, then the governing system of the Board of Regents could easily fall apart. Fortunately, Iowa's Governor Harold Hughes was a serious leader interested in seeing all the state's public universities grow in size and stature and he was not interested in petty turf wars. Furthermore, whereas Hilton and the longtime Iowa president Virgil Hancher detested one another (Hilton so disliked Hancher that he would not allow Iowa State officials to take rooms at Iowa's student union when the Board of Regents met in Iowa City), Parks enjoyed the respect and friendship of Howard Bowen, who had succeeded Hancher in 1964. In an effort to establish a more workable budget system, the Board of Regents undertook an extensive review of its policies in 1965 and 1966, and Parks made a compelling case for major changes. Years later, Bowen recalled that Parks "handled himself . . . with tact and grace and with humor but he was tough." "Actually," Bowen reflected, "I think I lost that battle, but we didn't quarrel with allocations after that."[11]

This pattern of mutual respect continued when Willard "Sandy" Boyd succeeded Bowen in 1968 and with Boyd's successor James Freedman. There were, to be sure, differences and tensions. When Iowa finally agreed, reluctantly, to schedule an annual Iowa–Iowa State football game, it insisted that five of the first six games be played in Iowa City. One reason for this was the small size of Iowa State's stadium, but when Iowa State built a new stadium in 1975, the rationale for playing the games in Iowa City no longer existed. In what would become a highly publicized squabble, Iowa's athletics administration refused to renegotiate the contract. This battle, however, should not obscure what was one of Parks's most important achievements as ISU president. He quietly established that Iowa State deserved the full support of the regents and the legislature and that ISU should not be relegated to a lesser status in the scramble for resources, and he did this while maintaining, and actually improving, relations with the University of Iowa.

The need for support was plainly evident. Every year more of Iowa's high school graduates were going on to college, and as enrollments at Iowa State rose, so did the pressure for new classrooms, more laboratories, and more dormitories. These pressures were made more severe by a backlog of building projects that needed attention in 1965. Many of Iowa State's facilities were simply too small and too old for a growing university with new aspirations. Furthermore, no one envisioned that enrollment would leap from 14,000 students in 1965 to 26,325 in 1985, and as the size of the student body grew, so did the need for a building program.[12]

From 1965 to 1986, a quarter of a billion dollars went into new buildings, additions to existing buildings, and major renovations. The projects included Bessey Hall, Carver Hall, the College of Design, Ross Hall, Kildee Hall, the College of Veterinary Medicine, the Agronomy addition, two library additions, the conversion of the old veterinary medicine college building into the College of Education, the music building, and many others. The Towers dormitories and the Richardson Court dormitories began to relieve the annual shortage of student living space on

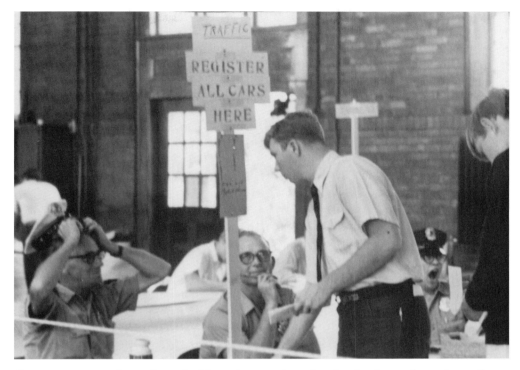

*For many years, Iowa State held student registration in the State Gym. Long lines of students formed to register for classes and also to pick up parking permits. (Used by permission of Iowa State University Library/Special Collections Department)*

campus. The Armory gave way to Hilton Coliseum in 1971 and Clyde Williams Field to the new football stadium in 1975.[13]

The construction amounted to the physical rebuilding of Iowa State. While there were only modest changes to the central campus, the rings of buildings surrounding Beardshear and Curtiss became a maze of concrete and red brick structures. Some faculty grumbled about money for "bricks and mortar," but the buildings were badly needed. Winning legislative approval was sometimes difficult, and this was particularly true of projects such as the music building. Music classes were being held in rooms across campus suited for little more than storage (after the football team moved out, there were even music classes in a room in Clyde Williams stadium). Still, members of the legislature asked why Iowa State needed a building in which to teach music. Thanks in part to heavy lobbying by Parks himself, the appropriation was approved, and the building was constructed overlooking Lake LaVerne.[14]

The most important of early construction projects was the completion of the four buildings that constituted the Iowa State Center. The center had been proposed as early as 1954, and it had become a formal commitment in 1962, when the university announced that the center would include a new basketball arena, a world-class auditorium, a continuing education center, and a smaller theater for theatrical productions. Just as important—and daunting—the project would be funded without using state revenues. In 1965, the center was an unfunded hope. Working one building at a time, however, the Iowa State Center was under way by 1967. A major gift from C. Y. Stephens made possible the auditorium that bears his name. It opened in 1970, and it was followed the next year by the arena named in honor of former president Hilton. They were followed in 1974 by the Fisher Theater, and a year later the Scheman Continuing Education Center completed the work.[15]

The opening of C. Y. Stephens Auditorium in September of 1969 attracted national attention when the New York Philharmonic Orchestra and conductor Seijo Ozawa agreed to travel to Ames for five concerts. A lecture by the historian Arthur Schlesinger Jr., a performance of *King Lear*, and a production of *Madame Butterfly* by the Chicago Lyric Opera Company soon followed. Whatever the event, the auditorium won instant praise. A music critic for the *Kansas City Star* wrote, "The hall itself was as interesting to the opening night audience as anything going on in it. It is an impressively bold and uncluttered architectural statement on the outside, and the interior, despite its size, establishes a rather surprisingly intimate atmosphere." The *Des Moines Register*'s Donald Kaul neatly caught the impact of Stephens when he wrote, "[The University of] Iowa was the school with class, with the high powered liberal arts school. Iowa State? Iowa State was for farmers and engineers . . . Well, Iowa City still has its charms, but concert attractions isn't one of them . . . and so, you Iowa State fellows, the next time an Iowa person is bugging you with 'Moo U.' and 'Silo Tech' jokes, ask him this question: 'Which Iowa school has a better concert hall than it has a football press box?' They'll know the answer."[16]

C. Y. Stephens and the Iowa State Center marked a new phase of Iowa State's history in other ways as well. Before 1965, private fund-raising at Iowa State was a limited undertaking. The center changed this. The Iowa State University Foundation had only been organized in 1962, and it had succeeded in securing few large gifts when C. Y. Stephens agreed to donate $1.1 million for the building of the nearly $5 million auditorium. About $7 million of the $19.5 million came from student fees for Hilton Coliseum and the rest from private fund-raising. For the first time in Iowa State's history, a major part of the university had been completed by relying largely on private support.

Of all the new buildings, additions, and renovations during his presidency, no project was more personally satisfying to Parks than the expansion of the library. Both he and his wife, Ellen, believed that a university library should be at the heart of a university, and Parks had made improvements in Iowa State's library a major priority. With the new addition, the library was finally able to house its increasingly impressive collection of books, journals, and archival materials as well as provide a convenient space for students to study. Quite fittingly, the building was named the William Robert Parks and Ellen Sorge Parks Library in 1983 to recognize their commitment to the library.[17]

More than just buildings were changing at Iowa State. Many of the thousands of students who arrived on campus each year continued to seek degrees in agri-

*Iowa State students of the 1970s relax between classes. (Used by permission of Iowa State University Library/Special Collections Department)*

culture, engineering, or the sciences, but thousands more were interested in business, architecture, design, education, and the social sciences and humanities. In 1965, for instance, the College of Agriculture had 1,978 students, and its enrollment would rise slightly to 2,461 twenty years later. The College of Science and Humanities, however, would climb from 3,427 to 8,087 during the same period. These changes reflected the changing economy and changing student interests. The new patterns of enrollment also prompted an expansion in the number of ISU's colleges from six to nine. The additions included Education in 1968, Design in 1978, and Business in 1984. In addition, from 1965 to 1986 forty new undergraduate majors and thirty graduate majors were added at Iowa State. These changes were part of an ongoing revision of the undergraduate curriculum that became less rigid with more options for students to fulfill general education requirements. To some extent, the changes reflected the greater emphasis on the social sciences and the humanities. History, Political Science, and Philosophy became separate departments with larger faculties. History added two doctoral programs, one in technology and science and the other in agriculture and rural life, which perfectly fit the university's larger strengths and interests. Meanwhile, new interdisciplinary programs became a larger part of both the undergraduate and graduate curriculum. Still another major change occurred in 1981 when Iowa State converted from a three-quarter academic calendar to a two-semester calendar.[18]

While contending with larger enrollments, the need for more campus buildings, and the quest to reshape Iowa State, new problems arose as well. With a few notable exceptions, university campuses before 1965 were rarely the scene of political activism or social protest. In the ten years after 1965, however, this changed and changed dramatically. Almost certainly no one anticipated at mid-decade the turmoil that was about to engulf Iowa State and other universities, although one hint of the looming problems appeared in the very issue of the *Ames Daily Tribune* that carried a picture of Parks in front of Beardshear Hall greeting well-wishers upon the announcement that he would be the next ISU president. A headline just below the picture read, "235 Americans Now Killed as Rebel Offensive Mounts." This was late 1964, and as the number of American soldiers killed in Vietnam rose in the years ahead, so did campus strife.[19]

Student protests during the 1960s and early 1970s had many sources. The sheer size and constant growth of the student body was one of them. Increasingly, attending a university meant living in large, overcrowded dorms, standing in lines to register, and taking notes in lecture halls that seated three hundred or more students. Of necessity, Iowa State and other universities became more bureaucratic and impersonal, and as they did, it became easier to see university hierarchies as remote and less interested in students. This growing distance made resentment and rebellion all the easier. These developments coincided with the emergence of a post-1960 youth culture seeking an unprecedented degree of personal freedom. The quest for greater choices, more control, and fewer rules took many forms. Some were trivial, some destructive. Students sought to lower the voting and drinking ages, lift moral strictures regarding sexual relations, experiment with drugs, and embrace new forms of cultural expression such as rock music. And, of course, there was the Vietnam War and the war-era draft, which bitterly politicized generational tensions.

In ways that few faculty, students, or administrators could have anticipated before 1965, universities became the center of youth protests. Iowa State was no exception. Many students never used drugs and spent more time complaining about the lack of parking spaces or cramped dorm rooms than they did about the Vietnam War. But many others were deeply engaged in either defending or protesting the war, and the conflicts threatened to consume the university and endanger its ability to function free of outside interference. The campus turmoil put universities, with their traditions of tolerance and openness, in a vulnerable situation. Students treated each rejection of their demands as evidence of the administration's backward and authoritarian nature. For much of the general public, however, each news story about sit-ins, protests, demonstrations, drug use, and sexual freedom seemed further evidence of moral decay, the creation of an unrestrained and unhinged youth culture, and the unraveling of American society. Furthermore, because of the vital role of universities in American society, both sides were determined to persevere. Outside of the university, the critics insisted that public tax dollars not be used to support or encourage attacks on American values and institutions. Inside the university, students and younger faculty demanded massive changes in student and faculty governance and sought to place the universities in the vanguard of political and social change. Caught in the middle were university administrations and their presidents.[20]

For the first year or two, what passed for protests and rebellion seem insignificant and even innocent in retrospect. In 1965, one of the most pressing issues was that of dormitory hours. At a time when eighteen-year-old men were registering for the draft and being sent to the battlefields of Vietnam, it seemed hardly appropriate for a university to tell students, male or female, when they should be in their dorm rooms. In response to student pressure, the residence hall system established what the *Ames Daily Tribune* called "the most progressive women's hours in the Big Eight."[21]

The fight over hours was but one example of new attitudes. The Kingston Trio and Stan Getz gave way to the folk rock group Peter, Paul, and Mary. And at concerts the haze of cigarette smoke gave way to the more acrid odor of marijuana. A full house cheered the black comedian, civil rights activist, and Vietnam War opponent Dick Gregory.

One 1967 event suggests the changing attitudes of the Iowa State student body. This was "Gentle Thursday" (although it was held on a Friday), which involved one thousand students in a "concentrated attempt to escape from reality." Students spread across campus engaging in "gentle" activities. One student put a television set on his head and peered back at the world. Another was painted red, yellow, and blue as fellow students brushed and spattered him with paint. Four dancers in white face makeup played croquet, without mallets, balls, or wickets. Four students carried a yellow submarine with "Gentle" painted on its side across campus before launching it in Lake LaVerne (where it gently sank). A ringmaster wearing a top hat and tails played a kazoo and gave directions. A coed wearing a policeman's jacket and white stockings kept order while a judge clad in a black robe, an Uncle Sam hat, and a long beard licked on an all-day sucker. At the armory, a naval gun was decked with pink and yellow polka dots and a pinwheel fastened to the end of the barrel. When asked what it all meant, one of the organizers said, "There are two kinds of happenings, some are serious, thoughtful, provocative; others are just for fun." Another of the organizers said "interpretation of a happening tells more about the interpreter than about the event. You have to find your meaning." This was a new Iowa State.[22]

Gentle Thursday was one thing, but the election of Donald R. Smith as president of the Government of the Student Body (GSB) in 1967 was quite another. Traditionally, GSB presidents had come from the well-organized Greek system, and they dressed and looked the part of the earnest student leader. Don Smith fit none of these traditions. His hair was long and unkempt; he wore a shaggy beard; he lived off campus and rode a Triumph motorcycle. He was also one of twenty-two Iowa State students who were members of the New Left organization the Students for a Democratic Society (SDS). Smith seemed to have walked onto campus from Haight-Ashbury rather than the small town of Rockwell City in northwest Iowa. But in fact Smith had come from Rockwell City and his parents were both Iowa State graduates. He had campaigned on a platform of complete student freedom outside the classroom, and he also advocated legalizing marijuana and eliminating marriage. Smith doubted he would win, but he promised, "If I am elected, this university is going to be dragged, kicking and screaming, into the 20th century." In an election featuring a high turnout (about 50 percent) he won by four hundred votes of the roughly seven thousand cast.[23]

*Don Smith, an engineering student, was elected president of the Government of the Student Body in 1967. Smith vowed to eliminate most university rules and regulations for Iowa State students. (Used by permission of Iowa State University Library/Special Collections Department)*

Smith instantly attracted the kind of attention of which no university president dreams. The *New York Times* profiled him as "The Bearded, Sockless Radical of Moo U." *Time* magazine and other newsmagazines did stories as well and wanted pictures of him arriving on campus atop his Triumph. Within the state, however, he was no curiosity. Members of the state legislature were furious. One said he was "nauseated" by Smith's election. Not to be outdone, another said he was "concerned and nauseated." (University of Iowa officials were delighted not to be the focus of the legislature's wrath. One administrator confided, "We're happy not to have him here. This is an appropriations year, you know.") The Council Bluffs *Daily Nonpareil* wrote that students didn't enroll at Iowa State "to challenge the existence of God, or the necessity of marriage in this modern world, or the justice of laws, prohibiting the use of drugs." Rather, they enrolled "to learn to be home-makers, farmers, engineers, veterinarians, teachers or other productive members of society. Nothing very exciting or shocking happened there; once in a while after a football victory . . . , the students threatened to drain Lake LaVerne. . . . But now one bearded, loudmouthed bonehead is trying to change all that."[24]

Smith was neither a bonehead nor a loudmouth. He was a soft-spoken young man and an excellent student who had nearly a straight A average in mechanical engineering. In public he was not much of a speaker, and in private he rarely invoked the lingo of SDS radicals (which meant, however, that he tended to label values and institutions that he opposed as "icky"). He had gravitated to the SDS because of his own commitment to the cause of civil rights and because of the influence of a young Iowa State history professor. Once elected, he pressed ahead with a list of demands for the Iowa State administration that included lifting all rules and restrictions on student behavior, limiting the university's power to dismiss a student solely due to academic failure, and granting students complete control over student fees. Parks listened politely to the list (Smith had presented them politely), but he refused most of them. Before Smith could press the case for his version of the twentieth century, however, he had to contend with an effort to impeach him over his views on marijuana. He chose instead to drop out of Iowa State, and, allegedly, he headed to California. His departure brought a sigh of relief from Iowa State officials and howls of delight from conservative critics. Charles Grassley, then a member of the Iowa legislature, reacted to the news by exclaiming, "This tickles me."[25]

Parks knew all too well from seething calls and meetings with members of the legislature and from the letters that poured onto his desk from parents and alumni that the growing evidence of student revolt could endanger Iowa State's ability to ward off outside intrusions that would undermine academic freedom. The counterreaction he feared became a reality when the Story County Grand Jury began to investigate Iowa State. Ostensibly inspired by the tragic murder of a female student, the grand jury's focus was, in reality, on drug use, draft evasion, and "moral pollution" at Iowa State. Don Smith's brief tenure as student body president clearly confirmed the existence of "moral pollution," as did Dick Gregory's campus appearance. Its fifteen-page report released in January of 1968 pointed to "concrete evidence of failures educationally and administratively in the Humanities" and insisted that radical faculty members were indoctrinating students with subversive ideas. The regents should act to prohibit the promotion of drugs, draft evasion, and premarital sex. They should ban speakers who are "liars, who blaspheme our flag, our heritage, our moral scruples." The report urged the regents, the state legislature, and the governor to eliminate "moral pollution by faculty and paid speakers" and by all "suitable means encourage moral improvement." It also called for an "increased emphasis . . . [on] the American ideal."[26]

The report, which went well beyond the legal jurisdiction of a county grand jury, drew immediate fire. Parks denounced it as "an unfair and grossly distorted picture" of the university. The grand jurors, he said, were seeking to censor ideas by controlling what the faculty taught and who might speak on campus, and he refused to allow them access to Iowa State records. Its proposals amounted to "a demand for censorship, restrictions on freedom to speak and freedom to listen, and rigid restrictions upon freedom of inquiry in our state university."[27]

The state's major newspapers criticized and even ridiculed the report and its charges. However crude and heavy-handed it may have been, it spoke to very real concerns harbored throughout the state. Each antiwar rally, each news story of a student burning a draft card, and each rumor of students flaunting older values raised the demands for some more forceful response that would erode the independence of the university and its ability to foster free inquiry.

Easily the most contentious and dangerous issue was the Vietnam War. The antiwar protests were smaller and less volatile at Iowa State than at other universities, but every year brought highly publicized antidraft rallies and antiwar marches. Many students and faculty members supported the war; many opposed it; many were torn, hoping it might somehow end. For the male students who were required by law to register for the draft and carry a draft card the issue was an especially difficult one. Some earned deferments, but for others there was the continual uncertainty about whether they might be drafted and whether they might be the next to return in a flag-draped coffin.

The initial protests were low-key affairs. In March of 1966, for instance, SDS and other antiwar groups (many with religious affiliations) sponsored a weekend-long protest that featured a teach-in, a "hootenanny of protest and freedom songs," and an open mike debate in which both pro-war and antiwar students and faculty could speak. As the war continued, however, teach-ins and hootenannies gave way to rallies against the draft (first to turn in draft cards and later to burn them), efforts to stop buses transporting draftees by forming human barriers, protests aimed at closing down the Story County induction center, and harassment and protests aimed at Iowa State's Navy ROTC unit.

These events sometimes produced poignant moments of generational conflict. When Dennis Ryan, a twenty-year-old electrical engineering major and the secretary of Iowa State's Young Democrats club, gave up his draft card (at the time a violation of federal law) at an antidraft rally in 1968, his father, E. B. Ryan, a Des Moines realtor, appeared at the rally demanding that his son's draft card be turned over to him. His son, he said, was a minor and was too young to make such a decision. Dennis Ryan, dressed in a coat and tie, as was his father, made a simple but forceful reply: "don't give it to him." When asked what he would do if Dennis should be arrested, E.B. Ryan replied: "Certainly I'd help him. . . . He's still my son."[28]

Each news account of an Iowa State rally or protest provoked angry letters of disbelief from alumni and parents. One leading member of the Iowa legislature vowed to cut the Iowa State and Iowa budgets because of antiwar activism. The Iowa attorney general denounced the universities for not acting to control "disruptive" students. As Parks had realized, the pressure to turn the universities into "political instruments" on both the left and the right was quite real and quite dangerous. Initially, Iowa State tried to impose rules limiting rallies and demonstrations and prohibiting the use of university buildings for such activities. After nearly fifty students violated the policy and were under review for expulsion, it was obvious that rigid bans were likely to incite more protests, more headlines, and more calls for action from outside the university.

Parks by his nature disliked conflict. He understood that confrontations invariably intensified what were already emotional issues and produced headlines that would render more compelling the demands for outside intervention. Hence he sought to defuse campus tensions. He appeased no one but listened to everyone. To the faculty and students, he urged "tolerance" and "openness" and insisted that these qualities should be essential features of a university even in difficult times.

*Iowa State students rallied in front of Beardshear to protest the Vietnam War, spring 1970. The students later marched to the ROTC field west of the Iowa State Armory. (Used by permission of Iowa State University Library/Special Collections Department)*

In this quest to avoid dramatic incidents, he was aided by Iowa's new governor, Robert D. Ray. Having just entered office in 1969 and somewhat new to politics, Ray faced strong pressure to follow the lead of other Republican governors and stop demonstrations with the use of state police or even the Iowa National Guard. Parks and Willard Boyd knew it was a huge risk to order onto a college campus police or troops untrained in handling civil disturbances. Parks, in fact, refused to bow to pressure to change Iowa State's established policy of not having the campus police carry weapons. The two presidents told Ray that if they needed outside help, they would ask for it. Ray agreed to this, and to his great credit, he did not overrule them.

Parks's ability to talk with angry students was made easier by his belief that the war had been a tragic mistake. "I thoroughly hated the war in Vietnam," he later recounted, and he made his views clear when addressing campus protests. When students rallied against the war in May of 1972, Parks spoke briefly to the 1,500 students on central campus in front of Curtiss Hall. To their applause, he said, "I am glad you care enough about peace in the world to attend this meeting, because we simply must find a way to end this war before it consumes and utterly destroys

*During VEISHEA 1970, people protesting the Vietnam War take part in the "March of Concern," near Union Drive. The antiwar protestors marched at the end of the VEISHEA parade. Later the marchers and others gathered near the Campanile, where President Parks addressed the crowd about the need for peace. (Used by permission of Iowa State University Library/Special Collections Department)*

the cohesion, the humanity and the moral fiber of this country." As he always did, he asked for peaceful actions. "I implore you to keep your actions and your protest meetings peaceful in every instance. Militant response and disruptive action tend to drive many people away from the cause of peace rather than attracting them."[29]

Perhaps the most serious challenges came in 1970 following the tragic deaths at Kent State, when the Ohio National Guard opened fire on students protesting the invasion of Cambodia. Over two hundred colleges and universities across the country had to suspend classes, end their terms early, or bring in police and National Guardsmen to maintain order. Parks labored to keep Iowa State open. To close down a university in the face of political pressure or because of uncontrolled turmoil was to challenge the place of higher education in American life. Universities had to be resilient enough to function in times of turmoil, and closing their doors might easily cede control to powers outside the university. Parks detested the war; he prized the university. He could not end the war; he could defend freedom of inquiry.

Kent State occurred just two days before the start of Iowa State's annual VEISHEA celebration, which raised immediate concerns about whether to hold the VEISHEA parade on the Saturday of VEISHEA. Students organized two different marches—one an antiwar March of Concern to follow the VEISHEA parade and the other a "Patriots" march in support of the Nixon administration and the war. Fearing a violent incident, Parks and Iowa State officials considered cancel-

*VEISHEA Planning Committee, circa 1975. Committees are elected by the entire student body to plan all activities held during the annual VEISHEA celebration. (Used by permission of Iowa State University Library/Special Collections Department)*

ing the parade, but instead the VEISHEA Central Committee announced a set of rules for the event that included prohibiting parade participants from carrying weapons or even replicas of weapons (which meant that the female drill team the Americare Stepperettes had to march the parade route pretending to be holding and twirling wooden rifles). On the day of the parade, perhaps as many as five thousand students, former students, faculty, and men and women opposed to the war gathered for the March of Concern. One faculty member, Richard Seagrave of Chemical Engineering, told the *Iowa State Daily,* "After being around this campus for 13 years, I've finally had a chance to participate in a Veishea activity that has some relevance." (Years later Seagrave would be named a distinguished professor and would also serve as Iowa State's interim president.)

Parks spoke to the marchers and said, "I am glad this rally is being held for peace. I know you are concerned, deeply concerned, about what happened at Kent State and recent developments in Southeast Asia. . . . If the University is not concerned with deep human problems such as bringing peace, then what should it be concerned with?" His comments were greeted with a standing ovation. One of the VEISHEA organizers wrote in 1982 that Parks "made probably [his] most impressive address since becoming President of Iowa State University. His words were rather brief, profoundly eloquent, and touched the spirit of the group in making the basic point that although more than 200 universities had closed or were closing for the rest of the term, Iowa State University would remain open; for that was the mission of Iowa State University as a place for reasoned discourse." When some of the marchers proposed to take over Beardshear Hall, Parks raced to Beardshear's steps to urge nonconfrontational protest instead. Taking over the main administration building, he knew, would create precisely the kind of incident that would bring National Guardsmen to Iowa State. In a brief but tense exchange, he succeeded in keeping the protest out of the building and on central campus.[30]

Fifteen years after the Kent State–marred VEISHEA, Parks reflected on Iowa State's Vietnam War era. "Some people think the big gain we made here," he said, "was getting out of [the sixties] without a big explosion of some sort but I don't think so. I think the big gain was we came out of it all without injuring academic freedom one bit." He was deeply proud of this, and justly so.[31]

ISU weathered the years of campus turmoil well, but the protests, the other crises that engulfed American society after 1965, and a less robust economy created a far more sour and pessimistic climate for higher education. From 1965 to 1986, Iowa State's budget steadily increased as budget income rose from $19 million to $338 million. During this period, the university became more heavily dependent on state appropriations, which accounted for 29.65 percent of the university's budget in 1965 and 36.4 percent in 1986. Dependence on student tuition and fees grew from 7.76 percent to 10.7 percent. Iowa State was a better-funded institution after 1965, but its funding was never sufficient to ensure sustained achievement. Some years were quite dire. In 1969 and again in 1983 and 1984 the university suffered major cutbacks in funding because of plummeting state revenues. Throughout the 1970s, the high rates of inflation ate away at the university's base budget and severely curtailed faculty salaries.[32]

The university responded to the funding problems by aggressively lobbying for higher state appropriations and by raising tuition and student fees. In hindsight, the tuition increases were modest and in terms of real dollars in-state tuition at Iowa State remained an excellent value in 1986, but to students and their families the steady increases (and increases in dormitory rates) were frustrating and a source of some degree of resentment. In the state legislature, the constant beseeching for more operating revenues, more buildings, and more research funds produced an angry backlash. Governors and legislators began to challenge the state's massive investment in higher education. The *Des Moines Register*, once a firm ally of the universities, began to portray the state's public universities as the "Pentagon of the Iowa budget," by which it meant that Iowa State and the other two universities had an insatiable demand for resources. There could never be enough.

The requests were, in fact, legitimate attempts to meet the needs of a larger student body, skyrocketing research costs, and more expensive requirements that all institutions were now beginning to meet such as rendering buildings accessible to men and women with disabilities. The disenchantment with rising tuition and the need for more resources reflected changing public attitudes. The optimism of the mid-1960s had given way to a national pessimism that was fueled by economic uncertainty and sluggish rates of economic growth. Faith in larger institutions of all kinds—government, business, and universities—eroded in the wake of Vietnam, Watergate, the energy crisis, and other national traumas.

The constant struggle for budgetary resources had important implications for Parks's hopes for Iowa State. Increasingly, governors and state legislators asked if the three universities were engaging in costly duplication of programs. For Iowa State, this charge was especially disconcerting because it was often aimed at Parks's efforts to create a more broad-based university. The evidence, moreover, hardly supported the charge. Compared to other states, Iowa's three universities had a surprisingly limited amount of duplication, and what did exist was often a product of student demand. Another issue that emerged in the funding wars was whether Iowa State should sell its television station WOI-TV, the ABC affiliate in central Iowa. Parks vigorously objected to this both on the grounds that the station was an economic asset and that the pressure to sell was an example of external political interference in the life of the university. He resisted pressure to sell the station just as he had resisted pressure to send the Iowa National Guard onto the Iowa State campus.[33]

The pressures for research funding had important effects as well. Erratic state funding and a dependence on limited state budgets forced research universities to rely ever more on funding from government contracts and grants and from private sources. It was increasingly the case that nothing lit up the eyes of a university budget officer or a university administrator as much as "indirect costs" and "grant overhead." These funds were becoming crucial to the success of a modern university. As they did, however, they reinforced the trend toward revenue-producing departments and colleges, and these were not the humanities. This trend also tended to reinforce narrow research emphases. The quest for grant dollars, in other words, moved Iowa State away from fostering a "new humanism."[34]

The scramble for research dollars could take odd turns. In 1977, for instance, Iowa State hosted the first ever International Conference on Iceberg Utilization, which included bringing to Ames a large chunk of an Alaskan iceberg. The purpose was to determine whether it was feasible to supply Middle Eastern nations with supplies of freshwater by chipping away at glacial icebergs. The conference was underwritten by the Saudi Arabian royal family. It generated national attention (and some gentle ridicule), but it was a testimony both to the mounting demand for new resources for research funding and to Iowa State's openness regarding research and inquiry.[35]

More in keeping with the university's scholarly pursuits was its contribution to the bicentennial celebration of 1976 by hosting the World Food Conference. The conference brought together a wide array of specialists from around the world to meet at Iowa State to discuss world food problems and how the world might produce and distribute food to eliminate hunger.[36]

The financial restraints notwithstanding, Iowa State's faculty continued to undertake a wide range of scholarly pursuits. Traditionally, Iowa State's best scholars were renowned for their ability to pursue research that combined sophisticated theory and practical applications to advance new fields of inquiry. This quality had characterized the work of such faculty stars as Henry Gilman in Chemistry, Frank Spedding in Physics and Metallurgy, Jay Lush in Animal Science, John Bremner in

Agronomy, and Oscar Kempthorne in Statistics. The faculty member who most brilliantly exemplified this tradition, however, was the economist Earl O. Heady. Born on a farm in western Nebraska, Heady had earned a Ph.D. in economics from Iowa State in 1945 and had then joined the faculty. A small man with a round face, Heady was modest and unassuming, but he was also ambitious, hardworking, and brilliant. Early in his career he combined new advances in economic theory with statistical methods to revolutionize the economics of farm management and agricultural production. He used this work as the basis for studying how farmers and the farm economy might adjust more rapidly to economic change. Then he turned to what was known as linear programming in an effort to develop complex computer-assisted models of the farm economy. He pressed the ISU administration for ever-larger IBM computers in order to handle his ever-larger economic models. This work and other lines of work led him to the study of world food problems and how poorer nations could feed themselves and a growing population. Graduate students flocked to him in small armies, and by the time health problems forced him to retire in 1983, he had trained 359 students who had come to him from around the world. He had also begun to advise governments on how they might address problems of food production. He worked closely with officials in India, Thailand, Indonesia, and Mexico, and with economists and agricultural officials in the Soviet Union, Hungary, Czechoslovakia, and other Eastern European nations. Knowledge, in Heady's view, should move beyond politics and international rivalries to address problems facing nations and the world. His aim was to find ways in which the world could feed itself, and his scholarly achievement was immense and established Iowa State as a foremost center of study of the economics of world food production and world food problems. Heady was a brilliant scholar, but his scholarship was always aimed at addressing economic problems, and alleviating world hunger was, he believed, the great challenge for agricultural economics and for institutions such as Iowa State.[37]

Athletics presented still another set of challenges from 1965 to 1986.[38] By the sixties almost all major public universities were heavily involved in fielding major athletics teams, and in the years after 1965 the emphasis (and overemphasis) on athletics in the university system would become more visible, more important, more costly, and more troubling.[39] Iowa State was to enjoy greater success in sports after 1965 than it had ever known, but with success came new problems as well. At the time, of course, Iowa State was a member of the Big Eight conference, and with the wonderful exception of Dr. Harold Nichols's wrestling teams, the Cyclones year in and year out finished in the bottom half of the conference standings. Bowl games, NCAA tournament appearances, and conference championships were not a part of the Iowa State experience. Since 1945, the football team had managed just three winning seasons. The basketball team had fared slightly better with nine, but with the exception of Bill Strannigan teams of the mid-1950s that starred Gary Thompson, it usually barely crept above .500. Some Cyclone players achieved all-conference and even All-American honors, but they were few in number. For Cyclone fans, "wait until next year" was a perennial lament.

Parks sought to build a strong Athletics Department as a part of the university. He knew well that the desire for winning teams could be corrosive, but he was no hypocrite. He enjoyed college sports and he understood that, like it or not, very often a university's best-known figures were not its talented faculty but its coaches and star players. This was true not just for alumni but also for state legislators and governors. His aim was to build an Athletics Department capable of fielding competitive and successful teams while also containing the immense pressures to violate rules and exploit student-athletes.

For Iowa State to continue as a member of a major conference would require the rebuilding of the Athletics Department. The changes began by hiring as athletics director Lou McCullough, a former Iowa State assistant football coach who had become a well-known assistant to Woody Hayes at Ohio State. A young assistant coach from Arkansas named Johnny Majors was hired as the new football coach in 1968 and a few years later Maury John, the highly successful Drake coach, took over the basketball team. When Hilton Coliseum opened in 1971, at a cost of $8 million, Iowa State had one of the nation's finest basketball arenas. Four years later, a new football stadium replaced the aging Clyde Williams Field.

After struggling for three years, Majors' 1971 team finished 8-3, with the three losses coming from the three teams that would finish the season ranked first, second, and third in the nation (Nebraska, Oklahoma, and Colorado). Led by linebacker Matt Blair and quarterback Dean Carlson, the Cyclones made their first postseason appearance in decades when they played Louisiana State University in the Sun Bowl. A year later, the team tied Nebraska 23–23 in Ames and played in the Liberty Bowl. For the first time in memory, Iowa State was gaining national attention in a major sport. Earle Bruce continued Majors's success during his five years at Iowa State with two bowl appearances.

Meanwhile, Iowa State's wrestling teams achieved outstanding success. Led by head coach Dr. Harold Nichols and star wrestlers such as Ben Peterson and Chris Taylor and the spectacular Dan Gable, Iowa State won six National Collegiate Athletic Association (NCAA) championships from 1965 to 1977. Gable was unquestionably the most brilliant Iowa State athlete of this period. As a wrestler, he combined intense training, spectacular skills, and an aggressive style to make him unbeatable. Or at least he was unbeatable until his very last collegiate match, when he lost in the NCAA championship in an upset that broke the hearts of Iowa State wrestling fans. The gymnastics team, coached by Ed Gagnier, added three more NCAA championships in 1971, 1973, and 1974.

The new facilities and the greater success did not come without controversy. To some critics, particularly among the faculty, Iowa State athletics had fallen victim to the nationwide craze to field winning teams regardless of the cost. With each big win, the pressure for more wins and more success increased, and the annual budget for athletics grew as well. One source of controversy centered on the new football stadium. Critics charged that the money could be better spent on other projects within the university, and when an angry Johnny Majors was quoted in the *Des Moines Register* as saying that he would like to punch one faculty opponent of the stadium project in the mouth, the issue embroiled the university.

By 1975, the stadium had been built, at a cost of $7 million, and although it was a decided improvement over Clyde Williams Field, it was, even by the standards of the mid-1970s, a modest structure that seated 42,500 fans and eschewed the opulence that was beginning to characterize sports facilities. It was funded through private donations and other sources without using any state appropriations. There remained, however, the question of what to name the stadium, and this issue proved even more controversial than building the stadium itself. One idea that quickly became popular was to name it for Jack Trice, an early African American football player for Iowa State who had died from injuries suffered in a game in 1923. Naming the stadium after Trice would honor his legacy and the contribution of black athletes to college sports.[40]

The debate quickly became contentious and emotional. The *Iowa State Daily*, many students, and some faculty backed the idea of Jack Trice Stadium. They were moved by Trice's death, and in the wake of Watergate and Vietnam there was a powerful appeal for breaking with the tradition of naming the stadium for a major donor or a university administrator. Outside of the university, alumni were less enthusiastic. Some saw the proposal as a political act and preferred to keep sports disentangled from political struggles. Others believed that the original opponents of building the stadium, having failed to stop its construction, were now trying to commandeer the stadium's naming. A university committee appointed by Parks and made up of faculty, alumni, and students rejected Trice Stadium for the more generic Cyclone Stadium, but the student members of the committee dissented, and in the face of student opposition, the issue festered and the stadium went without a name. The games went on in what became known as Iowa State's "no-name stadium." Eventually, the issue was resolved with the compromise of "Cyclone Stadium and Jack Trice Field." Still later it was renamed Jack Trice Stadium.

The controversies can be understood only in the context of the changing national mood of the 1970s. Whether to build a stadium and what to name it were issues that took on a new significance in the wake of Vietnam, Watergate, and the more divided America of the 1970s. They took on a powerful symbolic meaning about the purpose and direction of universities, race and race relations, and openness on the part of American institutions.

In these controversies, Parks tried to find a middle ground. While enjoying the newfound athletic successes, he was alarmed at the ever-more-intense pressure to yield winning teams and at the greed with which some universities reached for more lucrative television revenues. He successfully led the Big Eight universities to stop a proposal that would have undermined the NCAA's existing television contract, and possibly have undermined the NCAA's broader control of college sports, and he consistently advocated more aggressive enforcement of recruiting rules and reforms such as the so-called death penalty.[41] When the demands for gender equity in college athletics emerged as a major issue in the 1970s and 1980s, he urged greater resources for women's sports. In the traditionally male-dominated Athletics Department, Title IX was not a welcome development, and it would take time and some changes in key figures before women's athletics would become a major part of Cyclone sports.

Amidst the hype and often mindless hoopla that increasingly characterized college sports after 1965, some coaches and teams still managed to forge special bonds between a university and its varied supporters. One coach certainly did this at Iowa State, and his name was Johnny Orr. During his tenure, Orr would become Iowa State's winningest basketball coach: he would take six teams to the NCAA tournament and once reach the "sweet sixteen." The years he coached were not free of off-court incidents, and successful though he was, Orr's teams never won a regular-season championship (although they twice lost the championship game of the Big Eight tournament on last-second plays). Not every season was a winning season, but Orr's success transcended the number of games won or lost.

Some coaches demand reverence; others expect it. Orr earned it. He had come to Iowa State after many years as a winning coach at the University of Michigan, and to the *Des Moines Register,* the news of his hiring was an "ISU Stunner." When he arrived, Big Eight basketball was beginning to move away from a slow-paced, half-court style of play, and Orr's teams, particularly his best teams, pushed this transformation along with an aggressive game that featured man-to-man defenses and a fast-break attack. His Iowa State teams were often undersized, but led by players such as Barry Stephens, Jeff Hornacek, Jeff Grayer, and Fred Hoiberg, they compensated with superb team play and an infectious determination to win. Orr's combination of unusual wit, self-deprecation, fierce pride, and obvious respect for Iowa State's fans forged an endearing bond between a coach, his teams, and the thousands of Cyclone supporters who filled Hilton Coliseum. In thrilling matches with Minnesota, Iowa, Missouri, Oklahoma, Oklahoma State, and Larry Brown's Kansas Jayhawks, the Iowa State fans became an intangible but integral part of the game as they roared ever louder when Barry Stephens sank one of his arching jump shots or Jeff Grayer ripped a rebound away from a taller opponent or Jeff Hornacek passed or shot or did just about anything on the court. And each time Orr stomped his feet in disgust at an official's call, they bellowed in approval. As the cheering cascaded throughout the arena, the effect was almost magical. "Hilton Magic" was college sports at its best.[42]

When Parks retired in 1986, most of the entering freshman class of that year knew about the Vietnam War and the student protests of that era from what they had learned in high school history classes. Many of them had not even been born the year Don Smith had been elected GSB president. Most probably could not imagine Iowa State without the buildings of the Iowa State Center. Very few of them could explain how to use a slide rule, but most owned a pocket calculator, and they knew where to go on campus to find a computer terminal.

Iowa State had certainly changed. It was now awarding more degrees in history, philosophy, political science, and music than at any time in its history. The university's first doctoral degree in a humanities field was handed out in 1986 to a Ph.D. student in history. When he delivered the commencement address in May, Parks reflected to his call for a "new humanism" twenty years earlier and what had transpired since his inauguration. Iowa State was certainly a more broadly based institution, and it was certainly more attentive to learning in the humanities. He noted as well, however, that specialized and narrowly based training had continued, and the unified educational community he had envi-

*Iowa State University President W. Robert Parks late in his presidential administration. He served as ISU's top administrator from 1965 to 1986. (Used by permission of Iowa State University Library/Special Collections Department)*

sioned had not taken root. Very likely given the fragmented nature of modern knowledge and inquiry it could never be achieved in the way he had hoped. Still, Parks continued to hope that a humanistic perspective would one day inform learning and research at Iowa State and that the gap between scientific knowledge and social and humanistic knowledge might close. Iowa State, he told the graduating seniors, "must not be merely a university whose long-held motto has been 'Science with Practice.' We must be a university which also holds forward the motto of 'Science with Humanity.'"[43]

In the years after 1986, Iowa State continued to change, as Parks knew it would. He spent most of the next seventeen years in Ames quietly reading, enjoying Cyclone games, watching still more buildings go up about campus (and a few older ones come down), and seeing more books added to the Parks Library. When he died in the summer of 2003, he was buried in the Iowa State University cemetery beside his beloved wife, Ellen, and amidst the markers bearing the names of Beardshear and Curtiss and Friley and Hilton and Heady and many other men and women of Iowa State who had gone before him. It was a most fitting place of rest for a man who was deeply proud of Iowa State's past and who was ever hopeful for its future.

# Vignettes

## Student Leadership at the End of the Twentieth Century

In 1998, when Luke Foster arrived on campus as a National Merit Scholar and a recipient of a VEISHEA scholarship, he chose to major in biology. Within a short time, however, his friends teased that he was actually "majoring in extracurricular activities." In his first year, he participated in the Freshman Honors Program, the Student Alumni Leadership Council, VEISHEA, and FarmHouse fraternity. As a member of the President's Leadership Class, a group of thirty outstanding freshmen, Foster had the rare opportunity, in their weekly meetings, to discuss important issues and concerns with President Martin Jischke, as well as the Board of Regents, distinguished alumni, industry leaders, and the president of the Iowa Farm Bureau Federation.

For many students like Foster, college was about much more than academic training. Leadership training had become an essential part of student life. Toward the end of the twentieth century, as the job market became increasingly competitive, many young people came to campus expecting to gain practical experience outside of the classroom, whether it be through residence halls, Greek organizations, student clubs, internships, or part-time jobs.

By the late 1990s, students found a campus teeming with opportunity for involvement and leadership. In 1998, when Chris Lursen arrived on campus as a freshman, he became involved with Alpha Gamma Rho, a social fraternity for agriculture majors. Along with the men of the fraternity, he learned that leadership meant giving back to the community. He, along with other members, chaired various VEISHEA committees, helped with the blood drive, organized Greek Week activities, and held a car wash to raise money for Farm Safety 4 Just Kids, a farm safety organization. "We do a lot of community service," Lursen said, "because it's really good for us and it's good for Iowa State."

In 2000, as a member of the VEISHEA Community Service Committee, Luke Foster also gained valuable experience as a volunteer. That year, the committee sought to coordinate a group of four hundred Iowa State students to perform two thousand hours of community service before the VEISHEA opening ceremonies. Though it seemed to be a daunting task, Foster and the other members of the committee found Ames residents eager and thankful for the volunteer services.

Foster recalled, "We would contact local organizations like Youth and

*(continued)*

Shelter Services or Ames nursing homes. 'What would you like to have us do? How can we put in some hours?'" They put in time at elementary schools, assisted with a dance marathon, and helped organize countless other activities. They achieved their goal by the opening ceremonies of VEISHEA 2000.

Even if students did not always find the types of experiences they desired, they found they could create them. In 1998, when Paul Duncan arrived at Iowa State as a freshman majoring in transportation and logistics, he was disappointed to find that there was no organized railroad club. A train enthusiast since childhood, Duncan enjoyed model railroads and tracking real trains as they traveled across the country. He even set up a model train set in his dorm room. He soon became acquainted with other "railfans," who enjoyed watching the trains that rumbled through Ames. By his junior year, Duncan and several others took the initiative in forming the official ISU Railroad Club. Complete with a constitution and bylaws, the members were soon ready to plan trips to major railroad hubs in Kansas City, Omaha, and North Platte, Nebraska.

Duncan was no stranger to organization, time management, and leadership. He had long been involved with the Inter-Residence Hall Association, or IRHA. During his senior year, he served as president, representing 7,400 students and overseeing the 40-member IRHA Parliament. Issues facing the IRHA ranged from parking, food service, and washing machines, to setting up a Web-based resource for students living in the residence halls. Though he sometimes found the experience exhausting and often had to settle disagreements among members, he found the role of president to be personally rewarding.

"I'm representing people," he said in an interview during his senior year. "And I have people come up to me and say, 'Way to go, I'm really glad to see you guys work on this, or listening to us.' I go to floor meetings a lot and most IRHA presidents never even would have considered doing that. So I . . . just listen to people and find out what's going on. It's the best way."

As Chris Lursen looked back at his college career, he, like many of the students who pursued leadership opportunities at Iowa State, realized that the valuable lessons he learned would last a lifetime.

"I was told to take advantage of any opportunity I had and make the most of it," he said. "I think I have, with all the activities I've done, and I've prepared myself for the working world."

Jenny Barker Devine

# "An Incredible Experience": Students and Music in the 1990s

On December 31, 1999, as most Americans nervously awaited the new millennium, 190 members and alumni of the Iowa State Marching Band prepared to play "ISU Fights" and "Stars and Stripes Forever" in the London New Year's Parade. Though performers and groups from around the world participated, the Iowa State Marching Band was the only band to represent a four-year Division I college. Student and mellophone player Jeff Brown described it as "the trip of a lifetime."

From pep band to marching band, orchestra, choir, or even student rock bands, Iowa State students in the late 1990s found that participating in musical activities provided many unique experiences. Though music had always been an important part of student life at Iowa State, by the end of the twentieth century, it was easier than ever to travel, perform, and find common ground with fellow musicians.

Playing with the marching band was not without its "dirty work," however. At the end of each summer, Brown dreaded Band Camp, a four-day refresher and practice under the hot August sun. "We start practicing on music and hopefully learn the pre-game show, and work on music for half-time," he said. "It's a lot of tedious and strenuous work that I really don't like."

Yet the benefits of marching band far outweighed the rigors of Band Camp. After his memorable trip to London, Brown played with the band at the Insight.com Bowl in Phoenix, Arizona. And as a member of the pep band, he cheered on the men's Cyclone basketball team through all of their home games. Ultimately, he found that the band provided a ready group of friends for parties, games of Trivial Pursuit, bowling, and other activities.

"It's a lot more than just showing up for an hour and a half each day for practice," he said. "Usually you'll see a bunch of the same people in food service after practice. There's a lot of interaction between band people, inside and outside of band."

Not all students interested in music sought out university-sponsored activities. In 2000, when Dan Shea entered Iowa State as a freshman, he became involved with the Rock, a Christian student ministry through Stonebrook Community Church. Every Friday night, members of the Rock met for fellowship, listened to a speaker, and usually had a band provide music. Eager to join in and play the bass, Shea pestered members of the band by saying, "If you ever need a bass player, I can do it." Within a short time, the band members asked him to play with "the Rock Band."

*(continued)*

By the beginning of his junior year, Shea's band had new opportunities and a new name "the Lone Strangers." They played gigs at the Rock, the Beta Sigma Psi fraternity house, and for Destination Iowa State, a freshman orientation program at the Memorial Union. The following spring, the Lone Strangers played at the Towers Extravaganza, a festival near the Towers complex that included a carnival, food, fireworks, and a "Battle of the Bands." They provided warm-up music for bands playing at the Maintenance Shop at the Memorial Union, recorded several original songs, and produced their own CD.

What started as a group of friends playing for the Rock quickly became a band well known across campus. For Shea, playing with the Lone Strangers provided a wealth of new experiences. When the Lone Strangers played at VEISHEA, on the stage at Welch Avenue, Shea looked out to see a crowd of more than four hundred people listening to their music.

"We were right before one of the main acts and it was at the prime time of people being out there, and not being in the bars," he said. "It was just cool to look out at that many people and play for them."

Jenny Barker Devine

# Angie Welle: "Like No Other Player"

She finished her career as the leading scorer in the history of Iowa State women's basketball. She was the key post player on teams that posted consecutive records of 25-8, 27-6, 27-6, and 24-9 during her career. She could shoot, as her school record field goal percentage of .641 would attest. She could hit the boards and finished her career as the all-time leading rebounder in Iowa State history. But what set her apart from other players her size was that Angie Welle could run with anyone. A common sight was Welle beating slighter defenders down the court to receive passes from her teammates for a layup when the Fargo, North Dakota, native patrolled the post for head coach Bill Fennelly from 1998 to 2002.

Welle stood six feet four but ran like a guard. Very few centers could get out on the break like this All-American. Her quickness was just one part of her talent. Welle had great poise down low around the basket, utilizing a variety of pivot moves that often left opponent centers and forwards committing a foul in attempts to stop her. Welle had great court sense, and her ability to pass from the inside to an open teammate beyond the three-point arc played in perfect symphony with Fennelly's penchant for building great shooting teams. The fact that Welle was a southpaw further confounded opposing players who weren't accustomed to strong drives to the left of the basket.

Welle contributed right away, which she expected. As a freshman, she averaged 10.9 points and 6.8 rebounds. In Iowa State's historic 64–58 win over Connecticut that advanced the Cyclones to the Elite Eight of the 1999 NCAA Tournament, Welle played twenty-four minutes with 10 points and a team-high seven rebounds. Welle's sophomore season was one of further adjustment and she finished strong, averaging 15.4 points and 8.6 rebounds. The Cyclones posted a 13-3 record in the Big 12 in 1999–2000, tying for first, swept the field as the top seed at the league tournament, and then advanced to the Sweet Sixteen for the second straight season.

As a senior, Welle averaged 20.5 points and 11.3 rebounds despite being the main focus of each opponent's defensive efforts. There would be a bittersweet ending to Welle's senior campaign. Iowa State was the No. 3 seed in the 2002 NCAA Tournament and opened with a first-round win over Temple. But the Cyclones lost to Brigham Young in the second round in Hilton Coliseum.

Her statistics set the highest standard for those who would follow the All-American. She ended her Cyclone career holding records for points, field goals made, field goal percentage, free throws made, free throws attempted, rebounds, and blocked shots. Her career included fifty-four double-doubles

*(continued)*

and set eight school records for single-season play as a senior. There was always more to her than basketball, as she was academic all–Big 12 in each of her Iowa State seasons and academic All-American as a senior.

The success experienced by Welle and her teammates fueled skyrocketing fan interest in Ames. Iowa State averaged 3,775 fans per game the season before Welle's arrival in Ames. Her sophomore season, an average of 11,184 fans packed Hilton Coliseum. That figure increased to 11,370 in 2000–2001, as the Cyclones won twenty-seven games for the second straight season, beat Oklahoma 68–65 in the Big 12 Tournament, and knocked off St. Francis and Florida State in the NCAA Tournament.

Tom Kroeschell

## Chapter 4

# Strategic Focus and Accountability: The Eaton-Jischke Years

Charles M. Dobbs

The four decades after the Second World War greatly changed Iowa State University. There were many more students, faculty and staff, buildings, colleges, and academic fields of study. It seemed in the latter years of the Parks presidency that ISU would become a broad-based research university, much like the University of Iowa, as many Iowa Staters hoped. The succeeding era would be very different, in which key stakeholders—especially elected officials, business leaders, and the Board of Regents—would insist on strategic focus and increased accountability and on proof the university was concentrating its resources to achieve that focused mission. There would be many challenges adjusting the university to these new mandates, and these pressures would continue after the presidencies of Gordon Eaton and Martin Jischke had ended.

American higher education was changing greatly in the mid-1980s. Since the 1950s, taxpayers and their elected representatives across the nation generously supported public institutions of higher education and trusted those institutions to educate the coming wave of "baby boom" children as older boomers began flooding colleges and universities in the mid-1960s. Traditional campuses constructed new facilities and new institutions arose, all to deal with this surge of young people seeking higher education. By the 1980s, state legislatures were beginning to demand "accountability" as well as defined missions and measurable outcomes. With more competition for increasingly scarce state resources, legislators asked hard questions of the public universities they were funding. The "Rust Bowl," the farm crisis, and challenges in the economy of the 1980s only added impetus to this pressure for accountability. Iowa State University was not immune to this larger trend.

On July 1, 1986, Gordon P. Eaton officially began as the twelfth president of Iowa State University. Eaton recognized that the conditions under which Iowa State University had prospered in the Parks presidency had changed and that times called for a thorough review of the university. As he said when he interviewed on campus, "Iowa State's progress in the future is dependent on the university's ability to increase its resources" and "reallocating resources within the University would probably be necessary". The president of the Board of Regents,

John McDonald, in announcing the hiring of Eaton said that "he understands the need for re-emphasis on science and technology." Eaton noted the board "wanted the new president to get the university moving again."[1]

Eaton was a geologist and, along with great intelligence, brought a scientist's sense of accuracy and brutal honesty to the office. He earned his Ph.D. from the California Institute of Technology, had served with the U.S. Geological Survey, including as scientist-in-charge of the Hawaiian Volcano Observatory, and later as dean and then provost and vice president for academic affairs at Texas A&M University. Eaton, as many soon learned, was honest and forthright and spoke his mind to friends and critics alike. He also was personable and often walked campus, showing up unexpectedly at student events, to the delight of students. Administrators who interacted regularly with him enjoyed working with him. He brought Charles McCandless from Texas A&M and McCandless often served as the "bad" guy to Eaton's "good" guy. For an individual who regularly spoke his mind, Eaton remained surprised that the media would print his remarks on the front page; he often claimed that such statements would at best be printed well inside the newspaper in College Station, Texas, home to Texas A&M.[2]

He soon concluded that external trends, if not reversed, did not favor Iowa State University. The state's rural economy was in crisis, as was the family farm. Advances in agriculture rewarded larger and larger farms to take advantage of new, bigger, and more costly equipment, and to realize economies of scale, land holdings were concentrating. The continued mechanization of agriculture meant fewer and fewer people working on farms, and this led to the decline of many small towns dependent on the surrounding farm population for their economic vitality. In the 1980s, Iowa's population declined by nearly 140,000, and that devastated life in many farming communities. The so-called Rust Bowl decline in basic manufacturing, sadly, exacerbated the economic impact of the farm crisis.[3]

Eaton believed Iowa State had drifted off course. The Parks presidency had an optimistic view of Iowa's future; one sign was construction of the Towers Residence Area, well south of the main campus, to prepare for a satellite campus to educate an ever-increasing student population. This increase never materialized as Iowa's population decreased. Parks believed that Iowa could afford and wanted two broad, public research universities and he promoted the humanities to make Iowa State such an institution. In Eaton's view, however, Iowa State needed to focus strategically to have a few areas of recognized excellence or be mediocre in a great many areas. There also was a degree of complacency at the university. Iowa State dropped in the [old] Carnegie Endowment rankings of universities from Research I to Research II, reflecting a decline in research grants, nationally recognized faculty members, and the number of graduate students and graduate degrees awarded. The decline could lead to Iowa State becoming a second-class institution. Worse, neither senior administrators nor faculty admitted to the drift. Eaton felt that there were too many areas of "complacency, self-satisfaction, and contentment and, in some instances, even apathy."[4]

He had concerns about Iowa's economy and state financial support for the university. As Iowa's population and economy stagnated, Eaton recognized that the regents institutions generally and Iowa State specifically produced more graduates in key fields than Iowa's economy could absorb. Taxpayers were supporting the public universities to help prepare their children to move far away to find work in their fields of study. As Iowa's population declined, there would be increased pressure from community colleges and small private colleges to contain the public universities in the fight for limited state tax dollars and student enrollment, because student enrollment and the concomitant tuition and fees they paid represented the lifeblood of community colleges and small private institutions. As Eaton noted in an interview with *VISIONS* magazine, the university lost General Fund support most years between 1979 and 1986 yet continued its business without adjusting; there were three thousand more students, a reduction in state support of $30 million, and the university acted as if it were business as usual. University resources were overburdened.[5]

Eaton concluded the university needed to demand research excellence and to focus on practical research that brought new revenue to the university and improved Iowa's economy. Research excellence required excellent faculty, and Eaton was committed to raising faculty salaries and enhancing support for agricultural research, at which he believed Iowa State should excel. Iowa State had to focus on its traditional strengths in research while continuing to provide a first-rate and broad undergraduate education.

As President Eaton said in his inaugural address on August 25, 1986, "economic vicissitudes . . . are quite profound and in some ways as unsettling as those which overtook us during the Industrial Revolution." He continued, "we must therefore ask ourselves if our current mission, the size and distribution of our student body, our academic standards for admission, our present organizational structure, our traditional ways of approaching our basic tasks, and even some of those basic tasks themselves, are appropriate to the new and leaner times and to the new environment."

While challenging the entire university community, Eaton made clear that Iowa State would always provide excellent education, engage in first-rate research, and reach out to Iowans. "The dissemination of knowledge that already exists is not challenged as a basic obligation of a University, for it is the underlying stuff of the classroom lecture." Eaton wanted a stronger emphasis on education, including "the vital importance of an understanding of other cultures and their relationship to our global interdependence and global world economy."

But he worried about "intellectual self righteousness," especially "that applied research is not as worthy as pure research." And he called on the university to "reevaluate our commitment to research and reexamine our faculty reward system as it relates to the conduct of research, both pure and applied, as well as to our commitment to our programs of professorial research."[6]

In time, Eaton came to depend on a new set of academic administrators, including new college deans and an entrepreneurial head of federal relations, Michael Crow, who helped realize this strengthened commitment to research excellence. He noted that Iowa State should be "a beacon of hope" for national agriculture, a leader in biotechnology, and a force in the sciences. Eaton described the new Engineering dean, David Kao, as one who will "continue the invigorating research effort for a college that has not been as active as it might have been." He applauded new Agriculture Dean David Topel for his vision of value-added farm products and for increased international ties in the college.[7]

Eaton was blunt in describing the measures the university needed to take. At his first appearance before the ISU Faculty Council, Eaton stated that Iowa State needed to raise faculty salaries and decrease student enrollment, which required a long-range planning process to "prevent a repeat of the situation which has necessitated the first two needs." He stated that, in some cases, the university was not using research funds effectively, and he intended to find out who was accountable. He felt ISU was adrift and later stated that "admittedly, we used something akin to the electric shock therapy used to start a heart that's stopped." The *Daily Tribune* editorialized that "questions can be raised about Eaton's shake 'em up management style but there can be little question about his goals."[8]

Eaton relied on Michael Crow, who demonstrated great ability to work with Iowa's congressional delegation to establish a series of research centers somewhat apart from the regular academic organization of the university. Crow recognized the challenge: "the university was insufficiently robust as a research and discovery enterprise." He saw the crucial need to "transform the University from a slow-moving, agriculturally-focused institution to a rapidly-moving, broadly focused, research university." But Crow was also a lightning rod for controversy, and some faculty members were concerned about the establishment of new research centers. He came under fire from other academics "for developing projects for applied research and concepts that can be commercialized." Some critics on campus fumed about the emphasis on applied research as opposed to teaching. Crow left the university soon after the regents appointed Martin Jischke as president.[9]

Nonetheless, Crow's success raised a larger, continuing issue. Should the university recruit senior faculty in engineering, the physical sciences, the life sciences, and the animal sciences and let those individuals hire their research teams, including junior faculty members? Or, should the university hire a larger number of junior faculty members and hope that some of them would develop great research projects and prove successful? The two models reflected a trade-off, a concentration on research on the one hand and a more balanced view of faculty obligations on the other, and this trade-off lay beneath some of the faculty opposition to Michael Crow. Yet great research was occurring at the margins of departments, and traditional organizations might inhibit synergies at these margins.

Eaton believed the university needed a long-range strategic plan to complement the commitment to restoring research excellence. The regents wanted the public universities to identify their respective roles and avoid unnecessary duplication. As he stated on Iowa Public Television's *Iowa Press,* the structural changes will yield "a smaller, more sharply focused institution" that will be the nation's best agricultural research school in five years. He envisioned the long-range planning process to produce a very radical change in the organization of the institution. Or as Eaton stated, "when I started this process it scared the hell out of everybody; there hadn't been any change for twenty-one years."[10]

The process certainly left many faculty and staff uncomfortable. Task Force Director and Professor Jean Adams noted that "there is a sense of anxiety" about the plan's recommendations and also about the commitment to excellence, includ-

*Strategic planning was vital to Gordon Eaton's vision for improving the university. In 1989 he initiated a long-range planning process to refocus the university on science and technology and on research. (Used by permission of Iowa State University Library/Special Collections Department)*

ing orienting institutional rewards toward the demonstration of excellence. She told *VISIONS* magazine that she attributed the anxiety to the fact that "Iowa State perhaps was just too stable for too long. That's not meant to be critical of the Parks administration." Neither Adams nor Provost and Long Range Strategic Planning Committee (LRSPC) Co-Director Milton Glick seemed willing to assuage faculty fears over what appeared to be a largely top-down process and perhaps its predictable outcome. At a November 16, 1987, planning committee hearing, some faculty members expressed concern for the abandonment of the liberal arts and an overemphasis on science and technology.[11]

In November 1988, the LRSPC released the first and what proved to be the less controversial part of its report. It reaffirmed that Iowa State University should offer a broad general undergraduate education with focused strengths in graduate education and research. It confirmed the goal of developing centers of excellence in science and technology. But the details would come in the second part, which the central administration intended to release in February 1989.[12]

Even before the administration released the second part of the report, faculty members expressed concern. Some indicated they wanted the top priority of the university to be undergraduate education and took issue with Eaton's "leaner and meaner" vision of a high-tech institution emphasizing research to attract national money and attention.[13]

The LRSPC released the second part of the draft plan in early February 1989. The plan ranked departments and colleges by their quality and centrality to the university's mission. There were several dramatic recommendations, including reducing eleven academic departments in the College of Engineering to five and raising the annual average of $14,790 in externally funded grants then received per faculty member closer to the annual average per faculty member of $100,819 obtained at peer engineering colleges at research universities; making the College of Agriculture internationally competitive; and eliminating the College of Family and Consumer Sciences and the College of Design. It called for enrolling more adult and minority students, increased Extension Service work, centralized authority, interdisciplinary research, expanded graduate programs, and a vision of excellence.[14]

The draft aroused faculty fears and anger. University Relations Director David L. Lendt noted that there were months of work in this watershed report, and that it would restructure existing university assets, retool the university, and give emphasis to specific departments. Among concerns expressed were that setting a goal of becoming one of the top five land-grant institutions likely posed a bigger challenge than the university could achieve, that the liberal arts might be gutted (despite Eaton's assurances about the value of a general education) in favor of the hard sciences, and that Eaton was seeking to make ISU into a business of a sort for the state's economic salvation.

Faculty members were concerned that Eaton had his priorities out of line and certainly not in line with his predecessor. Pulitzer Prize–winning novelist and English professor Jane Smiley called the long-range planning report "a myriad of fantasies and misconceptions" and noted that "trust among faculty members has eroded" since its release. An ad hoc group of mostly retired faculty members, led by Bill Kunerth and Don Biggs, self-titled "The Committee on the State of Iowa State," criticized the second part of the planning report and President Eaton and Provost Glick. Later, this self-styled watchdog group criticized the central administration for a top-down management style and heavy-handed leadership, for not rewarding teaching, for unwise financial management policies, and for overemphasizing research. While the committee would lose some of its energy, it continued into the Jischke years, fading finally when Kunerth left Ames. The ISU Faculty Senate was skeptical of a "spirit of cooperation" with the administration until after it reviewed changes made in the long-range plan. As Professor Fred Williams noted, "I am exasperated how to respond via the Senate." There was even talk of a faculty vote of "no confidence" in the Eaton administration, which naturally concerned Dr. Eaton.[15]

Eventually, Provost Milton Glick announced the central administration would retreat from the more dramatic recommendations of the committee he cochaired. There would be no push to eliminate colleges, and Journalism seemingly avoided the axe. Or, as Eaton noted to the media, he wanted "anxieties relieved" and said he would use a less strident approach than the LRSPC.[16]

About this time, the Board of Regents announced it had engaged a consulting firm, Peat Marwick Main and Company, to review the three universities to find inefficiencies and duplications of effort. It seemed Board President Marvin Pomerantz wanted to head off legislative interference and assure Iowa legislators that the institutions were good shepherds of public funds. But he became a focal point for faculty anger and this anger migrated directly to Eaton and later to his successor, Martin Jischke. In the aftermath of the planning process, it seemed a case of overkill. Eaton and Glick defended the university's planning process, stating that "we're already lean and mean in terms of offerings; the question is: are we going to become anorexic?" If the regents ignore this process, Eaton noted "the credibility of our effort is gone." The consultants recommended consolidation in business, education, engineering, home economics, and journalism at the three universities, as well as eleven other departmental programs. The following fall, the university submitted its penultimate defense, noting that the programs under review were popular, unique, of high quality, and essential to the mission of a land-grant university. In the end, the regents largely rejected the major and most threatening recommendations, but did reduce the Journalism program and housed it entirely in the College of Liberal Arts and Sciences.[17]

With the environment on campus somewhat calmed, the university presented its first formal strategic plan. Eaton noted, "I sense a much more positive and upbeat attitude. Things are happy. People are affecting their own futures." In April 1990, Iowa State unveiled a plan to become the nation's top land-grant institution. Requiring increased state support, the plan called for ninety additional faculty members in key research areas, improved undergraduate education, a more diverse campus, twelve to fifteen premiere graduate programs, six hundred additional graduate students, better service to the state, and strengthened use of technology. The regents supported the plan and its aspiration to be the best.[18]

Eaton recognized the university needed its alumni and friends for a major gifts campaign to leverage the increased state resources he was seeking and the federal funds that were flowing to the university in research grants. In early 1989 the university finished preparations and launched its largest fund-raising effort, "Partnership for Prominence," a capital campaign with a goal of $150 million over five years. In February 1990, with the quiet phase at an end (the initial phase of a campaign during which nonprofits seek to raise at least 60 percent of the total goal), President Eaton noted that he was planning on spending as much as 50 percent of his time traveling across Iowa and the nation on the fund-raising campaign.[19]

Eaton paid a price for this commitment to strategic focus and research excellence. He noted, after he resigned, that his blood pressure had risen to over three hundred, a sign of his stress. One staff member recalled that a reporter for the *Ames Tribune* camped out on the front steps of Beardshear Hall to trap Eaton on his walk to the Knoll at day's end, and Eaton would sneak out a side exit to avoid the reporter. Critics, while few, were so vociferous and Eaton was so committed to correcting their many errors of fact and interpretation that a former Faculty Senate president called Eaton's "Occasional Notes" instead "Bullets from the Bunker." The university's first real effort at marketing backfired on campus. Eaton wanted a clear and consistent image across the state, and the result, in part, was the catchphrase "Iowa State Means Business," which was the title of many of his talks to

*Dr. Eaton determined that the university needed to fund-raise more aggressively in order to supplement state resources and federal funds. The campaign fund-raising executive committee shown here includes, left to right, sitting, Milton Glick, provost; Owen Newlin, Foundation Board president; President Eaton; and left to right, standing, Dayton Hultgren, executive director of development; David Lendt, director of information; Charles McCandless, executive vice president; and Warren Madden, vice president for business and finance. In this first-ever capital campaign, university leaders aimed to secure gifts of $100,000 or more. (Used by permission of Iowa State University Library/Special Collections Department)*

local chambers of commerce. It seemed to sum up to faculty critics what was wrong with his priorities.[20]

The backlash became so intense that, soon after becoming president of the Board of Regents, Marvin Pomerantz sent a very public and strong letter of support to Eaton. The *Ames Tribune* reported that "flurries of rumors and criticism circling an embattled Iowa State President Gordon Eaton may be dying down as critics say he is beginning to open the flow of information from Beardshear Hall." The *Tribune* reported Pomerantz wrote Eaton that "leaders who are asked to take charge of major institutions during times of significant difficulty and change are faced with extraordinary burdens."[21]

Eaton, to be sure, responded too often and too honestly to his critics. The *Des Moines Register* editorialized that "Gordon Eaton knows speaking his mind gets him in trouble but he does anyway." The premier issue of *VISIONS* noted, "in the

*Dr. Eaton meets with a group of students as they launch Alcohol Awareness Week (1985). (Used by permission of Iowa State University Library/Special Collections Department)*

eye of it all is a CEO leading the university his way . . . stirring up controversy and support, criticism and applause with his every step." He pointed out his opponents "leap wide chasms of logic" with their criticisms. Or, in one of his more famous retorts, "I look at the reputation of my critics and I'm not unhappy with the critics I have." "Typical Eaton; a Classic putdown," editorialized The *Daily Tribune.*[22]

Sadly, the critics made Eaton to be a bad person when he was extremely likeable, personable, and supportive of his colleagues and subordinates. A former Faculty Senate president said that "Dr. Eaton was a gentle and smart man who honestly had the best interests of the faculty at heart." A former secretary in the office stated that Dr. Eaton "treated everyone with the same courtesy and respect." She recalled that she enjoyed "the family atmosphere" in the President's Office. A former assistant noted that Eaton encouraged input, and this inclusive approach made his staff feel more valued.[23]

At the same time, students were changing, as were their expectations and values. They grew up in greater affluence than their parents, and they did not feel as connected to their communities. They were more alienated in many ways—the so-called Me Generation—and less likely to bond with the university through active involvement in campus clubs and organizations. These students born in the 1960s had less respect for authority and greater expectations. It was a volatile mix.

The most noticeable change was the VEISHEA riot of 1988. Since its inception in 1922, VEISHEA was supposed to show off Iowa State to the community and prospective students. Over the years, there was less and less recruitment and more and more partying and revelry. Thousands of young people came to town to party with their Iowa State friends. Early on Sunday morning, May 8, 1988, some individuals in a crowd of five thousand on Welch Avenue threw bottles, rocks, and bricks and even made a bonfire from furniture. To stop the riot, the police asked basketball coach Johnny Orr and football coach Jim Walden to urge the crowd to disperse and it worked. This larger riot followed smaller outbreaks the two preceding nights, which resulted in part from the authorities shutting down parties in the Campustown area. As *VISIONS* magazine noted, "VEISHEA will never be the same again." Or, as Eaton commented, the riots on May 6–8 gave ISU "a black eye for the entire nation to see." The *Daily Tribune* reported that it was "Welch Avenue's longest weekend . . . thousands ran wild, dozens arrested, others hurt in the riot." Ames residents awoke on Sunday morning to see the results of three consecutive nights of violence, vandalism, and excessive drinking. Eaton could not apologize enough: "ISU is deeply ashamed, embarrassed and disappointed in the involvement and it owes a profound apology to the taxpayers for the wanton destruction; it was mad and senseless behavior."[24]

And, there were challenges in athletics. The most notable one involved the football program and head coach Jim Criner. By fall 1986, a series of losing seasons dampened enthusiasm for football, and the decline in ticket sales affected the entire athletics budget. The NCAA investigated charges a former player made that athletic boosters offered loans to players, which, if true, were clear violations of NCAA regulations. The NCAA presented Eaton with thirty-three allegations of rules violations by ISU football and basketball teams. He was concerned about boosters because, as he noted, "a university cannot take any disciplinary action against a booster." The bad news continued, as two former ISU student-athletes alleged that football assistant coaches paid part of their university fees. Several football players were arrested for burglary in the rising tide of problems engulfing the program. Several more student-athletes lost their academic eligibility, several more quit the team, and the entire program seemed to be spiraling downward. In October the media reported several former players used credit cards stolen from an assistant coach. Six weeks later Eaton issued a statement: "The University will not tolerate violations of University or NCAA rules and intends to see that future violations do not occur," noting that ISU "intends to run a clean athletic program that is above suspicion." Athletics director Max Urick fired Jim Criner, and assistant head football coach Chuck Banker served as acting head coach for the remainder of the season. Eaton said that ISU was guilty of "major" NCAA violations and expected severe sanctions, which turned out to be two years of probation and loss of eight scholarships during that period. The university hired Jim Walden, from Washington State University, as coach, and he restored integrity but proved unable to win consistently.[25]

The university moved forward, and Eaton gave a series of interviews as he was concluding his fourth year, taking due credit for the achievements. He told the *Daily Tribune* that there were days when he wished he was "sitting out on a chunk of granite somewhere." But he noted real accomplishments, including better fac-

*Gordon Eaton assists in tapping new members for Cardinal Key, an honorary society that recognizes junior and senior undergraduate students, faculty, and staff who have demonstrated outstanding leadership, service, character, and scholarship as a member of the Iowa State University community. (Used by permission of Iowa State University Library/Special Collections Department)*

ulty pay, up 46.2 percent over four years, and the push for more research to regain Carnegie Research I status. He concluded that he was considering serving as president for a total of seven years and retiring no later than when he turned sixty-five.[26]

Then, suddenly and unexpectedly, Eaton announced his resignation. The headline read, "ISU Shocker: Eaton Resigns." Eaton told the university community and the media that he could not pass up the opportunity to return to science at a high level as director of Columbia University's Lamont-Doherty Geological Observatory.[27]

Media summaries of Eaton's achievements as president were predominantly favorable. The *Des Moines Register* editorialized that Eaton was able to destroy the old but did not stay long enough to build the new. James Flansburg noted that "the Iowa Board of Regents hired Gordon Eaton to administer the shock to Iowa State. . . . He did it mostly by forcing everybody to challenge the assumptions they'd been living with since 1965. . . . His job was to be the bad guy who dramatized the transition of the institution." *Register* editorial writer David Yepsen concluded that "Eaton wasn't an architect who built a world-class university, just a demolition expert who blew up a moribund one. First things first." Still, the media generally recognized all that Eaton had accomplished. The Cedar Rapids *Gazette* editorialized that "Eaton assumed his first university presidency at an enormously difficult time of transition, and acquitted himself well." The *Daily Tribune* commented that "Eaton increased faculty salaries, increased research and grants, put a new administrative team in place, and set the University on a new and sound direction." It also noted that "the school has benefited from his tutelage."[28]

The university community and Iowa soon became engrossed in the search for Eaton's successor. David Yepsen in the *Des Moines Register* wrote that Board President Marvin Pomerantz "is looking for someone to continue Eaton's battle to make Iowa State a leading land-grant university again. He's also looking for someone to move about faster than Eaton was moving." The *Register* reported that the "search panel may want someone just like Eaton: from the Midwest, strong academic background in the sciences, engineering or agriculture, continue to stress economic development, research and grants, reach out to alumni and donors, and be a good communicator."[29]

Meanwhile, Milton Glick served as interim president and promised to stay the course. Glick moved the university to operate under the guidance of the new strategic plan; he continued the fund-raising campaign Eaton had begun. The *Daily Tribune* noted that "Glick's contribution will be remembered." It included improving communications between faculty and administration, developing and fine-tuning the university's strategic plan, and spurring Iowa State's economic development efforts.[30]

The board selected Martin C. Jischke to be the thirteenth president of Iowa State University. The *Tribune* commented that Jischke "has a lot of enthusiasm for his new post, his new university, and his new state." Board President Pomerantz stated that Jischke "has impressive academic credentials, excellent communication skills, and is a proven leader." Faculty members, staff, and students at the University of Missouri–Rolla all commented favorably about him.[31]

Martin Jischke brought administrative experience, tremendous energy, great vision, and boundless enthusiasm to the position. A graduate of the Massachusetts Institute of Technology, Jischke had been a professor of aeronautics and astronautics, dean of the College of Engineering, and interim president at the University of Oklahoma and chancellor at the University of Missouri–Rolla. He interviewed candidates for senior line and staff administrative positions, indicating that the vacant position was not merely a forty-hour-a-week job, and he regularly worked weekends and late into the night. And he proved tireless in promoting the university, its faculty, its students, and its alumni.[32]

Jischke set forth his priorities at his installation. On October 13, 1991, he recalled Iowa State University's great and historic role in the land-grant movement, the cherished legacy of access and opportunity for higher education, the attachment of Iowans to education and the land and their quintessential modesty, and how Iowa State exemplified all these values. He called for a strengthened commitment to excellence. He noted the relationship of practical and liberal education, the centrality of learning, the need for civility, the obligation to research and to disseminate the fruits of that research, and the public trust that Iowa State University must continue to earn. He committed Iowa State to becoming the nation's best

*Dr. Martin Jischke was installed as the thirteenth president of the university on October 13, 1991. (Used by permission of Iowa State University Library/Special Collections Department)*

land-grant institution, and in succeeding years he established benchmarks to measure progress and drive the university to achieve this ambitious goal.[33]

Martin Jischke and his wife, Patty, opened the Knoll, making it a valued front "door" to the university. The demands on university presidents were changing greatly, including expectations of increased outreach, fund-raising, and influencing of political and business leaders. The Jischkes were an ideal team to take on these new obligations, more in line with private university presidencies, to reach out to elected officials, business leaders, key alumni, and donors. They entertained in grand style, hosting more than 250 events annually at the Knoll and many more elsewhere in Ames, in Iowa, and across the country, including breakfasts, lunches, dinners, afternoon teas, and evening dessert receptions. Some eight thousand people a year experienced the hospitality of the Knoll, and it gained a reputation of being one of the best "restaurants" in central Iowa.

Faculty, staff, students, and alumni had many opportunities to visit the Knoll. The Jischkes hosted holiday receptions for faculty, professional staff, and student leaders; they entertained department chairs; they hosted distinguished professors and university professors. Similarly, the Jischkes hosted alumni, donors, and friends of the university. Hundreds of Iowa State University alumni brought their children, the "legacy" program, to walk through the Knoll. Homecoming, Alumni Days, and the Order of the Knoll all meant heavy weekends of entertaining. There were lunches to honor donors and key alumni; there were invitations to business and political leaders; the Jischkes frequently hosted campus visitors before they

*Mrs. Jischke, known to all as Patty, is seen here arranging flowers she just cut from gardens on the grounds of the Knoll. The Jischkes opened the historic Knoll for many events and numerous visitors during their time at Iowa State. (Used by permission of Iowa State University Library/Special Collections Department)*

would give featured speeches. And Patty Jischke was involved in many community activities, and that brought additional guests to the Knoll.

Anthony Cawdron, the events coordinator at the Knoll, became a well-known and well-liked figure around the university and in central Iowa. The *Des Moines Register* called him "Iowa's 'King of Class'". Cawdron organized and oversaw more than 250 events a year at the Knoll and countless others on campus. He not only coordinated events with grace and style, but he gave countless talks to help students at Iowa State and 4-H kids around the state learn dining etiquette. He kept detailed notes, and guests knew that he would be cognizant of their dietary needs and provide a special and equally outstanding meal. It was a consummate performance that reflected dedication and hard work, and it helped make an invitation to the Knoll a treat for people on and off campus.[34]

Jischke continued the strategic plan that Eaton had barely begun, and he worked to make it the guiding document of the university. He believed it a workable blueprint to strengthen Iowa State's excellence while committing the institution to become the best land-grant university. In investing new funds from year to year, regardless of the source, he always committed them based on how they helped realize the goals of the plan.

Thereafter, in 1994, there was another exercise to develop a plan for 1995–2000, and in 1999, the same for 2000–2005. The *Daily Tribune* reported on the 1995–2000 plan that the "preliminary draft of ISU plan [was] similar to 1990 goals," for there was value in a consistent plan providing guidance on the university's direction. The plans continued Eaton's striving to become the best, with a stronger focus on undergraduate education.[35]

But the fears that dogged Eaton, research at the expense of education and narrow as opposed to broad focus, also dogged Jischke. Over time, a small group of faculty members and external critics would charge either that Jischke and Iowa State University not only favored research but downgraded the importance of teaching or that the university was selling its soul for corporate grants and contracts. Not surprisingly, the same group of faculty members who had complained about Eaton were concerned about the changes that were continuing or being initiated under Jischke.[36]

Jischke was committed to raising the visibility of Iowa State University in Iowa and the nation. He deeply believed in the land-grant ideal, and insisted that Iowa State University retain its strong ties to the people of Iowa. He also wanted Iowans to recognize that the university was a community of outstanding faculty, staff, and students, and he was very willing to serve as cheerleader for such a great university. He implemented programs to better connect the university and the people of Iowa and to raise Iowa State's visibility in national, academic, and research circles.

Jischke visited from ten to twenty Iowa communities each year; these were all-day trips. He would leave early in the morning, and he would typically make an industry visit where an Iowa State graduate would escort the president. He would stop at a local community project, perhaps a social service project or a cultural or tourism project. He would visit the local high school and speak with juniors and seniors about continuing their education and attending Iowa State. He would meet with the editorial staff of the local newspaper or make an on-air appearance on the local radio station. He would speak at noontime to the local service club or organization, visit an area community college, and cap off the long day with an alumni reception in the home of an ISU alumni couple. He also accepted virtually every speaking invitation, including serving as speaker at high school graduations or being the luncheon speaker for local chambers of commerce and service clubs, because they gave him an opportunity to promote Iowa State.[37]

Jischke also led new ISU faculty and staff on so-called Roads Scholars tours from Ames to the border of Iowa. Beginning in fall 1992, the trips took place during October and April each year; and, if there was sufficient interest, Jischke led one bus and (new) Provost John Kozak led another. The Office of the Vice President for External Affairs invited new faculty and staff members to join the president on a weekend bus tour to become better acquainted with Iowa and Iowans whose taxes so generously supported the university. As an example, on October 1–2, 1999, a bus with forty-five new employees traveled to southeast Iowa with stops in Knoxville, Oskaloosa, Drakesville, Bentonsport, Fairfield, Ollie, Sigourney, Pella, and Keosauqua. The group visited a high school, several private colleges, an Amish sawmill, a family hog farm, and a manufacturing plant as well as meeting with ISU alumni and local economic development officials.[38]

Similarly, Jischke assumed leading positions among research university CEOs.

*Framed by the columns of Beardshear Hall, Dr. Jischke presented a somewhat formal and imposing figure. (Used by permission of Iowa State University Library/Special Collections Department)*

Jischke's peers valued his abilities, and he was appointed to the Board of Directors for the National Association of State Universities and Land Grant Colleges, and thereafter to be president of the board; he served on the American Council on Education Board of Directors. In part, because of his initiative on recruiting National Merit Scholars, the National Merit Scholarship Corporation invited him to serve on its board. And, along with the president of the National Agricultural University of the Ukraine, Dimitry Melnuchuk, Jischke helped found the Global Consortium for Higher Education and Research in Agriculture, GCHERA, and was its first president. GCHERA held its first meeting in Amsterdam in July 1999 and brought together higher education, government, and industry experts from across the globe.

Still, there were very real challenges. A crisis in the state budget forced Jischke to act immediately upon assuming the presidency. He had to cut the budget and eliminate positions, including firing some employees, to balance the budget for the fiscal year that began literally days after he started his presidency. Initially, the state's budget crisis forced a 3.5 percent reduction or $5.9 million; it increased to $18 million, and eventually after five mandatory rounds of budget cuts in FY 1992, Jischke had to reduce the university's state funds budget by $27 million, lay off three hundred employees, and eliminate eighty-eight faculty positions.[39]

Thereafter, he worked hard to increase fund-raising and grants and contracts to provide other revenue streams to balance state funding. Jischke used discretionary spending to help encourage faculty research and a great many other initiatives. He would, in his words, "invest" in a project, and the practice paid off. Grants and contracts increased from less than $150 million in FY 1992 to nearly $220 million in FY 2000.[40]

The sale of WOI-TV had been simmering and in 1985 moved to the front burner. In December, the university defended the ABC affiliate on campus, noting that "the station has tangible assets worth $4.8 million, provides numerous services to the University, and is in the process of boosting its revenue." During the 1980s farm crisis, Governor Terry Branstad felt the state needed to exploit every revenue stream, but he agreed it was a decision for the Board of Regents, which then ordered the university to conduct a study about a possible sale and reinvestment of the proceeds within the university. The outcome, for a short time, was an effort to boost revenue for this perennially third-place station in the greater Des Moines news ratings.[41]

It was a difficult situation, and it caused a great deal of pain in the university community. In 1991, after years of debate about whether to sell the station, Jischke stated that he would begin considering offers. To many WOI-TV supporters, this move reflected the influence of the Board of Regents president, Marvin Pomerantz, a major business leader and strong Branstad supporter. It soon appeared that the board approved sale of the station to two local businessmen, Gary Gerlach (who, along with Michael Gartner, owned Partnership Press, which included the *Daily Tribune*) and David Belin, a well-known Des Moines attorney. They offered $12.5 million and promised to keep the station in Ames for at least five years. However, the regents decided to reopen the bidding owing to some questions about the bid process, and in that reopened process the local investor group withdrew and Citadel Communications of Bronxville, New York, offered $14 million, later reduced to $12.7 million, all cash. The regents accepted that offer by a vote of 6 to 3.[42]

There were a series of legal challenges until the plaintiffs exhausted all remedies and the sale took place. In June, opponents of the sale, "Iowans for WOI-TV," went to court for a temporary injunction. The court case began on August 25, 1992, and in late October, District Court Judge Ronald Schectman stopped the sale, a decision the regents appealed. Then Iowans for WOI-TV filed suit to stop the regents from going forward with the sale while the Iowa Supreme Court reviewed the case. Meanwhile, Jischke, speaking on *Talk of Iowa* on WOI Radio, stated he opposed the sale because it harmed the academic programs of ISU. "I recommended to the Board that the station not be sold," he stated, and "I have not changed that recommendation." On November 24, 1993, the Iowa Supreme Court reversed the trial court and gave the regents permission to proceed with the sale. At its monthly meeting in Iowa City on Wednesday, February 16, 1994, the board, whose membership had changed several times since the initial discussions began in 1985, voted 7 to 2 (the two ISU alumni on the board in opposition) to approve the station's sale to Citadel Communications. Citadel Communications took over the station on March 1, met with every station employee, and quickly fired twenty of them. The company then moved the station to Des Moines, where it remained firmly in third place in the local news ratings.[43]

At the same time, Jischke inherited Eaton's capital campaign, "Partnership for Prominence." When the fourth executive director of development in four years quit, Murray Blackwelder (who soon became president of the ISU Foundation) was hired. Blackwelder faced real challenges. He was the fifth director in as many years (one resigned only thirty-eight days into the job), and this instability in the senior leadership position affected the entire Foundation. The ISU Foundation was $600,000 in debt and had no unrestricted endowment (the earnings from which, for example, they could use to retire debt); a resident consultant neither secured major gifts nor built a solid fund-raising team among Foundation staff; the Foundation had to pay $1 million a year to retire the bonds for the Durham Center but had no strategy to raise money; and, finally, the five-year, $150 million capital campaign had stalled at $90 million in its third year. Blackwelder hired a strong group of fund-raisers and subjected proposals from academic units to feasibility studies to provide concrete information for alumni and friends of the university who were interested in helping with major gifts on those projects. He asked members of the board of directors and of the board of governors to make special donations to help retire the Foundation's debt. Finally he increased the Foundation's assets and its unrestricted endowment to help meet unexpected expenses. He created giving levels and clubs, such as the President's Club or the Campanile Guild within the larger Order of the Knoll, so as to recognize major donors.[44]

The result would be several successful fund-raising campaigns. The capital campaign, "Partnership for Prominence," with an original goal of $150 million, raised more than $214.5 million—one of the largest public university fund-raising totals at that time. It demonstrated the increasing professionalism of the Foundation, the effectiveness of Jischke and Blackwelder as fund-raisers, and the generosity and support of alumni and friends of the university.[45]

Soon after completing this campaign, the university began a limited Presidential Scholarship Campaign, with a goal of only $26 million. This campaign sought funds to compete for the best students and to encourage students facing challenges to attend Iowa State; it was in the spirit of access and opportunity, so cherished by the larger ISU community. The Lied Foundation Trust of Las Vegas, Nevada, made the transforming gift when Christina Hixson, its sole trustee, donated $5 million for the Christina Hixson Opportunity Awards, initially a one-year $2,500 tuition and fees scholarship to ninety-nine first-year students, one from each Iowa county, who faced very real challenges. The scholarship now provides for four years at Iowa State. This gift and the campaign resonated with donors, and the Foundation soon extended the goal to $50 million. When the campaign expanded yet again to a general capital campaign, Iowa State raised more than $104 million for scholarships. Put another way, more than eight thousand students currently receive scholarships from Iowa State University from these funds.[46]

Donors responded so strongly that the campaign expanded to a general fund-raising campaign, "Campaign Destiny," with a stated goal of $300 million. The new campaign, begun soon after the previous one, sought funds to provide scholarships; endow faculty chairs and professorships; help pay for new and renovated buildings, classrooms, and laboratories; and support the 1995–2000 Strategic Plan goals of becoming the best land-grant institution. By December 1996, the campaign raised $145 million. At the annual Order of the Knoll gala on September 18, 1998, Jischke announced the campaign had reached the $300 million goal twenty-one months ahead of schedule, and he extended the goal to $425 million by the campaign's close of June 30, 2000.[47]

Eventually, the university and the ISU Foundation raised $458 million. To cap the campaign, the university announced at a rally on the central campus on September 9, 1999, an amazing $80 million gift for an endowment in Agronomy. The donors requested anonymity, although the media worked to discover their names. The campaign was filled with "feel-good" stories such as Roy and Bobbi Reiman donating the initial funds to create the Reiman Gardens, a beautiful entrance to the campus; Bob and Diane Greenlee challenging the Journalism Department, now the Greenlee School, with a $9 million gift as part of an $18 million challenge to rediscover its greatness; Stanley and Helen Howe donating $6 million to help the university realize its dream of the Engineering Teaching and Research Complex with Howe Hall; and Russ and Ann Gerdin helping the College of Business establish its identity with a $10 million gift as part of a $35 million challenge campaign capped by construction of the Gerdin Business Building.[48]

Jischke also helped realize the strategic plan and its focus on transforming the university. The Plant Sciences Institute was a stunning example of this transformation. Jischke picked up where Crow had left off and proposed an institute with nine centers, some existing, some new, to bring faculty research together at the margins of disciplines, a truly global research center to explore the growing field of biotech-based crop research. Jischke stated he "felt it would expand Iowa's strong base of research and development in the plant sciences." He called for $400 million over ten years, including $10 million a year from the State of Iowa, which the university pledged to match with $10 million a year in donations and $20 million annually in new grants and contracts for research and discovery. The Plant Sciences Institute would more than meet its $20 million annual goal for grants and realize its $10 million annual goal for donations.[49]

Not every initiative succeeded. In 1994, Iowa State wanted the United States Department of Agriculture (USDA) to establish a National Swine Research Center to bring together federal hog research into one location in a state—Iowa—renowned for its production of hogs. The goal was to open a swine research farm southwest of Ames near Luther and a laboratory adjacent to the Soil Tilth Lab on campus. The proposal became a political football for years. Protest about possible contamination of Big Creek by the farm killed it, and eventually Congress approved constructing a building, turning it over to Iowa State University, but providing no funding for its ongoing operation. The university and Iowa pork producers managed a compromise where the Agricultural Research Service of the USDA provided $1 million annually and the Pork Producers provided a match, but the retitled National Swine Research and Information Center never realized its original dream.[50]

Still, the campus landscape changed considerably. During the Eaton years, the university opened the Agronomy Hall addition (although, for a while, there was no furniture or equipment in the new space), the Durham Computation Center,

On July 9, 1993, Squaw Creek flooded, subjecting the areas of the university on its floodplain to varying degrees of damage. This view, from the steps leading to C. Y. Stephens, looks toward Hilton Coliseum, where the floor was entirely immersed. (Used by permission of Iowa State University Library/Special Collections Department)

the Lied Recreation/Athletic Facility, and the expansion of the Applied Sciences Complex (ASC II and ASC III). The Jischke years witnessed an even larger construction boom. The university renovated a great many buildings, virtually gutting and rebuilding some of them, including Alumni Hall, Carrie Chapman Catt Hall, and the Student Services Building. Others were greatly expanded, including the Food Sciences Building, Kildee Hall, LeBaron Hall, the Seed Science Lab, and the Palmer Building. New construction included the Livestock Infectious Disease Facility at Veterinary Medicine, the Thielen Student Health Center, the National Swine Research Building, Molecular Biology, Howe Hall, the Gerdin Business Building, and the Administrative Services Building.[51]

There were unplanned events as well during Jischke's administration. In early summer 1993, nine inches of rain fell on the saturated South Skunk River watershed north of Ames, and as part of the great floods along the rivers feeding the upper Mississippi River, the South Skunk overflowed its banks and Squaw Creek flooded over Elwood Drive. Water flowed into the Lied Recreation Athletic Center, Maple-Willow-Larch Halls, the Iowa State Center, Hilton Coliseum (to the sixth row of seats in the parquet area), the Olsen Building, and Cyclone Stadium. The *Des Moines Sunday Register* called Hilton the "world's largest swimming pool."

When the waters receded, the university faced a challenge paying for repairs, but eventually the Federal Emergency Management Agency (FEMA) agreed that Elwood was an approved flood barrier and bore most of the cost of repair.[52]

Another negative situation occurred when, in 1995, Partnership Press, Inc., owner of the *Daily Tribune,* felt unfairly threatened by an expansion of circulation into the larger community on the part of the student newspaper, the *Iowa State Daily.* Partnership Press filed a lawsuit on November 27 claiming violation of state competition laws. That lawsuit and one filed against the university over its policy on limiting distribution of newspapers dragged on for nearly three and a half years. The court cases demonstrated an unfortunate distance between the students running the newspaper—including the Publications Board and the Editorial Board—and the journalism faculty whose offices were in the same building, Hamilton Hall. The students felt that the faculty, who sided with Partnership Press, cared little for them. In the end, Partnership Press won and, equally important, the student newspaper was determined to be an integral part of the university, not an affiliated organization, as the university claimed. This stance later threatened the independence of the ISU Foundation and the confidentiality of its records. The court decided that the university's desire to limit newspaper distribution on campus to control trash failed before constitutional protections of a free press and free speech.[53]

For many people, the university's intercollegiate athletics program was their connection to the university, and athletics faced very real challenges. NCAA Division I intercollegiate athletics had become a big business, and better-funded programs could provide better training facilities and greater academic support for their student-athletes and compensate their coaches better. For those reasons they were usually more successful, winning more games and championships. The result was bidding wars, and ISU, with many teams and one of the smallest athletics budgets among NCAA Division IA institutions, could very well lose.

Budget challenges caused Jischke to think of a new conference arrangement to increase athletics resources, and that led to formation of the Big 12 Conference from the old Big Eight and former Southwest Conferences. Big Eight Conference schools were located mostly in small states—for example, Iowa, Kansas, and Oklahoma—and lacked major media markets that would provide high-revenue television contracts, especially for football. This caused Jischke and Kansas State University President Jon Wefald to take the lead in bringing about the combination of Big Eight and four Texas institutions to form the Big 12 Conference in 1995. The initial television contracts for football and basketball resulted in distribution in 1996–1997, the first year of conference competition, of $54 million, an amount that nearly doubled by 2003–2004.[54]

Football was the engine that drove athletics, and there were problems in ISU football. Eaton and athletics director Max Urick had hired Jim Walden to replace Jim Criner as head football coach, and the team suffered through a series of bad seasons and weak attendance. After the 0-10-1 1994 campaign, Jischke, Reid Crawford, vice president for external affairs, and Urick's replacement, Gene Smith, reluctantly concluded they needed to replace Walden. Smith recommended Dan McCarney, an Iowan who was a senior assistant head coach at Wisconsin. Smith was able to fund-raise to upgrade facilities, including the new Jacobson Building, a natural turf field, the Press Tower and the Concourse Suites, and two practice fields. By fall 2000 the team went 8-3 and qualified for the Insight.com Bowl.[55]

There were issues in men's basketball as well. Johnny Orr expressed anger when he was not named a finalist for the athletics director position after the university let Urick go, and he threatened to resign as head basketball coach. After the 1994–1995 season, Orr decided to retire, and Smith hired Tim Floyd from the University of New Orleans. Floyd achieved great athletic success even though there were problems with some of the student-athletes he recruited. He left after several seasons and Smith then hired Larry Eustachy from Utah State University. Eustachy achieved even greater athletic success, but neither coach consistently drew more fans than Orr. Several of Eustachy's student-athletes had academic difficulties or problems with the authorities. Eustachy would leave the university in 2003.[56]

In the end, the financial challenges were too great and ISU had to cut sports. In March 1994, ISU athletics eliminated men's gymnastics and tennis and added women's soccer for financial and gender equity reasons. In late fall 1994, it appeared that the projected athletics deficit of $650,000 for FY 1995 might force elimination of baseball, men's golf, men's swimming, women's gymnastics, or women's tennis unless the Government of the Student Body approved an increase in student fees. Jischke decided to postpone the decision into spring 1995. The Special Student Fee Committee proposed adding a small fee to avoid eliminating any more sports; the Government of the Student Body approved the plan by a vote of 21–5; and by the end of the semester, it appeared that athletics had control over its finances and a sound plan in place for the future.[57]

One response to funding shortages was to rebuild enrollments, which Eaton had reduced. Students not only paid tuition but filled the residence halls, supported Dining Services, and made use of other auxiliary operations, all of which brought in revenue. In his fall 1994 convocation address, Jischke noted the drop in student enrollments below projections necessitated a $1.5 million midyear budget cut. Despite his concern, enrollments continued to decline, reaching a low of 24,431 in 1995. Jischke's new assistant vice president for enrollment services, David Bousquet, led the effort to turn around the decline in student enrollments. Iowa State soon enrolled among the most National Merit Scholars in the country. Recruitment became more personalized, more strategic, and included Iowa State faculty, staff, students, and alumni as well as community leaders. With greater attention to recruitment and new incentives to help recruit students, enrollments began to increase steadily, peaking at 27,898 in FY 2002.[58]

Jischke also wanted to recommit to the land-grant goal of access and opportunity for a broad range of potential students. He liked to speak of his own background and the benefit he derived from that principle. The innovative program funded by Christina Hixson is an outstanding example of this commitment to access and opportunity. Jischke also provided funds to increase recruitment of National Merit Scholars, National Achievement Scholars, and National Hispanic Scholars, so that Iowa high school seniors in those categories who chose Iowa State would receive a full scholarship. He provided funding for programs to recruit minority students to help diversify the student body. Finally, he established the

*Following tradition, Patty, Mary, and Martin Jischke waved at the crowd from the back of an open convertible at the annual VEISHEA parade. (Used by permission of Iowa State University Library/Special Collections Department)*

President's Leadership Class, a group of thirty outstanding first-year students, who met weekly at the Knoll; Jischke wanted to strengthen the leadership skills of ISU students to help lead the more than five hundred student clubs and organizations on campus as well as to contribute to the leadership capacity of Iowans after graduation. Sometimes leaders in business, government, and philanthropy would join the class and stay for dinner with the students.

Increasing enrollments allowed for a dramatic remaking of the university's housing system, which needed updating. The change began with a renovation of Maple Hall and a requirement that residents do well in class, be substance-free, and volunteer for a community service activity; when Maple Hall reopened, it was oversubscribed. Frederiksen Court apartments replaced the old Hawthorne Court. Thereafter the master plan called for construction of three suites-style buildings and a new dining center, Union Drive Community Center, the demolition of Helser North and South Halls, and the replacement of the Towers with a series of three-story apartment buildings. Jischke unveiled the plan at the June 1998 Board of Regents meeting. He noted that "most of Iowa State's residence halls were shaped for a different generation of students; living styles have changed considerably over those generations." After discussion, the regents approved the first phase. Even though students responded positively to the recommendations, after Jischke left and the university decided to reduce student enrollments, it backed away from many of the remaining plans, including renovation to Richardson Court and the replacement of the Towers with three-story apartments.[59]

There were other issues, to be sure. Each year after the 1988 riot, university and Ames community officials crossed their fingers during the annual VEISHEA weekend. Student involvement in VEISHEA committees and in official events declined; VEISHEA became more of an event for the Ames community and ISU alumni. Meanwhile, a troubling unofficial, unsanctioned VEISHEA based on alcohol and tottering close to outbreaks of violence became an unwanted companion to the officially sanctioned events.

In 1992 during VEISHEA there was another riot along Welch Avenue. After an arrest for public intoxication at Welch Avenue and Lincoln Way, a crowd of eight thousand revelers confronted the police, throwing rocks, cans, and bottles. There was considerable vandalism. The weather was warm, there was no rain, and the media contributed to an expectation of disorder among the celebrants, many of whom came from out of town for the weekend. President Jischke formed a Task Force on VEISHEA and it recommended organizing more events later into the evening, seeking to increase student involvement in these events, scheduling classes on VEISHEA Friday, and holding VEISHEA earlier in the semester so that bad weather would discourage youthful overexuberance.[60]

In 1994 the disturbance began at large parties along South Franklin Street. Tenants in some of the rental properties sold tickets enabling partygoers to enjoy as much beer as they could consume, the legal definition of bootlegging. When neighbors complained and the police arrived, revelers threw cans, bottles, and rocks at the police; they also damaged the nearby Ames Middle School track. Some twenty were arrested.[61]

Finally, in 1997, amidst an alcohol-fueled weekend, Uri Sellers was killed in an argument over a keg of beer at the Adelante fraternity house on Welch Avenue in Campustown. While there were fewer alcohol-related arrests than in past years, the murder shocked the Iowa State University community, even though neither the killer, nor his accomplice, nor Sellers were Iowa State students. Jischke appointed a VEISHEA Advisory Council, but he did not believe its recommendations, especially on alcohol, were sufficiently strong to prevent a recurrence of another tragedy or to assuage community concern. Jischke decided to continue VEISHEA only as an alcohol-free event, insist on a pledge from student groups to make VEISHEA safe and alcohol-free, and expand recreational opportunities to divert students from the temptation to binge drink and riot.[62]

The resulting "no alcohol" pledge seemed to work for the next several years. Jischke engaged in a review of VEISHEA and announced in early fall 1997 that he would allow VEISHEA to continue only if major student groups—for example, the Government of the Student Body, the VEISHEA planning committee, Inter-Residence Hall Association, Interfraternity Council, and the Pan-Hellenic Council—pledged a "dry" VEISHEA. The demand received great community support, and although they balked at first, student groups eventually pledged their support and VEISHEA was largely incident free for the next six years. During VEISHEA 1998 students complained about a police state atmosphere, and there was continuing resentment about alcohol and party rules.[63]

Other turbulence in these years arose when the dedication of Carrie Chapman Catt Hall seemed to bring relations with African American students to a crisis. A series of unrelated events indicated that perhaps the campus environment was less than welcoming to students of color. In 1992 a student hung Nazi propaganda on his dormitory room door; as a result, for the next several years students could not post materials on the outside of their doors. An ISU food service worker had a visible KKK tattoo on his arm, but later agreed to cover it at work. In fall 1993 an African American student, DeAngelo X, accused a history professor, Christine Pope, of racism in her teaching of African American history, and the charges roiled the campus. History graduate students literally checked registrations before admitting students to Pope's lectures. In spring 1994 GSB President Denis Klein vetoed GSB funding for the Mr. and Ms. Black ISU Pageant. When the university accepted a recommendation from various groups to rename Botany Hall after the great suffragist Carrie Chapman Catt, from Charles City, Iowa, who played a key role in securing passage of the Nineteenth Amendment, it led to protest about Catt's alleged racism and the insensitivity of the university.[64]

The result was the so-called September 29th Movement, and a great deal of campus ferment that inaccurately labeled Catt a racist. Led by three charismatic students, Milton McGriff, Alan Nosworthy, and Meron Wondwosen, the movement criticized women suffragists for their negative reaction to African American males receiving the right to vote with the Fifteenth Amendment (1870) while women had to wait another fifty years for the Nineteenth Amendment. An editorial board at the *Iowa State Daily* that promoted student activism, however inaccurately focused, and institutional leadership that did not want to be viewed as "beating up students" exacerbated this ferment. The students leading this movement misread and misquoted Catt's *Women Suffrage by Federal Constitutional Amendment* and claimed that Catt supported Jim Crow segregation in the American South. It was simply untrue, but for several years the movement dominated headlines in the local media. Eventually that tumult faded. The three leaders of the movement graduated, and the placement of a plaque outside Catt Hall brought a GSB review to a close.[65]

Perhaps, most of all, Jischke's intelligence and his forceful personality were the issue. In a university community of intelligent people, Martin Jischke was a remarkably intelligent individual. He read widely and could speak knowledgeably on a great many topics. He was so quick that often before someone could finish his or her point Jischke would interrupt to point out the argument's flaws. With his dark suits, lightly starched shirts, and his comfort in being president and with himself, he seemed overpowering. When he was introduced to staff, he often would ask, "What do you do for the University?"[66]

Some faculty members complained about the commitment to "become the best" and the concomitant commitment to applied research and grant activity. The Committee on the State of Iowa State continued to criticize the administration and a new group, facultyvalues@iastate.edu, provided a forum for dissent. To some, an institution of 26,000 students and 1,700 faculty members could never compete with such huge public universities as Wisconsin–Madison, Illinois, Purdue, and Michigan as well as the great University of California campuses and America's renowned private universities. To others, especially in the arts and humanities, the perception that rewards flowed to colleagues in other disciplines caused resentment.[67]

Nonetheless, as Eaton had, Jischke enjoyed broad support within the university. Two former deans noted that they appreciated working for him; when they had his support, they knew their respective projects would succeed; when they lacked it, they knew they needed to rethink their ideas. Many faculty members appreciated the new facilities, the investment in technology and the "Electronic Library," and the support they received for their interesting ideas. Jischke's decision to establish what eventually became the Center for Excellence in the Arts and Humanities symbolized his support for the creative efforts of faculty members across the university.[68]

In March 1999, then Iowa Senator Derryl McLaren began warning elected officials in both parties that there were profound budget challenges on the horizon. McLaren, chair of the Senate Appropriations Committee, said projections by the nonpartisan Legislative Fiscal Bureau demonstrated that "the gravy train has come to an end." Noting that no sector in agriculture was profitable, he said the budget projections were bad for the new governor, Tom Vilsack, a Democrat, who wanted to increase state spending by 6 percent and for statehouse Republicans who wanted dramatic tax cuts and reductions in state spending. Two years later the gap between budget projections and reality zoomed to $300 million, ushering in a series of very bad years for state government and for government-funded departments and agencies, including Iowa State University.[69]

Few listened to McLaren's voice of doom, and his legislative colleagues shunted him to the sidelines. He was assigned to the Senate Agriculture Committee and soon left for a position in the USDA. The Democrats appeared to be equally oblivious to the fiscal realities he had noted. Sixteen-year governor Terry Branstad had signed off on a 10 percent reduction in state income tax rates. He and successor Tom Vilsack approved other tax-cutting measures that, when fully phased in, totaled more than $800 million annually. In addition, Vilsack approved contracts with the American Federation of State, County, and Municipal Employees (AFSCME) union that increased unionized worker pay as much as 7 percent a year. He wanted money for K–12 education and teacher pay.[70]

Jischke believed McLaren's financial analysis; he was concerned about Vilsack's commitment to public higher education, a concern that succeeding years would bear out. Branstad had believed that public universities were critical for Iowa's economic development and quality of life. Vilsack, a graduate of a private college and a private law school, seemed to lack a commitment to public university education. Although the state budget increased slightly each year, the regents system suffered far more than its fair share of cuts as favored programs were funded.

At this time, Purdue University was looking for a new president. Although Jischke had earlier indicated he was not interested in leaving Iowa State, the state budget and governance challenge caused him to listen to Purdue's renewed inquiry. News reporters camped out at the small Ames airport to note a corporate jet

*President and Mrs. Geoffroy were among the many dignitaries who celebrated the tenth anniversary of the Reiman Gardens on September 17, 2005. (Used by permission of Iowa State University Library/Special Collections Department)*

with Purdue University tail numbers and wondered if Jischke was going to Purdue. The suspense ended on May 22, 2000, when Purdue University introduced Martin C. Jischke as its president-designate.[71]

Jischke took great pride in his achievements at Iowa State. He reversed a downturn in student enrollment, which would peak at 27,898 in 2002. There were initiatives to strengthen teaching and learning, including "Re-engineering Engineering Education" to make undergraduate education more active and more practical for students, "Extension 21" to help make ISU Extension relevant in the twenty-first century, the Plant Sciences Institute, Project LEA/RN (Learning Enhancement Action/Resource Network) to help faculty members develop an active learning environment for students, the Center for Excellence in Learning and Teaching, expansion of undergraduate computer labs, and an increase in international agreements leading to more study and internship abroad opportunities for students. Similarly, in 1995 ISU regained its status as a Research I institution from the Carnegie Foundation for the Advancement of Teaching. Also during Jischke's tenure, sponsored funding soared from $127 million to more than $200 million; campus construction boomed with ten new major buildings; and the university ranked consistently among the top U.S. universities in research productivity, including first in licenses and options on intellectual property and second in the number of R&D 100 awards from *R&D Magazine*. It was a great moment in Iowa State University history when a team of engineers and scientists completed the Atanasoff-Berry Computer replica project and the world's first computer worked once again. Less happily, the faculty-dominated Board of Directors at Iowa State University Press advised its sale, and the university administration accepted that recommendation. The resulting sale of Iowa State University Press to Blackwell Science, a for-profit scientific and technical publisher based in the UK, was highly unusual and controversial in the world of academic, not-for-profit publishing.[72]

The Eaton-Jischke years transformed Iowa State University. Much as Robert Parks helped strengthen the position of the arts and humanities, Gordon Eaton and Martin Jischke provided strategic focus and helped reposition Iowa State University as one of the nation's leading research institutions in engineering, the physical sciences, the plant sciences, and the animal sciences and as a major player internationally. There were, to be sure, individuals inside and outside the university community who decried the centralization that accompanied this strategic focus, the focus on science and technology, and the focus on research. However, generally, Iowa State faculty members, students, and alumni as well as Iowa opinion makers supported the strengthening of research and the commitment to applied research and technology transfer that would make ISU a major factor in strengthening the economy and improving the quality of life in Iowa. With more difficult economic times and with seemingly less support for the university in the state legislature after FY 2000, the future would again be challenging and new leaders would explore new solutions to age-old problems.

# Part 2

# Vignettes

## Winifred Tilden: Advocate

As men's intercollegiate athletic competition at Iowa State maintained its hold on the public despite the Great Depression, women at Iowa State had a variety of opportunities to participate in athletic competition within the college. In significant part these physical education offerings were possible through the leadership of Dr. Winifred Tilden. Tilden grew up in Ames. Her family was physically active, ahead of its time, enjoying parlor games, baseball, picnics, croquet, tennis, and lawn bowling.

Tilden was the head of women's physical education at Iowa State from 1904 to 1944. A strong advocate of athletic opportunities for women, she began her career as directress of physical culture, based out of the Speech Department. It was in this position that she stressed a progressive program of quality physical education for all women students.

During her tenure, she developed competitive sports for women and she affirmed the value of exercise. She founded the Women's Athletic Association and a women's "A" Club to provide direction for her program. Iowa State offered women's education and competition in field hockey, basketball, tennis, swimming, archery, and golf. Tilden's students numbered less than one hundred when she came to Iowa State but expanded to thousands by the end of her four decades of service.

Tilden's philosophy included teaching women sports they could play the rest of their lives, thereby giving them the skills to stay physically fit long after their college days. As early as 1914, Tilden employed a four-hole women's golf course just north of Lincoln Way where the Maple-Willow-Larch dormitories stand today. Men also used the course when the women weren't using it.

Tilden's efforts encouraged an environment that included more women competing in intramural athletics at Iowa State than at any other school nationally. Tilden brought to the Iowa State campus ideas she gained from her studies and travel internationally. It was from these travels that she developed a May Day Pageant and May Pole dances in 1911. These were a forerunner of the VEISHEA celebrations that began in 1922.

One of Tilden's lasting legacies on the Iowa State campus is the Barbara Forker Building. Tilden had long dreamed of a campus gymnasium for women. In 1938, Margaret Hall, the facility then used to house women's physical education, was destroyed by fire. The building had served as a women's dormitory and included a converted gymnasium and a women's

*(continued)*

swimming pool built in the 1920s. Tilden lobbied hard for the construction of a new facility, making her first request for funding in 1925. It would not be an easy battle and took years of personal lobbying by ISC student representatives. Tilden took her fight all the way to the state legislature before getting approval in 1939. The building, dedicated in 1941, makes up the south side of the Forker Building today.

Tom Kroeschell

# The Social Whirl, Circa 1940s

When Japan attacked Pearl Harbor on December 7, 1941, the lives of all Americans changed, including those of Iowa State students. Most college traditions continued through four years of war, but often these traditions were modified and, in some cases, eliminated. Dorothy Gross Hanson and Henry "Hank" Hanson shared some of their memories about their college days during World War II.

Students in the 1940s had far fewer freedoms than students in the twenty-first century. Hank Hanson has strong memories about the campus ban on alcoholic beverages in 1941 and 1942. He described it as "zero tolerance." If a student was caught drinking, Hank recalled, it resulted in a trip to Dean Maurice Helser's office for a "serious lecture on the evils of drink."

Hank also recalled that in the early forties, ISC had its own campus radio station, which sometimes featured a male student quartette, the Woodland Warblers, who sang "old favorites that one could sing along with."

Both Hank and Dorothy remembered that by 1942, with male students entering the military at an ever-increasing rate, many students decided to marry before the men left for war. And the war brought shortages: the Hansens recalled that the student newspaper cut back from an eight-page daily to a four-page daily. Some departments added summer school classes so students could graduate earlier.

Dorothy Hanson recalled that students' "social life centered around dances [where] students met and later married their partners of the Friday night dorm exchanges." Dances were typically held in the Memorial Union and usually required formals and corsages for women and tuxedos for men. Dorothy explained that since few students owned cars, they had to walk from the dorms and Greek houses to the union, "which meant the long gowns and delicate shoes could be a problem walking in winter." It seemed that there was a dance or ball for every occasion, including the Engineer's Ball, the Bomb Beauties Ball, the Christmas Dance, and the Junior Prom.

Dorothy remembered that in the early forties, many students had little money for anything but the necessities. As a result study dates were popular and, as Dorothy pointed out, "a way to mix studies with a touch of romance." Both the YMCA and the Union were popular student hangouts. Picnics were also popular. Dorothy recalled an old poem that usually appeared in some publication in the spring as students began to dig out blankets for spring picnics: "Spring is here; The Grass is riz; I wonder where; My blanket is." Given the limited resources, even blanket study dates were popular.

Dorothy Schwieder

# The Good Old Days

College students of the early twenty-first century would probably look aghast at the many policies and restrictions faced by students in the early 1940s, as well as the many inconveniences. Bonnie Gregg Calderwood shared remembrances about her college days in the early forties, which clearly set college students of the 1940s apart from students of today.

World War II created a student housing shortage at Iowa State, but even before the war, housing was limited. Bonnie recalled that during her freshman year in 1939, she lived in the Memorial Union. The small rooms assigned to students had originally been planned as hotel rooms; in 1939, four female students were typically assigned to each room. The students had some advantages, however, as each room had its own bathroom and telephone, which dormitory living did not include. The women's dining room was on the second floor of the Union, although the women usually ate breakfast in the Union Commons. A housemother also lived on the second floor and students there had the same hours and rules as in the ISC dormitories.

Once the war started and military training programs got under way, women students were often shuffled around to accommodate housing for the military. Bonnie began her sophomore year living in Elm Hall, but before long the women were moved to fraternity houses (most were empty since male students were entering the military) so V-12 naval trainees could live in Elm. Bonnie described the fraternity house as "old." "We had problems with mice and the plumbing was not dependable. Our housemother always urged us to make use of the college facilities before we returned to the fraternity." Although Bonnie did not smoke, many of her female friends did, but they were not allowed to smoke in the dorm; for that, they had to step outside. The reason given: the college's insurance policies would not allow it. But once military training programs got under way, the rules quickly changed, allowing men to smoke in the dorms.

Bonnie also recalled the need for frugality during the late thirties and early forties, given that most families were still recovering from the Great Depression. One way she and her freshman roommates coped was by sharing formals. All four women were about the same size so by wearing each other's formals, they always managed to have something different to wear to the many dances.

Dorms and Greek houses lacked the modern laundry facilities of today, and so many students sent their dirty clothes home to be laundered by "Mom." Bonnie remembered that every week she sent home a suitcase full of dirty clothes; a few days later, the suitcase arrived back in Ames, complete with clean, ironed clothing and, as a bonus, homemade treats.

Strict protocol existed in many areas of student life. During her freshman year, Bonnie decided to attend a high school reunion in her hometown. Careful to follow the rules, she went to Dean Maurice Helser's office to get approval for her absence from campus. With a serious demeanor, and after a few minutes of deliberation, Dean Helser allowed that it would be all right for Bonnie to miss a day or two of classes, and gave her a written statement of permission. At the same time, he dispensed some fatherly advice: he didn't think she would want to attend any later high school reunions. Bonnie recalled with a chuckle, "And I never did until my 50th."

Bonnie also reflected on the many social activities available to students in the early 1940s. Along with weekly dances, students could spend time in the Union—where many students played cards—and attend sports' events. Students had activity tickets that covered admittance to major sports events, including wrestling meets and football and basketball games. VEISHEA was a major event and required many hours of work to set up open houses and construct floats for the annual parade. Homecoming generated "a lot of excitement" on campus and included a big bonfire, usually located along Lincoln Way. If Iowa State defeated Nebraska, which apparently was the "team to beat," students celebrated. Bonnie added, "That didn't happen very often."

Dorothy Schwieder

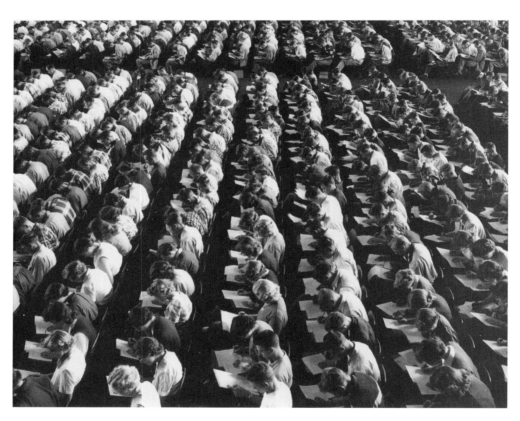

*Chapter 5*

# Loyal and Forever True: Student Life at Iowa State University

## Jenny Barker Devine

On a frosty winter evening in 1869, the president of the Iowa Agricultural College, Adonijah Welch, invited the students to an evening social in the chapel of Old Main. It was to be the first student social at the Iowa State Agricultural College, and Welch hoped to become acquainted with the students as both a teacher and as a friend. When the students gathered, however, he found them to be "awkward and uncouth, unused to society, and untaught as to social matters." The young men milled quietly around the windows and spoke in hushed whispers, while the young women "huddled together near the door, as if ready to flee when approached." At last, Mary Welch, the wife of the president, brought in a fine Italian music box and placed it on the stage. As students gathered around to marvel at the "tinkling music," they began talking and laughing. They found within one another a new community of friends. As students, they shared not only the struggles associated with course work but also the chill of poorly heated rooms in Old Main, homesickness, and a longing for familiarity.[1]

Since that winter evening, new students have arrived in Ames each year seeking more than lecture halls, laboratories, and textbooks. They have come from around the state, nation, and world in search of camaraderie and a community of like-minded individuals. They have come looking for new experiences and opportunities, lifelong friendships, and possibly a spouse. Over the years, the students of Iowa State have established governing bodies, athletic contests, academic honoraries, residential communities, religious organizations, volunteer groups, fraternities, sororities, and a range of clubs and societies to accommodate nearly every niche, belief, and activity—from oration to skydiving. They've shared the experiences of Homecoming, cherry pies at VEISHEA, and studying late into the night for final exams. Each class left an indelible mark. The student body has grown and changed over time, and traditions have come and gone. Yet all students have sought ways to transform their college campus into a home, a place where they become "Iowa Staters."

From the very beginning, Iowa State offered students a unique educational experience, shaped by vocational training and coeducation. Applicants were to be at least sixteen years of age, residents of Iowa, and of "good moral character." They obtained admission based on applications made directly to the president and passing marks on entrance exams. Throughout the 1870s, Iowa State offered only six courses of study: agriculture, horticulture and forestry, mining engineering, architecture, military tactics and engineering, and a course in general science for women. In addition to their studies, students were also expected to work either on the college farm or in one of its facilities. Though they paid no tuition, for many students, the meager wages they earned through manual labor paid for living expenses, room, and board.[2]

In March 1869, when the first 173 students arrived from across Iowa for the first regular term, they took up residence in Old Main. The building held administrative offices, classrooms, a chapel, the library, and student living quarters. Still in the midst of winter when classes began, students found Old Main to be chilly and sparse. Furnishings in each double room included two chairs, a wardrobe, a study table, and a washbowl and pitcher. The college provided bedsteads, but each student brought his or her own bed tick, which was filled with straw piled near the entrance of Old Main at the beginning of each term. Before the installation of gaslights and a central furnace, students studied by candlelight, often wearing "overcoats and mittens." John Boyd Hungerford, who graduated in 1877, recalled that the students who lived in Old Main rarely complained because most came from "farms and workshops," rather than the "white collared class." They were therefore "accustomed to the open spaces and cared less for the sartorial excellence than comfort and were satisfied with what was merely conventional."[3]

Administrators strictly regulated student life and kept exacting hours for chapel attendance, manual labor, study, classroom instruction, and social interaction. A steward, usually a faculty member, supervised life in Old Main, while a preceptress oversaw the women students. A matron further supervised the women's work in the kitchen, laundry, and bakery. These advisors concerned themselves not only with students' academic performance but also their personal habits. Lucy McAllister Whitney, a student enrolled in the first class, described how the first matron, Catherine Potter, would gently remind the women to retain good posture and use proper table manners.[4]

In 1871, Iowa State's first president, Adonijah Welch, wrote that no student who proved to be "idle and morally perverse" would be tolerated, that the "Iowa Agricultural College is in no sense a reform school." Yet he also believed that students should establish and follow their own rules. Welch strongly supported a system of self-government whereby students selected officers to represent each of the seven halls, or residential sections, within Old Main. The officers created rules governing study hours, activities on Saturday and Sunday evenings, general rules regarding personal conduct, communication between the sexes, the use of alcohol and tobacco (both of which were forbidden), and leaves of absence. The officers also formed a court to try students who violated these rules. The system established a long-standing tradition of student government at Iowa State.[5]

The first students and administrators recognized the need for organized activities to enhance the college experience. In November 1869, several students gathered in the chapel to form the Philomathaen Literary Society, an organization for both men and women, designed to give students training in public speaking, de-

*Members of the Crescent Literary Society, circa 1896, gathered regularly for oration, spelling bees, singing, and debates. Their activities, including contributions to the first student newspaper, the Aurora, served as the basis for student entertainment in the early years of Iowa State. (Used by permission of Iowa State University Library/Special Collections Department)*

bate, writing, and leadership. Administrators had positive views of literary societies since they provided students with structured, intellectual activities. Within a few years, students founded several new literary societies. In 1870, male students broke away from the Philomathaen to form the Crescent Society and the Bachelor Society as organizations for men only. In 1871, several women established the all-female Clioian Society. Literary societies remained popular throughout the late nineteenth and early twentieth centuries, and though some rivalries existed, members of different societies typically cooperated to provide entertainment for the entire college. In 1871, at the annual Dramatic Exercises of the Literary Societies, members of different organizations put together a show that included music, poems, and Shakespeare's play *Much Ado About Nothing*. Then, in 1873, the literary societies collaborated to publish Iowa State's first student newspaper, the *Aurora*.[6]

Though literary societies thrived, much suspicion surrounded Greek organizations. Fraternities and sororities flourished at eastern and southern colleges, yet they struggled to find acceptance in the Midwest. While literary societies promised intellectual and social development, nineteenth-century midwesterners considered the rituals and initiation practices of "secret societies," such as Greek organizations, to be undemocratic, anti-Christian, and elitist. In 1876, however, President Welch approved the establishment of one fraternity, the Omega Chapter of Delta Tau Delta. One year later, he approved the creation of the Iowa Gamma Chapter of the Pi Beta Phi Sorority, known at that time as I.C. Sorosis.

Within a short time, students unaffiliated with the Greek organizations resented what they believed were exclusive clubs, whose members received preferential treatment from faculty and administrators. Members of Delta Tau Delta and I.C. Sorosis were expelled from literary societies, and anti-Greek sentiments often appeared in the *Aurora*. One 1883 editorial in the *Aurora* declared Greek organizations to be "unmitigated evils" that should be "rooted out of the college."[7]

Tensions remained high throughout the 1880s, and on the evening of May 25, 1888, a riot, later known as the Cyanogen Affair, led to an eventual ban of the Greek system. That night, nonaffiliated students stormed a banquet held by Delta Tau Delta and I.C. Sorosis in the old chemistry laboratory building. Though the fraternity had obtained permission from the college administration to hold the banquet, more than one hundred students surrounded the building, threw rocks at the windows, and chanted, "Down with secret men!" They then released large quantities of highly toxic cyanogen gas into the room and locked the doors, trapping those inside. Once several partygoers fled through an open window, rioters pelted them with rocks and rotten eggs. Following the incident, many students demanded that Greek organizations be forbidden on campus. In 1891, Iowa State President William Beardshear finally eliminated Delta Tau Delta and I.C. Sorosis when conflicts between Greeks and unaffiliated students continued to disrupt classes and student activities.[8]

Over time, local clubs appeared that resembled Greek organizations, yet they served a much different purpose than traditional social clubs. In 1897, in reaction to the terrible food served in the Margaret Hall dining room, twelve students formed a local fraternity dubbed the Noit Avrats, or "starvation" spelled backward. Members of the Noit Avrats led a movement to establish boarding clubs, or groups that arranged for their own meals. The movement gained momentum in the fall of 1900, following a typhoid epidemic traced to infected milk served in Margaret Hall. While students complained and refused to pay their food bills, more groups appeared such as the Tri-Serps, another men's boarding club, and the S.S. Girls, a boarding club for women. In 1902, the administration closed the dining room and sold the equipment, and boarding clubs became a standard method of obtaining meals until 1912.[9]

Greek organizations were not officially welcome on campus until 1903, when Albert Boynton Storms took office as the president of Iowa State. Storms faced a rapid increase in student enrollment, as well as a student housing crisis precipitated by the burning of Old Main in 1902. At that time, the college had an enrollment of 1,334 students, but only 228 beds. Without a central dormitory, students struggled to secure rooms in boarding houses and private homes. In the fall of 1903, several students approached the president about starting a local fraternity and Storms realized that this presented one solution to the housing shortage. With their large chapter houses and internal organization, Greek organizations offered students better housing options, structure, and guidance. By the spring of 1904, Storms received approval from the Board of Regents to reinstate fraternities and sororities. Within a year, Iowa State was home to two national fraternities, Sigma Nu and Sigma Alpha Epsilon, as well as several local Greek organizations.[10]

As students scattered throughout campus and Ames as a result of the housing crisis, a small group of students established a new governing organization to co-ordinate activities and formulate rules. In 1904, eleven members of the senior class organized the Cardinal Guild. Members of the guild, who were appointed by the faculty, set about to uphold college traditions, shape college policies, create a welcoming atmosphere for visitors, coordinate student activities, and promote a "democratic college spirit at all times." At the 1904 spring commencement, the first president of the Cardinal Guild, A. R. Buckley, addressed the student body and declared that a modern college campus needed a strong student government. Buckley hoped to leave future leaders a "solid foundation" from which to build, but he could not promise an easy road ahead. He left it up to the underclassmen to carry on.

Throughout the early twentieth century, ISC enrollment experienced a steady increase, while the campus gained new buildings, better facilities, and a variety of graduate programs. By the 1910s, students enjoyed an array of traditions and festivals that celebrated various departments, including the Agricultural Carnival and the Engineer's Campfire. In 1907, the Women's Athletic Association sponsored the first May Day celebration. It featured Elizabethan themes such as "Ye Merrie Milk Maydes," and proceeds from all activities paid for women's athletic equipment. In 1910, the Engineering Division sponsored the first St. Patrick's Day festival, with a parade, songs and knighting ceremonies, a baseball game, and the crowning of the "Engineer's Lady."[11]

In April 1917, however, the pace of student life changed dramatically when the United States entered the First World War. Within days of declaring war, male students attended mandatory military drills from 11:00 to 12:15 each morning, then again from 4:00 to 6:00 in the evening. By the end of the school year, more than five hundred students left campus for either military service or jobs in industry and agriculture.[12]

Administrators also urged women students to take on wartime duties. On April 19, 1917, just two weeks after Congress declared war, the dean of home economics Catherine MacKay outlined a program of war work for women that included courses on hygiene and home care of the sick, knitting and sewing, emergency building, preserving vegetables, stock feeding, beekeeping, and poultry raising. Although women also participated in fund drives, the sale of liberty bonds, and customary female activities sponsored by the Red Cross and the YWCA, college administrators focused on impending labor shortages. To this end, they offered women's courses in agriculture and technical subjects, including a "tractor school" designed to train women in the use of heavy farm machinery.[13]

Almost overnight, the Iowa State campus came to resemble an Army post. Men performed military drills and donned the appropriate uniforms, while the women

*During the summer of 1918, in response to the mechanized nature of the First World War, Iowa State provided training for several hundred soldiers in the relatively new field of auto mechanics and machinery. (Used by permission of Iowa State University Library/Special Collections Department)*

formed a chapter of the Red Cross and tended to incoming soldiers. In 1918, the War Department developed a program to use college campuses as training centers for military draftees, and in April, five hundred soldiers arrived for eight-week training courses in blacksmithing, auto mechanics, and machinery. That summer, the War Department also formed the Student Army Training Corps, or SATC, which allowed college students of draft age to integrate their college education with military service. By the war's end, more than 1,200 students enrolled as SATC cadets. In addition to military drills, they took history and economics courses that emphasized the social and political causes of the war.

Thoughts of the students who enlisted in the military weighed heavily on the minds of those in Ames. Members of the faculty mailed out Christmas packages containing issues of the *Green Gander*, the campus humor magazine, and maple sugar candy. Soldiers also wrote to their former instructors and classmates about their experiences in training, long voyages across the Atlantic, and their first taste of war.[14]

The enormous influx of soldiers not only created many logistical problems on the Iowa State campus, but it also contributed to a devastating epidemic of the Spanish influenza. In October 1918, when the worldwide epidemic hit Iowa State, administrators suspended classes and quarantined the entire campus. Students could not leave campus, even to visit downtown Ames, without a special pass. The college hospital, just completed in April 1918, proved inadequate to treat the nearly 1,250 reported cases. As they set up makeshift hospital wards in State Gym and a church basement, an overwhelmed Dr. Charles Tilden, the college physician, called on all local doctors and nurses to assist in treating patients. By the end of the war on November 11, 1918, there were still nearly a hundred cases of flu on campus, though the *Iowa State Student* declared the deadly disease to be "literally stamped out." The epidemic lingered for a few more weeks, and between October 8 and November 27, fifty-one students died, all of them young men enrolled as SATC cadets.[15]

The end of the war marked a new era in student life at Iowa State. In 1919, the demobilization of soldiers on campus and the elimination of the flu epidemic did not mean an end to problems facing students. In 1918 and 1919, Frederica Shattuck, a professor of public speaking and the acting advisor to women, reported rampant disciplinary problems among women students. Young women were suspended for offenses such as playing games of strip poker, attending unchaperoned dances, and ignoring nightly curfews. Both men and women demanded greater freedom, and administrators struggled to enforce rules against hazing, truancy, and unsanctioned social activities.

In April 1919, the Cardinal Guild petitioned the Board of Deans to extend the hours during which dancing was permitted. At that time, students could hold dances only on Saturday nights until 11 P.M. The Cardinal Guild requested that dancing be extended to 11:45 P.M. on both Friday and Saturday nights. On April 5, 1919, students held an "All College Dance" and, even after the lights were extinguished, danced until midnight to protest the current restrictions. In an open letter to the students, a disappointed President Raymond Pearson wrote, "I can hardly bring myself to believe that good students in this college would intentionally violate a college rule." He reminded the students that as future leaders, their behavior should exemplify "law observance and good order." The students reached a compromise, however, and they gained the right to dance on Friday until 10 P.M. and Saturday until 11:30 P.M.[16]

Students in the postwar era had grand expectations, greater sophistication, and a tendency toward frivolity. The Jazz Age and the era of the flapper made its mark on the Iowa State campus. Young people sought more freedom through music, dancing, fashion, social activity, and athletics. The 1920s saw students organizing in greater numbers, evident in the creation of intramural athletics and major fund-raising campaigns for the construction of the Memorial Union. Since 1914, students had lobbied for a central building for student activities. In 1920, Iowa State students launched a million-dollar campaign to build the Memorial Union as a tribute to those who died in the First World War. By 1924, students and alumni held another fund-raising drive and finally raised $750,000 of the $1 million needed. The building, completed in 1928, offered students a modern facility for dancing, dining, and socializing.[17]

In 1922, the students of Iowa State further demonstrated their desire for campus unity by consolidating the various springtime celebrations into the first VEISHEA. The largest student-run festival in the nation was named for the various divisions (later colleges): Veterinary Medicine, Engineering, Industrial Science, Home Eco-

*The tradition of "tapping," or selecting members for Iowa State's two highest honorary societies, Mortar Board and Cardinal Key, continued as a special tradition for several decades. The names of new members were kept secret until the ceremony. After thirty years, at VEISHEA in 1952, the element of surprise was still part of the fun. (Used by permission of Iowa State University Library/Special Collections Department)*

nomics, and Agriculture. It included a parade, a carnival, and open houses that allowed each department to show off its wares. Over time, VEISHEA gave Iowa State students and alumni an opportunity to start and carry on beloved traditions: cherry pies, canoe races, and the VEISHEA queen contest.[18]

VEISHEA also celebrated students and their accomplishments. Beginning in the late 1920s, one highlight of VEISHEA was the "tapping" ceremony for Iowa State's highest student honorary organizations: Cardinal Key and Mortar Board. Founded in 1914, Mortar Board honored junior and senior women, while Cardinal Key, founded in 1926, honored junior and senior men who embodied the virtues of character, service, leadership, and scholarship. Only a small number of men and women could be initiated, and the selection process remained secret until the day of the "tapping" ceremony. Typically on the last day of VEISHEA, students gathered around the Campanile to learn who would be inducted. The active members and alumni stood in a semicircle under the Campanile and, one by one, members of both organizations searched through the crowd for new pledges. Once they

*At the Oak Lodge cooperative dormitory for men, everyone pitched in, donning aprons to clean the dishes after dinner. These students took tremendous pride in their cooperative dormitory and even put together annual scrapbooks. This photograph appeared in the 1935 Oak Lodge Annual. (Used by permission of Iowa State University Library/Special Collections Department)*

were "tapped," the new pledges returned with the active members to the Campanile, where they were introduced to the crowd.[19]

As with the rest of America, Iowa State fell on hard times in the early 1930s. Following the onset of the Great Depression, student enrollment fell 25 percent between 1932 and 1934, while state appropriations dropped 27 percent. In order to balance its budget, the college cut salaries and reduced its staff. In order to assist students, the administration established a book rental program, increased student loans, and employed greater numbers of students in part-time positions. Yet even those students who could afford to remain in school struggled to pay their expenses. Tuition alone ranged from thirty dollars to forty-five dollars per quarter. And while grants from the National Youth Administration funded many part-time on-campus jobs, these tended to fill quickly, leaving students to compete for off-campus and summer jobs.[20]

The formation of cooperative dormitories helped many to reduce student fees. Students could pay approximately twenty-five dollars per month so long as they shared the duties of cooking, cleaning, laundry, and household management. By comparison, room and board in residence halls and Greek houses cost roughly forty dollars per month. The first cooperative dormitories for women opened during the 1920s, beginning with Westgate Cottage in 1924, and Barton Hall and Freeman Hall in 1928. In 1931, 120 men established a cooperative dormitory in Oak Lodge, which quickly proved to be a financial success. By 1936, more than

300 students lived in cooperative houses, and though Oak Lodge was razed in 1938, the men simply transferred their program to Hughes Hall.[21]

Julia Faltinson Anderson, who graduated in 1941, recalled how students in co-operative dormitories worked one or two hours each day and rotated duties on a six-week schedule. She said, "One week you were cleaning the ground floor and first floor. The next week you would be preparing dinner. The next week would be third and fourth [floors] and then you would prepare breakfast . . . Then out of six weeks, you got a week of rest."[22]

Students further reduced costs by adopting inexpensive social activities. Student clubs and Greek organizations held fewer dances but hosted more "firesides," or evenings of casual socializing, dancing, singing, talks, games, and snacks. Intramural sports and intercollegiate athletics also grew in popularity. In many ways, the economic crisis allowed students to gain new freedoms. For example, during the 1930s, women gained the right to smoke in the Cyclone Cellar of the Memorial Union.[23]

Though the rules governing student life appear restrictive by today's standards, students of the 1930s recognized that they enjoyed unprecedented liberties. A 1936 article in the *Iowa State Student*, entitled "Fifty Years Ago Their Pants Were Narrow, So Were Their Liberties," stated, "To compare the Iowa State College of 1886 with that of today is comparing Sing Sing to a Cyclone Twister. By comparison, the liberality of 1936 fairly floors grandpa and his ex-collegiate wife." What did the future hold, the students wondered? The writer concluded, "If the fifty years ahead of 1936 bring as much change in the social rules of Iowa State as the past fifty years have done, only time and Buck Rogers can foretell what will be the situation in the year 1986."[24]

Only a few years later, as war once again seemed imminent, students and administrators realized that even greater changes were ahead. In a 1942 message to the students, Iowa State President Charles Friley wrote, "without question the next twenty-five years will prove to be the most challenging, the most interesting and the most difficult era in modern history."[25]

Even before America's entry into the Second World War, students were well aware of the impending crisis. The *Iowa State Student* featured daily articles on the worsening conflicts in Europe and Asia, as well as information regarding the military draft. Throughout 1941, students wrote lengthy letters to the editor debating whether the United States should even go to war. The Japanese bombing of Pearl Harbor on December 7, 1941, settled any debate, and with the rest of the nation, Iowa State went to war. The 1942 *Bomb* declared, "Iowa Staters will remember Dec. 7, 1941 . . . Sober-faced collegians immediately started shaping their plans to meet a grim, new life—one that called for sacrifices and a renewed pledge to fight vigorously for the preservation of democracy."[26]

Although men faced major decisions regarding the military and the draft, neither President Friley nor the student body expected the war to interfere with daily life on campus. On December 9, 1941, the *Iowa State Daily Student* reported that, with the exception of ROTC, no college campus would host military training programs. In contrast to the First World War, the *Daily* predicted there would be no armed guards, no military barracks, and no emphasis on the "teaching of military tactics."[27]

Students wished to contribute to the war effort, however, and in early 1942, President Friley organized the Student Defense Council (later the Student War Council), a committee of seventeen students to coordinate defense activities on campus. Whether it was working with the Red Cross, the United Service Organizations (USO), scrap drives, or fund-raisers, all students were expected to play a part. Members of the YWCA formed "knitting clubs" and sent care packages to soldiers containing homemade cookies, letters, and campus news. In January 1942, the Women's Panhellenic Council made "Defense Stamps" the theme of their annual formal, and sold defense stamp corsages, "attractively arranged and wrapped in cellophane," at the door. The following month, the Student Defense Council sponsored an All-College Taffy Pull to make candy for Iowa State men in military service. The council provided the necessary ingredients to thirty-four residence halls, Greek houses, and campus kitchens. In one evening, more than two thousand students made six hundred pounds of candy.[28]

Students also expressed much interest in the political and military aspects of the war effort. In 1942, approximately a thousand students attended an all-college lecture series entitled The Citizen and the World Crisis, sponsored by the Science Division. And throughout the conflict, the Student Defense Council promoted education through in-class lectures, the formation of discussion groups, and Coffee Forums. Beginning in 1942, faculty and students from the English and Speech departments presented a weekly program on WOI called Let's Talk It Over as a "rumor clinic" to dispel myths and rumors about the war.[29]

Despite earlier reports that Iowa State would not host military programs, in June 1942, the first naval trainees arrived on campus for instruction in the Electrical and Diesel Schools. Over the next few years, several thousand men prepared for military service at Iowa State through this program, as well as the V-12 Navy College Training Program and the Bakers' and Cooks' School. Though kept on rigid military schedules, naval trainees blended into student life as they participated in athletics, joined fraternities and clubs, and took part in social activities on campus. By 1944, the presence of military men was no longer novel, and a segment in the *Bomb* remarked that the men were especially welcomed by "lonely coeds," or "WAMS—Women Affected by the Man Shortage."[30]

For students not directly involved with the military, the war still shaped their college experience. Accelerated programs in engineering, veterinary medicine, science, and home economics allowed students to complete their degrees in less than four years and find employment in war industries. Iowa State offered courses year-round and at night. This, in addition to the introduction of military training programs, led to rampant overcrowding. The 1943 *Bomb* noted that although students filled classrooms to capacity at all hours, and the lights in campus buildings burned late into the night, students still found it difficult to get into their required courses.

Departments also altered their curriculum to reflect wartime needs. The Engineering Division offered courses on navigation and electronics ballistics, while the

*During the Second World War, thousands of young men attended Iowa State as military trainees in the Electrical and Diesel Schools, the V-12 Navy College Training Program, and the Bakers' and Cooks' School. Though they wore military uniforms and adhered to strict schedules, they became involved with social organizations and events on campus, like this 1945 dance in the Great Hall of the Memorial Union. (Used by permission of Iowa State University Library/Special Collections Department)*

Agricultural Division created intensive courses for women on dairy and poultry research. The Division of Home Economics developed specialized programs for women entering war industries, including engineering drawing, industrial cooking and nutrition, and an intensive course on the organization of wartime nursery schools. One of the most popular courses, Civilian Pilot Training, came out of the newly formed Department of Aeronautical Engineering.[31]

For the women of Iowa State, the war afforded many challenges as well as new opportunities. In 1943, housing for women became a problem when the naval trainees took up residence in Roberts, Birch, and Welch Halls. Many of the displaced women were relocated to fraternity houses, left empty by the fraternities that voted to go inactive for the duration of the war. This arrangement appeared highly unconventional to many young women and their parents, who worried that it would hinder the women's college experiences. When Lorris Foster prepared to enter Iowa State as a freshman in 1942, her father received a reassuring letter from Madge McGlade, the director of residence, that his daughter would find her room in the Sigma Alpha Epsilon house to be satisfactory. McGlade wrote, "The girls in no way miss college life living this way, in fact, I think they are very fond of the small groups and each one has a good housemother supervising the group."[32]

The 1943 *Bomb* noted that as women scattered throughout "fraternity houses and improvised boarding and apartment dwellings," they still managed to organize dances and social events, "keeping dorm life in some semblance of pre-war routine." Certainly, life during the war was far from routine for most Iowa State women. In 1941, only five women were enrolled as engineering majors. By the war's end, however, women gained entry into the sciences through such programs as the Curtiss-Wright program, which trained ninety-seven young women to work for the Curtiss-Wright Aircraft Manufacturing Company. Women also stepped into leadership roles on the VEISHEA Central Planning Committee and on all campus publications. In 1945, both the *Iowa State Daily Student* and the *Green Gander*, the campus humor magazine, boasted all-female staffs.[33]

For all of their contributions to the war effort and tolerance for wartime changes, however, students remained unaware of Iowa State's involvement with the Manhattan Project. The first public statement regarding the project appeared in the *Iowa State Daily Student* on August 8, 1945, under the extra-large headline, "College Does Secret Atomic Power Work." The article appeared two days following the bombing of Hiroshima, and the day before the bombing of Nagasaki, in Japan. And though the article assured readers that "at no time was the city of Ames or the surrounding territory in danger of being blown off the earth," some students expressed shock and concern. When she learned of the news, Phyllis Nuss, a junior in Home Economics, said, "Atomic power is a wonderful discovery, but I can't be sure we are better off to have it. Although it is wonderful, it is terrible in its destruction of human beings."[34]

One week later, following Japan's surrender, the peal of the Campanile, the siren of the power plant, the blaring of car horns, and the "wild screams and shouts" of students signaled the war's end. The University observed V-J Day with a convocation to remember the Iowa State students killed in the conflict, as well as a two-day holiday filled with dancing, extended curfews for both women and military men, band concerts, parties, and time for all students to reflect on the significance of the day. While the women of Gamma Phi Beta sorority marched triumphantly through their house singing "Onward Christian Soldiers," student John Hillis opted for a quiet two-day trip home to see his brother, returned to Iowa after spending two years as a prisoner of war in Germany. Still others postponed their celebrations until their friends, relatives, and sweethearts returned safely from military service.[35]

In the fall of 1945, students found a renewed interest in activities such as the Iowa State Singers, orchestra, academic organizations, religious groups, Greek life, parties with outrageous themes, Friday night dances, and concerts by big names including Duke Ellington and Louis Armstrong.

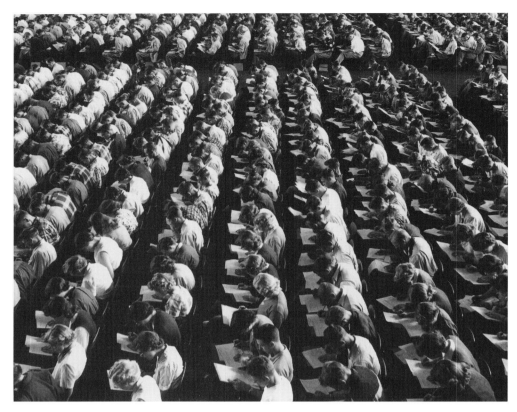

*After the Second World War, Iowa State enrolled record numbers of students. Without the facilities to handle this sudden increase, most students found themselves overwhelmed by long lines and crowded residence halls. These freshmen in the late 1940s crowded into the Armory to take placement exams. (Used by permission of Iowa State University Library/Special Collections Department)*

Yet the war had forever changed campus life. Thousands of servicemen returned home and flooded college campuses across the country. Not only did former students return to complete their degrees, but the GI Bill provided financial assistance to veterans, many of whom were otherwise unable to afford higher education. Student enrollment skyrocketed, from 3,407 in 1945 to 9,216 in 1946, and 10,114 in 1948. In 1948, when Frances Worth Pruitt arrived on campus as a freshman, she was overwhelmed by the large numbers of men returning from military service, many of whom still dressed in their olive drab clothing.

These men were typically older and seasoned by their military experience; they worked hard to earn their degrees, but they also challenged rules governing student conduct. Being of legal age, many drank alcohol without interference from the dean of students, Maurice Helser. In the years before the war, Helser sought out and punished students drinking at local taverns. Yet he could do little to stop the veterans from gathering at Traveler's Inn, where they enjoyed twenty-five-cent beers and reminisced about military life. Their influence even appeared in the

*Green Gander*, the campus humor magazine, which began to feature satirical articles about the military, photographs of pinup girls, and jokes that read, "'What was the hardest thing you learned at college?' asked the father proudly. 'How to open beer bottles with quarters,' replied his son."[36]

It was not the behavior of veterans, however, but rather their sheer numbers that had the most dramatic impact on campus life. To manage the rapid increase in enrollment, the college quickly erected temporary classrooms and student housing units, most of which were drafty and threadbare. New students struggled to find good housing, and the available apartments, residence halls, and Greek houses were filled beyond capacity.

Carl Rusk, who left Iowa State in 1943 to serve in the military, returned in 1946 to find his fraternity, Alpha Gamma Rho, "overflowing" with new members. To solve their housing shortage, the men of Alpha Gamma Rho moved a small building behind the chapter house to serve as temporary quarters for returning veterans. The solution was fleeting, however, because "the health authorities condemned it." [37]

Finding housing typically required creative solutions and a willingness to tolerate some hardship. In January of 1946, David Calderwood, an agricultural engineering major, took up residence in a second-story room of a building on the college poultry farm. As part of his rental agreement, he tended to the chickens and gathered eggs on Sundays.[38]

The fact that nearly half of the returning veterans were married further complicated the housing shortage. Prior to 1945, married students represented just 4 percent of the student population. Following the war, 21 percent of students were married. Throughout 1946 and 1947, the college constructed a neighborhood of trailers and military surplus Quonset huts, later known as Pammel Court. These structures tended to be cramped and extremely cold, and they held sparse furnishings constructed by state prisoners. Residents combated the chilly Iowa winters by piling dirt around the foundations of the Quonset huts and stuffing newspaper around electrical outlets.[39]

Though life in Pammel Court could be difficult, married student housing offered an affordable option to veterans who received just $125 per month for living expenses under the GI Bill. As they struggled to make ends meet, many wives of students found employment to support their families. Earle L. Hibbs, who graduated in 1948, spent any free time caring for his young child while his wife worked to provide a much-needed income. He recalled that his college days differed significantly from those of the younger, unmarried students. For Hibbs, there were "no fraternities, no wild parties, just work." Likewise, luxuries were few for John S. Baer, who graduated in 1949, and his wife, Sue, who earned thirty-five cents per hour working in the Visual Education Department. The young couple saved all week for a "Friday night splurge at the 'Maid Rite,' or a glass of beer with fellow students at a tavern near the railroad tracks."[40]

Though their lives were filled with hard work and family concerns, students and their families still sought to create unique communities on campus. This was especially important for the wives of male students, who were often unfamiliar with Ames and had little connection to the college. In February 1948, for example, the wives of men majoring in agricultural engineering formed the American Society of Agricultural Engineers Student Wives' Club. This new group served as a social organization while the women's husbands were in school and as a networking tool once their husbands graduated. The club held weekly meetings, potluck suppers, picnics, and a Christmas party.[41]

Iowa State administrators expected the number of married students to decline as veterans graduated and moved on with their families. Yet the number of married students remained high throughout the 1950s. By 1959, Harold Pride, the director of the Memorial Union, noted that the weekly social dances in the Great Hall had fallen out of fashion. Instead, students preferred group activities such as games and card tournaments that could include both students and their spouses.[42]

By the beginning of the 1960s, more students owned cars and enjoyed going off-campus. They expected to be treated as adults, a trend that gained momentum with the social movements of the 1960s. For Iowa State students, demands for change began in the student government and in the residence halls. During the late 1950s and early 1960s, the Cardinal Guild received increasing criticism for being nothing more than an exclusive "debating society," with unopposed elections and little power to shape university policy. In 1962, one student in the *Iowa State Daily* joked, "Cardinal Guild? What's that, a disease? Oh, I remember—that's the organization that doesn't do anything."[43]

That year, members of the student government sought greater legitimacy not only with Iowa State students but also the administration and the Board of Regents. They began in the winter of 1962 by holding an all-college referendum to change the name of the Cardinal Guild to the Government of the Student Body (GSB), a name that implied sophistication and authority. Shortly thereafter, members successfully persuaded the administration and the Board of Regents to make ROTC an elective, rather than a requirement for male students. An editorial in the *Iowa State Daily* declared that the GSB had finally "proven its worth." By the spring of 1962, candidates ran for office with a renewed energy and sought to address issues such as securing more funds from the state legislature, advancing the arts on campus, and study abroad programs.[44]

Perhaps no issue garnered as much attention as curfews for women students. For decades, students and members of the student government had petitioned to extend, and even abolish, women's hours. As late as 1959, while some grumbled and sent sarcastic letters to the *Iowa State Daily*, most women students still accepted the rules. That year, freshman Mary O'Conner said she didn't mind having to sign out when she left for the evenings because, she reasoned, in case of an emergency, "they have to know where we are." A year later, however, when the Cardinal Guild voted to extend women's weekday hours to 10:30 pm, a campus-wide survey revealed that 86 percent of Iowa State women supported the measure. Yet without the approval of the administration, the Cardinal Guild could not implement any real changes. It was not until 1966 that the Department of Residence took the idea seriously. That year, the women's residence halls were outfitted with magnetic locks, and all women (except freshmen, who still had a midnight curfew) received key cards to open the doors at all hours.[45]

By the mid-1960s, the civil rights movement, the youth movement, and dissent against the Vietnam War generated unrest and brought attention to social issues on college campuses across the country. Compared to institutions such as the University of Iowa, however, much of this change came slowly to Iowa State.

In September 1964, when Donald B. Siano arrived on campus as a graduate student in physics, he sought an antiwar organization similar to the one he knew as an undergraduate at Kent State in Ohio. At Iowa State, however, Siano found that student conflict still took the form of "panty raids," with men storming sorority houses and women's residence halls for the chance to capture "unmentionable" trophies. The only two student organizations with political leanings were the Young Republicans and the Student Committee on Racial Equality, or SCORE. The following year, when Siano and a handful of others organized a chapter of Students for a Democratic Society (SDS), they received a chilly, even hostile, reception from most students who tended to be supportive of the war in Vietnam.[46]

Even in 1967, many at Iowa State did not welcome radical politics on campus. In February of that year, students elected Don Smith, a mechanical engineering student, as president of the GSB. Smith, who ran on a platform of student rights, sported filthy t-shirts and jeans and a long, scruffy beard. He demanded a Students' Bill of Rights and a cooperative bookstore. Smith drew the attention of the national news media, and though he received the most student votes in GSB history, many students and faculty were hesitant to have him represent Iowa State. The greatest hostilities came from the Iowa General Assembly, whose members vowed to reduce funding to the university unless Smith was removed. They objected to his slovenly dress, his outspoken manner, and his radical idea that universities were merely "servants to industry and the military." When Smith told a reporter from *Life* magazine that he used marijuana, several students took out a full-page ad in the *Iowa State Daily* to discredit Smith's "anarchist" views, and started a petition against Smith that garnered more than 800 signatures in its first day (only 750 signatures were necessary to begin impeachment proceedings).[47]

The GSB started impeachment proceedings by April 18, but Smith resigned in the face of what he considered to be a "smear campaign," and eventually withdrew from the university. In his resignation speech, Smith stated that he never intended to "embarrass the University." He remained optimistic, however, and hoped that his replacement would "take advantage of the situation to build a strong and meaningful student government."[48]

Hints of change were in the air, however. In 1968, the administration began receiving complaints about war protesters at ROTC events, as well as the emergence of underground magazines geared toward the "hippie element." By May 1970, the campus climate had changed dramatically as students expressed heightened opposition to the Vietnam War and the military draft. The largest student demonstration at Iowa State took place in the days following the American invasion of Cambodia. Student protests against the war erupted across the country, and con-

*On May 6, 1970, student and antiwar activist Bob Bremley addressed a crowd of more than three thousand students gathered on central campus to voice opposition to the Vietnam War. (Used by permission of Iowa State University Library/Special Collections Department)*

tinued to grow after the Ohio National Guard opened fire on a crowd of student protesters at Kent State.

On May 5, 1970, following student protests on campus and in downtown Ames, the GSB voted to support a twenty-four-hour strike, to begin at noon the following day, as well as a mass rally. More than four hundred students attended the GSB meeting, filling the Great Hall of the Memorial Union, in order to support the strike. According to Jerry Parkin, the GSB vice president, not everyone was on board, especially with VEISHEA events set to begin that weekend. Parkin recalled that even though GSB President Jerry Schnorr "did not support the strike in any way," they "did come together in the end" and endorsed the protest.[49]

The following day, on May 6, 1970, more than three thousand students, armed with banners and signs, assembled in front of Curtiss Hall. That day, students sang "Give Peace a Chance," and chanted, "We don't want Nixon's war, we don't want any war!" They soon moved the protest to the Armory and the ROTC field to disrupt cadets' drill practices. From there, the demonstration grew to include four thousand protestors, who moved down to the intersection of Lincoln Way and Beach. While many sat down to block traffic, another one thousand students continued to downtown Ames, where they staged a sit-in at the Story County Selective Service Center. Although several students were arrested, demonstrations at the Selective Service Center continued for two more days.[50]

On Saturday, May 9, protesters joined the VEISHEA parade in a "March for Concern," despite fears that their presence would cause unrest. The parade took place without incident, however, and throughout the afternoon, approximately two thousand people gathered around the Campanile to continue their rally for peace.[51]

Many students attributed the peaceful nature of student protests to administrators who wished to create an open atmosphere. Thomas Goodale, the associate dean of students at that time, believed that Iowa State was fortunate to have "a unique trust between faculty, students, and the administration." He also realized that such trust could be "blown away over night." After observing the student protests, he said, "We do not need to come down hard on people. What we need is compassion and understanding and some way we've got to come together, that's all there is to it." Likewise, at the rally following the VEISHEA parade, Iowa State President Robert Parks told the crowd, "Bringing peace is the most important problem facing us. As president, I want to say you are going about it in the right way . . . If the university is not concerned with deep human problems such as bringing peace, then what should it be concerned with?"[52]

The social movements of the 1960s left a lasting legacy that affected all aspects of student life. One of the most visible changes occurred in the residence halls and Greek houses. By the mid-1960s, the Department of Residence had all but eliminated women's hours, and by 1969, Iowa State began its first experiment with coeducational housing. The new policy stirred little controversy and was a welcome change to many students. Administrators also favored coeducational housing because they believed it would generate greater interest in residence hall associations and activities. During the fall of 1969, a small group of women became the first to reside on one floor in Helser Hall. When the men of Foster House, also in Helser Hall, learned that women would soon be living on the floor below, the reaction was a jubilant, "Woopie!"[53]

The practice of hiring housemothers also became obsolete. In 1967, the Department of Residence began an "experiment" when they hired twenty-seven-year-old Nancy Gerdes, a graduate student in home economics education, to oversee the women living in Westgate Hall. Charles Frederiksen, the director of residence, was initially skeptical of having younger housemothers, simply because a graduate student could not devote as much of her time to the students as could an "older lady." Yet the experiment seemed to work, and within the next few years, graduate students filled the newly created position of "resident advisor." In 1969, for example, Sue Merkley, a graduate student in history and the resident advisor of Elm Hall, believed "younger women can relate to us more easily than the senior advisors."[54]

Many fraternities also faced major decisions when the university voted to end subsidies for housemothers in the Greek system. Fraternities unable to afford the salary simply did away with housemothers, while others replaced older matrons with female graduate students. These young women often viewed the role of housemother as a professional opportunity. In 1978, when thirty-year-old Katherine Andre applied for the position of housemother for Sigma Alpha Epsilon, she was looking for a job where she could apply her master's degree in recreation, work

*During the late 1960s, Iowa State administrators wanted to promote greater
diversity on campus and encouraged the creation of the Black Cultural Center.
In the foreground President Robert Parks appears with (left to right) Roy Snell,
Ellen Sorge Parks, Norman Thomas (the first manager of the BCC), Parks himself,
Amelia Parker, Dean William Bell, and Mrs. Bell, at the grand opening of the BCC
on May 17, 1970. (Used by permission of Iowa State University Library/Special
Collections Department)*

with young people, and spend time with her seventeen-month-old daughter, Elizabeth. Mother and daughter enjoyed much popularity not only amongst the men of
Sigma Alpha Epsilon but also among parents, who believed having a baby in the
house instilled a sense of responsibility in the young men.[55]

The social movements of the 1960s also generated interest in fostering greater
diversity on campus. By the end of the decade, the vice president of academic affairs, George Christensen, made efforts to recruit students from major metropolitan areas and the South, which resulted in an increasing number of African
American students. Yet many African American students encountered problems
adjusting to life in Ames. For example, in 1961, African American and international students reported rampant discrimination and extreme difficulties in finding good housing. One African American student reported that, without mention-
ing his race, he made tentative agreements with at least fifteen landlords over the
phone. "As soon as I finished calling," he said, "I started making the rounds and
found all the vacancies filled."[56]

Over the next several years, the civil rights movement brought greater attention
to racism and the need to promote awareness of African American culture and is-

sues on campus. To this end, in May 1969, the VEISHEA Central Committee made a $2,000 grant to support the development of a Black Cultural Center, or BCC. Opened one year later, and located at 517 Welch Avenue, the center hosted lectures and promoted events such as Black History Week. It also organized activities such as Sunday evening dinners, dance classes, and Kwanza celebrations.[57]

The BCC proved an immediate success. In 1976, BCC Director Delores Hawkins said the center provided a "home away from home" for many African American students. Hawkins found that many African American students from major metropolitan areas experienced culture shock when they arrived on campus, realizing for the first time "that they are indeed a minority." The BCC offered a variety of services and programs to ease the transition, including a library, children's programs on diversity, a newsletter, religious services, and even haircuts. Finding that few Ames barbers were familiar with African American hairstyles, and that the drive to Des Moines could be inconvenient, the BCC hosted an African American barber from Des Moines every two weeks.[58]

Women's issues also received greater attention than they had in the past. Queen contests at VEISHEA and Homecoming went out of fashion, and women's organizations sought greater legitimacy on campus. This became even more evident following the passage of Title IX of the Health, Education, and Welfare Act of 1972. Title IX prohibited public institutions of higher education from supporting programs or organizations that discriminated on the basis of sex. It had a wide-reaching impact on women's sports, education, and organizations. In 1975, both Mortar Board and Cardinal Key, the two highest honors organizations at Iowa State for women and men, respectively, announced that they would become co-educational.

Mike Bartosh, the president of Cardinal Key, said that members voted unanimously to accept women and the decision was made with little, if any, debate. The question proved more difficult for the women of Mortar Board, however. The president of Mortar Board, Dawn Smith, said that even when Mortar Board accepted men into their membership, the primary purpose of the organization would be to promote women's interests. She still believed in the benefits of "organizations just for men and just for women."[59]

Many women on campus shared this sentiment, and throughout the late 1960s and 1970s, students and faculty worked to establish a place specifically for women. It was not until 1981, however, after nearly ten years of organized efforts, that the Committee on Women requested and received a space on campus for a women's center in the Margaret Sloss House. Named for the first woman at Iowa State to be become a doctor of veterinary medicine, the Sloss House provided students with conference rooms, offices, and a central location for meetings, workshops, job postings, and information on health, child care, women's issues, and financial aid.[60]

By the mid-1970s, the campus climate had changed from the politically charged, uncertain days of the Vietnam era. For example, the practice of "streaking," or running naked through public places purely for shock value, took hold at Iowa State just as it had on campuses across the country. It stirred little controversy, however, because after the turbulent 1960s, "streaking" appeared to be nothing more than harmless fun. On the nights of March 6 and 7, 1974, more than a hundred Iowa State students frolicked about campus in the buff, playing Frisbee and leapfrog.

Neither campus security nor administrators intervened, and police arrested only two students who dared to bare it all in Campustown. On the morning of March 7, the *Iowa State Daily* ran an uncensored photograph on the front page featuring an unidentified male student wearing nothing but a carefree smile. Tom Quaife, the editor in chief of the *Daily* at the time of the incident, recalled how the student staff wrestled with issues of decency, but ultimately decided to run the photograph as it was. Quaife, who had been the editor for only one day, was fearful of losing his job. Yet when the issue appeared on campus, most students and other readers simply laughed. The *Daily* office received only three complaints, including one from the streaker himself, who suddenly lamented his newfound celebrity.[61]

In 1979, just nine years following the major student protests, *Iowa State Daily* editorial editor Angela Reilly looked toward the 1980s with some skepticism. She wrote, "We are the 'me' first generation: the politically apathetic, socially unmotivated, job-conscious product of the '70s. We've turned inward. After all the rallies and protests and mindless violence, we've perceived very little in the way of change."[62]

Life on campus had been transformed, however, and throughout the 1980s and 1990s, students continued to support time-honored Iowa State traditions while pressing for change. One of the most important changes in this period was a new emphasis on practical experience and leadership. Many students sought to gain new insights by participating in study abroad programs. In 1991, following the fall of the Berlin Wall and the end of the Cold War, students expressed an even greater interest in international issues and a desire to participate in study abroad programs. Students could study nearly any subject in a variety of international settings: agriculture in Brazil, political science in London, engineering in Germany, chemistry in Switzerland, business in Korea, and education in Jamaica. The number of students traveling abroad continued to grow. In 1992, 200 students studied overseas, and by the 1998–1999 academic year, this number grew to 862, many of whom received part of the $70,000 in scholarships from the university.[63]

For many students, going abroad was a deeply personal and eye-opening experience. In 1998, Jeff Hansen, then a student in international business, spent six weeks studying in Moscow without conveniences such as microwaves and hot water. "I came back a very humble person," he said, noting that he had never realized how he and his family members used much larger amounts of water and energy than necessary.[64]

Students also found new professional and academic opportunities on campus. In addition to having created a women's center, faculty and administrators wished to encourage more female students to pursue nontraditional careers. During the late 1980s, at a time when women accounted for only 8 percent of physics undergraduates, 12 percent of agronomy undergraduates, and 14 percent

*Interns for the Program for Women in Science and Engineering, like these two students in 1989, spent their summers working with faculty on a wide variety of research subjects. The internships provided many young women with opportunities to explore careers in the sciences. (Used by permission of Iowa State University Library/Special Collections Department)*

of computer science students, members of the ISU Committee on Women in Science and Engineering established the Program for Women in Science and Engineering, or PWSE. The new program offered scholarships and internship opportunities to female students majoring in science, engineering, or other technical fields.[65]

One of the most important aspects of the PWSE was its emphasis on practical experience. In 1987, PWSE began a summer internship program for women to complete research projects under the guidance of ISU faculty members in fields such as engineering, veterinary medicine, horticulture, botany, animal science, zoology, psychology, and food and nutrition. For many young women, this was their first exposure to work in scientific disciplines.

Gretchen Vogel entered Iowa State as a journalism major, but because of her experiences with the summer internship program, she switched to engineering. "I've always been interested in science and math and had success, but I never thought of engineering as a career. I always thought, 'What a terrible job.'" After two summers of interning under Ames Lab computer engineer Diane Rover and engineering professor Charles Wright, however, Vogel discovered that she truly enjoyed working in the field. The PWSE program proved highly successful, and by 2000, more than seven hundred women had participated in the internship program, while the number of women enrolled in either science or engineering at ISU increased by 50 percent, to 18–20 percent of those enrolled.[66]

For students in the early twenty-first century, ideals such as community and camaraderie proved to be just as important as they had been to students at the end of the nineteenth century. Yet twenty-first-century students arrived on campus with much different expectations than their predecessors. Most came from small, urban families and had always enjoyed technologies such as televisions and computers, as well as the privacy of their own bedrooms. Sharing a room in a residence hall with a roommate was an unfamiliar and daunting experience to many freshmen.

By the late 1990s, one way to ease the transition and to promote community was through learning communities, a program in which students with similar majors lived and studied together. Upperclassmen served as peer mentors while each community operated under the guidance of a faculty member. Within a few years of implementing the program more than two thousand Iowa State students (approximately 40 percent of the freshman class) participated in nearly fifty learning communities. Surveys found that participants tended to earn higher grade point averages and were more likely to remain in college than nonparticipants.[67]

The key to the program's success was its ability to combine the academic and social lives of students. Members of one agricultural community toured Pioneer Hybrid International, attended a play at Fisher Theater, organized tailgates before football games, and toured a no-till farm.[68]

As enrollment at Iowa State continued to grow throughout the 1990s and reached nearly twenty-seven thousand in 2000, students also found community through the creation of new organizations. By the beginning of the twenty-first century, students could find clubs and organizations to suit every niche, hobby, political perspective, issue, and lifestyle. And if students could not find a compatible group, they simply started their own. This was especially important for individuals who might otherwise feel marginalized or face discrimination.[69]

Beginning in the early 1990s, the Lesbian, Gay, Bisexual, Transgender and Allies Alliance, or LGBTAA, began sponsoring two annual events, National Coming Out Week in the fall and Awareness Week in the spring. Each event featured speakers, films, a dance, rallies, informational sessions, and "reverse Campaniling," which gave same-sex couples the opportunity to partake in a time-honored Iowa State tradition. The primary goals of such activities were to raise awareness, eliminate stereotypes, and eliminate the isolation felt by many homosexual students. Such change was slow in coming, however, and though membership grew considerably throughout the decade, the LGBTAA met with considerable resistance from students and alumni. In 1996, when the *Iowa State Daily* ran a photograph of two students "reverse Campaniling," the newspaper was flooded with letters objecting to the image. Editors of the *Daily* defended their decision and believed the photograph to be a "jolt of shock treatment for a conservative campus."[70]

Still, many students remained optimistic. In 1997, the LGBTAA, in conjunction with Lesbian, Gay, Bisexual, Transgender Student Services, or LGBTSS, launched the "Safe Zone" campaign, offering pink triangle stickers to faculty and staff supportive of homosexual students. Within the first few days of the campaign, more than 550 faculty and staff requested the stickers and displayed them in their offices. Then, in 1999, LGBTAA president Angie Chipman, then a junior in psychology, said, "If we reach one person, we've done our job."[71]

Whether they arrived in the 1870s, clutching a small bag of belongings in the back of a horse-drawn wagon, or towing a U-Haul full of life's "necessities" with their own car in 2000, Iowa State students have always sought community, friendship, and lasting memories. Just as W. A. Murphy, from the class of 1894, recalled his college days as "those happy days of youthful vivacity, of pleasant sensations, of delightful times," so too did Chris Lursen, who entered Iowa State as a freshman in 1998, describe his Iowa State experience as "the best years of my life." Looking back on his time as a student, Lursen concluded, "I don't think I could have done what I did at Iowa State anywhere else." Through the years, students have fostered camaraderie through the establishment of student governments, literary societies, athletic contests, clubs, and organizations. They lived and worked together in ever-changing residence halls and campus facilities. Though they sometimes stirred unrest and controversy, and have continually redefined what constituted "appropriate behavior," students strived to become, in their own way, true "Iowa Staters."[72]

# Vignettes

## Ed Bock: Everybody's All-American

One of the greatest players in Big Six Conference history, Ed Bock is the only Iowa State player to be inducted into the College Football Hall of Fame and was the Cyclones' first consensus All-American. Bock was selected to the first team of the Associated Press All-America squad as a senior. He was also invited to play in the East-West Shrine Game, the *Chicago Tribune* All-Star Game, and the Dallas Dream Game at the Cotton Bowl against the Green Bay Packers in 1938.

Bock started at guard for Iowa State in all twenty-six games of his career and earned all–Big Six recognition three times. He captained the great 1938 Iowa State team that included fellow ISU Hall of Famer Everett "Rabbit" Kischer at quarterback. Bock was a big reason the Cyclones finished with a 7-1-1 record that fall. The team opened the season with six straight victories, including wins over Nebraska, Missouri, and Kansas to earn ISU's first national ranking. College football in the 1930s was a rough game in the trenches.

"My three front teeth got knocked out by Sam Francis from Nebraska," Bock recalled in 1997. "He was quite a back. I tackled him but I caught his heel with my teeth. Iowa State said it would replace (the teeth). They made a special helmet with a face mask. It was the first one in the Big Six Conference."

"The college decided to replace my teeth at the end of the year, so I chewed up some wax and I molded some fake teeth. When I smiled or talked people really didn't know they were fake. I wore them during games. In the game against Kansas, I was wearing them and their back ran over me for a substantial gain. I was slow getting up and was on all fours and the referee looked at me. When he looked at me I spit out the teeth. He threw his flag and called unnecessary roughness on the runner as my 'teeth' lay on the field."

The No. 18 Cyclones beat intrastate rival Drake, 14–0, November 5 to move to 7-0. The Iowa Staters then traveled to Manhattan, Kansas, where they fought to a 13–13 draw, scoring on the game's final play. The tie set up a conference championship game in the season finale against Oklahoma in Ames. The Sooners prevailed over a Cyclone team that played without running back Hank Wilder, who was out for the season with a knee injury.

"I finished football in 1938 at Iowa State," Bock said. "I was offered $300 a month to play for the Chicago Bears [of the National Football League]. I turned them down because I wanted to go to graduate school to get my

*(continued)*

[master's degree] in mechanical engineering. [Iowa State] offered me $200 a month to become the line coach. I finished my degree and went to work at Monsanto for $120 a month. I was at a speaking engagement with baseball player Joe Garagiola. He introduced me and laughed, 'Ed, one more move and you would have been on relief.'"

Hardly. He would go on to be president at Monsanto.

Tom Kroeschell

# Ron Galimore: Perfect

Ron Galimore was just five years old when his father, Willie, was killed in a car accident. Willie Galimore was starting his eighth season as a star running back for the Chicago Bears of the National Football League. His second son, Ron, would take the family name to new heights, quite literally. Ron Galimore would prosper in a different sport as one of the best gymnasts ever.

Galimore transferred to Iowa State from LSU in 1979. He had won a pair of NCAA titles before coming to Ames. Under ISU head coach Ed Gagnier, Galimore would go where no gymnast had ever gone. Galimore won two individual NCAA titles on the vault, leading Iowa State to a second-place national finish in 1981. Ultimately he would win All-America honors nine times, placing in the all-around, vault, and floor exercise twice at the NCAA championships.

At the 1981 NCAA meet, after a chief rival had just tallied a score of 9.9 in the vault competition, Galimore demonstrated the depth of his talent and character. He saved the best vault of his career for that final performance as the last competitor, registering the first perfect 10 in NCAA history. Galimore would go on to earn a spot on the 1980 U.S. Olympic team that never got to compete because the United States boycotted the Moscow Olympic Games.

After retiring from competition, he served as an assistant coach at Iowa State. He would go on to work as national men's program director for the U.S. Gymnastics Federation. Galimore was a star performer. His leaping ability allowed him to soar higher than his peers in competition. His spectacular vaults were unique and brought people to gymnastics meets who had never seen one before.

Tom Kroeschell

175

# Clyde Williams: The Cyclone Patron Saint

Clyde Williams, a Sheldon native, had earned a dentistry degree at the University of Iowa while being the first player west of the Mississippi to make Yale coach and American football innovator Walter Camp's All-America team as a star back at Iowa. He practiced his trade briefly, but missed the competition enough that in 1906 he accepted a position as baseball coach and assistant football coach at Iowa State. A year later, Williams became the head football coach. His first Iowa State football team notched a 7-1 mark.

The 1907 season included a 20–14 win over Iowa and a controversial 13–10 win at Nebraska. The game in Lincoln, Nebraska, came down to a disputed drop-kick field goal by Iowa State that bounced over the goalpost and through the uprights. The referee disallowed the play, which would have given Ames a 13–10 victory. Iowa State protested what Nebraska called a 10–9 win. Iowa State appealed the next day to football coaching legend and rules guru Walter Camp. "Upon further review," Camp stated that the goal should have been allowed. "We Won," claimed the *Iowa State Student*. Both schools still count the game as a win. After beating Drake on Thanksgiving Day in Des Moines, the Cyclones declared themselves the state champions of Iowa.

Williams's contributions to the future of Iowa State athletics were profound. In addition to leading the football and baseball programs, he started the school's basketball program in 1908. A visionary on the gridiron, he was the first coach to utilize the forward pass, a major innovation that reduced the brute violence of the game. A visionary off the football field, he started lobbying to construct a new athletics field and gymnasium. Williams had a plan and would not deviate from his vision. For three years, he worked to secure a stadium site at the corner of what is now Lincoln Way and Sheldon Avenue. Up to that time, Iowa State had played its football games on a field located west of Morrill Hall where the Parks Library now stands.

By 1905, portable bleachers allowed nearly two thousand spectators to take in a Cyclone football game. Players would dress in the basement of Beardshear Hall and walk to the field. Offered other sites for a new field, Williams refused all alternative plots and after three years of negotiations, the field was graded in 1913 on the site of a prized peach orchard. A shortage of funds delayed further development, but in October 1914, Iowa State President Raymond Pearson recommended construction of a concrete bleacher at a cost of $35,000. The new facility, which seated 5,600, was known originally as State Field. The bleachers were built without state money, funded instead by a personal loan note. Williams was one of the six individuals who signed the promissory note. The note was paid off through money saved from gate receipts.

As he had refused alternative sites for the stadium, Williams refused compromise on appropriations for a new gym building. In 1914, Iowa State won a petition of full funding and State Gym was constructed at a cost of $150,000. The new facility included a basketball court, offices for athletics staff and physical education faculty, and a pool. It would be Iowa State's basketball home until 1946. State of the art when it was built, State Gym would house Iowa State coaches for more than eighty years. In addition to athletic competitions, the facility would host university convocations, operas, and other performing arts exhibitions. U.S. President William Howard Taft spoke there. In 1918, during the Spanish influenza epidemic, State Gym served as an overflow hospital for the collegiate community.

Williams's leadership rendered his appointment as athletics director in 1914 anticlimactic. He remained at Iowa State through 1919. At the age of forty, he went back to his hometown of Sheldon, where he joined friend and former player and assistant coach Homer Hubbard as a partner in an automobile dealership.

Williams's mark at Iowa State remains indelible. His football teams had a six-year record of 33-14-2. His four seasons as basketball coach had permanently established the sport in Ames. Williams was also head baseball coach. He spent eight years on the National Football Rules Committee, representing the Midwest on a panel that included gridiron legends Amos Alonzo Stagg of Chicago and Yale's Walter Camp.

Williams left Iowa State with an impeccable reputation. In 1912, an anonymous individual sent Williams a package containing Iowa's signals and plays just ahead of the Cyclone-Hawkeye football game. "Here are the plays and signals of the Iowa team and here is what we will do with them," Williams said to assistant coach Homer Hubbard, before tearing the pages to shreds. When Williams succumbed to cancer in 1938, Hubbard wrote a tribute that appeared in the *Alumnus* of Iowa State. "Great as an athlete, he became great as a coach," Hubbard wrote. "Great as a coach, he became great as a director. Great as a director, he became the patron saint of athletics at Iowa State, planning for years ahead to build its plant, removing a famous orchard, grading the grounds and raising, in part with his own money, the original $40,000 for its bleachers. All this because he was great as a MAN."

Tom Kroeschell

*Chapter 6*

# Athletics at Iowa State University

Tom Kroeschell

Intercollegiate athletics at Iowa State University (formerly Iowa State College of Agriculture and the Mechanic Arts) grew out of interclass competitions in a variety of events including track and field and baseball. Following a pattern at schools across the country in 1891, Iowa State President William Beardshear spearheaded the foundation of an athletic association to officially sanction Iowa State athletic teams. That was only the first step, however, in the development of a highly diverse sports program at Iowa State University. Through the years Iowa State would belong to many conferences including the Big Six, Big Seven, Big Eight, and eventually the Big 12. All major sports programs including football, basketball, track, wrestling, and gymnastics would undergo major expansion. By the 1970s, women's athletic teams would also have a major presence on campus. Today, the sports facilities are extensive and continue to expand as sports activities play a major role in campus life, the community, and the state.

In 1892, the football program at Iowa State College began in an inauspicious manner. A student, Ira Brownlee, formed the school's first football team. It was not an instant hit. The *Bomb*, the student yearbook, related that very few people knew of or understood enough of the game to watch or play it with enthusiasm.[1] But still, the sport caught on. One of the most unlikely Iowa State athletics pioneers was none other than George Washington Carver. He came to Iowa State as a graduate assistant in botany in 1891. Carver was the first African American to serve on the Iowa State faculty. The scientist who eventually became famous for his agricultural research was one of the Cyclones' first athletic trainers.

The first father of Iowa State football was a stout young man straight out of Cornell University where he had been an Ivy League star. Glenn "Pop" Warner had contracted with IAC to coach the school's football team in 1895. Warner, just beginning a coaching career that would span forty-four years and 313 victories, came to coach the team in late summer before heading to Georgia, where he had been named head coach.

Warner's team would put Ames on the college football map and leave a lasting legacy. The Iowans traveled to highly regarded Northwestern University for that school's season opener. Northwestern was a heavy favorite. The home team was in for a big shock. The visitors from Iowa led 30–0 at halftime and left Chicago with a 36–0 victory. The final outcome was so decisive that the *Chicago Tribune* carried a September 29 story with the headline "Struck by a Cyclone." The *Tribune* declared, "Northwestern might as well have tried to play football with an Iowa cyclone as with the Iowa team it met yesterday." The Cyclone nickname stuck, as Warner's team had literally made a name for itself.

In 1906 a former Iowa All-American came to Ames and would have a wide-ranging impact on the future of Iowa State athletics. Clyde Williams started at Iowa State in 1906 as baseball coach and assistant football coach; in 1907, he became head football coach. Among his many contributions was promoting the construction of a new football stadium and the construction of State Gym. He later became ISC athletic director.

The 1912 Iowa State football team shared a Missouri Valley Intercollegiate Athletic Association title with Nebraska with 2-0 league records. Iowa State had entered the conference in 1908, joining charter members Kansas, Missouri, Nebraska, and Washington of St. Louis. Drake joined the league the same season. It was a loose federation by today's standards, but formed by a desire for teams west of the Mississippi River to create a governing body like the Western Conference (now the Big Ten Conference) and eastern collegiate leagues. The conference would grow and eventually split into two leagues.

By the late teens, the Cyclones were putting top caliber athletes on the football field. Dick Barker was Iowa State's first All-American, earning honors from the *Chicago Tribune* in 1919. Polly Wallace, of Washington, Iowa, was the first Cyclone to be named first-team All-American after being tabbed by Walter Eckersall of the *Chicago Tribune* at center in 1920.

In 1922, Sam Willaman was hired as Iowa State's football coach. Willaman had been the head prep coach at East Tech High School in Cleveland, Ohio. He was signed to a three-year contract. Willaman brought with him from Cleveland three of his own players, Jack Trice and brothers Norton and Johnnie Behm. All three would make major contributions to the Iowa State football program and one would be forgotten and then later immortalized.

Jack Trice, the grandson of slaves, grew up first in Hiram, Ohio, and then in Cleveland. He selected animal husbandry as his Iowa State major. Married, he lived in downtown Ames with his wife, Cora Mae. His promising career ended tragically, however, when he was injured in a 1923 game at the University of Minnesota. He died two days later in Ames. A statue in his honor is located near the Jacobson Athletic Building, and since 1997, the football stadium carries his name, Jack Trice Stadium.

A key to the growing popularity of sports in America, especially the collegiate game, was the rise of radio. The first Iowa State football game to be broadcast on the radio occurred when Andy Woolfries did play-by-play of a Cyclone game in 1921 on the fledgling college radio station, WOI. Initially, only a few individuals had headset model radios. Woolfries called the first game almost by chance after station founder Harmon Deal backed out of announcing the contest. "It was only by accident that I broadcast the first football game," Woolfries said. "Deal had decided to put it on the air and I was to run the transmitter. At the last minute, Deal

*Iowa State's first African American student-athlete, Jack Trice was a promising player on the field and a successful student in the classroom. He died on October 8, 1923, from injuries suffered in his second career Iowa State College game. Since 1997 his name has graced Iowa State's football stadium. Trice came to Ames along with head coach Sam Willaman, who also brought to ISC fellow backs Johnny Behm (far left) and Norton Behm (right of Trice) from Cleveland. End Bill Nave (far right) of Burlington, Iowa, was killed on a bombing mission in World War II, one of at least thirty-one Iowa State letter winners who died for their country in the two world wars. (Photo courtesy of Iowa State Athletic Media Relations)*

sort of got the shakes, sort of mike fright and decided I was to broadcast it. Well I did, and I guess got by, only because there was no standard to compare it to."[2]

There were other ways of following the games away from Ames. A gridgraph system was used for capacity crowds at State Gym. The large graph had a football field marked on it with a ball that moved to the play-by-play sent via Western Union. It was in State Gym that Cora Mae Trice first learned of her husband's injury at Minnesota, watching the gridgraph.

In 1928, the ten-team Missouri Valley Conference broke into two leagues. Iowa State, Kansas State, Kansas, Missouri, Nebraska, and Oklahoma formed a new conference that the media nicknamed "The Big Six." The name stuck and the conference would prosper and grow through the next seventy-five years. After a winless 1930 football season, Iowa State turned to a former Hope College (Michigan) three-sport letter winner whose leadership would leave a lasting impact at ISC. That man was George Veenker, head basketball coach and assistant football coach at Michigan.

*Winifred Tilden enriched the lives of thousands of women at Iowa State College from 1904 to 1944. As Iowa State's head of women's physical education, she stressed a progressive program of quality physical education for all women students. Tilden's philosophy included teaching women sports they could play the rest of their lives, thereby giving them the skills to stay physically fit long after their college days. (Used by permission of Iowa State University Library/Special Collections Department)*

Veenker was a man of action and few restrained words. His teams produced immediately. To shake any vestige of previous Iowa State teams, Veenker dressed out his 1931 Cyclones not in cardinal and gold, but in the maize and blue of Michigan. His methodology seemed to connect with his players. Iowa State went into the final game of the season with an undefeated Big Six record after wins at Oklahoma (13–12) and against Kansas State (7–6) in Ames. The Cyclones eventually placed second in conference play. The unexpected turnaround earned Veenker national recognition.

While coaches and players got the adulation, there were several individuals who worked behind the scenes running Cyclone athletics on a day-to-day basis. One individual who saw firsthand the evolution of the Iowa State athletics program was Merl Ross. Hired by Clyde Williams in 1917 for sixty dollars a month as secretary for the physical training department, Ross was named ticket manager in 1924. By 1932, he had earned a position in the department as business manager. His accounting for the Iowa State 1933 football team's trip to Kansas underscores how times have changed. The team left Ames on Friday, November 17, in six automobiles, including cars driven by wrestling coach Hugo Otopalik, Dr. Edwards, former ISU football and intramurals director Harry Schmidt, basketball head coach Louis Menze, William Allender, and Veenker. The group of twenty-nine, including coaches, players, and staff, ate dinner in Excelsior Springs, Missouri, for $25.25. The team stayed at the first-class Kansas City Muehlebach Hotel. The two-night stay for twenty-eight totaled seventy dollars. After a 20–6 loss the team returned to Ames at 3 P.M. Sunday after dinner for thirty at a church in Leon at fifty cents per person. The entire weekend cost $382.58.[3]

A variety of sport programs continued to develop at Iowa State in the 1920s and 1930s. In addition to football, basketball, baseball, track and cross country, swimming, and tennis, Iowa State fielded a polo team. Starting in 1928, the Cyclone polo squads played other Big Six schools and its members could earn numerals sweaters and veterans a varsity "I."

It was during Veenker's tenure as football coach that the Iowa State–Iowa series in football was renewed for two seasons. The Cyclones suffered a 27–7 defeat at Iowa in 1933. That game only set the table for the 1934 showdown, which would go down as one of the greatest wins in school history.

Iowa came to Ames on October 20. The Hawkeyes, led by standout back Ozzie Simmons, took the Clyde Williams Field turf heavily favored. What the Iowa team had not counted on was Sioux City freshman Tommy Neal, who dashed for four touchdowns in a stunning 31–6 rout of the Hawkeyes. *Des Moines Register* reporter Sec Taylor was ebullient in his writing after the game: "Tommy Neal, an all-state high school midget of 155 pounds from Sioux City, Iowa; Fred Poole, a kicking fool from Ames High School and a troupe of their inspired teammates wrote football history here Saturday when they not only brought victory for Iowa State College over Iowa University but humiliated the Hawkeyes by piling up the almost unbelievable score of 31 to 6."

Poole, an Ames High graduate, punted twelve times for a 54.5-yard average. He consistently pinned Iowa deep in its own territory by kicking all but one of his efforts out of bounds and away from Simmons, a dangerous return man. The campus and the town of Ames celebrated long into the night as Cyclone fans, still reveling in the unexpected victory, milled around Campustown relishing the win with their friends. They would have to live off that feeling for a long time. Attempts to continue the rivalry were futile. The two teams would not meet each other again on the football field until 1977. Veenker later added athletics director duties to his football responsibilities.

By 1938, Iowa State's athletics physical plant included State Gym, which housed five basketball and volleyball courts, an indoor cinder track equipped with jumping pits, a white-tiled swimming pool, two large locker rooms, and administrative and coaches' offices. The East Stadium at Clyde Williams Field contained the wrestling room, six handball and squash courts, a golf driving net, two ping-pong tables, two locker rooms, and lecture rooms. Horseshoe pitching pits were located under the West Stadium. North of State Gym were seventeen full-sized football fields for intramural competition in flag football. In the spring, goalposts were exchanged for home plates and twenty softball fields. There were three varsity and freshman baseball diamonds, including the field on which Iowa State played intercollegiate baseball, just east of Clyde Williams Field. In addition to the outdoor cinder track within the stadium, locations near State Gym provided two practice putting greens, two lawn bowling greens, six outdoor handball or tennis practice courts, twenty-one clay and hard-surface tennis courts, and five all-weather horseshoe pitching courts.

Although the Iowa State football team had excelled in earlier years, not much was expected from the team in 1938. Yes, the Cyclones had the services of quarterback Everett "Rabbit" Kischer and one of the nation's best linemen in Ed Bock. But Iowa State had won only five Big Six games in the previous six seasons. Starting his second year as Cyclone head coach, "Smilin" Jim Yeager didn't put his team on the spot. "We're figuring on winning a game or two in the Big Six, and it might be any of the five," Yeager said. After dispatching Denver and Luther, Iowa State's team headed for Nebraska. Few expected a Cyclone victory. The Cornhuskers were 31-1-3 in Big Six play since 1931. Iowa State hadn't beaten Nebraska since 1919.

In Lincoln, Iowa State took a 2–0 lead after junior Paul Morin blocked a Cornhusker punt in the third quarter. Five minutes later Kischer took a lateral from Gordon Ruepke and dashed ten yards for a touchdown that gave ISC an 8–0 advantage. It wasn't over. Nebraska scored to make it 8–7, and the Cornhuskers were frothing at the mouth in front of more than twenty-eight thousand of their fans. Nebraska coach Biff Jones threw waves of reserves at Yeager's men, but as the *Des Moines Register* recorded, "Never did a team from Iowa fight for victory like the Cyclones did, and [when] it seemed they no longer could withstand the flow of Nebraska reserves, they kept right on fighting and got the sweet reward of the first Iowa State victory over the Cornhuskers in 19 years. Now even Yeager was excited. 'We've waited 19 years for this victory,' he said. 'I'm so excited I can hardly talk. I can't say anything too good for Kischer and Bock. They were great—and (Gordon) Reupke—the whole gang.'"

In Ames, students carried the celebration far into the night. The midnight curfew was joyously disregarded and fans scurried to meet the team, which arrived back home at 1:15 A.M. College officials declared that student behavior had been so good and, in light of the occasion, no one would be penalized. Missouri and Kansas were the next foes to fall. Only Veenker's 1931 squad had won more than two conference games. ISC then scored victories at Marquette and over Drake. The Cyclone winning streak back to the previous year now stood at ten games. The Cyclones scored on the final play at Kansas State for a tie that set up a showdown for the Big Six title against Oklahoma. A record crowd of more than twenty-one thousand fans packed newly named Clyde Williams Field and saw the Cyclones drop a 10–0 decision to a team that shut out every conference opponent. But what a season it had been. Bock was an All-American and several Cyclones were named all-conference.

The 1944 Iowa State football team had its own brush with greatness. Coached by NFL Hall of Famer "Iron Mike" Michalske, the Cyclones were 3-0 heading into a game at Missouri. There was another factor in Iowa State's football resurgence. Like all other aspects of college life, everything changed on December 7, 1941. The United States' entry into World War II would have a profound effect on Iowa State athletics. The most significant factor was the V-12 program. Iowa State's nationally

*A record Clyde Williams Field crowd of more than twenty thousand watched Iowa State's 10–0 loss to Oklahoma in the final game of the 1938 season. One of the greatest teams in Cyclone history, the Ed Bock and Everett "Rabbit" Kischer–led squad finished the season with a 7-1-1 record. (Used by permission of Iowa State University Library/Special Collections Department)*

regarded engineering program brought naval cadets into the V-5 or V-12 program. The naval trainees were eligible to participate in athletics for the Cyclones, regardless of age or previous college graduation. Iowa State teams during the war years had so many V-5 or V-12 student-athletes that when the Cyclones hit the road only a handful of individuals would not be dressed in a military uniform.

In 1944, the Cyclones finished a key game with a flourish. "We were trailing [at Missouri] 21–14 with only a few minutes remaining," Cyclone lineman Dick Cole reminisced. "As we got the ball at our own 20-yard line, we could hear the public address guy announce that there would be a victory celebration at the Student Union right after the game. I think it was . . . Joe Noble, our quarterback, who said 'It's not over. Let's show 'em we can go right down the field.' That is just what we did. Merry Warner went the last 20 yards for the touchdown, and the game ended in a 21–21 tie."[4]

The 1944 team was, literally, inches from glory. In a showdown with Oklahoma in Ames, Iowa State's bid for an undefeated season ended in heartbreak when Dick

Howard caught a short pass from Noble and was hit by a Sooner where the goal line met the sideline flag. The referee, standing on the fifteen-yard line, called Howard out-of-bounds on the one-inch line. Game films later showed Howard crossed the goal and when hit, pushed the flag back upright. Instead of winning 13–12, Iowa State lost 12–7. The loss would burden Michalske and his players long after the final gun sounded. The Cyclones rebounded to beat Nebraska 19–6 and previously unbeaten Drake 9–0. The 1944 Iowa State team still ranks as one of the Cyclones' best ever. It outscored its foes 203–39 and shut out five opponents. Michalske demonstrated his coaching ability and Jack Fathauer was named to the second team of Bill Stern's *Look* magazine All-America squad. Six other Cyclones were honored as all–Big Six selections.

The end of World War II brought back thousands of servicemen who sought a college education at schools across the country. Gone from Ames were the V-5 and the V-12 men. Colorado had joined the Big Six, making the conference the Big Seven. The immediate postwar period would be a tough one for the Iowa State football program. In 1946, fourteenth-ranked Oklahoma beat Iowa State 63–0. The disparity between the two teams forged the 630 Club, the forerunner of the National Cyclone Club, as Iowa State fans worked to financially upgrade and make the Cyclone football program competitive.

The 1949 Iowa State football team, led by wide receiver Jim Doran of Beaver and the able contributions of quarterback Bill Weeks, proved its worth. Against one of Oklahoma head coach Bud Wilkinson's best teams, Doran set a National Collegiate Athletic Association (NCAA) record with 203 receiving yards on eight catches, including an eighty-seven-yard TD pass. Iowa State's final victory in that 5-3-1 season was a 21–8 win over Drake in Des Moines. The game drew the largest crowd ever to see a game at Drake Stadium (18,311).

Jim Myers's departure after the 1957 season as head football coach sent Iowa State looking for another gridiron leader. The Cyclones settled on UCLA assistant Clay Stapleton. Stapleton was familiar with the single-wing football schemes the Iowa State players had been learning under Myers. In Stapleton's second year, injuries and departures cut the 1959 roster down to thirty players. It was a close-knit group. The Cyclones routed Drake 41–0 in the season opener on a muddy field on a Friday night in Drake Stadium. As the team filed into the locker room, trainer Warren Arial greeted them by saying, "here comes the dirty thirty." The players liked their new tag. It became the talk of Iowa the following week when sports information director Harry Burrell included the nickname in his game story of Iowa State's 28–12 win at Denver.

Back from 1958, the team's leaders were back Dwight Nichols and fullback Tom Watkins. The duo would make the Dirty Thirty a household name across the nation, ranking second and third, respectively, in NCAA rushing. The Cyclone defensive efforts, which included the play of future Ohio State head coach John Cooper, pitched consecutive shutouts at Colorado (27–0) and at Homecoming against Kansas State (26–0). The race for the Orange Bowl was on the line when Iowa State boarded its jet for an October 31 game at Kansas. Heavy fog forced the

Cyclones to fly back to Des Moines and board buses that did not arrive in Kansas City until 2:30 A.M. Despite the lack of sleep, Iowa State battled Kansas to a scoreless draw until the Jayhawks scored on a fifteen-yard fourth-quarter rushing play to win the game 7–0. Despite the loss, Stapleton was proud of his team. "How can you help but be proud of these kids? he said. "Off the field I'd rather be coach of the Dirty Thirty than President of the United States."

The following week against Nebraska, Watkins returned the second-half kickoff eighty-four yards for a touchdown as Iowa State beat the Cornhuskers, 18–6. In one of the coldest contests in ISU history (wind chill 11 degrees), Iowa State dispatched San Jose State 55–0. The 7-2 Cyclones prepared to meet Oklahoma November 21 in Norman, Oklahoma. A victory in the season finale would mean a tie for the league title and the school's first-ever Orange Bowl berth. Many ISU fans were among forty-seven thousand spectators who saw OU jump out to a 21–0 halftime lead. ISU closed the gap to 21–12 after three quarters, before a forty-eight-yard Prentice Gautt TD run secured a 35–12 Sooner victory.

Although the Cyclones were denied an Orange Bowl berth, Nichols had proven himself to be one of the toughest and most productive players in school history as the first Iowa Stater to rush for more than two thousand yards in his career. Nichols, who had spent four years in the Navy before coming to Ames, was the perfect catalyst for a team that averaged only 179 pounds per man. He earned All-America honors in 1959, his second straight season as the third-most productive rusher in college football. Nichols was the first man to lead the Big Eight in total offense three straight seasons in nearly twenty years. Watkins, second nationally in rushing in 1959, would be a 1960 All-American as Iowa State put up a second consecutive 7-3 season. The 14-6 two-year mark was Iowa State's best effort in back-to-back seasons since the 1916–1917 campaigns (10-4-1).

Nichols's departure did not leave the cupboard bare. The 1960 team was led by Watkins but included a sophomore named Dave Hoppmann. Despite missing several games, Hoppmann led the Big 12 in rushing and ranked fifth nationally in that category. The signature win of that season was ISU's 10–6 win over Oklahoma in Ames, the first Cyclone victory over the Sooners since 1931. In 1961, Hoppmann and his mates beat Oklahoma for the second straight season, 21–15, in Norman. The consecutive wins over OU were an aberration. Indeed, Iowa State was 5-63-2 against Oklahoma in the twentieth century. It was against Kansas State in 1961 that Hoppmann compiled a Big Eight record 271 rushing yards. He earned first-team honors in 1961 and 1962, finishing his career with a Big Eight record 2,562 rushing yards. Stapleton's last years as head coach included All-American performances by fullback Tom Vaughn (1963) and offensive tackle John Van Sicklen (1964). Vaughn was a great return man and all-purpose yards producer. He was an all–Big Eight choice as a fullback in 1963 and as a defensive back in 1964.

To find his replacement as head football coach in 1967, Stapleton, now athletics director, went looking for a young, enthusiastic coach who could garner support for the Iowa State football program. He had his heart set on an assistant coach at Arkansas who had been an All-American back at Tennessee, Johnny Majors. Fortunately for Iowa State University, Majors decided to accept the job.

The Cyclone football program was buoyed by Major's enthusiasm and popularity. His first teams struggled in a rapidly improving Big Eight Conference. Despite the challenges, Iowa State took a 6-3 record into its 1971 Big Eight finale against Oklahoma State. Due to final exams, ISU's first teams didn't practice together all week. It didn't matter. Iowa State laid to rest any doubts about their ability by scoring on a forty-nine-yard pass on the game's first play. They routed the Cowboys, 54–0, the biggest-ever Cyclone win over a conference opponent. Led by quarterback Dean Carlson, running back George Amundson, and linebacker Keith Schroeder, ISU accepted its first-ever postseason bowl bid, an invitation to the Sun Bowl in El Paso, Texas. Iowa State lost the game to quarterback Bert Jones and the LSU Tigers, but finished the season with an 8-4 record, the most wins compiled by a Cyclone team since 1906.

Iowa State had been ranked for weeks in 1972 as the Cyclones played host to No. 3 Nebraska. Amundson had switched to quarterback for his senior season and thrived, throwing for a school record 2,110 yards and seventeen touchdowns. The game came down to the last minute. With a defense led by Marv Krakau, Iowa State trailed just 23–17. In maybe the greatest last-minute scoring drive in Iowa State history, Amundson completed four passes, the last to wide receiver Willie Jones deep in the east corner of the south end zone for the tying touchdown. A missed extra-point attempt forced a draw. But Majors's squad was ranked twelfth, the highest Associated Press poll rung in ISU history. An invitation to the Liberty Bowl followed the next weekend. After the bowl game, Majors told his team he would be taking the head coaching job at Pittsburgh. For Iowa State it would mean new challenges. Iowa State athletics director Lou McCullough turned to the head coach of Tampa, Earle Bruce. The new coach would put his own distinct mark on ISU football.

Ground was broken for Iowa State's new football stadium in 1973. Two years later, Iowa State beat Air Force, 17–12, on September 20, 1975, in the completed facility. Iowa State Stadium cost $7.6 million. The facility originally seated forty thousand but capacity grew to fifty thousand with the addition of north and south end zone bleachers. Dialogue about an appropriate name for the stadium stretched over twenty years. An effort to name the facility Jack Trice Stadium for the fallen ISU student-athlete first made headway when the Iowa Board of Regents voted in 1984 to name the field within Cyclone Stadium Jack Trice Field. This did not fully appease those working on memorializing Trice's name. In February 1997, the Board of Regents approved a university request, changing the name of the stadium to Jack Trice Stadium. The stadium remains one of the newest and most modern in the NCAA and its location is unique for the thousands of parking spaces adjacent to the facility.

Led by Dexter Green, Iowa State's diminutive but driven sophomore tailback, 1976 was a season to remember. The Cyclones headed into the last home game of the season, against Nebraska, with a 7-1-1 record. With Nebraska having scored to close within 17–13, Iowa State's Luther Blue took the ensuing kickoff and returned it ninety-five yards for a touchdown and a 24–13 lead. The Iowa State defense took over from there as the Cyclones beat the Cornhuskers, 37–28. ISU was ranked fourteenth nationally the following week. A 42–21 loss at No. 16 Oklahoma State the last week of the season cost Iowa State a bowl bid. Despite the snub, Bruce would say that his bicentennial team was the best of his trio of eight-win units. Green, a sophomore, rushed for 1,074 yards. ISU had a strong defense as well. Safety Tony Hawkins was an all–Big Eight selection. Brothers Mike and Maynard Stensrud and fellow lineman Tom Randall lifted Iowa State's level of play. The Stensrud and Randall names would figure large in Bruce's accomplishments in a stretch of twenty-four wins in three seasons.

Despite their 1976 accomplishments, the Cyclones were picked to finish sixth in the Big Eight before the 1977 season. Iowa State won three of its four nonconference games, although the defeat at Iowa in the first meeting between the two schools in forty-three years truly stung. But once fans had their first taste of the Iowa State–Iowa game, there was no going back, and the series continued. Iowa State went on to post eight wins and earn a Peach Bowl bid. More than twelve thousand ISU fans traveled to Atlanta to see North Carolina State beat ISU, 24–14. The following season, Earle Bruce's squad rebounded from a 0-3 conference start to win eight games. The Cyclones were again bowl-bound, losing 28–12 to Texas A&M in the Hall of Fame Bowl. Bruce confirmed after the game that he would take the head coaching position at Ohio State, his alma mater.

The Iowa State football program underwent several highs and lows after Bruce departed for Ohio State. Head coach Donnie Duncan's tenure (1979–1982) at ISU produced three straight wins over Iowa, including a 23–12 victory in 1981, Iowa's first trip to Ames since the 1934 game. Jim Criner (1983–1986) followed. Criner resigned late in the 1986 season. The Jim Walden era (1987–1994) was marked by several high points despite a smaller squad hurt by NCAA penalties before Walden's arrival. The biggest moment came on November 14, 1992, when Iowa State fourth-string quarterback Marv Seiler keyed the biggest upset in Cyclone history, a 19–10 win over seventh-rated Nebraska. The Huskers had ripped Kansas and Colorado on consecutive weeks before heading to Ames. Seiler rushed for 144 yards, including a 78-yard fourth-quarter run that set up Iowa State's only touchdown. The game marked the only time in the coaching career of Nebraska's Tom Osborne that the Husker coach lost a game to a team that finished its season below .500 (4-7). The Cyclones beat No. 18 Kansas State in Ames in 1993. But Iowa State was 0-10-1 in 1994, setting the stage for a dramatic turnaround in ISU football fortunes.

On November 23, 1994, ISU athletics director Gene Smith introduced Wisconsin defensive coordinator Dan McCarney as the new head football coach at Iowa State. "We will bring back respect, we're going to bring back winning, we're going to bring back fun; we are going to turn [Jack Trice] Stadium into one of the most exciting places to play in college football," McCarney said at his first press conference.

You couldn't blame people for being skeptical; Iowa State hadn't had a winning season in nine years and hadn't gone to a bowl game in sixteen seasons. Progress was slow early. Iowa State was 13-42 in McCarney's first five seasons. A pair of brothers from Miami, Florida, Troy and Darren Davis, highlighted McCarney's first years. Troy was a first-team All-American and became the fifth rusher in collegiate history to eclipse the 2,000-yard barrier, finishing 1995 with 2,010 yards. He earned his trip to New York's Downtown Athletic Club and was fifth in the

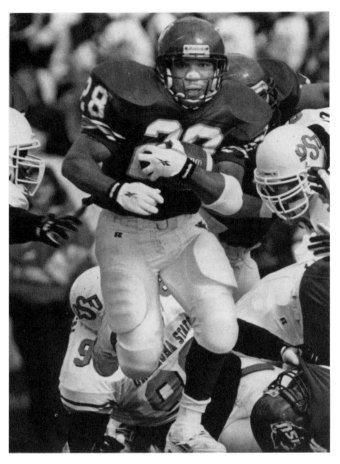

*Iowa State's Troy Davis was the first collegiate player to rush for more than 2,000 yards in two seasons. The Miami, Florida, native rushed for 2,010 yards in 1995 and finished fifth in Heisman Trophy balloting. As an All-American tailback, he rushed for 2,185 yards as a 1996 senior, finishing second in the Heisman Trophy race to Florida's Danny Wuerffel. (Photo courtesy of Iowa State Athletic Media Relations)*

Heisman voting. Troy was at it again in 1996, leading the nation in rushing, including an incredible 378 yards on forty-one carries with four touchdowns in a 45–31 win over Missouri in Ames. By season's end, Troy had rushed for 2,185 yards on twenty-one touchdowns. Iowa State was 2-9 in 1996, but Troy finished second to Florida's Danny Wuerffel in the Heisman voting, the highest showing ever by a Cyclone.

If one game could be used as the turning point in the McCarney area, it would be September 12, 1998. Iowa State traveled to Iowa City to face a heavily favored Iowa. The Cyclones had lost fifteen straight times to their intrastate rival. ISU had not won a road game in seven years. That all changed on a beautiful day in Kinnick Stadium. Darren Davis ran for 244 yards on thirty-seven carries and the ISU defense allowed just three first downs by rush in a convincing 27–9 Iowa State win.

McCarney's 2000 team affirmed Smith's decision to stick with his head coach by posting a 9-3 record, including a 37–29 win over Pittsburgh in the Insight.com Bowl, ISU's first-ever bowl victory. Quarterback Sage Rosenfels developed into one of the nation's best quarterbacks and with tailback Ennis Haywood and defensive linemen Reggie Hayward and James Reed, the Cyclones posted their most wins since 1906. All four would play in the NFL.

Clyde Williams had started Iowa State's men's basketball program in 1907. There was some initial success but ISC was just 14-62 in the Missouri Valley Conference through a five-year span ending in 1928. The program needed new blood.

For the 1928–1929 season, the Cyclones chose a disciple of pioneer round-ball strategist Dr. Forrest "Phog" Allen to head the Iowa State men's basketball program. That man was Louis Menze. His first team produced the first winning record in seven years. It was the start of consistent success that Iowa State would experience under Menze.

Iowa State's first basketball All-American might not have come to Iowa State if not for a school newspaper ad for basketball tryouts. A six feet four inch prospect from Everly, Waldo Wegner immediately caught Menze's attention. Menze liked what he saw in Wegner and worked diligently to develop his basketball skills. The effort paid off. With Wegner in the post playing every minute of every game after his initial collegiate contest, the Cyclones became one of the Midwest's best teams. In 1935, Wegner led Iowa State to the first of four Big Six titles that the Cyclones would produce under Menze. A record 3,800 fans were shoehorned into the gym to see Iowa State score a 41–33 New Year's Day win over Iowa.

"We played our games in State Gym and the first two years that I played, you could have come in and had plenty of space to sit," Wegner recalled. "It wasn't very big crowds early on, but when we started winning and it looked like there might be a possibility of us being in the upper half of the conference, it started filling in. The last half of the year, they were hanging from the rafters."[5]

The basketball program's rise under Louis Menze continued. The Cyclones won a second Big Six title for their coach during the 1940–1941 season as Iowa State tallied a school-record fifteen wins. Big man Gordon Nicholas and all-star Al Budolfson led a balanced attack that featured four players who averaged over seven points per game.

In 1943–1944, Menze again had a team poised to make a run at the league title and maybe more. The Cyclones blitzed their opponents during the season, finishing 13-3 overall and 9-1 in the Big Six. Of ten players on the roster, eight were naval trainees while two were civilians. The team was led by twenty-three-year-old Price Brookfield, a Navy V-5 aviation cadet who had previously earned All-American honors in his senior season at West Texas State. But there was a catch. The Navy had a rule for all of its trainees stating that a naval cadet could not be away from his base for longer than forty-eight hours. This was key. Iowa State was extended a bid to the NCAA Tournament, which was just six years old and in direct competition with the National Invitational Tournament (NIT). Iowa State initially rejected a place in the tournament. Brookfield was due to be shipped for further training as early as Friday, March 10. But a backlash from the team and the student body made the athletic council reverse its decision. The Navy gave some assurance that the cadet could travel to play Pepperdine in Kansas City in the tournament's first round. The school expected that if Iowa State won both its Kansas City games, the whole team would be eligible to travel to New York for the NCAA championship game.

Iowa State beat Pepperdine, 44–39, holding the Waves to a season-low point total. The Cyclones then dueled Utah, which, having lost in the NIT, accepted an NCAA bid. Utah beat ISU 40–31. As a sidelight to the game, the Navy had told Iowa State officials the morning of the Utah contest that the Cyclone cadets would not be allowed to go to New York for the championship game. Officials at both schools were then notified that, win or lose, Utah would advance to the Big Apple. "Naturally our players were disappointed at the turn of events, and so were we," Veenker said. "However, Navy rules are rules and although we want to see the NCAA Tournament continued it is no importance in comparison with the job that confronts the Navy and everybody else."[6] Despite the tournament ups and downs, Iowa State's 1944 team had made history, advancing to what is now known as the Final Four.

Iowa State basketball struggled in the early 1950s. Enter Bill Strannigan. Hired from Colorado State, Strannigan was a personable individual who immediately demonstrated his basketball-coaching prowess, leading ISU to its first winning season in seven years with an 11-10 record for the 1954–1955 season. The Cyclones were led by junior Chuck Duncan and a sophomore guard named Gary Thompson, who would become the leader of Strannigan's hard-nosed teams for the next two seasons. ISU became one of the biggest surprises of the 1955–1956 collegiate campaign. Thompson earned first-team all-conference honors as the Cyclones broke the school record for wins in a season (18-5) and finished tied for second (8-4) in the Big Seven, one game behind Kansas State. The string of successes included victory at No. 8 Vanderbilt and three wins in Kansas City to win the Big Seven Holiday Tournament. It marked Iowa State's first conference tournament crown and helped propel the Cyclones into the national spotlight. Iowa State appeared in the national rankings for the first time in school history and was ranked No. 19 in the nation in the final International News Service poll.

With virtually all his top players returning, expectations were riding high in Strannigan's third season (1956–1957). Thompson was heralded as one of the best players in all of college basketball and junior forward John Crawford was returning after an outstanding sophomore season in which he averaged 13.5 points and 9.7 rebounds. Crawford was the first African American basketball player in Iowa State history and joined the Cyclone squad because of Strannigan. ISU jumped out to a 7-0 record and a No. 14 national ranking before losing its first game of the season on a last-second shot (58–57) to Wilt Chamberlain and his top-ranked Kansas squad in the first round of the Big Seven Holiday Tournament. With the loss to KU behind them, the Cyclones vowed revenge against the Jayhawks when they arrived in Ames on January 14. In arguably the greatest victory in ISU basketball regular season history, the Cyclones defeated No. 1 Kansas 39–37 on a last-

*Gary Thompson's Iowa State legacy spanned a half century. An All-American basketball player, he scored 1,253 points from 1954 to 1957. His on-court success preceded a long career as basketball color commentator on national, regional, and Iowa State network television. (Photo courtesy of Iowa State Athletic Media Relations)*

second shot from Don Medsker, as Thompson outscored Chamberlain 20–19. The Cyclones registered what remains the only Iowa State win against a team ranked No. 1 in the Associated Press poll.

The win helped ISU achieve its highest ranking in school history (No. 3) and put the Cyclone basketball program in the national spotlight. Iowa State ended the season at 16-7 and finished third in the Big Seven (6-6), as Thompson earned first-team All-American honors and Big Seven Player of the Year accolades after averaging 20.7 points per game. Strannigan was picked to coach the West team in the East-West Shrine All-Star Game at the conclusion of the 1957 season, where his star pupil Thompson helped his West squad come away with a 64–60 victory.

Strannigan's fourth year (1957–1958) with ISU was yet another outstanding season for the Cyclones, as attendance records and sellout crowds were the norm in the Armory. Crawford paced ISU with 14.1 points per game average, as the Cyclones finished 16-7 overall and 8-4 in the Big Seven, tying for second place for the second time in three seasons. ISU was once again ranked in the top twenty during the season, marking the third straight year under Strannigan's watch where the Cyclones achieved top-twenty status. Crawford was named first-team all–Big Seven for his performance in 1958.

Strannigan had been courted by a number of top schools for his coaching services throughout his five years in Ames, turning all of them down and honoring his commitment to the Cyclone program. However, after the 1959 season ended, an offer from his alma mater, Wyoming , was too powerful to resist, and Strannigan packed his bags and moved to Laramie. Strannigan's three-year run at ISC from 1956–1958 still ranks as one of the greatest periods in the history of Cyclone basketball, with Iowa State amassing a 50-19 overall mark, a 22-14 Big Seven record, and finishing second, third, and second in the tough Big Seven Conference. The first two Big Eight basketball players to score more than six hundred points in more than one season were the legendary Wilt Chamberlain and a 6-8 Iowa State post player from Brooklyn, New York, named Don Smith. Smith, the 1966 Big Eight Conference Newcomer of the Year was the league's player of the year in 1968.

By graduation, Smith had broken nearly every major Iowa State school record including points and rebounds in a game, season, and career. The Cyclones finished third in the Big Eight in Smith's senior season, which preceded a ten-year NBA career.

Iowa State basketball struggled after the Strannigan years. ISU then looked just twenty-eight miles to the south, to Drake, where its basketball coach, Maury John, had led the Bulldogs to four Missouri Valley Conference titles and three NCAA Tournament appearances. John was made an offer he couldn't refuse to take over the basketball program in Ames. The two years previous to his arrival at Iowa State in 1971, Iowa State posted a 17-35 record. John hit the ground running. In his second season, the 1972–1973 Cyclones won sixteen games and posted a 7-7 Big Eight record. Early in the 1973–1974 season, John was told he had inoperable cancer. One of six coaches in Iowa State history to post a winning career record, he died on October 15, 1974, at the age of fifty-five. His brief tenure demonstrated there was new potential for basketball success in Ames.

In 1980, after the resignation of head men's basketball coach Lynn Nance, Iowa State athletics director Lou McCullough began a national search for a replacement. McCullough brought ten coaches to Ames for interviews. He leaned on several individuals for advice. One was Michigan head coach Johnny Orr. The Wolverine coach was a national figure in college basketball. A two-time National Coach of the Year, Orr led his team to Big Ten titles in 1974 and 1977. His 1976 team made the NCAA Championship final. In mid-March, Orr came to Ames in a bid to help Iowa State find a new coach. He ended up taking the job himself.

Thus began a remarkable chapter in Iowa State history. Orr's first three teams had losing records as he steadily built his program. It didn't matter. Attendance continued to climb as Orr's gregarious personality and blunt humor made him an Iowa favorite. His entrance onto the Hilton Coliseum court, made to the "Here's Johnny" theme of the *Tonight Show Starring Johnny Carson*, was a national basketball staple. A favorite moment of his grand entrance was the reaction of the opposing coaches, who could only dream of such fan devotion. His contacts helped bring players like Barry Stevens and Jeff Grayer from Flint, Michigan, to Ames.

The Cyclones made the NIT in 1984. In 1985, with Stevens and Grayer, who would finish their careers as the top two scorers in school history, Iowa State received its first NCAA Tournament bid in forty-one years. In the season before Orr's arrival, an average of 6,470 fans attended each Iowa State basketball home game. By the 1985–1986 season, Hilton Coliseum was sold out for all of ISU's thirteen home games—all won by the Cyclones. Among the catalysts in Orr's program was point guard Jeff Hornacek. Recruited without a scholarship, Hornacek blossomed into one of the premier point guards in collegiate basketball. Hornacek, who had gone from working at the Dixie Paper Cup Company near his LaGrange, Illinois, home to the all-time Big Eight Conference career assist leader, combined with Grayer, center Sam Hill, and Gary Thompkins to boast a record of 20-10 heading into the NCAA Tournament in Minneapolis. In the opening game against Miami of Ohio, Hornacek hit a twenty-five-foot shot with two seconds left in overtime for an 81–79 ISU victory. Iowa State would then face its coach's former team, the Big Ten champion Michigan Wolverines. Michigan, coached by former Orr assistant Bill Frieder, was ranked fifth nationally with a 28-4 record. Iowa State outquicked the Wolverines, who had no answer for swingman Ronnie Virgil's seven-of-eight effort from the field. Iowa State led most of the game, but the score closed to 64–63 with 1:19 left. Then Hornacek hit a streaking Elmer Robinson for a dunk and a monumental win in Iowa State men's basketball history, the biggest of Orr's Cyclone career. Iowa State lost to North Carolina State in the Sweet Sixteen game in Kansas City, Missouri, but the Cyclones were now a program of national caliber. The man who had amazed basketball experts by taking the head coaching job at Iowa State could now say "I told you so."

Orr went on to coach Iowa State to NCAA Tournament bids in 1988, 1989, 1992, and 1993. His legacy, however, can't be measured by his school-record 218 victories. Orr's persona was even bigger than his basketball coaching achievements and he put Iowa State athletics on the national map.

Iowa State surges in basketball, as well as in wrestling and gymnastics, were aided by the addition of an exceptional new arena, as the fourteen-thousand-seat James H. Hilton Coliseum opened in 1971. Hilton Coliseum was a part of the massive Iowa State Center project. It proved to be an ideal collegiate sports facility that gave ISU teams a decided home court advantage. Under head coach Johnny Orr, the Hilton mystique earned the moniker "Hilton Magic." Hilton's acoustics fostered deafening noise. ISU basketball fans each have their opinion of what was the loudest night in Hilton. Some would say the February 15, 1992, game when the Cyclones erased an eighteen-point halftime deficit and a ten-point margin with 6:09 remaining to beat No. 2 Oklahoma State, 84–83, in overtime. Justus Thigpen helped the Cyclones close a seven-point deficit with 1:49 left in overtime with three straight three-pointers. OSU's Darwyn Alexander was fouled with two seconds remaining and had two shots to win the game, but missed both attempts as players from both teams felt the court shake. Lafester Rhodes's fifty-four-point effort to beat No. 7 Iowa on December 19, 1987; Fred Hoiberg's seventeen straight second-half points to upend No. 3 Kansas, 69–65, on January 14, 1995; and Texas' Mike Boddicker missing two free throws in the final seconds to preserve a 78–77 ISU win over the eleventh-rated Longhorns on February 14, 2004, all qualify as undisputedly deafening moments.

*Ames native Fred Hoiberg was dubbed "the Mayor" by fans and teammates, af-
firming his status as a hugely popular All-American basketball player. He finished
his career with 1,993 points. Hoiberg's four-year Iowa State career (1991–1995)
included three NCAA Tournament berths and three wins in four years over rival
Iowa. He then went on to a ten-year NBA career with Indiana, Chicago, and
Minnesota. (Photo courtesy of Iowa State Athletic Media Relations)*

Following Orr's retirement, the national standing of the Cyclone men's basketball program was sustained by a coach from New Orleans University who had wavered before accepting the ISU head coaching job. His name was Tim Floyd, and
his teams etched their own standard of excellence.

Floyd's first team featuring forward Fred Hoiberg, center Loren Meyer, and forward Julius Michalik was ranked most of the 1994–1995 season, compiling a 23-
11 record and making the second round of the NCAA Tournament. Hoiberg,
dubbed "the Mayor" by his teammates because of his popularity in his hometown
of Ames, finished his career as Iowa State's No. 3 all-time leading scorer with 1,993
points. His most memorable game came that season against No. 3 Kansas. Hoiberg
scored seventeen straight points en route to a thirty-two-point effort as Iowa State
upset the Jayhawks, 69–65, before a wild, sold-out Hilton Coliseum.

Floyd's greatest coaching job would be the 1995–1996 team. With the departure
of Hoiberg and several fellow seniors, Iowa State was picked for last in what would
be the final Big Eight Conference basketball season. The Cyclones, featuring new-

comers including guard Dedric Willoughby, forwards Kenny Pratt and Shawn Bankhead, center Kelvin Cato, and holdover point guard Jacy Holloway, surprised everyone with a 24-9 record and 9-5 Big Eight Conference mark. The season included a 56–55 win over No. 5 Kansas in Kansas City, Missouri, for the championship of the last Big Eight Men's Basketball Tournament. With his starting lineup returning for the 1996–1997 season, Floyd's Cyclones were 22-9. NCAA Tournament wins over Illinois State and Cincinnati put ISU into the Sweet Sixteen, where Floyd's team lost on a last-second overtime shot against UCLA.

In 1994, Big Eight Conference presidents invited four teams from the former Southwest Conference—Texas, Texas Tech, Texas A&M, and Baylor—to join with the Big Eight schools to form a new conference, the Big 12. The new league was in a better television revenue bargaining position than either of the former conferences. It was a double-edged sword. Iowa State athletics would benefit from additional television and other conference revenue. It also raised the stakes for ISU coaches, who now had to contend with additional top-notch competition. When Floyd left Iowa State for the head coaching job of the Chicago Bulls, ISU athletics director Gene Smith chose Larry Eustachy of Utah State to head the ISU men's basketball program.

If ever selecting a zenith moment in Iowa State athletics history, it would be hard not to focus on March 2000, which included the thrilling end of Eustachy's second season. Several Cyclone programs were peaking at the right time. The Iowa State men's basketball team, picked by one preseason magazine to finish last in the Big 12, was a national story under eventual AP National Coach of the Year Larry Eustachy. The Cyclones meshed as a team. Marcus Fizer, a junior from Arcadia, Louisiana, was wreaking havoc on opponents with his strength in the post, leading the team and the Big 12 in scoring with a 22.8 points per game average by season's end. Point guard Jamaal Tinsley would break Jeff Hornacek's ISU single-season marks for assists and steals. Off-guard Kantrail Horton was the heart and soul of the Cyclone defense, making sure the top scorer on the opposing team was working for every shot. Senior Mike Nurse thrived at off guard and forward Stevie Johnson was Mr. Automatic, hitting on 66 percent of his shots.

The team raced through the Big 12 season with a 14-2 league record. In the Big 12 Tournament in Kansas City, Missouri, ISU beat Baylor, Oklahoma State, and Oklahoma in Kemper Arena, called "Hilton South" by many fans because of the decidedly pro-Cyclone crowd made up of fans from across the country. The NCAA made Iowa State the No. 2 seed in the Midwest Region, the school's highest-ever seed. Iowa State beat Central Connecticut (88–78) in the Metrodome ("Hilton North" with thousands of Cyclone fans migrating to the facility in Minneapolis, Minnesota). Iowa State beat Auburn 79–60 in the second round. Then it was on to Auburn Hills, Michigan, for a "Sweet Sixteen" battle against UCLA, which had routed Maryland in its previous game. ISU had lost to the Bruins in three previous NCAA Tournament games. But Iowa State put history behind it, whipping UCLA, 80–56—a landmark win in school history. Fizer, Johnson, Nurse, and Tinsley each scored fourteen points. The biggest challenge was next. Top-seeded Michigan State would face Iowa State just forty minutes from its East Lansing, Michigan, campus. It was a great game. Iowa State led 59–52 with 5:15 left. The Spartans pulled within 61–60 with less than four minutes remaining. A controversial charging foul on Paul Shirley that took a basket away and gave the center his fifth foul was the turning point. Michigan State went on to win, 75–64. It would be difficult not to call the 1999–2000 Cyclones the best team in school history. A school-record thirty-two wins, a No. 3 national ranking in the final coaches poll, and Big 12 regular-season and tournament championships make for memories that will last Iowa State fans a lifetime.

At the same time that March, head coach Bill Fennelly's women's basketball squad was playing like his best team. The night before the Iowa State men beat Oklahoma in Kemper Arena for the 2000 Big 12 Tournament title, the ISU women rocked Municipal Auditorium in a tournament-clinching win over Texas. Cyclone women's NCAA victories in Hilton Coliseum over St. Francis (92–63) and then Florida State (85–70) followed. The ISU men's basketball team was boarding its charter jet for a quiet ride home hours after losing to Michigan State when word reached the plane that the Cyclone women had fallen in their Sweet Sixteen game of NCAA Tournament, losing to Penn State 66–65. The month had begun with huge March 1 road wins, for the men at Texas Tech (87–79) and the women at Texas (72–65). The ensuing twenty-four days were like no other time in Iowa State sports history.

If the world's oldest sport is wrestling, then Iowa was a cradle for its competitive rise in North America. It should be no surprise that Iowa State's first wrestling coach, Charlie Mayser, posted a 36-3 record, including a string of twenty-two straight victories. Facilities were simple. The team would work out on mats at the far ends of State Gym's basketball court. The sport was hugely popular on campus. Students camped out a day in advance to be the first allowed onto the bleachers. Every meet in 1921 drew at least 3,000 fans, and 4,500 fans watched the Cyclones against Penn State.

Mayser's assistant coach and legacy, Hugo Otopalik, was head coach at Iowa State from 1924 until 1953. Otopalik expanded Iowa State's wrestling stature, organizing the AAU Wrestling Championships in 1927. A year later, under his leadership, Iowa State played host to the first NCAA Wrestling Championships. Otopalik was also the head coach of the 1932 U.S. Olympic team. He would coach Glen Brand, the first of five Iowa State Olympic wrestling gold medalists.

In August of 1953 a strong-minded coach arrived on the Iowa State campus to take over leadership of the ISC wrestling program. He was a native of Cresco, Iowa, and had come to Iowa State from Arkansas State, where he had served as wrestling coach, assistant football coach, assistant basketball coach, head swimming coach, head track coach, head trainer, and intramural director. His name was Dr. Harold Nichols. Nichols would literally change the concept of coaching the sport, teaching all-out wrestling with the full intention of pinning the opponent if possible. Relentless attack, he believed, would eventually wear down even the most talented competitor. His impact locally was immediate. His impact nationally started to show itself in 1957 with a third-place NCAA finish. The Cyclones were second in 1958 as Ron Gray (147) and Les Anderson (130) won Nichols's first individual na-

*Dan Gable's achievements truly transcended his sport. The 1972 Munich Olympic Games gold medalist wrestled to a 118-1 collegiate career record and a pair of NCAA titles under coach Dr. Harold Nichols. (Photo courtesy of Iowa State Athletic Media Relations)*

tional titles. Led by, among others, three-time NCAA champion Larry Hayes, the Cyclones posted four national championship runner-up finishes and two third-place efforts. For Nichols, being on the victory stand while Oklahoma State or Oklahoma stood on the top of the championship platform was not enough.

It all came together in an unlikely way in Laramie, Wyoming, on March 26, 1965. Figured out of the running for the team title after a disappointing semifinal round, the Cyclones roared back in the consolation matches, winning several head-to-head duals against Oklahoma State competitors. Veryl Long (147) and Tom Peckham (177) both won NCAA championships as Iowa State won its first NCAA national team title since 1933. ISU won NCAA team titles in 1969, 1970, 1972, and 1973. Featuring multiple NCAA champions like Jason Smith (1969–1970), Chuck Jean (1969–1970), Carl Adams (1971–1972), and Ben Peterson (1971–1972), the Iowa State wrestling program had established itself, not just in the U.S. collegiate wrestling ranks, but internationally. If Nichols altered the philosophy of collegiate wrestling, a young man from Waterloo, Iowa, would be the vessel of change that would stifle any doubters and transcend the sport as a competitor and coach for two generations of fans, wrestlers, and coaches. His name was Dan Gable.

Iowa State captured its second consecutive NCAA title at Northwestern University in 1970 after claiming the school's first Big Eight title since 1957. Three Cyclones won individual crowns, but Gable was not one of them. Heading into the championship match at 142 pounds, Gable's high school and collegiate record was a combined 181-0. But Gable ran into Washington's Larry Owings, who pulled off one of the greatest upsets in college sport, winning the match 13–11. Gable's collegiate career was over, but he had only started building an unequalled legacy. Iowa State won another NCAA title in 1972. Carl Adams (158), Ben Peterson (190), and 440-pound heavyweight Chris Taylor won individual titles. Peterson and Gable won Olympic gold medals at the 1972 Munich games and Taylor won a bronze after a controversial semifinal loss. Iowa State wrestling had reached the mountaintop of collegiate and international competition. In 1977, Nichols won his final NCAA crown, led by 190-pound champion Frank Santana.

In the spring of 1985 Harold Nichols announced his retirement. After coaching six NCAA title teams, seven Big Eight championship teams, thirty-eight NCAA individual champions, and ninety-one Big Eight titlists, he was ready to step aside. Under Nichols, the Cyclones added eleven NCAA second-place trophies and eight NCAA team third-place awards. His career dual meet mark at Iowa State is an untouchable 456-75-11.

Under young former ISU national champion Jim Gibbons, the 1985–1986 team had an auspicious 19-1 dual season. Gibbons's young team jelled in 1987. A 23–12 win over Iowa marked the first back-to-back victories by the Cyclones over the Hawkeyes since the 1937–1938 seasons. ISU tied for the Big Eight championship and was dominant at the NCAA meet, compiling a 36-7 record in the tournament. Billy Kelly (126), Tim Krieger (150), Stewart Carter (158), and Eric Voelker (190) won individual titles en route to the school's first NCAA team crown in a decade.

In 1992, Iowa State athletics director Max Urick named Arizona State head coach Bobby Douglas as head coach to replace Gibbons. Douglas, another wrestling legend, led Iowa State to NCAA runner-up finishes in 1996 and 2000. In 2000, the seven-time Olympic coach, who helped Cyclone Kevin Jackson win a freestyle gold medal in 1992 in Barcelona, Spain, as U.S. head freestyle coach, was named national collegiate Coach of the Year. Sophomore Cael Sanderson led ISU with his second NCAA 184-pound title. Sanderson's brother Cody was second at 133 pounds; Joe Heskett (165) and Zach Thompson (197) also placed second and Trent Hynek (HWT) placed third. Sanderson would go on to finish his career as the only undefeated (159-0), four-time NCAA champion in collegiate history. A 2004 Athens Olympic gold medalist, he would eventually replace his coach as the leader of the ISU wrestling program.

On June 23, 1972, U.S. President Richard Nixon signed Title IX. The law would have enormous impact upon girls and women who dreamed of competing for their schools in athletic competition. Women were already competing at Iowa State University, though on a different plane than their male counterparts.

The Iowa State women's physical education department organized the Women's Intercollegiate Sports Association in 1968. The program initially offered five sports

*Cael Sanderson won a freestyle wrestling gold medal at the 2004 Athens Olympic Games. That achievement capped a competitive career in which the Heber City, Utah, native became the first undefeated (159-0) four-time champion in NCAA history. Sanderson would go on to be named the sixth Iowa State head coach since the program began in 1916. (Photo courtesy of Iowa State Athletic Media Relations)*

including fencing, field hockey, gymnastics, tennis, and volleyball. Sixty-four women participated the first year on a budget of $1,148.56. The softball team qualified for the 1971 College World Series after playing just two games. Under head coach Pat Noe, Iowa State finished second. There was steady growth and in 1971 the Association of Intercollegiate Athletics for Women (AIAW) formed to regulate collegiate competition for 280 charter schools. ISU success was almost immediate. There would be steady progress through July 1, 1979, when Iowa State women's intercollegiate athletics was incorporated into the Cyclone Athletic Department. This merger was a giant step in upgrading competitive collegiate opportunities for women at ISU.

The Cyclones had a run of titles claimed by the Cyclone women's cross-country and track programs in the late 1970s. The coach responsible for Iowa State's rise in prominence was Chris Murray. Under his direction, Iowa State won the first four AIAW national cross-country titles, also sweeping the Big Eight Conference championships. Murray, a former Canadian Olympian, would guide fifteen athletes to All-America honors. Among his pupils were native Iowans Debbie Esser and Peggy

*Morocco's Nawal El Moutawakel (far right) came to Iowa State as a relative un-
known. Just twenty months later the 1984 NCAA four-hundred-meter hurdles
champion became the first Muslim woman and first Arabic woman to win a gold
medal at the Olympic Games, taking first place in the four-hundred-meter hurdle
event at the 1984 Los Angeles games. Here she acknowledges the cheers of Iowa
State fans after being honored for her Olympic success with (left to right) fellow
1984 Cyclone Olympians Moses Kiyai (Kenya, jumps), silver medalist Sunday Uti
(Kenya, four by four-hundred-meter relay), and U.S. silver medalist Danny Harris
(four-hundred-meter hurdles). (Photo courtesy of Iowa State Athletic Media
Relations)*

Neppel. Esser was the first athlete in AIAW history to capture four consecutive titles in one event, the four-hundred-meter hurdles. Neppel led Iowa State to the
team title at the first AIAW national cross-country meet as the inaugural individual
champion. She would run on three more national champion teams.

Iowa State's women's cross-country team continued to thrive after Ron Renko
succeeded Chris Murray in 1979 and kept the Iowa State women's cross-country
and track and field programs among the best. Renko coached twenty All-
Americans and fourteen individual Big Eight Conference champions and led the
Cyclones to two Big Eight cross-country titles and one AIAW national championship during his tenure. In just his second season as women's track and field and
cross-country coach (1981), the Cyclones captured the Big Eight title and national
championship (AIAW) in cross country. ISU's Dorthe Rasmussen won the individual titles at both the Big Eight and AIAW meets, becoming just the second Cyclone
in school history to win an individual cross-country national title. One of Renko's
top all-time performers was Nawal El Moutawakel. Renko and his staff brought in

El Moutawakel in 1982 from Casablanca, Morocco. The hurdler had one of the greatest seasons ever for an ISU athlete in 1984, winning the NCAA four-hundred-meter hurdles title and earning All-America honors in the four-hundred-meter dash by placing fourth. She followed her outstanding NCAA performance by winning the gold medal at the 1984 Olympics in Los Angeles.

The 1985 Iowa State cross-country team was an unknown unit. ISU failed to make the national meet for the first time in its ten-year history in 1984 and the Cyclones still had a relatively young team. Renko shocked the cross-country world by rallying the Cyclones to one of their most successful seasons. ISU finished first or second in all nine meets during the season, led by freshman Jill Slettedahl and junior Bonnie Sons. The duo finished seventh and eighth, respectively, to help the Cyclones place second at the Big Eight Championship and the pair placed fifth and seventh, respectively, to pace ISU to the NCAA District V title.

Prior to the 1985 NCAA cross-country meet, Renko was extremely proud of his NCAA District V championship team but recognized the top talent that his ISU squad would face at the NCAA championship on November 25 in Milwaukee, Wisconsin. Renko still hoped for a sixth-place finish, if everything came together. ISU exceeded all expectations, with the Cyclones finishing runner-up at the NCAA meet. Bonnie Sons and Jill Slettedahl were named All-Americans, finishing twenty-fifth and twenty-ninth, but ISU received outstanding performances from all its runners. Sue Baxter, a freshman from Brentwood, England, finished thirty-second; Julie Rose, a junior from Ashford, England, placed forty-second; Sheryl Maahs, a junior from Spirit Lake, Iowa, placed forty-fifth; and Tami Colby, a freshman from Boone, finished forty-eighth.

Iowa State and Renko were ecstatic with their finish as the team members boarded three Iowa State University–owned planes to take them back to Ames. Poor weather in the central Iowa area that Monday evening forced the planes to land in Des Moines rather than Ames. One of the planes, which carried Renko, assistant coach Pat Moynihan, Baxter, Rose, Maahs, student trainer Stephanie Streit, and pilot Burton Watkins, developed problems as it was preparing to land in Des Moines. The plane crashed in icy conditions in a neighborhood two miles from downtown Des Moines, killing all on board.

The tragic loss of lives stunned the Iowa State community. ISU President Robert Parks ordered that campus flags, including the flag of Great Britain (Baxter and Rose's native country), be flown at half-mast the following Tuesday, and scholarship funds were established to honor the victims. On December 4, 1985, more than 5,500 people attended a memorial service at Hilton Coliseum to honor Renko and the crash victims. ISU dedicated a plaque for permanent display at the Iowa State Cross Country Course to honor Renko and the crash victims for their dedication to Iowa State University.

Iowa State launched its women's basketball program in the 1973–1974 academic year. The team practiced four days a week for ninety minutes. The program had a budget of $1,059.79. The team stayed at a motel only once. To save money, the volleyball and basketball teams used the same uniforms.

The program continued to develop under coach Lynn Wheeler. The Cyclones were 20-8 during the 1975–1976 campaign. On December 1, 1976, ISU beat Drake, 71–65, in the first women's basketball game to be played in Hilton Coliseum. Wheeler faced major challenges running the program. She taught four classes in the physical education department. AIAW rules specified that coaches could not contact high school student-athletes. A coach had to wait until a potential recruit contacted him or her. Among Wheeler's best players was Pat Hodgson. The Glenwood, Iowa, native was the first one-thousand-career-point scorer in school history. A two-time All-American in track and field, she was the first Iowa State player to compete professionally.

In 1984, Iowa State hired former Miami of Ohio coach Pam Wettig to head the women's basketball program. The program had won just four games the year before she arrived, but Wettig won twelve games in her first Cyclone season. In the 1985–1986 campaign, Iowa State went 19-9 and Wettig was named Big Eight Coach of the Year. The sparkplugs of the team were point guard Jane Lobenstein, who earned first-team all-conference honors, and post player Stephannie Smith, who averaged 17.2 points per game. Wettig also coached Iowa State's best player of the decade, Tonya Burns. A six feet one center from Leo, Indiana, Burns owned or shared thirty-three Cyclone records at her career's end. Her No. 42 was retired following her senior season. A three-time all–Big Eight selection, she tallied 1,789 career points and set a Cyclone record with 42 points against Nebraska in 1984.

Iowa State's women's basketball team struggled into the 1990s. The Cyclones were seventh once and last in the Big Eight Conference three times during the four-year stretch.

In 1995, Iowa State athletics director Gene Smith hired Davenport native Bill Fennelly to coach the ISU women's basketball program. The William Penn graduate had turned the Toledo women's basketball program into a winner. Fennelly won his first Iowa State game, 82–55, over Idaho. A grand total of 653 people watched. If they only could have imagined what would happen next. Picked to finish last in the Big Eight, the 1995–1996 Cyclones went 17-10. Fennelly's second team went 17-12 and earned the first NCAA Tournament berth in history.

The program really took flight in the 1997–1998 season. Led by transfer point guard Stacy Frese and veteran post players Janel Grimm and Jayme Olson, Iowa State roared to a 25-8 record. Among the biggest wins was a 74–57 victory over Iowa. The win over the Hawkeyes marked the first time that fans sat in the balcony of Hilton Coliseum for a women's basketball game. With Grimm (1,449), Olson (1,799), Frese (1,494), and freshman Megan Taylor (1,866), the 1997–1998 Cyclones boasted four players who would finish their careers as one-thousand-point scorers. The Cyclones were no longer a secret. Iowa State drew more than 5,000 fans six times during a season that climaxed with NCAA first- and second-round victory home games that drew 9,221 and 9,705 fans against Kent State and Rutgers, respectively.

With Frese, Taylor, and freshman center Angie Welle the Cyclones were 25-8 in the 1998–1999 season. A Hilton crowd of 12,337 watched Iowa State beat Santa Clara in the first round of the 1999 NCAA Tournament. A second-round win over Oregon drew 11,719. The Cyclones' NCAA Tournament wins in Ames set the

*Jenny Condon's Iowa State career (1987–1990) ranks as one of the best in Cyclone softball history. The outfielder earned All-America honors and still owns single-season school records in hits (77), triples (10), and runs (45). A 1995 Pan American Games gold medalist, Condon is the ISU career leader in hits (216), battling average (.351), triples (24), and runs (120). (Photo courtesy of Iowa State Athletic Media Relations)*

stage for their biggest victory of all. In the Sweet Sixteen round played in Cincinnati, Iowa State beat top-seeded Connecticut, 64–58, to advance to the NCAA Mideast Regional final against Georgia, giving Fennelly his 250th career victory.

Iowa State defeated Texas in the championship of the 2000 Big 12 Conference basketball tournament and advanced to the NCAA Sweet Sixteen for the second straight season with tournament victories over St. Francis and Illinois.

"I had a good friend in coaching tell me when I took [the Iowa State] job that I was committing professional suicide by coming here," Fennelly later said. "[A few years] later he called me to tell me we were ranked ahead of Tennessee and Louisiana Tech."

In 1895, the Iowa Intercollegiate Baseball Association was formed by Iowa State, Drake University, and the State University of Iowa. Iowa State won the initial competition for the $40 Silver Bat Trophy. In the initial season, Iowa State prevailed over Grinnell, 8–5, in the first official game in Iowa State history. Iowa State tied with Grinnell in IBA competition in 1893.[7]

From 1938 to 1974, Iowa State baseball was Cap Timm. His teams earned two berths in the College World Series. In 1957, Iowa State won the Big Seven Conference and made the series for the first time. The team's biggest stars were catcher Dick Bertell and shortstop Gary Thompson. Bertell was a two-time All-American who would later play seven years in the major leagues for the Chicago Cubs and the San Francisco Giants. Gary Thompson was every bit as nifty fielding and hitting the baseball as he was shooting the basketball. The "Roland Rocket" earned baseball and basketball All-America honors, the first such honoree in Iowa State history.

In 1970, Timm's Cyclones won the school's first Big Eight title and qualified for the NCAA College World Series. Iowa State repeated as Big Eight champs in 1971. Figuring large on both teams was Larry Corrigan. The Cyclone was recognized as an All-American as a pitcher with an 8-1 record in 1970. Incredibly, he was the Iowa State catcher in 1971 and again earned All-America honors by hitting .349. Corrigan would return to Ames as the Cyclones' head coach from 1981–1984.

Another two-sport baseball All-American was Mike Busch. At six feet five, 250 pounds, Busch led Iowa State teams that were third in the Big Eight in 1989 and fourth in 1990. He was also an All-American tight end in football. In 1991, ISU tied for third in the Big Eight, led by All-American and Golden Spike finalist Tom Vantiger.

The State Gym pool played host to a proud Iowa State swim program. In the first eleven years of the Big Six Conference, Iowa State won six team titles, shared two others, and posted three runner-up efforts. In 1939, George Haldeman and Roger Adams were the first All-Americans in Big Six history. In 1941, Iowa State turned to Jack McGuire to take over the reins of the Cyclone swim program. In his first year, McGuire's Cyclones won a fifth straight Big Six title. The redheaded graduate of Iowa would lead the Cyclones to nine conference team titles, including his last ISU team in 1977. Among his all-time best were All-Americans Jon Mixdorf, Bob Brown, and Jim McKevitt. McGuire also oversaw the construction of the pool in Beyer Hall, across the street from State Gym. In the new building, ISU hosted the 1965 NCAA championships at the state-of-the-art facility. In the 1980s, Cyclones Scott McAdam and Eric Hansen would streak to All-American status under ISU swim coach Bob Groseth. Under Trip Hedrick Iowa State remained nationally competitive, winning the 1995 Big Eight Conference championship. Hedrick was Big Eight Coach of the Year and the Cyclones placed twentieth at the NCAA meet.

A permanent Iowa State fixture had its birth in 1935. That is when work began in the North Woods bordering the campus. Opening in the spring of 1938, the Iowa State golf course had been constructed by moving tons of soil in what was part cow pasture, part orchard, and part heavy wood. Four thousand trees were cut down and five thousand others planted on the course, which was designed by the legendary golf course architect Perry Maxwell. The facility played host to the 1949 NCAA championship, in which a golfer from Wake Forest named Arnold Palmer was a tournament medalist.

In the late 1930s and early 1940s, the Cyclone golf team was led by the outstanding brother duo of Bill and Max Hall. Billy was conference medalist in 1939 and Max won the Big Six individual crown in 1941. Max was the first Cyclone to qualify for the U.S. Open, competing in the 1949 U.S. Open at the famed Medina Country Club near Chicago. Iowa State won conference titles in men's golf in 1940, 1947, and 1953.

In 1954, a group of students that included Pep Council president Chuck Duncan brainstormed on how to build more school spirit and approached Collegiate Manufacturing of Ames about creating a school mascot. Since the consensus was that one "could not stuff a Cyclone," a bird figure using the school colors (cardinal and gold) was the eventual choice. Duncan and the Pep Council then got the green light from longtime Cyclone Ray Donels, ISU alumni director "Red" Baron, and longtime sports information director Harry Burrell. A cardinal-like bird was introduced at the 1954 Homecoming pep rally. A contest was held to determine the cardinal's name. The entry "Cy" won. Cy is short for Cyclones, and the cardinal figure represents the school colors as well as the original Iowa State nickname. Donels and Burrell were longtime contributors to Iowa State athletics, Burrell serving Iowa State as sports information director from 1941–1978. Donels and former ISU footballer, swimmer, and National Cyclone Club Director Mal Schmidt (1992) both earned honors as Cy's Favorite Alum, recognizing their accomplishments in and loyalty to the advancement of Iowa State athletics.

As the 1950s segued into the 1960s, a former All-American Michigan gymnast, who was the first Canadian to represent that country in his sport in the 1956 Melbourne Olympic Games, sent letters out to every U.S. college that did not have a gymnastics program, looking to build a team from scratch. Iowa State answered that call in 1961 when Ed Gagnier was chosen to start the program. Success was almost immediate. Led by Brent Simmons's 1971 national title efforts in the parallel bars and the high bar, Iowa State won the first of three NCAA team championships. Simmons, who won six Big Eight titles and was a four-time All-American in the Cyclones' initial NCAA title season, won the 1971 Nissen Award as collegiate wrestling's top gymnast. Gagnier also coached one of the greatest athletes in Iowa State history and a member of the ISU Letterwinners Hall of Fame charter class, U.S. Olympian Ron Galimore.

The first true international caliber track star to run in an Iowa State uniform was Ray Conger. Conger won conference titles from 1925–1927. In 1927, he raced to victory in the national collegiate mile. He went on to set a world record in the 1,000-yard run and an American record in the 1,500-meters. The 1928 U.S. Olympic Trials 1,500-meter champion in 4:01.2, he would own a victory over track and field legend Pavel Nurmi.

By the 1980s a driven, savvy head coach was bringing Iowa State's dormant men's cross-country and track programs back to life—and then some. Bill Bergan, a Waterloo, Iowa, native, became Iowa State's head cross-country coach in 1971 after the team had finished in the Big Eight Conference's lower division for eleven straight years. When he became head track coach in 1976, the Cyclones had finished last or next-to-last in the Big Eight Conference outdoor meet for twenty-one straight years. The turnaround would be astounding. After Bergan assumed command, Iowa State won twenty-five conference titles. The cross-country teams won ten Big Eight crowns in fourteen years. Before his arrival in Ames no one could have dared imagine Iowa State boasting the nation's top cross-country program. But it happened, twice.

In 1989, Iowa State won its third straight Big Eight title and went into the NCAA championship at the U.S. Naval Academy in Annapolis, Maryland, as the odds-on favorite to win the team title. They didn't disappoint. John Nuttall and Jonah Koech dashed to a one-two individual finish. Five Cyclones placed among the meet's top twenty-three finishers to give Iowa State an NCAA title. A balanced team effort secured the 1994 NCAA title on a cross-country course in Fayetteville, Arkansas. Part of Iowa State's cross-country legacy is the ISU Cross Country Course, which hosted the 1995 and 2000 NCAA championships as another point of pride in the Iowa State running program.

A full accounting of Bergan's success would bury one in a flurry of numbers. Still, some of those numbers are world class and worth remembering. In addition to world champion Yobes Ondieki, Bergan's pupils included Olympic silver medalist Danny Harris. As an eighteen-year-old freshman, Harris was precocious on the biggest track and field stage. After winning the 1984 NCAA four-hundred-meter crown, the Perris, California, native, who first came to Iowa State to play football and run track, raced to the silver medal at the Los Angeles Olympic Games. He finished second to the legendary Edwin Moses in the final, the same week El Moutawakel claimed gold in the women's four-hundred hurdles.

Iowa State had additional Olympic sports success in the early 1990s, including winning the 1993 Big Eight Conference women's golf championship. Led by Shelley Finnestad, the first women's conference golf medalist in school history, and two-time all–Big 12 selection Beth Bader, the Cyclones were NCAA regional qualifiers from 1993 to 1996.

As the Cyclone basketball programs soared at the end of the twentieth century, Iowa State's women's gymnastics program was on a steady rise through the national ranks under head coach Amy Pyle. Kim Mazza's perfect ten effort at the 1997 Big 12 Championship was a prelude for even greater team success. Led by

All-Americans Betsy Hamm, Kelli More, and tough-as-nails Big 12 champion Sissy Huey, the Cyclones made the 2000 NCAA championship and finished eighth nationally. The program continued its flight under head coach K. J. Kindler.

By 2000, there was no question that athletics was a major fiscal operation at Iowa State. The university's athletics budget had grown steadily to reach $18.1 million for eighteen varsity sports by the turn-of-the-century. Expenses were outrunning revenue. Iowa State had dropped men's tennis and men's gymnastics after the 1994–1995 season. The loss came four years after Glen Wilson had won the 1990 Big Eight Conference men's singles title, the first time a Cyclone had claimed the championship since 1946. In 2001, fiscal issues led to the elimination of baseball and men's swimming from Iowa State's athletics program.

Iowa State athletics in more than one hundred years of competition had spanned the rise of newspapers, radio, television, and the Internet. From the Missouri Valley to Big Six, Big Seven, Big Eight, and Big 12 Conference the constant at Iowa State was that the school was a place where special people could make a difference. Over the years, the achievements of its coaches and student-athletes underscore that fact.

# Vignettes

## George C. Christensen: An Agent for Change

In August 1971, the vice president for academic affairs, George C. Christensen, told the graduating seniors they had lived through a period of tremendous change. He listed numerous examples, including the protests against the war in Vietnam, elimination of women's hours, and controversies with the Government of the Student Body. He concluded that while no one had all of the answers to the new problems confronting society, he was "certain that change is a crucial component of a university's function and responsibility."

Change was a topic very familiar to Christensen, who came to Iowa State in 1953 as an associate professor of veterinary anatomy. Born in New York City in 1924, he attended Cornell University, where, in 1953, he earned a Ph.D. in veterinary medicine.

In 1958, he left his post at Iowa State to become head of veterinary anatomy at Purdue, but returned five years later, in 1963, to become dean of the College of Veterinary Medicine. In 1965, on the same day that Robert Parks began his term as the president of Iowa State, Christensen became the vice president of academic affairs, a job he kept for the next twenty-two years. Then, from 1987 until 1989, he served as the executive director for international affairs.

In that time, Christensen led efforts to recruit more minorities and women, and he was involved with the creation of several new departments, as well as the colleges of Education, Design, and Business. He initiated planning for the present facilities of the College of Veterinary Medicine, and promoted policies such as faculty improvement leaves, foreign travel grants, and a semester system, rather than a quarter system. As the executive director for international affairs, he established several programs for students and faculty to gain new experiences at universities in Europe, the Middle East, China, Taiwan, New Zealand, Africa, and Latin America. Ultimately, he played a crucial role in transforming Iowa State College into Iowa State University.

Christensen's philosophy was one of keeping the university relevant to new trends in education, the workplace, and society as a whole. He often worked from the bottom up, looking to students, faculty, and staff to ask, "Where are we missing the boat? And how can we do better?" In a 1973 commencement address, he spoke of his "zeal for the people-to-people approach," and encouraged the graduating seniors to "give yourselves to others on a person to person basis," to share skills, talents, and experiences.

Throughout his time as vice president for academic affairs, Christensen promoted openness and diversity on campus. He met regularly with members

*(continued)*

211

of the Government of the Student Body and consistently sought student's opinions regarding policy changes. During the late 1970s, when Iowa State adopted the semester system, Christensen worked closely with students on various committees for more than two years in order to carry out a seamless transition away from the old quarter system. Students raised a number of concerns about credits, curriculum, textbooks, and residence hall agreements. The team of students and administrators worked so effectively to resolve these issues that once Iowa State adopted the semester system, representatives from other institutions visited campus to see how it was done.

Though he met many challenges, perhaps one of his greatest was recruiting more women and minorities as faculty, staff, and students. For Christensen, this simply seemed the "right thing to do," if Iowa State were to compete in an increasingly diverse society. Beginning in the 1960s, minorities still struggled to find adequate housing in Ames, and most women served as "tokens" on faculty and student committees. To foster greater diversity, Christensen encouraged departments to look beyond closed networks when looking for new faculty. This meant instituting new hiring practices and advertising outside the university for potential candidates, particularly at African American and female colleges. He also encouraged efforts to recruit more African American students from cities such as Chicago, Detroit, and East St. Louis, as well as in the South.

Throughout the 1970s and 1980s, Christensen also worked closely with the University Committee on Women to address women's concerns, establish the Margaret Sloss Women's Center, and broaden women's educational opportunities. When he first arrived at Iowa State, Christensen noted that women simply did not have a "presence" on campus, and as students, they were relegated to the College of Home Economics. Over time, however, as more women joined the faculty and created programs such as the Program for Women in Science and Engineering (PWSE), he noticed that female students gained mentors and positive role models. And slowly, things began to change.

In 1953, when Christensen began his career at Iowa State, it was a college of just 7,780 students. The College of Veterinary Medicine had few, if any, female students. At the time, most women simply did not apply to the program because they were discouraged from doing so by parents and teachers. By the time he retired, however, the majority of students in the Veterinary Medicine program were women. Moreover, by 1989, Iowa State was a top research institution with an enrollment of more than 25,000, and an open and diverse campus.

On July 31, 1997, Iowa State President Martin Jischke renamed the road around much of the College of Veterinary Medicine as George C. Christensen Drive, in honor of an administrator who strove to bring out the best of Iowa State. As Christensen told the graduating seniors at their commencement in 1971, "The university is not a mere collection of buildings. It is people, people drawn together to learn from each other. The university is life, and life is constant change."

Jenny Barker Devine

# Yobes Ondieki: World Champion

Yobes Ondieki set a world record in the ten thousand meters, becoming the first man to run the distance in under twenty-seven minutes. He shattered the existing mark by more than nine seconds at the Bislett Games in Oslo, Norway, on July 10, 1993. Many track experts considered Ondieki's mark as the greatest distance race ever run up until that time.

Ondieki, the five-thousand-meter world champion in 1991, captured four Big Eight titles, three in cross country, while at Iowa State. He led the Cyclones to conference track and cross-country titles in 1983 and 1984. The Cyclone distance runner received All-America honors six times, earning NCAA runners-up honors three times and third-place honors three times. Ondieki placed among the top three runners at the NCAA cross-country meets from 1983 to 1985. The Kenyan won every cross-country meet he competed in during the 1983 and 1984 seasons, except the NCAA championship. During his Iowa State tenure, Ondieki was the only performer in Big Eight Conference history to win or take part in setting five all-time conference bests. He competed as part of the 1981 Cyclone 4 x 1,600-meter relay team that established an NCAA and Big Eight record. Ondieki still maintains a hold on three Cyclone records.

The obstacles he overcame as a Cyclone magnified the distance runner's greatness. Ondieki was hampered by injuries throughout his collegiate career. During the 1982 cross-country season, he was sidelined in a cast with a leg injury. Despite not having run for over three weeks, Ondieki had the cast removed the day before the competition and captured second place at the Big Eight cross-country championships.

Ondieki placed fourth in the five thousand meters at the 1992 Olympic Games in Barcelona. He also participated in the 1988 Games in Seoul. Ondieki qualified for the 1984 Olympic Games in Los Angeles, but was unable to compete because of a leg injury.

Tom Kroeschell

# "Tradition with a Vision": Iowa State Traditions

Late one night during the fall of 1998, after hours of connecting lengths of PVC pipe, twisting chicken wire, and arranging piles of cotton batting, the women of Kappa Delta sorority stood back looked regretfully at their Homecoming lawn display. The structure they designed to be a giant, mystical crystal ball looked more like a "big snowball or a cotton puff."

In keeping with the theme "Tradition with a Vision," the women of Kappa Delta, in cooperation with Kappa Sigma fraternity and FarmHouse fraternity, planned an elaborate lawn display with the crystal ball surrounded by all of the essential Iowa State traditions: Cy, the mascot; the zodiac in the Memorial Union; Lake LaVerne; Lancelot and Elaine, the regal swans; the Campanile; the water tower; and the *Fountain of the Four Seasons*. As it was, however, the lawn display, with its giant "cotton puff," failed to inspire hope that Kappa Delta could win the competition.

Kathryn Craig, who coordinated the lawn display, had worked tirelessly to secure donations for the purchase of materials. She had made countless late-night runs to Wal-Mart, which was open twenty-four hours, for additional fabric, glue, and paint. Though dismayed at the outcome of the crystal ball, she was not about to give up. After spraying glitter all over the cotton batting, she and a friend stayed up until 4 A.M. painting, cutting, and gluing fabric stars, with the hope that stars would lend the "cotton puff" a hint of mysticism. Though they made a valiant effort, the lawn display could not compete with those of other fraternities and sororities. Nonetheless, Craig was not discouraged. "We had a whole lot of fun building it," she said, "and we had a great time that year."

Ask Iowa State students or alumni about their favorite memories of their years on campus, and they are sure to include traditions such as Homecoming and VEISHEA, Varieties, athletic events, Campaniling, canoe races, and the holiday tree-lighting ceremony. These traditions have helped new students to connect with the past, while allowing alumni to return and reaffirm their connection with their alma mater. While it is not always clear how some traditions began, students passed them down through the years until they simply became a part of life at Iowa State.

Some traditions are without clear origins, or even plausible explanations. For example, true Iowa Staters never walk directly through the front door of the Memorial Union. They immediately and carefully step to the side of the raised zodiac set into the floor of the entrance, and they become visibly annoyed by the occasional freshman or visitor who traipses over it. Yet it is not reverence for art and architecture that keeps the students from walking over the zodiac, but the fear of a curse that all who touch the zodiac will fail their next exam. The origin of the curse is uncertain, since the Memorial Union architect, W. T. Proudfoot, intentionally designed the raised, bronze zodiac to be polished and worn down over time as a symbol of science overcoming superstition. At the current rate of wear, it will be more than one hundred years before the brass symbols of the zodiac are level with the concrete floor.

Campaniling, or kissing your sweetheart as the bells toll midnight under the bell tower, is another tradition without a definite beginning. One could assume that Campaniling, this important rite of passage that transforms Iowa State women into "official coeds," began as early as 1899, upon completion of the bell tower. But it was hardly mentioned in student publications until after the Second World War, when the administration extended women's weekend curfews to after midnight. By the end of the twentieth century, Campaniling became a less intimate affair with the introduction of "mass Campaniling" during Homecoming and VEISHEA. Then, hundreds of couples gathered at once, while single persons scouted the crowds for willing partners.

The lore of Iowa State is filled with tales of students forming friendships, achieving lofty goals, and often, finding love. Whether quirky, boisterous, silly, or solemn, unique campus traditions foster community, connect students and alumni to the past, and enable students to become true Iowa Staters. Traditions change over time, however, and as students adapt some of the best-loved events and customs to their own tastes, old rituals have taken on new characteristics.

Jenny Barker Devine

*Chapter 7*

# Iowa State Faculty:
# The People and the Disciplines

Amy Bix

Before World War II, Iowa State was a relatively insular college with a relatively small faculty. This fact permitted the school to run its business in an unbureaucratic manner and to concentrate on doing a few things well. Decision making was essentially centralized in the administration, leaving faculty free to concentrate on teaching, learning, service, and a certain amount of research. Matters such as hiring, promotion, and tenure decisions were handled in a fairly informal method, relying on word of mouth through a somewhat opaque process. Faculty members sometimes learned about their raises only from newspaper articles, while decisions on promotion were handled inconsistently. The rights and responsibilities of faculty were vaguely understood, but nowhere spelled out explicitly, and practices varied widely across colleges and between departments.

After war's end, Iowa State underwent dramatic changes, paralleling the evolution of many other state schools and private institutions. Faculty size grew dramatically throughout the second half of the twentieth century, paralleling the school's overall growth and its expansion into new areas of undergraduate and graduate teaching. Characteristics of the faculty body also changed. In the prewar years, many faculty had stayed at Iowa State after receiving their degrees here and worked their way up the ranks. But especially by the 1970s, as ISU placed a new emphasis on diversity and a new priority on research, professors came to Iowa State from a wider geographic range of institutions. The need to compete with other universities, particularly as measured by standards such as the *U.S. News & World Report* annual ranking of colleges, intensified a focus on quantifiable comparisons such as the percent of faculty holding doctoral degrees.

As the college grew into a university, faculty governance became more problematic. More than ever, Iowa State had to wrestle explicitly with questions about how faculty positions could best be represented to the larger community and how the faculty could give input on institutional matters. Moreover, the faculty did not always speak with one voice; priorities and concerns differed between disciplines, ranks, and, of course, individuals. The expansion and increasing complexity of faculty governance structures illustrated the perceived need for better lines of communication and decision making. In years when state budget cuts strained university resources, faculty became increasingly involved with institutional finances and with decisions about institutional directions. Inevitably, such trends

*Iowa State College students working in zoology and physiology laboratory with faculty member Oscar Tauber, circa 1944, examining a model of brain and skull structure and blowing into a spirometer to measure lung capacity. (Used by permission of Iowa State University Library/Special Collections Department)*

altered the relationship between the faculty and the administration; communication was not always smooth, and perspectives did clash.

Throughout the immediate postwar years, Iowa State had no faculty governing body, other than the local chapter of the American Association of University Professors (AAUP). The college seemed sufficiently compact to enable most issues to be resolved within divisions, with the president and provost calling on advice as necessary to make institution-wide decisions. Iowa State professors, associate professors, and administrators comprised the General Faculty, but quarterly meetings of this unwieldy group could not provide a practical opportunity for any sustained discussion or careful analysis, and this group's power came only from custom rather than law.

A 1949 AAUP chapter report on faculty participation in administration spurred an initiative to establish a Faculty Council, which was approved by voice vote in a General Faculty meeting in February 1954 and backed by new Iowa State president James Hilton.[1] The Basic Document establishing the council specified that it was "responsible to the General Faculty (the official body of the Iowa State

College)." The newly created organization was intended "to facilitate communication between the faculty . . . and the President, Deans and other administrative officers" and to "conduct studies and make recommendations concerning matters of educational policy and faculty welfare affecting the College," through its monthly meetings.[2] The council was composed of twenty faculty, four elected for two-year terms from each of the college's five divisions, with one member per rank (professor, associate, assistant professor, and instructor). The council would have the power to advise and recommend, but not to legislate or finalize policy decisions.

The first council chose history professor Norman Graebner as its first chair and immediately took up an important question of faculty prerogatives, the expense of attending professional and scientific society meetings. Conducting a survey of Iowa State divisions, a council committee discovered that about 40 to 45 percent of staff members had attended at least one national or regional meeting in 1953–1954, a trend the council wished to encourage, to keep faculty knowledge and skills up-to-date for strength in both teaching and research. Divisions followed no consistent policy on financing travel, and the council recommended setting a uniform expense allowance for one meeting per year per person (giving divisions the option of funding additional trips out of division money). In a sign of division administrators' discomfort with establishing across-the-board policies, this standardized travel-policy proposal met resistance from deans and remained unresolved.

Reflecting this early concern for securing and enlarging faculty development opportunities, the council also proposed establishing a sabbatical program enabling staff to pursue advanced studies, conduct research, write, or gain industrial or professional experience. After sending a questionnaire to other colleges, the council reported that fifty-eight out of eighty already had such leave programs and that Iowa was the only state in the Big Seven Conference without sabbatical arrangements. However, the Iowa attorney general ruled that sabbatical leaves would violate the Code of Iowa mandate that salaries be paid only for services rendered. Sabbaticals did not become permissible until 1965, with passage of a bill in the Iowa legislature specifically enabling this.

More fundamentally, council members realized with dismay that Iowa State had no commonly understood and accepted set of principles establishing rights and responsibilities of faculty. Vital business such as new appointments, promotion and tenure, termination, and academic freedom rested on habit and chance, rather than clear and uniform procedure. Faculty had no written source of information on such basic matters as fringe benefits. As Iowa State grew in both size and complexity, the council felt, fairness demanded compiling and distributing policy information uniformly to guide both administrators and faculty. The council proposed to print a *Faculty Handbook* to serve this need, and the administration appointed English instructor Hazel Lipa to help draft it.

In preparing this handbook, Lipa and other faculty immediately encountered the difficulty that on matters such as consulting, they had no existing statements to serve as starting points. The council developed its own suggestion that Iowa State allow and indeed encourage a reasonable amount of outside consulting by faculty, since this advantageously introduced faculty and departments to new ideas and valuable experiences. The committee declined to impose strict limits for time spent on consulting, suggesting only that department heads intervene if academic functions suffered.

Searching for information about promotion policies and criteria, the handbook committee compiled what material it could find, citing informal statements from the divisions of Veterinary Medicine and Engineering. The College of Home Economics had a more formal document specifying that all staff members were expected to demonstrate not only classroom excellence and interest in teaching but also "personal attributes" including "health and moral character," "emotional stability," "intelligent loyalty, . . . cooperation, . . . broad perspective and a sense of humor."[3] The college specified that instructors should hold a master's degree or equivalent and might be considered for promotion to assistant professor after three to six years, depending primarily on teaching effectiveness. Doctoral degrees were required for associate professorship in certain fields of home economics and for full professorship.

Intangible individual situations and difficulties in evaluating work between different fields made it unwise or even impossible to write inflexible university-wide promotion policies, the council warned. Yet at the time, the term "merit" seemed "almost meaningless since it is not defined in writing even in the broadest terms." With no avenue for appeal if they felt unjustly rejected for promotion or raises, faculty became subject to department heads' mercy and whims. Frequently, staffers only learned they had been promoted when lists appeared in the newspaper or only discovered they had been granted a raise upon opening their paychecks. "The apparent lack of uniformity in initiating promotions and salary increases with no formal notification to the individual concerned . . . can lead to . . . rumor and lowering of morale." The council recommended that all divisions establish and publish general promotion policies with as much consistency as possible. It praised the Chemistry Department for informing all new hires about its system, which involved appointing a committee of full professors to evaluate staff and make promotion recommendations. The council called the similar system in the Economics Department (explained in a document of just three short paragraphs) one of the best and most impartial.

In writing the handbook, the council noted significant differences in how divisions operated in matters such as governance. The Engineering Division operated primarily through a cabinet, while the Agriculture Division had sixteen faculty committees, an administrative council, an inside advisory committee, and an outside advisory committee. Engineering faculty met quarterly in a general assembly, while Veterinary Medicine held monthly faculty meetings.

Even the essential notion of academic freedom had no official written protection, the council observed. Its own draft statement declared that a "staff member has in common with every other citizen the privilege to exercise the full rights and responsibilities of citizenship, advocating that which he believes to be best for the society in which he lives."[4]

Publication of the first *Faculty Handbook* did not settle all issues of faculty rights and responsibilities. In subsequent years, the council returned to unresolved questions, such as how and when department heads should be evaluated and, reexam-

*Iowa State students conferring with Kenneth R. Marvin, professor of technical journalism, circa 1949. (Used by permission of Iowa State University Library/ Special Collections Department)*

ined issues such as consulting. Some faculty grumbled about having been arbitrarily barred from legitimate opportunities, but a 1963 council report concluded that consulting policy seemed sufficiently "flexible and permissive."[5] Though the council saw no evidence of abuse, it recommended modifying policy to require each staffer to report annually on time spent on consulting, the nature of such work, and the source of outside pay, giving Iowa State information that might be needed "to defend itself against [any future] charges of conflict of interests."[6]

While preparing the *Faculty Handbook* and continuing discussions of faculty privileges and duties represented a major accomplishment, the Faculty Council of the late 1950s and early 1960s addressed many other issues suggested by faculty members, administration, and students. The council met with the Cardinal Guild to discuss teacher evaluation forms, problems of cheating and absenteeism, and the idea of exempting seniors with high grades from final exams to increase participation in graduation activities. Additional topics under discussion included campus lighting, library carrel and reserve policies, school spirit and alumni relations, women's dormitory hours, dorm fire safety, WOI Radio and TV programming, class schedules, the need for a resident psychiatrist, the quality of teaching by graduate students, preservation of Pammel Woods, and the quarter-system versus semesters. The council perennially grappled with problems of campus pedestrian, bicycle, and vehicle traffic, not to mention faculty unhappiness with parking arrangements. Council members met occasionally with state legislators, as in 1958, for informal discussion of campus needs for space, clerical help, and higher salaries (especially so that the school could compete with industry for engineering staff). In 1959, the council's Executive Committee gave President Hilton an important endorsement for his plan to rename Iowa State a university.

Faculty Council provided a vehicle for individuals to express resentment of traditions and expectations that they considered burdensome, particularly in light of growing attention to research. In 1959, a few faculty members asked to be excused from the time-consuming duty of ushering at the five annual commencement ceremonies, but the Commencement Committee resisted, saying that faculty presence in formal regalia created a favorable impression on attending parents.

Despite its active agenda, Faculty Council already seemed inadequate to some observers by 1955. Authority resting in the General Faculty excluded the voices of instructors and assistant professors. Examining alternatives, committees toyed with ideas for a faculty senate with departmental representation, but worried about the unwieldiness of such a large body. Decisions during the 1960s expanded the council to forty members, to provide wider input and relieve each member's committee burden. Representation for this enlarged council was initially determined by a remarkable formula involving the square root of the total number of eligible staff within each college (later made proportionate to each twenty-five or one hundred faculty in each unit).

Inevitably, council's discussion about Iowa State internal policy reflected concerns and trends in national higher education. Most notably, the postwar years represented a period when opportunities for federally sponsored research expanded rapidly, particularly in connection with military technology and from the newly established National Science Foundation. Iowa State soon faced the problem that some departments, particularly in agriculture, science, and engineering, had greater access to government grants and industry contracts than did the humanities and most of the social sciences. "Numerous areas in the physical and biological sciences are so well funded that applications of mediocre as well as outstanding merit may be successfully activated," the council noted, but "a large proportion of the faculty lie in a grantless nether world . . . unable to properly fulfill their potentialities as teacher-scholars and they suffer reputationwise."[7] Iowa State declined to bar faculty from accepting grants, providing there were no restrictions on publishing results (except for national security reasons). Council members noted that the universities of Missouri, Wisconsin, and Illinois all had fairly generous mechanisms to support research in fields such as history. One faculty member quoted a letter from an Illinois colleague saying that money for research assistants and typing is "not hard to get. Since so much money rolls into the sciences, and engineering, the university is happy to support research in those areas where money is harder to obtain."[8] Administrators sympathized, but declared that Iowa State simply did not have research funds available for distribution.

*Iowa State professor Frank Spedding (right), head of the Institute for Atomic Research, with visiting Russian crystallographer Dr. N. V. Belov and Iowa State chemistry and physics professor Robert Rundle, circa 1960. (Used by permission of Iowa State University Library/Special Collections Department)*

Amidst the post-Sputnik national prioritizing of science and the cold war investment in military technologies, Iowa State was able to claim a sizable share of federal research dollars. The Atomic Energy Commission chose Ames as the site of a major research facility, a development that originated from the work that chemistry professor Frank Spedding had done for the government during World War II on methods of producing pure uranium. After the war, Iowa State created an Institute for Atomic Research, headed by Spedding, to focus on metallurgy and materials science, rare-earth element chemistry, and nuclear energy. Operating the AEC's Ames Laboratory, the institute brought together faculty from physics, chemistry, engineering, biology, and other disciplines, allowing graduate students and even undergraduates to participate in research. Agriculture faculty investigated the effects of radioactivity on swine, while veterinary faculty conducted radioisotope studies. The institute acquired AEC funds for building construction, for a nuclear reactor, for a seventy-million-volt synchrotron, and sophisticated labs for handling radioactive material.

Other faculty members also undertook ambitious and exciting research during the 1950s and early 1960s. Veterinary staff conducted radiology research in deep X-ray treatment of animal diseases. The presence of the United States Department of Agriculture (USDA) National Animal Disease Laboratory facilitated investigations of swine brucellosis, hog cholera, and other livestock problems. Engineering faculty worked with the Iowa Highway Commission to investigate construction methods, highway materials, bridge design, and soil mechanics. Home economists researched the latest frozen foods, statisticians mapped American farms, and the Center for Agricultural Adjustment addressed the economic and social challenges facing farm families. Research and outreach work took on an increasingly international flavor; ISU Home Economics professors traveled to India to teach and help develop college programs at Baroda University. ISU's Agriculture faculty worked with projects in Lebanon, Brazil, Ecuador, and many other countries, while the Tropical Research Center studied corn production in Guatemala to create improved hybrids. Such research led to tangible results, including the development of diethylstilbestrol, a new feed for beef cattle. Advanced scientific research demanded the latest expensive equipment; in addition to its atomic research equipment, postwar ISU also acquired a larger reflector telescope, an electron microscope, and the high-speed "Cyclone" digital computer.

ISU faculty in the postwar years adjusted curriculum offerings to reflect the growth of new knowledge and the interest in new disciplines. During the 1950s, the Agriculture Division added studies in entomology, plant pathology, and fish and wildlife management, plus new business and industry-oriented classes. Engineering added new curricula in metallurgy and in engineering science; Home Economics developed a restaurant management major and textiles and clothing merchandising. A number of new courses directly incorporated the latest cold war science; Veterinary Medicine taught biomedical electronics, Aeronautical Engineering created new courses on rocketry and space engineering; and Electrical Engineering added courses on transistors. The growth of commercial television led to new courses on production and programming.

The excellence of some ISU researchers earned national recognition. In 1945, chemist Henry Gilman became the first Iowa State faculty member elected to the National Academy of Sciences; he was joined in 1952 by Spedding and in 1967 by animal geneticist Jay Lush (who was also awarded the National Medal of Science by President Lyndon Johnson in 1969 for his work in scientific animal breeding).

While internal matters such as faculty rights and responsibility policy occupied most of the council's time, there were other intrusions of outside concerns. Reflecting cold war tensions, the council in 1959 recommended that Iowa State maintain a blood-type index for all workers, to screen potential blood donors rapidly in the event of an emergency. This era brought the mobilization of the civil rights movement and in 1962, the Student Committee on Racial Equality approached Iowa State to discuss means of handling problems of discrimination. The university had already become concerned about prejudice in access to off-campus student housing, and an ad hoc committee appointed by President Hilton recommended restricting university rental listings to only property owners pledging not to discriminate by race, religion, color, or national origin. Noting that they had heard that some minority faculty experienced difficulty finding housing, Faculty Council supported creation of a Human Relations Committee to address cases of discrimination and educate the community about race relations.

By the mid-1960s, ISU faculty noticed that the school's growth had spurred jeal-

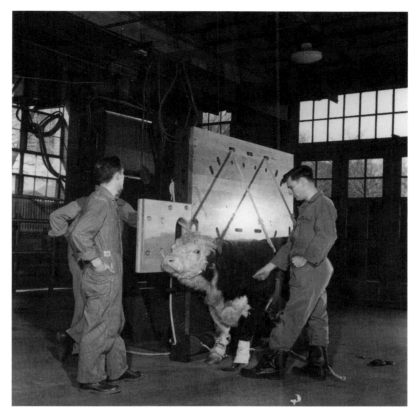

*Iowa State students and faculty member Mack Emmerson, head of the Department of Veterinary Obstetrics and Radiology, conducting deep X-ray treatment on a herd bull, circa late 1950s–early 1960s. (Used by permission of Iowa State University Library/Special Collections Department)*

ousies and morale problems, due to unhappiness with teaching loads, lack of research support and travel money, pressures caused by faculty absences on leave, and related strains. Students too felt the stress; in 1966, Faculty Council distributed questionnaires asking about their academic experiences. Most of the eight-hundred-plus responses expressed satisfaction that exams and grading were fair, but resented the stress on memorization rather than learning, especially in large classes. Undergraduates complained about incompetent and apathetic graduate-student instructors, particularly in mathematics classes. One student referred to the system as "mass production" and another compared it to being "ground through a giant machine." Agriculture and Vet Med students were pleased with their academic advising systems, but only 10–25 percent of Home Economics upperclassmen said they were satisfied, and 60–70 percent of Engineering students considered the system inadequate. Students wanted personal attention, feeling uplifted when faculty made themselves available for conferences and feeling hurt if professors broke appointments or failed to recognize an advisee in the hall. Most considered the current size of ISU to offer a good variety of people, courses, and cultural advantages.[9] But Iowa State faced the risk that larger size and complexity might undermine the quality of undergraduate education, as well as put extra demands on faculty and administration. As it turned out, during the late 1960s and early 1970s, such internal tensions and uncertainty would be exacerbated by larger concerns, especially the threats of student unrest and political dissention.

By the late 1960s, Iowa State (like many schools around the country) witnessed a trend for campus residents and observers to question and redefine relationships between students and faculty, between students and administration, between faculty and administration—and the relationship of all three groups toward the local, national, and global communities.

In April 1968, the Faculty Council began reviewing a national AAUP statement on the rights and freedoms of students, which emphasized a university's duty to cultivate free expression and free inquiry among students. Reports linked rising campus unrest to young people's resentment of being marginalized and silenced on campus and in national affairs. The AAUP statement supported students' right to challenge classroom information, criticize institutional policy, and participate in academic policy decisions as constituents. ISU's Faculty-Student Relations Committee followed this lead, encouraging department heads to give undergraduates representation on department committees, share information on faculty qualifications, and confer with students on curriculum planning and in advisory meetings. Surveys showed that a significant number of Iowa State students wanted greater involvement in university affairs, the committee said, and departments such as Statistics and Sociology had already acted on commitments to incorporate student opinions.[10] "As ISU increases in size, the isolation of faculty from students becomes an even more serious problem," the council warned, and "events at Columbia . . . make it quite clear that isolation leads to an atmosphere in which students, faculty and administration are inclined to overlook their common interests and [lead to] a 'class struggle.'"[11]

A few faculty rebelled, complaining that student interest was fickle and nonrepresentative and that faculty and administrators abdicated their responsibility by giving students a voice in decisions. Engineering teacher William Larsen criticized the committee for racing to mollify those students ready to condemn institutions as evil and treat authorities as antagonists. Larsen compared student-faculty relations to marriage, a partnership "with very different roles." He praised experimental engineering courses where professors guided students to solve real-life technical problems as the proper means of promoting student-faculty communication. Larson recommended revitalizing teaching to promote the student's development and self-fulfillment inside the classroom, rather than "involving him in peripheral areas such as university administration."[12] Nevertheless, Faculty Council declared its intent to protect student rights, recommending that instructors not be informed which students enrolled in their classes on a pass-fail basis and recommending that ISU refuse to disclose student status to local selective-service boards without student authorization.

In supporting students' right to participate in faculty and administrative business, professors also insisted that faculty views deserved greater weight in institutional decision making. In 1967, ISU's Faculty Council voiced alarm that ISU's long-range campus-planning process did not allow enough faculty input on facilities planning, future program expansion, or optimum enrollment size. Reflecting a conviction that by definition, faculty held a different perspective on such questions than administrators, one professor noted, "Good university planning can only come about by each element in its community having an appropriate voice."[13] President Parks offered to nominate faculty to sit in on meetings with architectural consultants, but council criticized this as insufficient representation. Professors also spoke of demanding more say in appointment of department heads and deans, to counter administrators who opposed change; President Parks responded that often it was faculty who settled for "comfortable mediocrity" and that "faculty involvement often leads to overcomplication."[14]

Over subsequent months, ISU's Faculty Council became swept up in state and nationwide debates over whether and how to control student behavior. After radical guest lecturers such as performer-activist Dick Gregory shocked a Story County Grand Jury into condemning Iowa State's political climate, the council joined President Parks and the Board of Regents in defending controversial speech as part of an intellectually open academic community. After legislators proposed requiring instant dismissal of any student or faculty member convicted of inciting or carrying on a riot, the council declared the importance of protecting the right to study or teach through academic due process with impartial appeal channels.

ISU's Faculty Council tried to walk a fine line between praising students' political energies and condemning violence, between recognizing the unusual campus climate and protecting students and faculty who wished to continue normal work undisturbed. While encouraging student activism, the council rejected demands that professors *must* enable this by suspending regular educational practices, defending professors' right to continue class work they considered important. As activists nationwide began planning Vietnam Moratorium Day events demanding an end to violence, ISU had to decide whether to join some other schools in canceling regular classes on October 15, 1969. While neither supporting nor rejecting the moratorium, the council encouraged faculty to participate in "activities that illuminate and examine this controversy" and devote "some or all" class time (if appropriate) to discussing Vietnam. The council urged faculty not to penalize absences, but also asked students to respect professors who had previously scheduled exams that day.[15]

After May 4, 1970, when Ohio National Guard troops shot Kent State students protesting American aggression in Cambodia, killing four young people, enormous protests erupted at schools around the country and many colleges closed early. ISU's Faculty Council commended students for responding responsibly "when headlines and broadcast time were there for the taking by a sensational act, and when the individual catharsis of rowdy disdain for community values through violent confrontation was a distinct possibility." Like their counterparts nationwide, some ISU students felt compelled to leave school immediately to undertake political activity, and the Government of the Student Body asked ISU to pass special rules releasing students from final exams. In a specially called meeting attended by hundreds of faculty and students, the council objected that making blanket provisions would "intrude upon the most significant relationship . . . in the university . . . between the student . . . and the instructor," denying the pro-

*Graduate students in Iowa State's Food and Nutrition program work with faculty member Frances Carlin (second from right), studying differences in jelly consistency for a course in experimental cookery, circa 1953. (Used by permission of Iowa State University Library/Special Collections Department)*

fessor's freedom "to award to students in his classes the grades earned." The council suggested that situations should be negotiated individually, under existing rules; when possible, professors should accommodate students who requested special arrangements to postpone or end work early, while students should understand that some faculty could not offer any "practicable alternative" to finishing the entire course as planned.[16]

During summer 1970, as sentiment among young people nationwide grew increasingly volatile, Iowa's Board of Regents held hearings on campus disorder. Opposing suggestions that schools impose external authority to enforce discipline, ISU's Faculty Council recommended a "conservative" philosophy "in that we feel no drastic change in policy is called for"; although "campus tensions" presented a "real and present threat," ISU's administration, faculty, and students had a proven ability to govern themselves.[17] When the board adopted a code of personal conduct authorizing school presidents to ban any student, employee, or visitor who disrupted university functions, ISU faculty complained that the language was vague and "dangerously arbitrary." They resented the insistence on ruthlessly cleansing the university of all troublemakers, which imposed a "standard of uniformity . . . alien to the tradition" of free expression. "The public should be made to realize that we are conducting an educational institution, not 'running a prison,'" history professor Harold Sharlin declared.[18]

Yet faculty realized they had a public relations problem: they needed people to "recognize that the university is not a 'monster that gobbles up its taxes and its children.'"[19]

Some observers accused professors of fomenting rebellion, abusing classroom privileges to "lead astray . . . impressionable" youth.[20] The regents responded by requiring each university's faculty body to develop a faculty ethics statement. ISU's council delicately faced thorny questions, such as whether professors could use class time to discuss unrelated subjects or make known their own political beliefs.

Meanwhile, professors simultaneously felt besieged from within the university, as rumors spread that ISU planned to build a new football stadium. Council members denounced this as a misplaced priority during a period of tight financial resources and questioned the quid pro quo allocation of preferential seating to private contributors. President Parks agreed that academics must take precedence over athletics and that "Iowa State should not become another Nebraska," but stood up to the council to defend the need for a bigger, better stadium.[21] Faculty Council had previously skirmished with the Athletic Department over faculty rights to tickets and facility use and over the problem of sporting-event attendees commandeering faculty parking spaces. Complaining that ISU was being pushed to field increasingly expensive, nationally ranked teams, professors cited stories about coaches interfering in the grading of athletes or helping them submit ghost-written papers. But other faculty cheered stadium construction, and Faculty Council backed away.

It would be an internal faculty dispute, however, that ultimately led Faculty Council into crisis. In May 1972, after Nixon's decision to mine North Vietnam's harbors, the council passed a motion to recognize popular concern about the war by initiating petitions condemning escalation. The petition, signed by over 230 ISU faculty, was printed in June's *Congressional Record*, where Iowa's Senator Harold Hughes called it evidence that "opposition to our military adventurism in Southeast Asia continues to flow deeply in the conscience of the Nation."[22] But more than two dozen ISU faculty objected that the council had no jurisdiction to engage in such political activity without the General Faculty's authorization. Tarnishing the university's image with controversy risked a backlash in which government might slash appropriations, Professor Charles Black warned; California's legislature had already denied salary increases to that state's faculty, supposedly to punish their militancy. ISU's Faculty Council defended itself, saying that the council itself had not voted against Vietnam policy, that the petition had come from individual faculty, none coerced into signing, that the national AAUP had already set precedent for debating the war, that the petition exemplified responsible citizenship, and that ISU was already politicized through issues such as ROTC, TIAA-CREF, and agribusiness. But the faculty body sided with the critics, voting to require the council henceforth to confine its scope to internal university matters.

A shaken and disillusioned council retreated, to focus on problems such as continuing ambiguity in ISU's personnel guidelines. "In the minds of many faculty

*Iowa State students in the Agriculture College study meat cuts and quality in laboratory section, no date. (Used by permission of Iowa State University Library/Special Collections Department)*

. . . tenure policy is still not clear," the council noted, and even those administering procedures felt confused. A survey of twenty-two departments showed no consistency; "many use the faculty handbook as authoritative, others use the Office Procedures Guide (which . . . contains conflicting information)."[23] A 1974 survey showed that more than 70 percent of the departments did not have any document available to faculty that specified evaluation procedures or promotion criteria. More than one-quarter of ISU departments did not routinely advise faculty about the results of their annual evaluations, and some faculty only learned through reading the *Faculty Newsletter* that their promotion had been approved.[24]

Meanwhile, the University Committee on Women (created in 1971) called on ISU to ensure adequate representation for women on groups deciding university policy and to "create a climate" in which female students, staff, and faculty would enjoy "opportunities comparable to those of men . . . with similar abilities and interests." In a 1974 survey, 45 percent of ISU's female faculty reported seeing gender discrepancies in salary (outside Home Economics and the women's physical education department, where women constituted a majority). Thirty percent perceived gender bias in promotions, and a roughly equal number complained about deliberate or unintentional discrimination by male colleagues in professional interactions and informal judgments.[25] Over subsequent months, women faculty mobilized to open discussions (with mixed results) about maternity leave policy, day-care availability, part-time-faculty rights, and creation of a women's studies curriculum. A 1980 Faculty Council report noted that more than one-third of ISU departments still had no women in tenured or tenure-track positions, which "represents a serious lack of role models for female students and may adversely affect student enrollment in nontraditional fields." It pointed out that women's representation was concentrated at lower faculty ranks (only 9 percent of women were full professors, versus 37 percent of the total faculty) and that at each level, female faculty earned lower salaries than men.[26]

Throughout the 1970s, ISU faculty became increasingly troubled by the state educational climate and the danger of political interference in academic affairs. They felt pressure to explain and justify their existence, particularly when critics attacked professors for spending insufficient hours in class. The typical university workweek extended longer than forty hours, the Board of Regents replied, considering time required for writing and updating lectures, preparing tests, grading, and advising students on academic work and professional prospects. "Is a judge at work only when he presides formally over . . . the court? Does a minister work only during the hours he conducts religious services?" Good teachers also needed time for research, the board declared, since "if the professor is to be a true guide to learning, *he must keep constantly at the forefront of knowledge.*"[27] Yet politicians threatened to force new priorities on professors, whom they criticized for de-emphasizing teaching; in 1973, Representative Charles Grassley introduced a bill proposing that faculty should not be judged by the quantity or quality of publications they produced. Media attention hinting that ISU scientists enjoyed too-close relationships to agribusiness forced the university to defend its consulting policy and strengthen its surveillance to prevent abuse and conflicts of interest.

By the late 1970s, ISU faculty became especially demoralized over financial issues, particularly given the way double-digit inflation had eroded salaries. To pressure the legislature, the council compiled reports showing how much faculty pay had fallen behind the cost of living. Between 1969 and 1978, they noted, average real salaries for ISU faculty had fallen between 17 and 22 percent, even as all state residents' real per-capita personal income rose over 28 percent. "Real salaries paid to professors . . . in 1979–80 are nearly equal to what the University paid associate professors in 1969–70."[28] The council emphasized the direct cost to recruitment and retention, when ISU could not offer competitive salaries to the most talented people. A 1977 survey of faculty who had left ISU since 1974 identified salary as their main cause for resigning; more than half of those who moved to another university or government received substantial raises, while 60 percent of those faculty who jumped to private industry increased their salary by more than 20 percent. Engineering departments reported particular trouble finding talented candidates for vacant positions, due to continued salary slippage. "Graduating students with bachelor's and master's degrees often receive starting salaries that

*Iowa State researchers, including Electrical Engineering professor Alvin Read (far right), work with a specialized gas laser, circa 1960s. (Used by permission of Iowa State University Library/Special Collections Department)*

exceed the salaries of the faculty who have educated them. . . . Deteriorating faculty salaries tend to dampen student enthusiasm for graduate training."[29] Some ISU faculty flirted with the idea of collective bargaining to restore their negotiating power, but failed to win many converts.

Taking a broader perspective, the 1960s and 1970s had brought growth to some areas of ISU in terms of faculty numbers, physical facilities, research development, and student enrollment. Some science, agriculture, and engineering faculty particularly benefited from consulting opportunities and grants from federal agencies such as the Atomic Energy Commission (support of the Ames Laboratory), the Department of Agriculture, and the National Science Foundation. This funding supported investments in graduate students, postdoctoral staff, and the expensive equipment crucial to let ISU keep abreast of the latest knowledge and techniques in high-tech fields. By 1969, Iowa State ranked twentieth among all U.S. universities in research expenditures. President Parks defended the institution's call on state funds as justified, stating that seed money proved essential for attracting more federal and foundation dollars. However, not all disciplines enjoyed equal chances to share such resources, and uneven expansion imposed extra costs on certain departments. Teaching loads had risen, as had the student-faculty ratio, from sixteen to one in 1959 to nineteen to one in 1980. The colleges of Design, Engineering, and Science and Humanities felt especially stretched by overcrowded classes. ISU filled classrooms with many adjunct or temporary appointees, who comprised over 23 percent of faculty by 1985.

Like their counterparts at schools nationwide, ISU faculty began to devote special attention during the 1970s to environmentally oriented research, focusing on projects such as pesticide exposure, biological methods of pest control, and handling of animal waste. The new environmental concern also matched student interests; in 1971, ISU offered over eighty environment-related classes, with almost 2,200 students enrolled just in environmental biology courses. In 1972, ISU opened the World Food Institute, studying worldwide nutrition problems and their solutions.

ISU expanded the scope of its degree programs during the 1960s and 1970s. Between 1960 and 1969, enrollment in the College of Science and Humanities increased by 163 percent, thanks in large part to curriculum expansion. The university created separate majors in history, government, and philosophy, as well as a music major and a Ph.D. program in psychology. In 1980, the regents approved creation of the first humanities doctoral program at ISU, the graduate program in the history of technology and science, which had a natural link to ISU's historic emphasis on engineering and science; it awarded ISU's first Ph.D. in the humanities in 1986.

In the 1980s, the state of Iowa experienced a devastating farm crisis, which greatly affected the state's financial situation and resulted in budget reversions for state institutions. At Iowa State the reversions only intensified faculty frustration that financial difficulties threatened to undermine ISU quality and alarm that the state's commitment to higher education was tenuous. A few years of sizable salary increases for faculty failed to compensate for preceding declines, leaving their 1988 purchasing power below that of their 1968 counterparts (even factoring in benefits). For comparison purposes, President Gordon Eaton had identified a set of public land-grant universities with missions similar to ISU's (the universities of Arizona, California-Davis, Illinois, Minnesota, Wisconsin, North Carolina State, Ohio State, Texas A&M, Michigan State, and Purdue). Within this "Peer Eleven" group, ISU paid the lowest salaries at all ranks except instructor by 1988, and the gap was widening.[30]

With recognition of how much ISU had changed over recent decades came gradual acknowledgement that it was time to restructure faculty governance. Between 1960 and 1983, ISU had expanded from 553 full-time-equivalent (FTE) faculty to 1,255 FTE. This growth made the council imperfectly representative; some departments rarely or never had one of their members elected, hindering the flow of communication and fostering apathy. Council members plaintively commented, "There is a continued need for a procedure at ISU to make known to the rest of the university community the wishes, hopes, dreams, and needs of the faculty."[31] ISU's council, as a purely advisory body, clearly lacked power, but indeed, faculty nationwide during the 1980s became bitter over a perceived loss of respect and lack of influence in campus planning.

Some professors noted that redefining university-level governance would not solve department or college-level problems; furious at already feeling overburdened, some simply wanted to be left alone to teach and do research. The idea of switching to a Faculty Senate with departmental representation seemed attractive, especially given that the College of Science and Humanities had already instituted an elected representative assembly to study curricula and approve changes, review college priorities and programs, and advise the dean on budget and policy matters. In April 1988, the General Faculty voted overwhelmingly in favor of creating a Faculty Senate with legislative authority for academic and educational policy, centered around departmental representation.

The governing document of the new Faculty Senate specifically gave faculty the opportunity and charge to cooperate in university decision making. This philosophy of "shared governance" codified the postwar trend toward formalization of policies and procedures, expansion of input, and faculty assertion of their rights and responsibilities.[32] Yet the new governing structure did not magically relieve all tensions in faculty feelings about the direction in which ISU was heading. By the end of the 1980s, ISU salaries had slightly recovered in comparison to peer institutions, but such progress had been purchased at the price of leaving many open faculty lines vacant (even as the size of university administration kept expanding, some faculty complained). Moreover, faculty remained concerned about lack of funds for supplies and services, equipment purchase and repair, support staff, and building maintenance. At a time when the cost of keeping library shelves stocked with the latest books and journals kept rising, as did the need for expensive computer and communications technology, tight budgets threatened to eat away at the intellectual and physical infrastructure necessary to research and teaching.

The late 1980s also witnessed the intensification of ISU institutional self-studies and outside analysis, driven by both internal direction and external pressure (a trend common at universities nationwide). This frenzied scrutiny distressed many faculty, who feared it both reflected and facilitated a drive to cut back on programs and to demand that the university implement economies of scale to do more with fewer resources. Plant pathology professor Harold McNabb, a veteran faculty leader, called ISU's 1989 Long-Range Strategic Planning Study "ludicrous," with its proposals for reorganization of departments and disciplines.[33] Other faculty feared that the study's recommendations overemphasized a narrow science and technology focus serving industry and agriculture, leading the university away from its historic land-grant character and its broader social mission. They complained that far from representing a constructive analysis leading to creative innovation, the planning process had been reactive, hurried, fragmentary, and divisive.

The 1989 organizational audit conducted by the accounting firm Peat Marwick Main and Company, at the regents' behest, further alarmed many faculty, especially with its recommendations for eliminating "duplication" at Iowa universities by terminating ISU programs in journalism, industrial engineering and industrial education and technology, and education doctoral study. ISU had long faced the

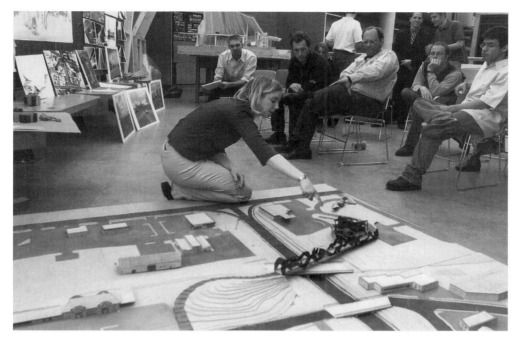

*Faculty and students in the College of Design observe and evaluate a project presentation by ISU second-year architecture student Amanda Sanders in 2001. (Used by permission of Iowa State University Information Technology Services)*

danger that financial stringencies would force it to jettison certain programs, but faculty protested that monetary considerations, political interests, and talk of "efficiency" could not be permitted to override factors of intellectual quality and student demand.

At a deeper level, faculty perceived that fiscal and political pressures were changing ISU in fundamental ways, too rapidly for many observers' comfort. Iowa officials increasingly demanded that ISU demonstrate tangible contributions toward state economic development, expanding the value of its applied science and technology research even as state support of that research threatened to keep shrinking. Amidst alarm that ISU had slipped from a Carnegie Research I university to the lower Research II category, the administration sought to restore its institutional stature by placing new stress on faculty research. Faculty in departments such as English, with large "service teaching" responsibilities to students across colleges, felt especially squeezed by heavy teaching loads and low status. (Moreover, a 1990 ISU study showed that faculty salaries were particularly low in departments heavy on undergraduate teaching.)

In 1991 and 1992, ISU faced further reductions and reversions of state funds, even as President Martin Jischke and Regents' President Marvin Pomerantz spoke about transforming ISU into the nation's premier land-grant university. Some skeptical faculty questioned what measures would be used to judge "the best" institution and wondered how ISU could compete against schools in larger and wealthier states. "While the rhetorical statement of being the best land grant university has great appeal, . . . such competitive enthusiasm must also be tempered by a recognition of budget realities to avoid fostering cynicism among the faculty," one report noted.[34]

Faculty not only in English but across campus (and not only at ISU) felt pressured by changing expectations and the need to juggle competing roles as teachers, researchers, and university community members. Standards for promotion and tenure kept rising, and many faculty became demoralized by seeing colleagues' promotion and tenure cases denied. Taking the expression "publish or perish" to new extremes, science and engineering faculty were evaluated in terms of their ability to land large research grants and publish large numbers of papers in refereed journals. Promotion for faculty in departments such as History became contingent upon publication of research monographs. In a 1992 survey, 51 percent of ISU faculty felt that the pressure to publish reduced the quality of teaching; 31 percent disagreed.[35] Professors were pressed to assume increasingly heavy and numerous responsibilities on university committees and other administrative chores, more Extension work, and more mentoring of both students and junior faculty, without a sense that such service would be rewarded by raises or promotions. ISU faculty felt that they were already serving more students while accomplishing more research on a nationally competitive level. "From fall 1986 through spring 1991, the university lost 172 FTE faculty . . . 8.8 percent. Since enrollment declined by only three percent during that period, the faculty experienced a reduction in number 2.5 times greater than the reduction in students. At the same time, sponsored funding increased by 131 percent."[36]

Ironically, even as faculty experienced these multiple demands on their time, politicians and the public attacked professors for spending only six to eight hours a week in the classroom. In 1992, a U.S. House Committee issued a report complaining that even as tuition rose faster than inflation, students were paying more and getting less at public colleges that sought to compete with the Massachusetts Institute of Technology (MIT) and Harvard by hiring research "stars" who avoided the classroom and delegated instruction to teaching assistants.[37] Tracking of workload data showed ISU faculty working an average 56.7 hours per week and spending 8.3 hours in the classroom.[38] Faculty felt that they were unfairly maligned by critics who failed to comprehend the multiple demands for investment of their time; to convey this message to the public and to the regents, ISU produced "A Day in the Life of a Faculty Member," a videotape following chemical engineering professor Charles Glatz as he moved among teaching undergraduate classes, working with graduate students, doing research and extension work, and participating in meetings.

Calls for public accountability pushed faculty members to devote more time to interacting with students, both inside and outside of class. Such demands accelerated as ISU followed the business world's infatuation with the philosophy of Total Quality Management. In the effort to satisfy political demands to demonstrate efficiency and to compete for students, ISU hired TQM experts who instructed faculty to regard themselves as suppliers, pushing themselves toward continual improvement to satisfy the demands of students, their parents, and the public. Many faculty scoffed at the jargon and feared that treating students as consumers might

*ISU Political Science professor Steffen Schmidt (middle) appears on CNN for a live interview with Crossfire journalists Paul Begala and Tucker Carlson as part of the media attention focused on Iowa in the weeks preceding the 2004 presidential election caucuses. (Used by permission of Iowa State University Information Technology Services)*

lead to a focus on numbers (serving the most customers) and on catering to student whims, rather than meeting solid standards of academic excellence. But in 1992, the Board of Regents requested that Iowa universities develop three-year plans to enhance faculty effectiveness and productivity. ISU pressured faculty to teach more evening, weekend, and off-campus classes to meet needs of nontraditional students and strive to improve retention, especially of minority students. In 1993, ISU opened its Center for Teaching Excellence, which ran orientation workshops for new hires, organized seminars where faculty could compare notes on classroom experiences and discuss both the theory and practice of pedagogy, and offered faculty individual consultations to help improve their teaching. Together with other offices on campus, the Center for Teaching Excellence helped faculty think through issues of incorporating diversity into the classroom, adopting new teaching techniques, and incorporating new classroom technologies.

Questions of how ISU could best handle issues such as diversity roused debate on campus and became spotlighted in a 1993 controversy where radical black students protested the content of ISU's African American history course and challenged professor Christine Pope's position as a white woman teaching that class. Amidst much agonizing, ISU tried to emphasize the need to give students freedom to question and faculty freedom to teach in a learning environment free from harassment. Faculty Senate voted to support Pope's right to teach African American history "as she deems appropriate for the goals of the course" and to ensure that nobody besides registered students could attend class without the instructor's permission. But the incident underlined minority students' expressions of unhappiness at ISU, their feelings of being unwelcome and devalued, and the challenges that created for recruitment and retention.[39]

Despite such upheavals and the hand-wringing over ISU's direction and financial restrictions, a 1992 survey showed that 20 percent of faculty considered ISU a "very good" place and 66 percent "fairly good". Ten percent rated the intellectual environment as excellent, 50 percent good, 30 percent fair, and 9 percent poor. About one-third felt they were better off in their ISU faculty roles than five years ago, one-third said worse.[40]

Even as ISU changed, the fact remained that many faculty were good instructors and enjoyed teaching, and that many were good researchers and produced work of international renown. The 1990s accelerated the trend toward internationalization of the university, in both teaching and research, and ISU expanded programs working in Eastern Europe and the former Soviet Union. The 1990s also continued the postwar trend toward "big science," the evolution of science and engineering to large-scale collaborative research that entailed large expenses for equipment, staff, and support and committed faculty to spend time in grant writing and administration. Increasingly, faculty in the social sciences and humanities also needed computers and other equipment for research and teaching.

Iowa State's faculty body had almost doubled over the course of less than fifty years; there were 900 faculty members in 1953, and 1,781 in 1999. Along with growth came a regularization of policy; although individual cases might occasionally still prove thorny, by the 1990s, ISU had set procedures to clarify terms of appointment, expectations for tenure, and evaluation for promotion. The original 1958 *Faculty Handbook* had been just over 50 pages long; by 1998, the *Faculty Handbook* had ballooned to almost 140 pages, covering personnel policies, salary and benefits, academic freedom and academic misconduct, conflict of interest and consulting, grading and graduation requirements. Faculty had to familiarize themselves with new sets of rules, such as ISU's Code of Computer Ethics, reviews of research using human subjects or live animals, and inclusive-language policy.

By the 1970s, demographic diversity of the professoriate emerged as a particular concern. Attraction and retention of female and minority faculty were issues of nationwide concern, but presented particular challenges in the rural Midwest. Starting in the 1980s, Iowa State's University Committee on Women conducted intensive surveys of hiring and employment conditions for female faculty. In a 1982 survey, they obtained information about the existence of sexual harassment on campus and then proposed policy on this issue. Progress was slow; a 1984 study showed that eight out of fourteen female administrators at ISU worked in the Home Economics College and that the proportion of women on the teaching faculty had not grown between 1971 and 1972 and 1981 and 1982, hovering around 18 percent. The lowest representation of female faculty came in Engineering (2.4 percent) and Agriculture (5.5 percent); the library was at 66.7 percent and Home Economics at 79.6 percent. Analysis showed that after controlling data by faculty

*In 2002, Religious Studies faculty member Whitney Sanford shows students through the virtual-reality Hindu Temple that Sanford developed for ISU's C6 virtual reality system in collaboration with Engineering faculty member Carolina Cruz-Neira. The technology offers users a sense of being visually surrounded by the simulated environment, supporting education in religious and cultural diversity. (Used by permission of Iowa State University Information Technology Services)*

rank, women earned about 90 percent of salaries of men at the same rank, and salaries were particularly low in departments with large numbers of female faculty.

Throughout the second half of the twentieth century, ISU's faculty had debated not only local issues but also national questions including student unrest, discrimination against minorities, and the employment of women. While most ISU professors by no means embraced radical stands, they could not and did not ignore national political and social issues.

Teaching and research underwent a transformation over the years, driven by institutional growth, by new opportunities, and by the changes in students and faculty themselves. As the university sought to raise its national profile and intellectual status, faculty members came under increasing pressure to publish in leading peer-reviewed journals, to author scholarly books, and to secure research grants, often totaling hundreds of thousands of dollars. Of course, Iowa State was not alone in the "publish or perish" trend or in the race for research funding that altered the nature of higher education across the country. Expansion of graduate training into new departments created both new opportunities and new strains on resources. The decades brought new teaching technologies, from television-based courses to Web-centered instruction and PowerPoint lectures. While many of the questions about what defined an educated student did not change, the answers did change. Even as faculty members concentrated more attention than ever on research accomplishments, the university also institutionalized expectations and resources for teaching excellence. The position of the arts and humanities had expanded, yet the distribution of financial and other resources often still followed Iowa State's historic emphasis on science, engineering, and agriculture. Years of difficult financial conditions had created strain, as the university sought to cope with the rising cost of health care, journal subscriptions, scientific and computing equipment, and maintenance. Iowa State University had emerged as a very different place from the old Iowa State College, and the faculty remained a key piece of that evolution.

## ACKNOWLEDGEMENTS

I would like to express my gratitude to Dorothy Schwieder, Gretchen Van Houten, and to the staff of the Special Collections Department of the Iowa State University Library. Particular thanks to Tanya Zanish-Belcher, Becky Jordan, Michele Christian, Melissa Gottwald, Brad Kuennen, and Teresa Morales.

# Vignettes

## The Dutch and Tiny Show

On the afternoon of March 27, 1962, Shelby County farmers attended a special meeting at the Harlan Theater to get the latest information about controlling Canada thistle, quack grass, and corn rootworms. There were numerous inducements to attract farmers, including free coffee, donuts, and parking, as well as a fashion show for wives at the American Legion Hall. But the big attraction was what farmers, journalists, and Extension people called "The Dutch and Tiny Show." Extension Botanist Erhard P. "Dutch" Sylwester (1906–1975) and Extension Entomologist Harold "Tiny" Gunderson (1913–1971) were the leading authorities on Iowa crop pests in their respective fields. Sylwester and Gunderson left their offices in ISU's Morrill Hall every winter and spring to conduct pest control meetings across the state. For approximately three hours at each meeting, Dutch and Tiny discussed the previous year's weed and insect pest problems and provided guidance to farmers who wanted to get the most out of their investment in pest control techniques.

When Dutch and Tiny talked, farmers listened. They were unrivalled experts who conducted interesting meetings, in part because farmers cared about the subject matter but also because of who they were. Sylwester was thickset and of medium height, while Gunderson was tall and thin. Sylwester once stated that Gunderson "spoke with chosen deliberation, quietly, directly, to the point." His rich, baritone voice was "uniquely Gunderson," in the words of the editors of *Wallaces' Farmer*. Sylwester was just as unique. Everyone who knew him or heard him speak referred to the distinctive German inflection of his tenor voice. The two men used slides, transparencies, and other props to illustrate their talks. At one wintertime meeting, Gunderson brought in several frozen corn stalks, gathered the crowd, and slit the stalks open lengthwise. In the warm room the previously frozen corn borer larvae began to come alive and wiggle, showing farmers how the pest could endure an Iowa winter if farmers did not do a good job of shredding cornstalks and plowing them under in the fall.

Both men joined Iowa State College in the 1930s, Sylwester in 1935 and Gunderson in 1939, arriving at a time when pest control was on the cusp of massive change. Thanks to U.S. government research during World War II, two new chemicals were available to Americans after the war. The first, commonly known as DDT, was a powerful insect killer that helped the military control insects such as mosquitoes and lice that were disease vectors for typhus and malaria. As a result, military forces in training, staging, and combat

(continued)

zones were far less likely to die or be debilitated by disease than they were from accidents or enemy combatants. The second chemical, known as 2,4-D, was a weed killer that simulated naturally occurring hormones within plants that caused them to grow themselves to death. War Department officials hoped to use this chemical as a tool in biological warfare, although the war ended before it could be used in combat areas. In 1945 farm experts, journalists, and farmers themselves were excited about the prospects of these chemicals to help reduce populations of insects that limited gains in livestock or preyed on crops and weeds that competed with crops for sunlight, moisture, and soil nutrients. Sylwester and Gunderson were ready to help farmers use these new techniques.

Dutch and Tiny were articulate promoters of chemical agriculture, but throughout their careers they insisted that it was only one part of the pest control picture. Sylwester urged farmers to plant crop seed free of weed seeds, prepare the seedbed with clean plowing, cultivate cornfields, mow pastures, and utilize numerous other cultural and mechanical techniques to control weeds. Herbicide, he argued, was the "ace in the hole" to supplement other techniques, not replace them. Similarly, Gunderson urged farmers to clean up manure piles to prevent fly populations from surging and to chop cornstalks in the fall and plow them under to deny crop pests such as European corn borers a place to spend the winter. He counseled farmers to use chemicals with caution, especially after the U.S. Food and Drug Administration began to clamp down on insecticide residues in meat and dairy products. Gunderson was not just concerned about public safety; he cared about the farmers who produced those commodities for their livelihood.

Both men also cared deeply about the welfare of all Iowans and believed that chemical techniques would not only make farming more profitable but also help homeowners, businesses, and local governments deal with pest problems. Farmers who boosted crop yields and livestock gains by using pesticides simply maximized their investment in all the other expenses of raising crops and livestock, including seed, fuel, and harvesting costs. Ironically, the chemical techniques they urged farmers to use sometimes had unanticipated and harmful consequences. Many farmers misused chemicals, applying too much or too little, even applying the wrong chemical or one that was deemed too hazardous to use on livestock. Furthermore, as farmers succeeded in controlling dominant pest species with pesticides, other species that were resistant to the chemicals such as the western corn rootworm and giant foxtail moved in. Some Iowans voiced concerns about the presence of pesticides in ground and surface water as well as in the food supply as chemical farming techniques became common. Reflecting on his career in an interview published in 1972, Gunderson stated that the move toward a more ecological perspective in agriculture was generally positive. "The outcry against pesticides has caused me to look at the problem from several angles and change my thinking," he noted. Gunderson did not, however, believe that DDT should be banned, since it was a valuable production tool when used properly. Sylwester was also convinced of the importance of herbicide, and wrote long and spirited letters to editors of farm magazines, newspapers, and to people across the country who challenged him on the appropriateness of chemical techniques. He claimed that pesticides were here to stay and the best solution was to use them wisely. Gunderson and Sylwester embodied the spirit of public service and endeavored to assist Iowans on and off the farm to improve their lives.

J. L. Anderson

# "The Voice of Friley Hall":
# The Beginning of College Radio at Iowa State

At 5 P.M. on October 17, 1949, the men of Friley Hall turned their radio dials to 640 AM to hear the inaugural broadcast of KMRA, Iowa State's first student-run radio station. Three students and radio enthusiasts, Cedric Currin, Chuck Hawley, and Maurice Voland, had set up the makeshift radio station, consisting of just two turntables, a small transmitter, and a public address system, in Currin's room in Niles House, on the fourth floor of Friley. For the men of Friley Hall and the students of Iowa State, however, the newly founded KMRA served a much greater purpose than mere entertainment. In many ways, the radio station helped promote cohesiveness and community among Iowa State students during the turbulent postwar years.

The tiny radio station operated on a transmitter with two tubes and an output of only thirty watts. With no antenna to speak of, KMRA relied on the radiators and steam pipes running through Friley to transmit its broadcasts. Though it was just a small-scale operation, KRMA enjoyed a partnership with WOI, the local Ames station operated on the Iowa State campus. After WOI signed off 640 AM at 5 P.M., KMRA took over the frequency. Student disc jockeys provided news, sports, and music approximately thirty to forty hours each week, during peak study hours, from 5 P.M. to 11:30 P.M. Monday through Friday, and until 2 A.M. on Saturdays. The first programs included such titles as *Armchair Serenade, Sports Rhythm, Symphony Hall,* and *A Date with a Turn Table.*

Within a short time, the station grew to require a staff of twenty-four students, and proved so popular that it needed a more permanent location. It moved from Currin's room into a broom closet, Room E67, in Bennett House, where it stayed only a short while. Not only was the closet too cramped, but residents in nearby rooms complained that the hall phone rang constantly with calls from listeners requesting songs. The station moved two more times, first to a basement room in Stange House, and then to the kitchenette room across from the Main Lounge of North Friley. With each move, the station grew in size and sophistication. In June 1950, KMRA became KMRI (nicknamed "crummy" by the men of Friley Hall), and its programs could be heard across campus.

In 1951, however, the success of KMRI nearly compromised the existence of the station. The electrical engineering students in charge of maintaining the equipment continually worked to upgrade and improve the signal, that is until one evening in February 1951, when radio listeners several miles from campus tuned in to an Iowa State basketball game, believing the broadcast to be coming from WOI. The Federal Communications Commission, or FCC, found that KRMI had exceeded its broadcasting area and forced the station off the air until the students could better control its signal.

Before long, KRMI was back on the air and had moved once again to the newly constructed Friley Annex. Plans for the 1951 addition to Friley Hall included a room specifically for a student radio station, and KRMI staffers were given $4,000 with which to design the studio and purchase equipment. Housed in Room 1205, KRMI had, without a doubt, become a permanent fixture at Iowa State. Dr. Julian C. Schilletter, the director of residence at Iowa State, regarded student radio as "the biggest step toward coordinating the student body in my twenty-seven years on campus." Just twelve years later, in 1961, when the station once again changed its name to KISU, it boasted a staff of thirty-five disc jockeys to spin records and fifteen newscasters to keep students in the know. Certainly the station that was on the air for nearly 120 hours per week had come a long way from three students and two turntables.

Since its humble beginnings in 1949, the student-run radio station at Iowa State changed its call letters several times, from KMRI, to KISU, to KPGY, KUSR, and finally, KURE. It moved to different locations around campus and had more than its share of close calls with the FCC for surpassing its broadcasting area. Yet KURE continues to serve the Iowa State community by broadcasting music and news not only over the airwaves but also on the World Wide Web. It reaches out to students by hosting events such as the KUREfest and Battle of the Bands, and it carries on the Kaleidoquiz, a twenty-six-hour trivia challenge that has been an Iowa State tradition for more than forty years.

Jenny Barker Devine

# Dan Gable: The Road to Gold and Black

The most internationally known of all Iowa State's student-athletes, Dan Gable set a standard of excellence as a competitor at West Waterloo High School, as a Cyclone, in Olympic competition, and as one of the greatest coaches in collegiate history. Gable's 64-0 high school record only set the table for what he would accomplish at Iowa State and beyond. Gable captured the imagination of the wrestling world as a collegian at Iowa State. The Cyclone compiled a career mark of 118-1 at ISU. He won his first 118 college matches, an NCAA record, before suffering his only defeat in the NCAA finals as a senior. He was a three-time All-American and a three-time Big Eight champion. Gable led the Cyclones to national championships in 1969 and 1970 and a Big Eight Conference team title in 1970.

Gable went on to earn titles at the Pan American Games, the Tbilisi Tournament, and the World Championship. He won an unprecedented six Midlands Open championships and was the meet's outstanding wrestler five times. Gable earned international fame in 1972, winning a gold medal in freestyle competition at the Munich Olympic Games. On the way to the medal, he didn't surrender a single point.

The Cyclone standout was named the nation's outstanding wrestler in 1970 by the American Athletic Union and again in 1971 by the U.S. Wrestling Federation. He was named Amateur Wrestling News Man of the Year in 1970. Gable was inducted into the USA Wrestling Hall of Fame in 1980 and the U.S. Olympic Hall of Fame in 1985.

Following his career as a wrestler, Gable became one of the most prolific coaches in the history of organized sports as head wrestling coach at the University of Iowa. Gable's wrestlers captured fifteen NCAA titles and twenty-one Big Ten championships. The incredible record included nine straight NCAA titles from 1978 to 1986. Gable served as head coach of the U.S. Olympic team in 1980, when the United States boycotted the Moscow Games, and in 1984 in Los Angeles. The 1984 team won seven gold medals.

Tom Kroeschell

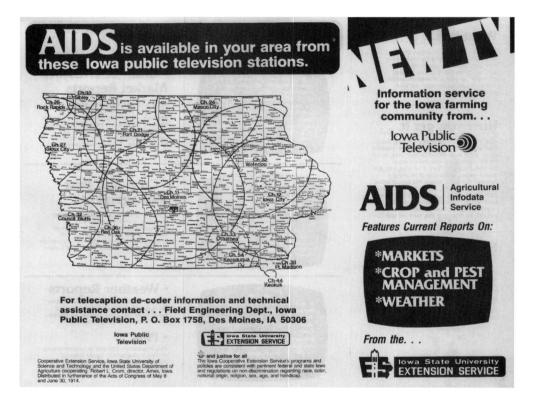

*Chapter 8*

# The People's University: Iowa State Cooperative Extension and Outreach

## J. L. Anderson

Iowa State University is about more than what happens in Ames. From its beginnings in 1858, Iowa State Agricultural College and Farm was dedicated to improving the lives of Iowans. At first this was a mix of classical and practical knowledge in the college's classrooms, barns, and fields in and around Ames, but over time the college became a force for meeting Iowa citizens in their own homes, farms, and communities. As Iowa State University approached its 150th anniversary, Extension remained one of the most important means of carrying the knowledge generated by highly trained specialists to people who used technology to make a living while helping people of all ages enhance their lives.

Since World War II, Cooperative Extension at Iowa State has continued to change in terms of programs and instructional techniques, but the primary mission has remained the same: serving Iowans. From the early years of the Farm and Home Development Program of the 1950s to the Expanded Food and Nutrition Program of the 1960s, to Extension's work in Integrated Pest Management in the 1980s and beyond, Extension has adapted and responded to changing circumstances.

The flexibility and creativity demonstrated at all levels of Extension work is one of the great themes of the Extension story. Extension changed as technology and communities changed. Leaders at the state and local level found ways to deal with the rise of the automobile, farm mechanization, population shifts, and the growing emphasis among commodity producers on responding to the needs and wants of consumers. In the postwar world, Extension leaders continued to use personal contacts, demonstrations, and classrooms to get important information to Iowans. However, they also used new technology to teach and reach clients. Today, Extension is more complex than ever before as it mirrors the complexity of Iowa and American society. Extension leaders focused more on building the capacity of individuals and families to learn and develop rather than simply assisting people conduct specific projects. This increasing sophistication has been a defining characteristic of Extension in the postwar period.

While the focus of this chapter is Cooperative Extension in the years since 1940, it is important to understand the antecedents of modern Extension work. A small land-grant college in Ames grew into a major university, and along the way began to work beyond the boundaries of the college. The desire to reach out to rural people of all ages was a national phenomenon in the late 1800s, but Iowans played an important part in changing the ways farm families produced commodities and met the needs of family members.

Many Americans in the late nineteenth and early twentieth centuries believed that society could be improved. There had been significant American reform movements in the past, most notably crusades to abolish slavery and to rescue the nation from the evils of alcohol consumption, but the period historians label the Progressive Era (1890–1920) was characterized by a drive to reorganize society along the lines of efficiency, scientific knowledge, and leadership by experts. Reformers believed that democracy would flourish in America's new industrial and urban society only if people accepted the need to eliminate waste and inefficiency in all aspects of society, from the governance of cities to the factory floor to farmhouses and fields. Many farm youths left for the cities and their promise of regular pay, "bright" gas or electric lights, and educational opportunities, in addition to entertainment and cultural opportunities. Urban progressives saw the trend of rural to urban migration and feared that only the most ignorant portion of the rural population would remain on farms and would be unable to meet the food and fiber needs of America's rapidly growing cities.

Most rural Americans did not share this view. They believed that their problem was not one of inefficient or wasteful production. Instead, they perceived low commodity prices and dishonest middlemen such as railroad magnates, grain merchants, meatpackers, and implement manufacturers as their biggest obstacles to prosperity. Farmers saw their fortunes rise and fall with the weather, insect infestations, or any number of problems beyond their control as industry leaders fixed prices for goods and set railroad rates, and meat packers offered a price that farmers could take or leave. To most farmers, increasing production in this system would exacerbate their problems rather than ease them.[1]

A vocal minority of reformers, however, urged farmers to improve the quality of their products and to increase production as a means of survival. Beginning in 1870, Iowa Agricultural College and Farm (IAC) President Adonijah Welch and college farm superintendent Isaac P. Roberts conducted farmers' institutes to disseminate new, scientific information about agriculture to farmers across the state. As historian Earle Ross noted, "None of the early land-grant colleges made a more immediate or persistent effort to serve their state" than IAC. After the first three-day institutes at Cedar Falls, Council Bluffs, Washington, and Muscatine, college leaders continued the tradition through many of the remaining years of the nineteenth century.[2]

College leaders cooperated with the Chicago, Burlington and Quincy Railroad to improve the farmers' institutes by putting them on wheels in 1904. The railroad provided designated coaches for exhibits and brief lectures to promote new farming techniques, most notably selecting and planting high-quality seed corn. Iowa State faculty member Perry G. Holden organized the first four-car exhibit in which he extolled the virtues of testing seed for germination rates and producing corn to uniform standards of ear length, number of rows of kernels, and kernel size, just as livestock producers used breed standards. Holden called the exhibit the Seed Corn Gospel Train, mimicking the itinerant revival preachers such as Ames native Billy Sunday, but with the gospel of agricultural improvement rather than the salvation of souls. By 1911 an estimated 939,000 people had boarded one or more of the mobile classrooms. Holden also assisted with the development of an agricultural short course. Dean of Agriculture Charles Curtiss organized the first short course in Ames in 1901, but Holden helped farmers in Red Oak create the first off-campus course in 1905. It is unclear just how much farmers learned from the farmers' institutes and short courses. Many people probably attended to view the spectacle or to see neighbors and friends, but the large number of attendees suggested that there was some interest in improving agriculture or, at the very least, seeing what people at the college were doing.[3]

Holden found inspiration in the example of Seaman Knapp, president of Iowa Agricultural College from 1880 to 1886. During his tenure in Ames, Knapp emphasized practical education to supplement course work. He resigned from IAC and took a job with a land developer in northern Louisiana. The developer wanted Knapp to teach farmers who migrated to Louisiana from the Midwest how to raise rice. Knapp hired a group of agents to do the fieldwork of teaching rice culture to farmers. In 1903, after several years of boll weevil infestations in Texas cotton fields, the United States Department of Agriculture (USDA) hired Knapp to replicate his system on a countywide basis in Texas. The idea of teaching through demonstration rather than through lectures or texts was a powerful one. Instead of demonstrating on a government-owned farm, Knapp convinced a few farmers to try new techniques on their own property, believing that they would become the most persuasive promoters of improved farm practices. Holden, supported by the Iowa Grain Dealers Association, the *Des Moines Register*, and the farm magazine *Wallaces' Farmer*, successfully lobbied the state legislature to pass the Extension Act of 1906, which provided state funds for lectures, short courses, and corn judging competitions. Holden was Iowa's chief spokesperson for changing the ways farmers operated.[4]

In 1912, a crop specialist for Iowa State College of Agriculture and Mechanic Arts (renamed from IAC in 1898) named M. L. Mosher helped change the way the state conducted Extension work. Mosher believed that Iowa should use a system of county agents, with local funding to pay part of the salary of the agent, but with the agent answerable to the state Extension Service. At that time, funding came from local businesses and the Farm Bureau, a new organization dedicated to improving farm productivity. In 1913, the legislature authorized the county agent system and authorized county supervisors to levy a tax to support the new organization.[5]

Meanwhile, the state Extension Department organized the Iowa Boys and Girls Club. Begun in 1909 and modeled on the work of Jessie Field Shambaugh in southwest Iowa, the purpose of the clubs, in the words of its promoters, was to extend "the benefits of the agricultural college to the young people of Iowa and to interest them in farm and home life by practical courses of study, effective organization and competitive contests." Membership was open to young people aged twenty and under. Participants signed up for free courses that would last the entire year. Courses of study for 1912 included the acre corn-growing contest (in which participants competed to raise the best-quality and largest crop on one acre of land), the pig contest, home gardening, preparation of vegetables and fruits, sewing, and poultry growing. The subject matter of the courses reflected the fact that adults expected farm youths to train for their adult lives on the farm. Reaching young people was a critical part of Extension work, since Extension promoters believed that many adults would never adopt improved farming techniques or were incapable of doing so. Teaching youngsters meant breaking the cycle of rural disdain for increasing production through the application of scientific techniques.[6]

The dedication of individuals such as Iowans Seaman Knapp and Perry Holden and many others across the country helped convince Americans and their representatives in Congress that farmers needed and wanted help. In 1914 Congress passed and President Woodrow Wilson signed the Smith-Lever Act, which created a national Extension Service based at America's land-grant colleges. This new legislation created a partnership between the USDA and the new state Extension agencies, with accompanying federal money for the organization and administration of the Extension Service at the state level.[7]

From the 1910s through World War II the state Extension Service based at Iowa State grew rapidly. Before the Smith-Lever Act, Iowa had six county agents in the field to carry the message of improvement from Perry Holden and the other college-educated professionals at Iowa State, the USDA, state agricultural experiment stations (authorized by Congress in 1887), and Extension offices in other states. By 1940 there were several hundred Extension faculty and employees in Ames, in addition to county directors in all ninety-nine counties. Furthermore, there were home demonstration agents and youth agents in almost every county. Home demonstration agents taught women about nutrition and improved techniques in homemaking, while youth agents encouraged farm children to use the best practices in homemaking and farm production to prepare themselves for productive adult lives on the farm.[8]

Extension agriculture programs of the years before World War II focused on improving crop and livestock production, although there were numerous specialized programs as well. Some county agents focused on promoting alfalfa as a forage crop that also helped build soil fertility, while others worked to test seed corn for germination. Extension experts in Ames provided guidance and expertise to county staff who, in turn, responded to local conditions. Short courses and farmers' institutes continued to be important in the interwar years, with short courses in 1924–1925 including sessions for cement products manufacturers, laundry operators, and radio amateurs in addition to courses in farm management, poultry, and dairy production.[9]

Women were important participants in Extension work in the 1920s and 1930s. Extension home economists encouraged farm women to improve the health and well-being of their families by using new techniques in food preparation and preservation, sewing, home furnishing, and decorating. In response to concerns about malnutrition in the countryside, county home agents told Iowans to be sure to consume milk every day, to eat raw vegetables or fresh fruit several times per week, and to breast-feed their babies. After federal funding became available in 1921, home economists set up "well baby clinics" for people to bring in their babies for physical examinations. Educational meetings in clothing construction and nutrition were among the most important programs, according to Iowa farm women. As one woman commented after the 1925 Farm and Home Week, she wanted to run her house instead of having it run her. Extension provided expert advice in scientific household management to improve efficiency in the home. Furthermore, there were few formal opportunities for farm women to get together outside of church circles, and women were often eager to gather for work and leisure. Farm women found that participating in Extension programs strengthened their social connections with women who shared similar lifestyles.[10]

During the Depression years of the 1930s, Extension played an important part in implementing government agricultural programs. In response to poor commodity prices, U.S. Secretary of Agriculture Henry A. Wallace administered a federal acreage reduction program in which farmers who participated received government payments. County agents were in a unique position to promote this program, which limited corn acreage and hog production. They spread the news, urged farmers to sign up, and assisted them in completing the forms. After 1936 government payments were tied to farmers' implementation of soil conservation practices on their farms. Again, Extension leaders arranged for demonstrations to show farmers how to reduce erosion while increasing productivity. Many people lived in desperate poverty during the 1930s, and Extension was there to help. Home economists helped women make do with what they had and reduce household expenditures, which was critical work during years of low income. The USDA and Extension also worked together to create a program for people to make mattresses to improve the quality of their lives. One Southern Iowa county agent recalled that in just one year residents of his county made over a thousand mattresses. Other programs included efforts to increase home canning of vegetables and meats to reduce household food costs.[11]

World War II ended the period of hard times on the farm, at least for a while. The demand for farm products increased as the United States mobilized, first to assist allies and then to meet the needs of our own military and civilian population. In 1942 Congress guaranteed minimum prices for farm products that were far better than anything people had seen since World War I. Government policy of the New Deal took land out of production to help boost prices, but now farmers were only limited by the amount they could grow with available labor and equipment. While farm families endured separation and loss during the war, in general, wartime conditions were good for farmers who survived many years of low commodity prices and poverty.[12]

Cooperative Extension played an important role in assisting farmers to meet wartime food and fiber needs. The home economists encouraged farm women to grow and preserve more food for the family. This work was especially important

*A county Extension director consulted with a farmer about increasing production and controlling costs during World War II. Meeting the nation's food and fiber needs during the wartime emergency put a premium on the specialized knowledge of Extension professionals. (Used by permission of Iowa State University Library/Special Collections Department)*

considering the wartime rationing program and resulting food shortages that affected all Americans. County directors assisted in meeting the labor shortage by organizing community members, advertising, and cooperating with a federal labor importation program that brought workers from Mexico and Jamaica to obtain enough workers to meet aggressive production goals. Extension staff members hosted machinery repair schools to help farmers make old equipment last longer since manufacturers focused on production of war materiel rather than consumer goods. Some 4-H clubs even pursued projects that aided the war effort, most notably selling war bonds. Producing high-quality livestock was a valuable pursuit in wartime as well as peacetime, so club members made direct contributions by continuing with individual projects.

As early as 1940 Extension leaders urged farmers to increase production. They took the message to the people with new pamphlets and leaflets containing information about growing soybeans and flax to help offset dwindling imports of edible oils and rope. Home Extension agents paid close attention to health and nutrition issues to ensure that farm family members were able to keep working or serve in the military. County directors attempted to recruit labor to deal with special needs at harvest time. From running advertisements in newspapers and radios to helping federal officials place foreign workers on farms, Extension leaders did what they could to make sure that precious food and fiber crops made it from the field to market. While Extension staff members encouraged farmers to produce more, probably the most decisive factor was the promise by Congress to keep farm commodity prices high for two years after the war.[13]

The Extension Service clarified its organizational structure in 1942, changing the names and designations of the old county agent, home demonstration agent, and club agent. According to R. K. Bliss, director of Iowa State Cooperative Extension, those positions would thereafter be called county Extension director, county home economist, and Extension associate. The new titles reflected a growing level of professionalism in attitudes about Extension work. Among several changes that year, Extension leaders required the county home economists to have two years of experience as a high school teacher in vocational home economics or as an associate in county Extension work. Sarah Porter Ellis, the state home demonstration agent leader, voiced her objections to the new plan, pointing out the double standard that no such qualifications were required of the county Extension director, who would act as supervisor for the home economists.[14]

Agriculture was far different in 1945 than it had been when the war began. Farmers had some money in the bank or in wallets and purses. Since 1942 farmers experienced a relative degree of prosperity for the first time since the collapse in commodity prices in 1932. They used much of their income to pay off debts on land, buildings, and machinery such as tractors. Unlike World War I, there was no rush to expand landholdings, flocks, and herds. Farm families emerged from the war with little or no debt and some money in the bank. This money could be used to invest in modernizing farm operations in the home, barns, and outbuildings, as well as fields, lots, and farmyards. Furthermore, farmers had access to new technology that would further transform agriculture, and Extension professionals were there to help farmers adjust to changing times.

Many of the new elements of farming were due, in part, to an aggressive government research program during the war. In the 1930s fruit growers used a synthetic hormone to promote uniform ripening of fruit. Users recognized that applying too much of the chemical, called 2,4-dichlorophenoxyacetic acid (2,4-D), would actually kill the plant, which was bad news. A scientist at the University of Chicago, however, recognized that this herbicidal property could be useful when the chemical was applied to weeds. A government program developed this chemical to use on enemies, but the war ended before that happened. Manufacturers turned to enemies in the United States, namely weeds that competed with crops for habitat, moisture, sunlight, and soil nutrients. The government also developed another chemical to use on insect pests, dichlorotrichloroethane (DDT). This nerve agent was useful in controlling body lice on soldiers and civilians—lice that served as disease vectors for typhus—as well as for controlling mosquitoes that infected service personnel with malaria at military installations in Asia and the American South. Once again, at the conclusion of the war agriculture was a ready market for insecticides to stop pest species that damaged crops and livestock.

Extension professionals played an important part in alerting farmers to the possibilities of this new technology. Extension botanists and entomologists provided information and even contributed articles to farm journalists, who, in turn, pub-

*This group of farmers from Guthrie County gathered on January 22, 1957, for a meeting with Harold "Tiny" Gunderson, Extension entomologist. Meetings such as this one were important components of Iowa State's outreach effort. (Used by permission of Iowa State University Library/Special Collections Department)*

lished that information for farmers to read. Extension botanist Erhard P. "Dutch" Sylwester and extension entomologist Harold "Tiny" Gunderson became two of the most recognized extension men in Iowa. During the winter months they conducted meetings across the state to let farmers know about the proper use of herbicides and insecticides and the balance between chemical techniques and more traditional pest control methods. Farmers who heeded the advice of pest control experts as well as Extension agronomists and livestock specialists frequently increased production without expanding acreage or enlarging herds.

The number and variety of short courses and field days multiplied in the postwar period. A few examples show the change from the mid-1920s, when 4,205 people attended twenty-four courses, to the 1968–1969 program year, when 26,123 people attended numerous courses in Ames and another 10,052 people participated in noncredit short courses and conferences off-campus. In the late 1960s, ISU sponsored driver's education classes, civil defense trainings, a session for school bus mechanics, and the more traditional agricultural production offerings such as soybean workshops, pesticide application short courses, and a conference on sheep feeding and nutrition, as well as a "Lady Land Owners School" for widows who found themselves confronting new challenges in working with farm tenants.[15]

The 1940s and 1950s not only brought new information to Iowans but also brought the information through a new medium—television. In 1950, Iowa State

*This promotional leaflet from 1959 highlights the cooperative nature of Extension work and the importance of Extension expertise. Local business leaders, corporations, and Extension professionals collaborated to bring the latest information about farm technology and other issues to the public. (Used by permission of Iowa State University Library/Special Collections Department)*

became the first educational institution in the nation to own and operate a television station as well as the first television station in Iowa. Television at Iowa State had been in development for years, however. President Friley explored the possibility of obtaining a federal broadcast license in 1941 when he approached the Federal Communications Commission about the requirements for obtaining a license. There is no record of any more work on the issue until 1944, when Friley appointed a five-member committee to "consider the present and future aspects of radio and television as these may pertain to the various activities of the College."

The first broadcast was in 1950 and subsequently Extension staff utilized WOI television for a variety of programs. In late 1951, for example, WOI-TV produced sixteen regular shows, including *Your Home Hour,* a program of news and features for homemakers coproduced by Home Economics Extension and the college's Division of Home Economics. Observers on and off campus were excited about the potential of broadcasting.[16]

Broadcasting, however, was not new to Iowa State. Beginning in 1921 radio became part of Iowa State's mission to serve the people of the state. That year the Electrical Engineering Department put a one-hundred-watt radio station called 9YI on the air, which became WOI in 1922. WOI was not an Extension project, per se, but it was an important tool that Cooperative Extension and Iowa State used to fulfill their mission of educating the people of Iowa and improving the quality of their lives. In 1949 WOI added FM broadcasting to enhance the station's cultural programming. As a 1965 policy statement for WOI indicated, one of the primary purposes of WOI-TV was to help extend the university to the public. While the station's advisory committee concluded in 1977 that there was no formal arrangement with the Extension Service, Extension personnel were the primary source of public service programming created by ISU.[17]

During the 1950s, the Extension Service faced numerous challenges, including organization issues and changes in farm technology. The old arrangement by which the Farm Bureau Federation supported the activities of Extension agents ended in 1954 by order of the U.S. secretary of agriculture. The special relationship between the Farm Bureaus and the Extension agent was critical to generating local interest and financial support for the agent, but it was also a source of conflict. The agent was simultaneously an employee of the Farm Bureau and the state, making it difficult to always know whose interests the agent represented. In 1955, the Iowa legislature responded by making the agents state employees. New county councils were organized to carry on the work of the old Farm Bureau county boards, but the councils were now open to all farmers, not just Farm Bureau members.

Another major challenge for Extension was that farming had become more complicated. The federal government required farmers who participated in commodity programs to practice soil conservation techniques. With new technology such as pesticides and fertilizers as well as new machines such as bulk dairy systems, forage choppers, and combines for the corn crop, farmers faced a bewildering array of choices to make in conducting their operation. The Kepner Report, issued by the USDA and the Association of Land-Grant Colleges and Universities, addressed this growing complexity as it related to the education of farmers. The authors of the report stressed that farmers wanted new knowledge to increase production and profits. As the number of Extension specialists multiplied, however, it was more difficult to take the advice of many specialists and create a plan for an individual family. Rather than helping farm families with many different projects, the idea was that Extension staff members could help families choose projects that complemented each other and best utilized family labor and resources.

The Farm and Home Development Program (FHDP), created in 1952, was a program that addressed the changing conditions on the farm. As one farm journalist wrote, "Farm and home development is aimed at helping farm folks make business decisions . . . It is an attempt to tie recommended practices together in a way that best fits your own farm situation." Extension staff members targeted young families during the 1952–1953 year, offering "ideas, information, and counsel," but encouraging families to make their own decisions and to implement them. County directors exercised flexibility in the ways they conducted the program, with some focusing on record keeping and others on improving communication between husbands and wives. In some families, women kept the books and paid the bills while the men made decisions about operating the farm or making major purchases. While many women accepted this arrangement, other women and Extension leaders recognized that women lived with the consequences of those farm management decisions and that they should have a greater voice in making them. Ultimately, the FHDP accepted men and women as equal partners in the farm enterprise.[18]

The FHDP was especially valuable during the mid-1950s because farm prices were often stagnant, while farming had become much more costly. Analysts called this situation a "cost-price squeeze" in which farm profits did not keep pace with farm expenses. As a result, the 1950s was a decade when many people left farming. While some of these people did so because of old age or retirement, many people found that they did not want to make needed investments in their farms or did not have the financial resources to do so. Cooperative Extension published pamphlets that showed farmers how to cut costs on their farms and how to determine if a particular operation on the farm was profitable.[19]

In the 1950s, Extension added new areas of work in addition to the traditional issues of increasing production and improving farm business practices. Extension leaders looked outward and recognized that Americans were citizens of the world as well as of their local, state, and national communities. This new world was one of improved productive capacity and lifestyles, but it was also very challenging. Among the many changes of the postwar years (and the 1950s in particular) was the development of the cold war with the USSR, its Eastern Bloc allies, and the People's Republic of China. Civil rights agitation in Congress and at the grass roots attracted national attention. In Africa, Asia, and South and Central America, people joined together to overthrow the colonial governments that had ruled since the late 1800s. In the mid-1950s, Extension responded to these changes by conducting discussions of global issues titled Understanding Asia and American Foreign Policy. Extension leaders wanted to help people become better citizens of their respective communities by understanding global affairs and countering traditional midwestern isolationism.

By the late 1950s, it was clear to Extension leaders the degree to which rural Iowa, just like the rest of the world, was changing. Over the previous decade, a record number of Iowans left farms for better opportunity in towns and cities in Iowa and beyond. Farming was more complicated and expensive, but there were other changes as well. A greater percentage of young people graduated from high school and attended college, allowing them to have more career options than previous generations. Iowa communities were in the midst of change, and as a result, Extension refocused, paying more attention to the interconnections between farms and small towns as well as rural and urban areas.

In 1957, Extension launched the Our Changing Agriculture program, a series of discussions that addressed the ways in which these demographic shifts and new social realities would affect Iowans. Encouraged by the success of the discussions of 1957, Extension launched the Challenge to Iowa program in 1958. Associate Director of the Extension Service Marvin Anderson stated that "The goal of the program was to make every Iowan aware of the changes that were actually taking place and to encourage him to approach the challenge in a constructive way." Approximately forty thousand Iowans participated in discussion groups that included people from rural and urban areas. Many ideas came out of these discussion groups, but Iowan's top three concerns were economic growth to create new jobs and increase income, improving public school education, and expanding higher education in the state. Similarly, in the spring of 1961 Extension began another statewide discussion titled the Iowa Future Series, focusing on citizenship, economic growth, and the future of families, communities, and agriculture.[20]

The results of these discussions became apparent in changes to Extension's organizational structure and programs during the 1960s and 1970s. One of the first developments was a statewide reorganization in the 1960s to better meet the needs of Iowa's changing population. In 1961 Extension officials and Iowa State University leaders joined with business and community leaders to create TENCO, a ten-county Extension region in southern Iowa. The new program reflected the economic and social conditions of the postwar period. Simply put, this multi-county area was a place in which residents bought and sold goods and their labor. With automobiles and improved communications, people no longer worked, shopped, and sold commodities just within their own county. Instead, there were subregions within the state that reflected the ways in which people lived, worked, and played. If Extension would continue to be relevant to Iowans, it was important to reflect these significant social and economic changes.

TENCO was an effort to revitalize the ten counties around Ottumwa, which had been wracked by economic change. Coal mining, agriculture, and business were declining rapidly in this area. School enrollment had dropped. TENCO leaders focused on agriculture, industry, education, and recreation. They urged farmers to improve livestock production techniques, particularly focusing on the cow-calf herd. Iowa State Extension's regional approach was a true innovation in extension work. As historian Dorothy Schwieder explained, TENCO was "one of the first programs in the nation to put rural development on a regional basis." The regional approach as demonstrated by TENCO became the new supervisory structure for Extension; all twelve areas were in place by 1969, each with an area director to supervise county-level staff and coordinate work between counties, the area, and the Ames campus.[21]

The regional approach helped get highly trained experts closer to the people. The pace of technological change in agriculture was so rapid that farmers needed

THE ECONOMIC BASE OF TENCO

IOWA STATE UNIVERSITY of Science and Technology
COOPERATIVE EXTENSION SERVICE
Ames, Iowa . . . . . . . April 1964 . . . . . . RAD-31

*In 1961, Iowa Cooperative Extension created TENCO, a pioneering multicounty effort to reorganize Extension work on a regional basis. TENCO represented a recognition of the importance of significant changes in the state, including the growth of urban areas at the expense of rural areas. (Used by permission of Iowa State University Library/Special Collections Department)*

better access to expertise. As a writer for the state agricultural yearbook stated, "Area organization was designed to bring more specialized extension educators into closer contact with the people." The new position of area director was the leader of the various county staff members within the region. The county Extension director (CED) was often trained in Ames, but was a generalist rather than a specialist. For over a generation, the CED answered inquiries and served as a conduit between the experts in Ames and farmers. The CED now put the farmer in direct contact with experts who specialized in the field of inquiry. For example, Jim Johnson, Hardin County CED, earned an M.S. in ruminant nutrition in the 1960s but could make no claims of specialization in agronomy or entomology. Each area included Extension specialists in livestock, business management, area development, youth work, and farm and home development. Agribusinesses also provided expert advice on their projects with field men who frequently knew more

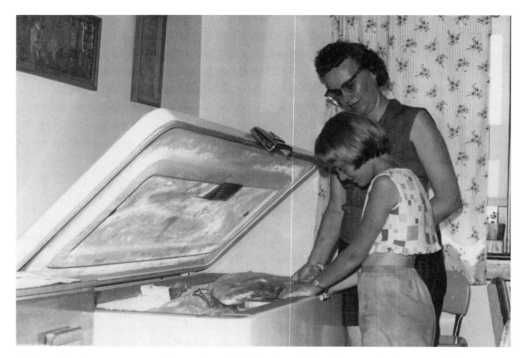

*Extension home economists, circa 1960, helped families make the transition to new food storage technology and techniques such as home freezers and freezing through the Family Living Program. (Used by permission of Iowa State University Library/Special Collections Department)*

about their particular product or field than the CED who remained a generalist. CEDs continued to play a role in advising farmers on production issues, but they increasingly assisted farmers in getting expert advice rather than providing it themselves.[22]

Home economists also faced many challenges in the 1960s. The FHDP faded in importance as county directors and home economists moved on to other projects, especially as farm prices recovered in the late 1950s. It was often difficult to get farm women to commit to Extension programs in the 1960s as more farm women began to work outside the home. The primary emphasis of Home Economics Extension in the 1960s was the Family Living Program. Much like the FHDP of the 1950s and early 1960s, the idea was that the family was a unit, and that programming should address the family rather than individual family members. Family Living Program topics were organized into six areas of mental and physical health, management, housing, consumer information, human development, and community and public programs. Still, many of the Family Living Programs resembled the work home economists performed for years, including seasonal fashion, sewing with new (synthetic) fabrics, foods, and child care. The Expanded Nutrition Program began in 1969 to train and guide "family food aides," who would teach low-income families about proper diet and nutrition. In many cases, these food aides were recruited from the same socioeconomic groups that the program served.[23]

*Youth work has always been an important part of the Extension mission. These 4-H participants developed technical and communication skills as they prepared their project. By the 1970s 4-H focused more on personal development, even though projects remained an important part of the 4-H experience. (Used by permission of Iowa State University Library/Special Collections Department)*

Youth work underwent important changes in the 1960s, as well, although the projects of the 1960s often resembled projects of the 1950s. Extension leaders wanted to refocus youth work from a project-centered approach to one that emphasized personal growth and skill development and leadership. Leaders also wanted to break down some of the distinctions between traditional "boy" projects such as livestock and crop production and "girl" projects such as sewing, food, and decorating. As Dorothy Schwieder noted, however, "this change was often difficult to accomplish." The popularity and success of traditional projects made it difficult for leaders and young people to change 4-H.[24]

Back in Ames, the university expanded its outreach function under the leadership of President W. Robert Parks. Parks believed that the benefits of public investment in the entire university should be taken to all of the people. The university created the office of dean of Extension in 1966 to lead what would be called University Extension. Parks appointed Marvin Anderson, the former director of Iowa Cooperative Extension Service, as dean. Anderson was a longtime veteran of Extension work both in the field and at Iowa State who served as dean until 1974. The new plan for University Extension joined four different university departments together: Cooperative Extension, Engineering Extension Service, the Center for Industrial Research and Service (CIRAS), and the Agriculture Short Course

Office. All of the previous outreach efforts would be managed by one office to better coordinate those efforts. This change reflected the view that Extension should be more than simply home economics and agriculture and that the university needed a modern organizational structure to utilize resources most effectively.[25]

For much of the 1970s agricultural production received the largest share of Extension resources. Farm issues were prominent in local, state, and national headlines, especially as they related to public concerns about the use of pesticides, residues in soil, water, and animal tissues, and problems of manure and fertilizer runoff. Extension hosted a series of public forums in each of the twelve Extension areas to educate farmers and the public about the risks of pesticides and farm wastes as well as the best practices to mitigate those risks. Meanwhile, state and county Extension staff focused on improved techniques in crop and livestock production.[26]

Community resource development was an important part of the Extension program in the 1970s. The attention given to communities increased as farm population declined. The effects of that decline could be seen on the main streets of small towns across the state as shops and businesses closed. The 1950s marked the rapid acceleration of this trend, and not surprisingly, Extension community development programs became more important during those decades. In 1971 Extension created the Regional Rural Development Center at Iowa State University to focus on the problems faced by a particular area in the state and to help communities come up with solutions to their problems. The first area to receive attention was a nine-county region around Fort Dodge.

The 1970s marked a major shift in Home Economics Extension. For years the local home economists selected programs from a manual compiled by the state specialists in developing their annual work plans. According to Elizabeth Elliott, who became head of Home Economics Extension in 1977, the old program was designed to address a specific problem with subject matter provided by a specialist. The new program was more focused on the big picture of decision making. Furthermore, Home Economics Extension leaders determined that a large portion of program resources were tied up in one-on-one meetings with clients and staff members. As Dorothy Schwieder noted, while "this approach produced a high level of client satisfaction, it also represented an inordinate amount of time devoted to a single client." Extension leaders replaced the old approach with monthly workshops, which included large group meetings in the morning and consultations with specialists in the afternoons.[27]

Extension home economics reflected the changing concerns of Iowans. From a program perspective, the Expanded Food and Nutrition Program took on greater importance, addressing the problem of low-income housing by providing information on government-assisted housing. Operation Ship Shape was an attempt to instruct low-income families in the best methods in home repairs. As energy costs increased in the 1970s, Extension leaders attempted to help families control or reduce spending on utility bills. Home economists instructed people in the installation of insulation, storm doors, and storm windows to reduce energy consumption and conducted analyses of home energy costs with and without energy-saving modifications. The Home Energy Audit Program reached thousands of households

*In the 1970s, 4-H was more inclusive than it had been in the past. In addition to traditional agriculture and homemaking projects, 4-H leaders reached out to urban constituencies and minority populations. This photo is from a 4-H cross-cultural camp in 1976. (Used by permission of Iowa State University Library/Special Collections Department)*

in the attempt to improve energy conservation and save money. An analysis of the program in 1981 indicated that 65 percent of all program participants adopted one or more energy-saving techniques in their home. Furthermore, a growing percentage of families included two working adults, which meant that more people chose to dine away from home, making it more difficult to provide healthy food choices for families. Food and nutrition programs, targeted to families at all income levels, accounted for a large share of Extension spending in the 1970s and 1980s.[28]

In the 1970s, Extension 4-H leaders also reached out to urban youth as the trend toward urbanization and suburbanization continued. There had been 4-H programs for urban children in other parts of the country, but in the 1970s this became an area of emphasis for program leaders. From 1970 to 1976 enrollment in beef projects only increased by 21 percent while enrollment in nonfarm projects such as creative arts and child care increased by 876 percent and 543 percent, respectively. The growth in these project areas reflected a fundamental shift in Iowa's population.[29]

The most important development in reaching out to urban and suburban youth was the change in emphasis in 4-H from the traditional project to the person. In the early days of Extension, this orientation on projects made sense, since part of the purpose of youth work was to persuade the next generation of farmers of the value of improved production practices in an age when many adults did not see the value in those techniques. In 1971, C. J. Gauger, state leader of Extension youth programs, explained that in the postwar period, this was an inappropriate strategy. He claimed that "we placed the emphasis on the wrong end of the halter." Gauger explained that the new approach was based on projects that "develop a more mature, well-rounded individual."[30]

In spite of the new focus on individuals as well as urban people and urban problems, Extension remained committed to meeting the needs of farm families. Farm men and women believed that the Extension staff members still played an important part in rural communities. Opinion polls showed that although county directors made fewer visits to farms and that home economists met with fewer clients one-on-one, the percentage of farmers who contacted Extension representatives was still high in the early 1970s. Dean of Extension Marvin Anderson reported that he was pleased that so many people continued to rely on Extension even as it reorganized into area offices and increasingly dealt with urban issues. As Anderson explained, each staff member now served seven counties instead of just one, which meant that each employee served many more people than in previous years. The changes in Extension organization and program did not undermine public confidence in its ability to serve Iowans.[31]

Throughout the 1970s, the tremendous out-migration from agriculture combined with a continued cost-price squeeze meant that farmers scrambled for more land and invested in new machinery and buildings to gain economies of scale. As a result, land prices began to soar, which gave farmers better access to credit since they had more collateral. Farmers borrowed money to purchase land and invest in new equipment. The downside to this trend was that in the early 1980s commodity and land prices fell, which meant farmers did not have the income to meet expenses and pay their debts.

University Extension was there when agriculture crashed in the 1980s. Extension professionals helped deal with the suffering and dislocation resulting from the farm crisis as they simultaneously continued to labor on production issues, youth work, home economics, and community development. As Iowa State University agricultural economist Neil Harl demonstrated, farmers who had the highest debt-to-asset ratios were the most vulnerable during the agricultural crash. This included younger farmers and those who were most aggressive about expansion, including those who invested in new land and machinery to accommodate the entry of new family members into the farm operation. Farmers were at risk because of a combination of federal policies that encouraged inflation, high interest rates, and large budget deficits. All of these factors exacerbated the farm debt crisis that occurred when commodity and land prices were low.[32]

While Extension was powerless to raise commodity prices, it could help farmers learn how to cope. The Cooperative Extension solution was the application of business principles, just as it was in the 1950s. In 1984, Extension launched the ASSIST program to raise awareness about farm problems, conduct management assistance and counseling for farm families, coordinate community support for farmers, and provide short courses in farm finances, among other subjects. A series of home study pamphlets from 1984 titled *Stress on the Farm* provided advice on numerous topics, including stress management techniques, understanding depression, and resolving family conflicts. Extension also cooperated with the Iowa Department of Human Services and the United Way of Central Iowa to establish the Iowa Rural Concern Hotline. Callers could get referrals to agencies that could help with problems relating to the farm crisis. The ASSIST program and the hotline were invaluable to many people. Thousands of farmers participated in these programs, which met emotional needs as well as material needs. In just five months of 1985 over 3,700 callers, most of them men, used the hotline. Ninety percent of all callers were concerned about financial issues. As agriculture suffered, so too did the Extension Service. Falling tax revenues meant reduced budgets for Extension. In the mid-1980s, Extension cut staff from approximately 430 employees to 370.[33]

Other aspects of Extension dealt with changing conditions during the 1980s farm crisis. Home Economics Extension also dealt with the farm crisis. Family specialists assisted with workshops in budgeting and finances. Extension specialists believed that families who needed housing improvements should not be neglected even in lean times. Extension professionals helped families take on low- or no-cost makeovers by moving furniture or reallocating living spaces. In 1985, Iowa Extension staff received a grant to develop a program to offer more in-depth assistance to families in crisis called Taking Charge in Changing Times. As one participant recalled, the purpose was not to offer solutions but to listen and to help families decide what their priorities were. With Extension's assistance, many families who were immobilized by their problems began to resolve them.[34]

Meanwhile, the agricultural crisis exacerbated the problems of rural communities. More people left farming, Main Street businesses failed, school enrollment declined, and churches struggled with smaller, aging congregations. Extension leaders conducted meetings throughout the state to help towns cope with these problems. For example, in Liscomb Extension leaders led discussions to help people there decide if it was a good idea to form a community corporation to create a grocery, restaurant, and service station. Community members purchased $40,000 worth of shares in the project. That money, combined with a loan from the Small Business Administration, enabled them to build their project. Extension set up Community Economic Development workshops to assist community leaders in attracting or creating new businesses. Over sixty communities participated in this program by 1988.[35]

As farmers and Extension professionals struggled with financial problems and the changing nature of rural communities, farm production remained one of the top priorities for Extension. As Dean of Extension Robert L. Crom noted in 1983, "The delivery of Extension education programs to farmers in all ninety-nine counties is recognized as aiding them in maintaining high corn (121.0 bushels/acre) and soybean (37.5 bushels/acre) yields in 1982, a year of adverse environmental conditions." Extension leaders worked with soybean producers to plant in narrower rows to increase yields and farm income. A soybean workshop in the sum-

*Iowa State University Extension has always been about production agriculture. Farmers at field days like this one in 1986 learned about new production techniques such as conservation tillage and no-till, appropriate plant populations per acre to maximize yields, integrated pest management, and ways to reduce harvesting losses. (Used with permission from Iowa State University Extension)*

mer of 1985 addressed a wide variety of problems and issues confronting farmers who raised that crop.[36]

Extension was also present as farmers adjusted to new concerns about chemical technology in the 1970s and 1980s. Many farmers used chemical fertilizers and pesticides without formal training in application techniques or in-depth knowledge about the ways in which these chemicals could affect people and ecosystems. There had been highly publicized problems associated with pesticides in Iowa and the nation by the 1970s, including the presence of new pests that tolerated chemicals, the rise of pesticide-resistant species of plants and insects, and the contamination of surface and ground waters. Furthermore, by the seventies and eighties scientists better understood some of the long-term health hazards of chemical use. Extension became a leader in promoting safe handling and application of chemicals. In the late 1970s, Integrated Pest Management (IPM) became an important program component as university-based agricultural experts, farmers, and concerned citizens became aware that pesticides could be as hazardous as they were helpful. IPM was a strategy that combined cultural, biological, and chemical control techniques rather than simply relying on chemicals. Statewide monitoring of pest populations helped extension professionals recommend that for some farmers it was not cost-effective for them to treat some of their corn acres for insect pests, thereby reducing the amount of toxic chemicals entering the soil and water.

Extension also responded as federal regulatory agencies tightened rules on the use of antibiotics and sulfa drug residues in livestock products. In the mid-1980s, Extension veterinary programs helped reduce the amount of sulfa drug residues in swine carcasses.[37]

Along with the shift in emphasis from chemical control to IPM, Extension leaders focused on creating an agricultural system that was more sustainable than that which had emerged in the immediate aftermath of World War II. While sustainable agriculture has been defined many ways, the concept is rooted in the idea that farming relied too heavily on nonrenewable fossil fuel–based inputs of fertilizer, pesticides, and fuels. These inputs were expensive in terms of farm finances and the long-term health of ecosystems. Accordingly, when the state legislature created the Leopold Center for Sustainable Agriculture at Iowa State in 1987, a key component was the use of the Extension Service to disseminate information about alternative farm practices as well as crop and livestock systems that could provide livelihoods for Iowans and possibly avoid some of the pitfalls of modern production agriculture. The traditional field days, short courses, and other activities of the Extension Service continued in the 1980s, even as the specific techniques of raising crops and livestock changed.

During the 1980s, Extension and Iowa State University developed innovative information-sharing programs that utilized the latest technology. Computers were valuable tools for helping farmers and homemakers understand their operations. From 1979 to 1981, Home Economics Extension offered a "computer-assisted program" to help people determine if they could afford to own their own home. In 1982, Extension cooperated with the Agricultural Infodata Service and Iowa Public Television to televise "real-time" information regarding weather, crop conditions, pest infestations, and commodity prices for eighteen hours per day. EXNET, a computer network, was designed to get information from the university to Extension staff members and subscribers across the state.[38]

Developments in telecommunications technology also shaped the ways in which Iowa State reached out to people across the state. The Telebridge system was a creation of the regents institutions to enhance distance learning at Iowa State University, the University of Iowa, and the University of Northern Iowa through teleconferencing and telecourses. At Iowa State, Extension accounted for most of the Telebridge use, which is not surprising considering that university-based Extension staff members needed to be in regular contact with county and area Extension staff as well as the fact that Extension was the institution within the university most dedicated to outreach. Although some departments within the university utilized the telecourse program, eventually university leaders discontinued the program. They found that new conditions decreased the demand for telecourses, including the rise of the community colleges, which met the needs of many students who had used the telecourse. Furthermore, there was a lack of participation in the program by Iowa State faculty, who sometimes perceived that telecourses were inferior to more traditional courses.[39]

The 1990s brought continued sophistication and expansion of Extension work. Beginning in the 1980s, a growing portion of Iowa families chose to educate their children at home. To help families provide high-quality education to their children

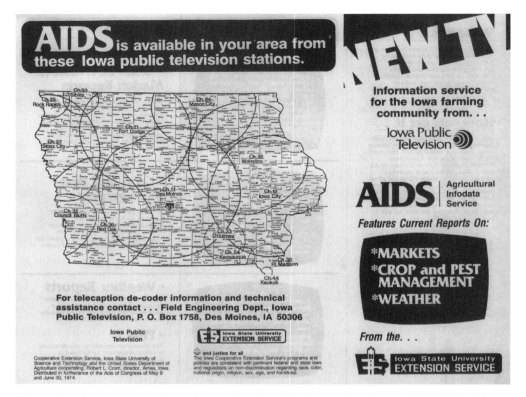

*Changing times meant changing technology for Extension. Iowa Public Television and Iowa State Extension cooperated to create the Agricultural Infodata Service. This service provided farmers with "real-time" information about weather, crop conditions, pest infestations, market reports, and commodity prices for eighteen hours every day. (Used with permission from Iowa State University Extension)*

in specialized subjects, Extension created the E-SET program. The E-SET program (Extension-Science, Engineering, and Technology Youth Initiative) was designed to provide assistance to traditional teachers as well as families who homeschooled their children. In 2000, over eight hundred trained educators instructed twenty-two thousand Iowa youth in a variety of programs called Marsville, Robotix, Bridges, and Toys in Space, which focused on science and design.[40]

Extension remained relevant to Iowans, even as the state's population became more urban and suburban. From 1990 to 1996 residents of fifty-nine Iowa counties chose to increase funding for Extension. Part of this grassroots support was tied to the widespread appeal of youth programs. One such popular program, Growing in the Garden, designed for children in grades K–3, provides students opportunities to learn about plants and food production. Other programs demonstrate that Extension is relevant to current concerns. In the aftermath of the disastrous flooding that occurred across the state during the summer of 1993, Extension hosted a conference titled "After the Flood: Assessing, Repairing, and Rebuilding Basements," which focused on drainage issues and health risks from mold and mildew, as well as the special issues relating to different building mate-

*The Fire Service Institute provided training to thousands of Iowa firefighters, community leaders, and students over the years. (Used with permission from Iowa State University Extension)*

rials. The audience included home builders and remodelers, insurance adjusters, and others who worked with homeowners.[41]

Community development continued to be a major thrust of Extension in the 1990s. The long-standing Fire Service Institute provided courses and training to thousands of firefighters from across the state every year. In addition to leadership training and community planning, Extension to Communities also conducted the Iowa Municipal Clerks Institute and Academy, which has provided training in communications, finance, personnel procedures, administration, and governance to clerks and finance officers from Iowa municipalities since the 1970s. Each year Extension trained thousands of community leaders and helped create jobs across the state in rural and urban areas.[42]

Even though Extension remained committed to families, youth work, and community development, the proportion of funding for those program areas declined in relation to earlier levels. Agricultural programs continued to attract the largest portion of funding, totaling almost 39 percent of funds in 1996. But work for families accounted for 17 percent, youth and 4-H spending was only 11 percent, and business and industry projects were 9 percent, while community projects totaled only 9 percent. Still, one of every five Iowa young people participated in Extension programs, even as the proportion of spending on those programs declined.[43]

New communications technologies have been central to Extension's educational mission. Television continued to be a part of Iowa State's outreach until the university sold the WOI television station in 1994. It was a controversial decision that aroused great passions among supporters and opponents of the sale. As television faded in importance to Iowa State Cooperative Extension after the sale of WOI, the Iowa Communications Network and the World Wide Web were important new tools for Extension in the 1990s. The State of Iowa launched the Iowa Communications Network to improve access to education across the state by providing specially equipped classrooms in each county and in selected locations. In 1996, students from Iowa, California, and Pennsylvania participated in ISU Extension's first virtual classroom via the ICN, while a two-day video conference on beef nutrition reached 1,100 U.S. and Canadian participants at forty sites. Iowa State University Extension established a presence on the World Wide Web in 1994. Web courses became an important part of the university's outreach throughout the 1990s. Iowa State offered its first Web courses in 1996, and in 1998, Extended and Continuing Education offered a total of 266 distance learning courses for credit, nineteen of which were conducted via the Web in the fall of that year. A partnership with the Iowa Farm Bureau Federation and Lighthouse Communications would help provide Internet service to rural Iowans. Extension leaders were optimistic that improved communications technology and Internet connections would improve rural access to educational opportunities.[44]

In addition to changes in the techniques and technology of delivering programs, Extension reorganized again. In 1997, local county Extension councils formed the Iowa Association of County Extension Councils (IACEC). Previously, each county Extension council stood alone, but with the new organization county councils could coordinate their efforts. This paid off as the legislature permitted the councils to accept grants, contract for educational services, and accept new sources of funds. According to the 1998 Annual Report, these changes allowed the councils "to diversify revenue sources and become more entrepreneurial."[45]

Extension's entrepreneurial emphasis of the late 1990s was no accident. When Stanley Johnson became vice provost for Extension in 1996, he recognized that Extension would need to find new sources of revenue. Johnson previously served as the director of the ISU Center for Agriculture and Rural Development. Johnson introduced a more entrepreneurial approach to funding Extension, pursuing more grants and implementing more user fees for Extension services, even as state appropriations increased during his tenure.[46]

By 2000, one of the most noteworthy changes in Extension was the growth in complexity and breadth of the outreach mission. Improving farming and household work in the late 1800s and early 1900s often meant convincing farmers to use fertilizer, invest in purebred livestock, or introduce labor-saving machinery in the home. Even as recently as World War II, many farm families clung to old techniques, in part due to their desire to minimize cash outlays or to simply farm the best way they knew how to farm. But new technology, shrinking per-unit returns on crops and livestock, and the massive migration from farms to towns and cities meant that farmers had to adjust to survive. Farming was more complex and so was Extension. More people lived in urban areas, and Extension adapted to meet the needs of urban people. New instructional technology enabled Extension to serve traditional clients and to reach new ones.

A quick survey of the Cooperative Extension Web site revealed the extent to which Extension work had changed just since 1945. Extension to Communities offered leadership training in cooperation with the League of Iowa Cities. In partnership with the United Way, Extension created the Nonprofit Management Institute in 1999, which helped professionals develop skills such as strategic planning, marketing, and fund-raising. Extension's Community Vitality Center was devoted to understanding the ways in which communities preserved or enhanced employment opportunities and quality of life issues as well as sharing that information with communities across the state. The Partnering Landscape and Community Enhancement program assisted communities in assessing needs and developing plans to revitalize communities.[47]

ISU Extension actively worked with businesses to spur economic development through Extension to Business and Industry. Extension's Center for Industrial Research and Service (CIRAS) provided information and technical assistance in engineering, management and other fields to Iowa manufacturers. Furthermore, the Iowa Manufacturing Extension Partnership, a group of businesses, trade organizations, state agencies, ISU, and community colleges, provided technical assistance and training to help Iowa businesses increase productivity and enhance their competitiveness.

Extension to Families continued to strive to improve the quality of home and family life for Iowans. Nutrition programs remained popular, with almost twenty-three thousand adults and youths participating in nutrition education programs in 1997. Iowans demanded help with financial management, as thousands of people participated in workshops, one-on-one consultations, or computer credit analyses. Extension to Families offered a range of programs from food safety courses for youth and senior citizens to parenting education classes, addressing concerns that Iowans face regardless of age or whether they live in urban, rural, or suburban areas.[48]

Continuing education and communications services played an important role in serving Iowans as well as University Extension as an organization. Distance learning for credit and noncredit courses served people in almost every Iowa county. The communications services office developed promotional and training materials for all Extension departments, creating and distributing items for Iowans and people around the world. Extension confronted the demands of the digital age by working to enhance access to the Internet for Iowans, allowing them to have improved access not only to the expertise and resources of Iowa State but also the World Wide Web.

Youth development remained a vital part of Extension work. Leaders continued to stress the development of life skills that strengthened each participant's sense of belonging, generosity, independence, and mastery. Approximately one-fourth of Iowa young people were involved in 4-H Youth Development programs at the end of the twentieth century. The programs ranged from Growing in the Garden, targeted to kindergarten through third grade, to 4-H clubs. Youth programs focused on connections between agriculture, natural resources, food, and people. As always, the 4-H program relied on the generosity of thousands of adult and youth volunteers.[49]

Last, and certainly not least, agriculture and natural resources programming continued to be the largest area of Extension work. From training pesticide and manure applicators to the Master Gardener Program, Extension reached hundreds of thousands of Iowans. Most of these people participated in workshops, attended field meetings, received newsletters, or called Extension hotlines, while some learned via Web stream or individual consultations. All of the issues farmers faced in the years after 1945 remained at the turn of the new millennium: low or stagnant commodity prices, the need for more education and skill development, the desire to modernize in order to cut per-unit production costs, and the pressure to expand acreages, herds, and flocks to gain economies of scale. These were the areas of expertise that Extension professionals had developed since its inception.

Iowa State Extension changed and adapted as it grew from the early efforts of Adonijah Welch, Seaman Knapp, and Perry Holden to the diverse network of people and programs of today. Even though Extension became far more complex than any of its early practitioners could have envisioned, it was remarkably similar in at least one important respect. Extension leaders were still driven to help Iowans change their lives through education. People of every age group, socioeconomic class, or ethnicity gained something through their involvement with Cooperative Extension. Conceived when most Iowans and other Americans lived on farms, Extension was designed to help rural people produce efficiently in an urban age. Extension played an important part in helping rural people make informed decisions about farm production and lifestyles. But to most Iowans of the post–World War II period, Extension was about much more than farming. By 2000, few people were involved in production agriculture, and only a sizable minority of Iowans lived in rural areas, but Extension remained relevant to Iowans as they worked, played, and enhanced the quality of their lives.

# Vignettes

## Art on Campus: A Historical Overview

The Iowa State campus art scene experienced a cultural renaissance in the 1930s. Iowa State College's President Raymond Hughes (1927–1936) believed that beauty was not only an essential part of everyday life but that beauty in the form of the arts was integral to learning, creating educated citizens who would be successful in local and world affairs. He supported and encouraged the fine and applied arts on campus, instituting visual, performing, and literary arts curricula across the academic landscape. On January 26, 1928, President Hughes appointed the College Art Committee, composed of Dr. Edward S. Allen, chairman and professor of mathematics; Joanne M. Hansen, professor of applied art; A. H. Kimball, professor of architectural engineering; and P. H. Elwood, Jr., professor of landscape architecture.

The Iowa State of 1933–1934 was small: with 3,784 students and 360 faculty and staff, it was located in a town of 10,260. Interdisciplinary endeavors were common and today's art-filled campus is a result of collaborations of artists, engineers, architects, agriculturalists, administrators, and students. The "artistic campus" was a common campus goal and achievement, inspired by the belief that beauty would elevate the intellectual mind and the moral fiber of the community.

In 1928, Iowa State College had joined in cultural meetings with the American Federation of the Arts, who had been active in Iowa as early as 1923. This symbiotic relationship proved fruitful in many ways, providing touring exhibitions, national speakers, critics and artists, and information on the national art scene. This association may have led to a relationship with the Carnegie Foundation, which soon would provide funding for ground-breaking arts projects at Iowa State College. In 1934 Anson Marston, dean of engineering, accepted the challenge of incorporating art appreciation into engineering, thereby providing a dramatic change in college curricula that supporters hoped would extend to all campus disciplines. This project began with thirty lectures for faculty and students. Many of these lectures were also presented as part of a WOI Radio series, thereby extending arts education and appreciation statewide.

Building on a practice of purchasing reproduction works of art that were then installed in the classrooms and corridors at ISC, Hughes expanded his scope in 1932 and began purchasing original works of art for campus. This included paintings from Iowa artists, some of whom participated in Grant Wood's Stone City Art Colony and later worked under sponsorship of the

*(continued)*

Public Works of Art Project (PWAP). Hughes soon took the giant step of commissioning original works of art, including portraits of historically prominent Iowa State faculty, alumni, and administrators. These commissioned works became the foundation of the University Art Collection, today known as the Art on Campus Collection. In 1933, at the depth of the Great Depression, Iowa State dedicated a newly commissioned campus portrait approximately every other month.

In 1928, just as the newly completed Memorial Union was opening, Zenobia Ness and Harold Pride developed the Iowa Artists Salon, an exhibition immediately following the Iowa State Fair art exhibition. The Iowa Artists Salon, held each year in the Memorial Union, concluded with an artist dinner and expressed Iowa State's sincere appreciation to the artists for their contributions to the college and the state. Grant Wood was a participant in these exhibitions and dinners as well as a reluctant speaker. These annual exhibitions and dinners and the resulting personal relationships may have been the impetus for Iowa State to commission, in 1934, the mural cycle *When Tillage Begins, Other Arts Follow*. Grant Wood accepted this commission at the apex of his national popularity and career. Within a few months, in January 1934, Christian Petersen was hired to sculpt the mural cycle *The History of Dairying* for the new Dairy Industries Building.

During the 1930s, Iowa State College was a leader and indeed a national model for commissioning and integrating the visual arts on campus to create a beautiful, inspiring center of learning. During the seven-month lifespan of the Public Works of Art Project in 1934, four hundred mural projects across America were created by both well-known and nearly anonymous painters. Murals, both local and national, became populist symbols of cultural renewal during a very painful economy. Grant Wood's murals for the Iowa State Library won immediate praise in national media such as *Time* and *Fortune* magazines.

In 1934, Christian Petersen (1885–1961) became the nation's first permanent campus artist-in-residence; in 1937 he was appointed assistant professor in the Applied Art Department. Fulfilling his life's dream, Petersen continued his teaching and sculpting at Iowa State until his retirement in 1955, and even then maintained a campus studio. In all he sculpted twelve major works for the campus and created hundreds of studio sculptures. He taught thousands of students from all disciplines. The students' love and appreciation was evident when, in 1951, they dedicated the Iowa State *Bomb* to him.

Two other artists-in-residence followed, Joanne M. Hansen (1949–1950) and Dwight Kirsch (1965). Only Kirsch's residency produced a permanent, site-specific mural. That mural is located at Kildee Hall. The College Art Committee, later known as the University Art Committee, continued to function in the 1950s, 1960s, and 1970s but with diminished vigor in acquiring campus works of art and integrating art across the campus. It focused instead on securing varied exhibitions for several campus locations. The National Endowment for the Arts was created by Congress in 1965 and inspired another artistic renaissance. By 1975, Iowa State partnered with the National Endowment for the Arts and commissioned Iowa artist Frederic Rennels to sculpt *Prairie Tetons*, a heroically scaled sculpture in a contemporary and abstract style.

In 1979, the state legislature, responding to the leadership of John Murray, an Ames attorney and state senator, passed legislation that created the State of Iowa Art in State Buildings Program. This legislation required that one-half of 1 percent of capital construction funds be used to acquire public art for all new state buildings. This requirement was a major factor in reviving the acquisition of public art for the Iowa State campus.

In the academic year of 1975–1976, Iowa State opened two new campus museums, the Brunnier Art Museum and the Farm House Museum. The University Museums was designated in 1980 as the campus unit responsible for administering the State of Iowa Art in State Buildings Program, which became one of several methods for purchasing campus public art.

In 1982, the University Museums created and formalized the Art on Campus Collection and Program, encompassing the acquisition, education, care, and conservation of Iowa State's public art collection across campus. Today the Art on Campus Collection is the nation's largest campus public art collection with nearly five hundred major public works of art and additions of about twenty-five new public works annually. The Art on Campus Collection includes aesthetic objects, aesthetic landscape design, and architectural sculpture and ornamentation. It is a program that enriches the cultural, intellectual, and scholarly life of Iowa State University and the citizens of Iowa by developing, educating about, and maintaining a collection of works by recognized artists of our time and by preserving our historical public art traditions. It is inventive in both its curatorial consistency and its all-inclusive working processes based on the democratic, land-grant mission.

Warren R. Madden and Lynette L. Pohlman

# Reiman Gardens:
# New Growth of an Old Tradition

Horticulture was one of the original programs of study when the Iowa State College of Agriculture and Farm opened to its first class of students on March 17, 1869, and a horticulture garden has been a part of the campus since 1914 when the Horticulture Building was constructed. In the 1960s, the garden was moved to a three-quarter-acre site on the northeast side of the campus, where it remained until 1993, hemmed in by streets and parking lots, and in the shadow of the university's power plant.

That changed significantly when Iowa State alumnus Roy Reiman and his wife, Bobbi, of Greendale, Wisconsin, led a complete transformation of the horticulture garden, in size, location, scope, and character. The Reimans provided the initial gift of $1.3 million to move and expand the gardens to a five-acre site southwest of Jack Trice Stadium and at the Elwood Drive entrance to the university's South Campus. Construction began in October 1993 and the Reiman Gardens, named in Roy and Bobbi's honor, were dedicated on September 16, 1995.

One of the reasons that site was selected was because it allowed room for future expansion, which the Reiman Gardens have done. With additional gifts from the Reimans and other alumni and friends, and with support from the local volunteer group known as the Reiman Gardens Co-Horts, Reiman Gardens now covers fourteen acres, making it the largest public garden in Iowa. It features eleven different garden areas, including a children's garden, herb garden, home production garden, and a national award-winning rose garden. Facilities include a conservatory with auditorium, domed tropical botanical center, meeting rooms, gift shop, café, work and laboratory rooms, the Christina Reiman Butterfly Wing (named for Roy Reiman's mother) and butterfly incubation area, the quaint cottage-style Hunziker House for small-group activities, and the original John Mahlstede Horticulture Learning Center.

With its growth, the Reiman Gardens has become a major visitor attraction for Ames, bringing approximately 120,000 visitors annually. Although no longer administered by the Department of Horticulture, Reiman Gardens maintains close connections with many of Iowa State's academic programs, including Horticulture, Plant Sciences, Landscape Architecture, Entomology, Institution and Resource Management, Marketing, Communications, and Human Sciences. Between twenty and twenty-five classes each semester use the gardens for class work, and nearly fifty students are employed by the gardens, gaining experience in a variety of areas related to the operation and management of the Reiman Gardens. The gardens also support many of Iowa State's student organizations, including the Hort Club, Turf Club, Forestry Club, and Entomology Club, by hosting their fund-raising activities and employing club members for on-site projects.

John R. Anderson

# Nawal El Moutawakel: Trailblazer

Nawal El Moutawakel arrived at Iowa State in January of 1983. No one could have imagined that this young woman would break momentous barriers for women around the world. The Moroccan had left Casablanca and although fluent in Arabic and French, she was still learning the art of English as she arrived in Ames on a very cold January day. El Moutawakel was recruited sight unseen, by assistant women's track coach Pat Moynihan and head coach Ron Renko. Switching from distance running to sprint hurdle events, El Moutawakel had made a fortuitous decision to concentrate on running the four-hundred-meter hurdles, one of the toughest events in track and field. By 1983 she ranked among the top thirty hurdlers internationally.

There were immediate challenges beyond language and culture shock. Just six weeks into her stay, she was belatedly told by her family that her father, who had encouraged his daughter to compete in running shorts when much of the Muslim world discouraged athletic competition of this nature, had died. Her brother came to take her back to Morocco. She stood her ground and decided to stay at Iowa State.

Her life changed forever in 1984. She won the four hundred meters at the Big Eight indoor track and field championships, and earned All-America honors in the hurdle at the NCAA indoor meet. Her outdoor season changed the world. The Big Eight outdoor four-hundred-meter hurdle champion, El Moutawakel won an NCAA championship in a meet record 55.84 seconds and was fourth in the four hundred meters.

El Moutawakel's performance made her the only woman on the 1984 Moroccan Olympic team. Her biggest fan was the country's king, Hassan II. He told her before the games that she could win a gold medal in Los Angeles. Dealing with those expectations, she made history. The Cyclone raced to a victory not forecast by track and field journalists. Her time of 54.61 in the first such race in Olympic history was a personal best. As she toured the track for a victory lap she did so as the first Arabic and first Muslim woman to win the gold medal. Her victory made her a national hero. King Hassan II declared that all girls born on that day be named Nawal. She persevered at Iowa State, despite the loss of Renko and Moynihan in an ISU cross-country plane crash in 1985. She also overcame an injury to compete again for the Cyclones.

El Moutawakel has served as Morocco's secretary to the minister of social affairs, responsible for youth and sport. In 1999, she was named managing director of the Foundation of Moroccan Bank of Foreign Trade for education and environment. She was the first women from a Muslim nation named to the International Olympic Committee. Her international reputation earned her the position of chair of the International Olympic Committee commission charged with evaluating the bids to host the 2012 Olympic Games among applications by Paris, New York, Moscow, Madrid, and eventual winner London.

Her international stature was affirmed when El Moutawakel was selected to carry the Olympic flag into the stadium during the opening ceremonies of the 2006 Torino Winter Games.

Tom Kroeschell

*Chapter 9*

# The Practical and the Picturesque: The Iowa State Campus

Peter Butler

Those who have visited Iowa State University campus more than likely hold a strong image of the place in their minds. Whether their visit included a stroll on central campus, a romantic moment at the Campanile, an evening of performance at the Memorial Union, or a sporting event at Jack Trice Stadium, the inspiring qualities of campus are not easily forgotten. The evolution of campus as a place reaches back into the nineteenth century, an age of transcendent poetry and the growth of a national conservation ethic. This history delves into the motivations of individuals whose imagination and creativity are expressed in the spaces and places of the university. And it rests on the values and traditions of Iowa State University as an embodiment of the spirit of the people of Iowa.[1]

Recent recognition has come to the campus as it was identified as one of the most beautiful campuses in the country. Central campus has been recognized by the American Society of Landscape Architects as a significant contribution to the history of design. The individuals and collaborators that created the order, the spaces, the buildings, the plantings, and the patterns that can be seen today began with a very simple question. How can Iowa State Agricultural College reflect the values of the state of Iowa? In many ways, the campus still retains the integrity of the early design decisions. Through one hundred and fifty years of development and change, demolition and construction, and staggering growth in the student population, a visit to campus today reveals the layers of the history that resulted in a stunning landscape.

Iowa State Agricultural College, from its beginnings, was an experiment in a new model for academic institutions. The need was for an institution modeled around the practical development of the state's citizens in the areas of agriculture and engineering. The physical campus reflected these very pragmatic directives and relationships.

The original site chosen for the college included many of the vegetation types of Iowa: woodland, prairie, and riparian areas, along stream banks. Cultural landscape forms, as laboratories for learning, also had a strong place within the campus plan including pasture, orchard, croplands, and windbreaks. Blending the built forms with the natural forms created the balance between nature and humanity

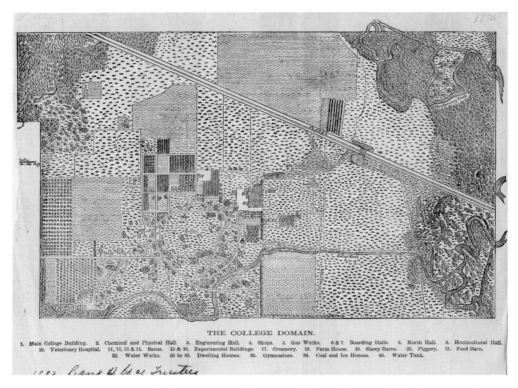

THE COLLEGE DOMAIN.

1. Main College Building.   2. Chemical and Physical Hall.   3. Engineering Hall.   4. Shops.   5. Gas Works.   6 & 7. Boarding Halls.   8. North Hall.   9. Horticultural Hall.
10. Veterinary Hospital.   11, 12, 13 & 14. Barns.   15 & 16. Experimental Buildings.   17. Creamery.   18. Farm House.   19. Sheep Barns.   20. Piggery.   21. Feed Barn.
22. Water Works.   23 to 32. Dwelling Houses.   33. Gymnasium.   34. Coal and Ice Houses.   35. Water Tank.

*This 1883 plan shows the basic organizing principles of the original layout of campus. The curvilinear central campus is surrounded by the grid of the working agricultural landscapes with occasional woodlands along the perimeter. (Used by permission of Iowa State University Library/Special Collections Department)*

that Dr. Adonijah Strong Welch, the college's first president (1868–1883), sought to express. Essentially this expression may still be considered the ideal image of Iowa as depicted by Grant Wood: voluptuous rolling fertile cropland meeting a wooded river valley, open prairie, and the simple structures of the farmstead—a working landscape that balances development with natural systems and celebrates the ingenuity, progress, and respect for nature of an agrarian society.

The Farm House, the first building on campus, at one time would have been evocative of this ideal vision. Placed along a slight ridge to the east and north of the central open prairie, the Italianate structure was an example of the Iowa vernacular architecture, or common building style of the era. The construction was completed by day laborers, reflecting the level of craft available locally. In line with the practical mindset of the college's founders, much of the building materials were found locally, and the bricks were made on campus. In the late nineteenth century, the Farm House would have been surrounded by gardens, orchards, and croplands with expansive views in all directions. Today, the restored building is surrounded by more recent construction, though it still evokes the relationship between the new settlement of Iowa and the open spaces of the prairie.

President Welch was the principal designer of the first campus developments,

*A common sight in the early years of life on campus would have been sheep graz-*
*ing on the turf of central campus. (Used by permission of Iowa State University*
*Library/Special Collections Department)*

and his influence may be observed today. English landscape gardeners Lancelot "Capability" Brown, Humphrey Repton, and John Claudius Loudon promoted the ideals of the naturalistic and picturesque landscape and the need for the integration of "natural" landscapes with more functional needs. In the United States, Andrew Jackson Downing, Frederick Law Olmsted, and Calvert Vaux were instrumental in transferring these ideals to North America. President Welch was attuned to these trends and considered them to be basic values necessary to the successful development of human environments.

Agricultural facilities would be sited to the east and engineering facilities to the west. The connecting grounds took the form of a grand parklike open space and meticulously composed corridors with masses of trees that framed views, spaces, and buildings.[2] The circuitous road, encompassing the open space and linking Old Main to the Farm House and working agricultural landscapes, guided the siting of early campus buildings: Old Main (1868), Morrill Hall (1891), Margaret Hall (1895, burned 1938), and Botany Hall (1892, now Carrie Chapman Catt Hall). The Campanile, built in 1897, served as a focal point for the early buildings radiating around it. In Welch's time the view to the east from Old Main (now the site of Beardshear Hall) would have been quite open to Squaw Creek. Orchards, vineyards, and croplands could have been seen to the north and east, and sheep may have been grazing the prairie grasses and forbs. Today, walking down the

*President Welch's concepts of framing views and corridors through the massing of trees is evident in this 1911 view from Curtiss Hall across central campus to the west. (Used by permission of Iowa State University Library/Special Collections Department)*

grand staircase from Beardshear Hall, looking east across central campus, one sees the massings of spruce, pine, and larch trees and the majestic oaks framing the Campanile and Curtiss Hall. Welch's concepts of framing of views and open space still remain, though not reaching beyond the central space.

H. H. McAfee, a horticulturalist and expert in nursery development, selected and grew plant materials for use on campus. McAfee had acquired national prestige as the first secretary of the American Forestry Association and as a grounds for experimentation, the campus was ideal. Many saplings were brought from the surrounding natural environment including the Squaw Creek and Skunk River riparian woodlands. Welch's philosophies in plant selection, using local varieties that were close at hand, is shown in this statement made to the State Horticultural Society in 1885: "Fifteen years of growth have beautified the college lawn with a variety of tree forms, most of which, I am glad to say, are common ones, for I love common things and common characters whose aspect never varies in any vicissitude of fortune or weather."[3] The original campus planners' visionary philosophies in planting design, including the use of native species of local origin, are considered "sustainable" landscape practices today.

The actual construction and planting of the campus grounds was completed in large part by student labor. The curriculum in landscape design of the era included eight hours of labor per week to be completed by students. Mythic stories hold that Welch would determine locations for plantings by throwing potatoes in a selected area, providing a random, organic quality to groupings. Students would seek out the potatoes, then excavate and install the trees. In time, Welch's goal of "the creation of an extensive natural landscape on the college grounds" was fulfilled.

Presidents Chamberlain (1886–1890) and Beardshear (1891–1902) inherited, and built upon, the designs of President Welch. In a description of the college in the *Iowa Normal Monthly* in February 1889, President Chamberlain referred to the campus as "one of the most extensive in the West; a beautiful park where the principles of landscape gardening have been so carefully obeyed as to please the eye and cultivate the taste."[4]

During Beardshear's presidency construction of buildings increased and affected the density of campus, requiring landscape changes. After two fires (1900 and 1902) destroyed a majority of Old Main, the central campus building, President Beardshear and the college's Board of Trustees brought Chicago landscape architect O. C. Simonds to campus in 1902. Simonds, the only midwestern charter member of the American Society of Landscape Architects and author of *Landscape Gardening* (1920), was known for his appreciation of the prairie landscapes of the Midwest and for the use of native plants in design. His philosophies sustained many of Welch's traditions in naturalistic campus development. Here, Simonds's main task was to generate plans to direct further development of campus grounds to accommodate growth in enrollment and to site new buildings proposed for construction, including the new central college building, now named Beardshear Hall.

The era's architectural style focused on the classical revival as expressed by the Columbia Exposition in Chicago in 1893. Beaux Arts buildings drew from Greek and Roman architectural ideals of symmetry, ornamentation, and proportionality. Columns, pediments, and ornate cornice designs are characteristic elements of the style as seen in Beardshear Hall, Curtiss Hall, and Marston Hall. The integrity of central campus was maintained as open space, and development was limited to the adjacent edges. Though views to the east were still open in 1902, the campus buildings, oriented to the central lawn, became more introverted toward the central grounds. Today, this northern edge has yet to be intruded upon with Morrill Hall, MacKay, Catt Hall, and Horticulture still retaining the margin between open space and development. And Curtiss Hall, built in 1909, defines the east edge of central campus.

The classical style of the campus architecture in the early 1900s influenced the design of the campus landscape beyond the siting of campus buildings. In 1906, renowned landscape architect J. C. Olmsted was brought to Iowa State College upon recommendation of A. T. Erwin (Horticulture). The Olmsted brothers, who had inherited the landscape design practice of their father, Frederick Law Olmsted, became well-known through their planning of city park systems in Boston and Seattle, and their design for the Capitol and White House grounds in Washington, D.C. Olmsted's recommendations for the direction of campus development called for overlaying an urban pattern on the pastoral landscape. The primary proposal was for the installation of a grid that would capture the central campus space as a quasi-urban park and extend academic rows to the north, east, and west of central campus. The plan, which focused on creating density while retaining open space, was rejected by the college with the exception of a few points: the siting of Curtiss Hall (Agriculture Hall, 1909) in alignment with Beardshear Hall to the west across central campus and the resituating of the interurban railway to the north of Margaret Hall along present-day Osborn Drive. With the siting of Curtiss Hall directly east of Beardshear an edge was defined that would guide development of central campus's adjacency for perpetuity.

The early 1900s were dominated by extensive new construction of significant structures, many of which define the architectural identity of campus today: Marston Hall (Engineering Hall, 1903), Beardshear Hall (Central Building, 1906), Alumni Hall (1907), Curtiss Hall (Agriculture Hall, 1909), Engineering Annex (1910), MacKay Hall (Domestic Technology, 1911), Lagomarcino Hall (Veterinary Quadrangle, 1912), Gilman Hall (Chemistry Hall, 1913), State Gymnasium (1913), Lyon Hall (West Hall, 1914), and Horticulture Hall (1914). Lacking firm acceptance of Olmsted's plans, the development of campus fell to the Building and Grounds Committee, primarily its secretary, Professor Erwin. Erwin, a founding member of the Iowa Forestry and Conservation Association, sought to retain the informal, picturesque organization of campus, contrary to the Olmsted proposal. The projects of the period focused on practicality and function. Roads were expanded and reconstructed to accommodate the burgeoning automobile traffic and paths led deliberately to newly constructed structures. Erwin has been considered a primary designer of the campus, having taken into consideration Olmsted's and Simonds's recommendations, and overseeing a significant period of growth.

The siting of new buildings followed the general layout of campus with engineering buildings and facilities to the west and agriculture to the east. From cen-

*The Veterinary Quadrangle (now Lagomarcino Hall) courtyard reflects the trend of creating more enclosed spaces within the buildings of academic disciplines. (Used by permission of Iowa State University Library/Special Collections Department)*

tral campus, the new Veterinary Quadrangle extended to the north. This development reflected a trend in creating smaller scale open spaces between buildings. Horticulture facilities were also grouped to create relatively enclosed courtyard spaces between the greenhouses, labs, and main buildings. Directly west of Beardshear, a campus quadrangle was formed with a strong axis defined to the south by Alumni Hall, and to the west by Marston Hall. The scale of these quadrangles was subordinate to central campus, reinforcing its significance. Adding to this hierarchy, the architectural styles of new buildings became more subdued as they moved farther from central campus and the ornate Beardshear Hall, Catt Hall, and Curtiss Hall. Primarily clad in Bedford limestone around the central campus area and clad in brick moving outward from central campus, the hierarchy of campus developments was reinforced materially. Bedford limestone, imported from Indiana, was used in many civic buildings in the Midwest and East and was considered a prestigious building material because of its uniform texture and soft, workable nature.

O. C. Simonds returned to campus in 1914 for a two-year appointment supported by funds donated by LaVerne W. Noyes (class of 1872). Noyes, who had become wealthy through the invention and manufacture of farm equipment, was

*The picturesque views of Lake LaVerne created inspirational drawing opportunities for students of landscape architecture. (Used by permission of Iowa State University Library/Special Collections Department)*

interested in donating his expertise and financial assistance to a campus improvement project. Of special interest to Simonds was the southern edge of campus at Lincoln Way (then Boone Street), where he envisioned the development and maintenance of a naturalistic area. Within the context of other developments occurring on campus, the construction of Lake LaVerne followed the previous ideals of the picturesque, establishing a parklike space within the increasingly dense campus, and connected Simonds with the Olmsteds' work in Boston. There, the Emerald Necklace included a series of ponds that functioned in storm water drainage and filtration for the surrounding streets. Lake LaVerne is essentially a storm water management device, an infrastructural element serving also as a public amenity. The lake was completed in only four months, though in following years it became silted with sludge and required further work, completed in 1933 by the Civilian Conservation Corps. In the 1920s, Lake LaVerne provided a stunning entry to campus from the nation's first transcontinental highway, the Lincoln Highway. Today, it remains one of the most celebrated and identifiable landmark spaces on campus. Recent renovations sought to solve problems of algal bloom caused by nutrient-rich sediment. Improvements included reconstruction of the north shore, installation of aerators, realignment of storm sewers, and construction of a swan nesting island to ensure the comfort of the trumpeter swans, Sir Lancelot and Elaine, the lake's most famous residents.

After the visit from J. C. Olmsted and the reengagement with O. C. Simonds, the college looked within for planning in guiding new developments. As campus grew to the north, the framework for organization of campus by discipline remained intact. On Osborn Drive fundamental sciences buildings were constructed including Gilman Hall (Chemistry, 1913), Science Hall (1916), and Physics Hall (1923). C. H. Scheman, in providing a general statement regarding the planning of campus in 1916, described the vision for future development of an introverted campus: "Eventually the main or central campus will be surrounded on three sides by stone buildings and it is planned to have it open toward the south except for the Campanile and the trees."[5] Of course, the south did not remain open for long, with the construction of the Memorial Union in 1928. A great deal of discussion regarding the development of a memorial to fallen soldiers in World War I ended with the decision to build the Union. Appropriately, the site selected for the structure is on axis with Catt Hall and the Campanile, and along with Curtiss and Beardshear Hall, reinforces the central focus of the university.

In the 1920s and 1930s, Professors P. H. Elwood (Landscape Architecture), A. T. Erwin (Horticulture), L. H. Pammel (Botany), and A. H. Kimball (Architectural Engineering) were the key players in designing new campus projects. They brought with them an understanding of the history of campus design, new sensitivity to the automobile's needs on campus, and a passion for plant materials. The departments of Forestry, Botany, and Horticulture worked tirelessly in the collection of a wide range of species that were hardy enough to survive Iowa's cold winters and hot summers, and to experiment with planting materials from around the world. The campus served as a laboratory for students of Botany, Forestry, Horticulture, and Landscape Gardening. Simonds recommended a naturalistic planting scheme while stressing the need for a diverse palette of plants. The campus was fast becoming a world-class arboretum and the labeling of trees and shrubs was suggested. Scheman writes, "during the spring and fall, classes of students can be seen studying the trees and shrubs on almost every day."[6] Landscape Gardening students of the period were still required to do the work of maintaining existing plantings and installing new landscape plants as a portion of their course work.

The reduction of expansive views on campus led to a focus on the detailed design of spaces at the scale of the garden. The focus on local vegetation collected by Welch along Squaw Creek and brought as saplings to occupy campus had changed to a Victorian mentality of the collection of exotic specimen species. The planting of a variety of species together, with sequential bloom, was choreographed to reveal natural processes. Enhancing the image of campus in springtime, so that students would leave for summer vacation with a positive image of the grounds, was a special concern of the landscape planners. Emergent bulbs and early blooming species were planted densely to create the explosion of spring color that is witnessed every year during the April VEISHEA festival, a great homecoming and community event on campus.

Interest in a forested area on the northwestern edge of campus began to grow in 1920. A use for the tract of land, which could not feasibly support crops or pasture, had been debated through the years. It had been suggested that the timber be harvested and that the area be improved as a park, but the costs of such projects outweighed the benefits. The research of L. H. Pammel, professor of botany, who had played a central role in forming the Iowa Forestry and Conservation Association and later in developing a conservation plan for the state of Iowa in the 1930s, led President Raymond Pearson to designate the area as a managed park. College Park, later named Pammel Park (1939), was to be managed by a committee consisting of representatives from the departments of Botany, Forestry, and Landscape Architecture. The preserve became a living laboratory for classroom instruction and research. It has been managed as a preserve for those purposes ever since and provides important recreational space for students. Hikers, strollers, and mountain bikers can be seen enjoying the park year-round, spotting spring wildflowers and admiring fall foliage.

Another of these naturalistic, picturesque places on campus is the Knoll. The Knoll began as the home of the president of Iowa State. It was built and inhabited by President Beardshear in 1901. The significance of the hill east of the Memorial Union is in its landscape. The landscape of the Knoll serves as another of the areas that define the image of the university along its most traveled thoroughfare, Lincoln Way, and through the twentieth century with Lake LaVerne to the west, demonstrated the dominant natural aesthetic values of campus development. Over the years changes to the area were discussed, including a possible transition to higher-density development. Privacy for the president and the president's family was the central concern. Women's dormitories to the east, the expanding Memorial Union to the west, and the constant traffic on Lincoln Way created undesirable conditions for habitation. Suggestions for reuse of the site included a transition to "administrative and student services, an art gallery, bookstore, museum or expansion of the Memorial Union, or a school of design, music, or drama."[7] However, the committee formed to study reuse of the area added that "the site of the Knoll, including the surrounding area, is one of the remaining natural beauty spots on the campus."[8] It was decided to preserve the area and save it from new development. Over time, the Knoll area became as valuable to student instruction as Pammel Park, and groups of students can still be observed examining mature trees and shrubs surrounding the residence, which was remodeled in 2000.

During the thirty-year period from 1920 to 1950, the campus experienced major growth and urbanization. While density of buildings increased, the open spaces of campus were shrinking and intensifying. President Hughes, in 1932, requested that all academic units report on their future needs with a focus on potential physical growth of departments. This report led to a new design for cam-

*In 1922, many of the landmark buildings on campus had been completed, and central campus remained an oasis within the growing campus. (Used by permission of Iowa State University Library/Special Collections Department)*

pus to facilitate the extraordinary expansion that would be seen in the coming decades. Professors Elwood and Kimball analyzed the collected survey data and began planning for major expansion. They realized a need for careful articulation and positive use of campus space. The siting of new buildings and the compartmentalization of spaces required strong coordination in order to retain the fluidity of movement on campus for growing populations of students, while also accepting that automobiles were a force to be reckoned with.

Elwood and Kimball developed a "Twenty-Year Development Plan 1935–1955" for campus spaces and facilities, envisioning a 300 percent increase in enrollment. The faculty designers planned circuitous routes for automobiles on campus that sought to separate them from pedestrian traffic. The campus was growing out from central campus, and designating loop roads to carry the bulk of commuters and students was a top priority, as was parking. Another priority was linking campus to the city of Ames through the development of stronger transportation routes and identification of potential natural resource connections, Squaw Creek in particular. Elwood and Kimball realized the need for programming, or determining specific uses and activities, for campus spaces. Academic use areas remained consistent with the first planning efforts with agriculture to the east, engineering to the west, and science and humanities to the north along Osborn Drive.

Residential and physical education facilities would be located to the south of central campus with the men's facilities to the west and women's to the east. Between these residential areas would be found the administrative and social use areas (Alumni Hall and the Memorial Union). Passive recreation areas were to be located within Pammel Park, along College Creek, and at the heart of the grounds:

central campus. Elwood and Kimball realized the need to define spatial organization on campus by academic discipline. They acknowledged some of the same concerns related to campus sprawl put forward by J. C. Olmsted thirty years earlier. In unifying spaces for disciplines the functionality of the campus environment would be enhanced and pedestrian movement would be limited to specific zones. The designers also recognized the need to program a space that would intermingle the interests of the university and the residents of Ames. This area, the seed for the Iowa State Center, was envisioned to include a stadium, museum, and theater.

Two phenomena led to many new projects on campus, the Civil Works Administration (CWA) work program and World War II. Under a federal program that provided for unemployed artists in the 1930s, internationally renowned artist Grant Wood (artist of murals in the Parks Library) was appointed head of the Public Works of Art Project for Iowa, which was later named the Civil Works Administration. The most noteworthy examples of CWA projects on campus are those of Christian Petersen, who was campus artist-in-residence from 1935 to 1961 after being brought to campus by Grant Wood through the Iowa CWA program in 1934. The trend toward urbanization and geometric design of campus spaces put forward by Elwood and Kimball complemented well the display of sculpture. Works by Petersen included relief sculptures on the exterior walls of the Dairy Industry Building (1934), defining the edges of the plaza. This space, in particular, is reflective of the intimate, precise new campus spaces allowing for circulation and movement while providing secluded eddies for study, socializing, and people watching. Other outdoor works by Petersen included the *Four Seasons Fountain* (1941) at the north entrance to the Memorial Union, the *Marriage Ring* (1942) adjacent to MacKay Hall (Family and Consumer Sciences), and *Gentle Doctor* in the College of Veterinary Medicine. Christian Petersen's final work, before retiring in 1955, was *Conversations,* a monumental sculpture. Three limestone sculpture groups that depict college life are placed along a freestanding wall, located on the grounds of the Oak-Elm Residence Halls. The detail design necessary for the creation of specialized spaces on campus took on an urban feel. This creation of outdoor rooms and smaller-scale spaces provided opportunities for the display of artwork.

The celebration and installation of artwork on campus is one of the great traditions of the university that had its roots in Grant Wood's era of the 1930s. Through the initiative of President Raymond Hughes, the collection of artwork became a mission of the university. Outdoor sculptures, sited within the exterior spaces of campus, have been collected since the days of Christian Petersen. The twentieth-century sculptures of nationally and internationally recognized artists (including Beverly Pepper, Luis Jimenez, and Andrew Leicester, among others) are found in niches as diverse as the open foreground to the College of Design, tucked away in the courtyard of the Agronomy Building, and in the mall area between Black Engineering and the Laboratory of Mechanics Building. These works of art provide inspiration when discovered by the watchful eyes of students, faculty, or visitors to campus. Whether one comes upon the dynamic human forms of William King's *Stride* at Lied Recreation/Athletic Facility, Jimenez's thought-provoking po-

*Christian Petersen's Four Seasons Fountain, north of the Memorial Union, is one of many artworks created during the 1930s and 1940s. The artistic legacy of this period lives on through the Art on Campus program. (Used by permission of Iowa State University Library/Special Collections Department)*

litically charged *Border Crossing* on the central lawn, or Leicester's strangely haunting *G-Nome Project* figures peering down from atop Molecular Biology, the pieces give pause to consider the human condition and enrich the experience of campus.

Partnering with the federal government in developing significant research has led to many new developments. In the 1940s the campus benefited from federal funding related to World War II. Investment in capital projects included an addition to the Armory (1941), Office and Laboratory Building or "the Link" (1947), and Spangler Geotechnical (1949). The campus became central to research and development in atomic energy. Professors Frank H. Spedding (Physical Chemistry) and Harley Wilhelm (Metallurgy) led efforts in the discovery of new methods for melting and casting uranium for the federal government, promoting the college to new heights in national significance. The pressing need was to extract pure uranium for use in a nuclear reactor at Stagg Field in Chicago.[9] Their research enabled the development of the atomic bomb, generating over one thousand tons of uranium for use in the research. This breakthrough led to the construction of the United States Atomic Energy Commission's Ames Laboratory (1949), the Metallurgy Building (1949), and Spedding Hall (1953).

The National Animal Disease Laboratory (1961), another federally funded project, extended campus even further, to the eastern limits of Ames, along Dayton Road. These facilities represent a strong partnership between Iowa State University and the federal government. The main mission of the laboratory was to reduce economic losses caused by diseases in the livestock and poultry industries. In 1956, a federal appropriation of $16.25 million enabled the construction of the facility. Today, the National Animal Disease Center (NADC) continues research on livestock and poultry and is one of the largest such animal research centers in the world.

Notable federally funded buildings followed the precedent of the Ames Laboratory, including, among others, Applied Science I (1956), Agronomy Lab (1961), Applied Science II (1990), and the National Swine Research and Information Center (1997). The connection between university research and the greater progress of the nation can be seen in the continued federal investment in university development.

The growing density and complexity of campus proper continued into the 1950s and 1960s. The college employed a supervising architect and superintendent of grounds to guide campus development. Designs sought to maintain the historic landscape character of campus while facilitating an increasingly complex university scheme. Preliminary design of new buildings and their integration with existing campus forms was a primary concern. Guidelines were set in order to retain the integrity of campus design and reflect the values established in the character of campus buildings. The arrangement of buildings facing central campus, and their subordination by requiring a gray tone finish, set them back from existing landmark architecture. Guidelines were set for the development of a street grid with ninety-degree corners and symmetry in street plantings. The campus designers adhered to the rigidity of town development, providing a strong framework for unprecedented architectural and landscape expansion. Administratively, the Campus Planning Committee was established (1955). The committee controlled the physical development of campus, including the location of future buildings and needed improvements to vehicular and pedestrian circulation.

The 1950s was truly the decade of the student. Competition in recruiting led to the extension of student services and an updating of student housing on campus. On-campus housing was in high demand. New projects included the completion of Westgate Dormitory (1955), Linden Hall (1957) women's dormitory, and Helser Hall (1957) men's dormitory. Hawthorne Court apartments (1956) at Pammel Court were built to house the families of married students, attracting the new alternative student and families of veterans attending via the GI Bill. The old Dinkey (a train service between the college and Ames) station functioned as a bookstore and post office until the bookstore moved into its new quarters in the Memorial Union in 1958. Spaces for student interaction were also being developed on central campus. The Hub (1959), a new student social space and snack bar, was built in a portion of the area that had been formerly occupied by the bookstore. Terrace additions (1953) completed at the Memorial Union extended outward toward

Lake LaVerne and provided a festive space for students attending concerts and other social and political events.

After all-time record enrollments were reached in 1962 (10,877), major changes in the physical form of campus were needed. New classroom spaces, residence halls, and transportation improvements followed. Temporary buildings that were constructed during World War II still dotted the quadrangle between the library and Alumni Hall. They were retained into the 1970s to facilitate increases in student population and other administrative needs, but would soon need to be replaced by permanent structures. Transportation improvements included widening Lincoln Way from Beach to Sheldon Avenue to four lanes; Stange Road was widened to four lanes from Osborn Drive to Thirteenth Street; and Bissell Road was widened from Union Drive to Pammel Drive. These transportation improvements worked in combination with the development of new residence hall construction.

The architectural styles of the era were dominated by the modern movement. On campus the construction of pragmatic, utilitarian structures dominated. These buildings are characterized by their simplicity, built of unadorned concrete and glass. All nonessential decoration was removed, with the emphasis being placed on balance and regularity. The "Suitcases" residential complex (1967) was completed on Storm Street and construction began on the Wallace Road complex, or the "Towers." University Village provided high- to moderate-density housing on Stange Road, supplying five hundred units in 1968. These developments extended campus to the south and north, continuing the trend of outward growth. Even with these new residential developments, housing on campus remained problematic. In 1973, residence halls were filled to capacity with over eight thousand undergraduates, and students needed to find temporary housing.

With the huge growth in the student population, classroom overcrowding was another concern. Pearson Hall (1962) and Electrical Engineering's Coover Hall (1970) were completed, addressing these concerns and providing new office space for the increasing faculty population as well. Pearson and Coover halls were constructed off of central campus and were built of brick, following the previously established guidelines requiring that new buildings be subordinate to the landmark structures of central campus in scale and material. Ross Hall (1973), another example of the modern style though it is actually constructed of limestone, was inserted north of Curtiss Hall. Originally sited north and nearly in line with the west facade of Curtiss, after much debate, the new building was set back from the openness of central campus, retaining the historic development patterns. A new college including the departments of Applied Art, Architecture, and Landscape Architecture was formed, and the resulting Design Center (1978, now College of Design) was constructed, again in the modern style of clean concrete and glass, but with the added feature of a vaulted glass ceiling.

In 1968, the firm Johnson, Johnson & Roy, Inc., published a guide for the continuing physical development of campus; and in 1972, Iowa State became a pedestrian campus when the State Board of Regents approved closing sections of cam-

*Unprecedented growth in the student population required the construction of new residence halls, including these modern structures on Storm Street completed in 1967. (Used by permission of Iowa State University Library/Special Collections Department)*

pus streets to automobile traffic during restricted hours, in order to accommodate bicycle and pedestrian traffic. The university needed to grow out of central campus in dramatic fashion. Because of the Squaw Creek floodplain to the north and east, and Clear Creek and residential development to the west, growth was focused to the south and east of campus. The construction of the U.S. Route 30 bypass created opportunities for such growth to occur. With the construction of Elwood Drive, campus was linked to U.S. Route 30 to the south. The green fields along Elwood Drive allowed expansion of residence halls, recreation facilities, and Veterinary Medicine Research facilities. Squaw Creek was to be managed as a greenway, a corridor defined by the natural resource of the waterway and recreational uses in park spaces and trails. With the development of trails and city park facilities within the floodplain, the university and the city created a partnership that links campus to Ames through recreation.

These developments to the south and east of campus contributed to plans for the most significant new campus development since its creation in the 1880s. The Iowa State University Foundation began plans for Iowa State Center, a multipurpose development that would signal a new era for campus. The concept for the de-

*Construction of the Iowa State Center began in 1965 with the fund-raising of the Iowa State University Foundation and was completed in 1975. (Used by permission of Iowa State University Library/Special Collections Department)*

velopment sought to create facilities that would bring nationally renowned performers, artists, and conventions to campus. It also sought to expand athletic facilities that were in dire need of improvements to keep pace with conference competitors. Through the generation of private funds, the dream of an Iowa State Center became a reality with groundbreaking ceremonies in 1965. After four years of construction, C. Y. Stephens Auditorium was finally inaugurated in 1969. The Iowa State Center Coliseum was dedicated shortly after in 1970. The third unit of the center, the Fisher Theater, was dedicated in 1974 by President Parks. The Scheman Continuing Education Building (1975) completed the Iowa State Center.

Elwood Drive was officially opened in 1970, bringing travelers directly off of U.S. Route 30 into campus through a new interchange. Elwood Drive and the Iowa State Center became the primary gateway to campus, creating a progressive image to visitors from around the globe. Named after P. H. Elwood, the route fulfilled his vision for a main loop arterial linking Lincoln Way, Hyland Avenue, and Thirteenth Street and providing the necessary circulation routes for automobile, pedestrian, and bicycle traffic. Another significant contribution to southern campus expansion was the plan for new Veterinary Medicine facilities. Construction

*Iowa State University Research Park serves as an incubator for research and development, connecting the work of the university to business and industry. (Used by permission of Iowa State University/Instructional Technology Center)*

began in 1968 and was completed in 1976. When seen from the highway traveling east and west, the new facilities defined the image of campus for thousands of daily travelers. The Veterinary Medicine facility was laid out as a campus entity itself, separated from the original lines of the university, though contributing strongly to its culture and image.

With the completion of Elwood Drive and the new interchange from U.S. Route 30, land use considerations around the interchange enabled the university to reinforce its positive image and create new opportunities for development. In 1974, a private corporation, Gateway Center, Ltd., was formed in order to direct improvements at the interchange. The land was owned by the Alumni Achievement Fund, whose main purpose was to reinforce the positive image of the university at its main entry through high-quality developments. These developments included Gateway Center, a sophisticated hotel and convention complex, and the Iowa State University Research Park, a thriving incubator for technological research, laboratories, and businesses.

Another new development at the southern gateway, Reiman Gardens, was actually transplanted from another location on campus. Horticultural gardens have existed at Iowa State since 1914. The present-day Reiman Gardens south of Jack Trice Stadium is the third location for the horticultural gardens. The first location for the gardens was north of the Farm House and across Knoll Road northwest of the Landscape Architecture building. The construction of Agronomy Hall (1952) and Bessey Hall (1965) resulted in the gardens being moved in 1968 to a three-

*Reiman Gardens, the third location for horticultural gardens on campus, provides a stunning gateway to campus from the south. (Used by permission of Iowa State University/Instructional Technology Center)*

quarter-acre site north of the power plant on the northeast corner of the campus. In the early 1990s the possibility of moving the gardens to a more visible location was realized. In 1993, alumnus Roy Reiman and his wife, Bobbi, generously made the donation that initiated phase one of the new gardens. The gardens were officially dedicated in 1995. Their location is strategically placed between Elwood Drive and Beach Avenue south of Jack Trice Stadium. The fourteen acres that the gardens cover with the recent addition of the conservatory complex and the Christina Reiman Butterfly Flight House, which opened in November 2002, provide a dramatic entrance to the Elwood Drive gateway to Iowa State University.

In 1992, the university brought celebrated Sasaki Associates, Inc., to campus to create a new master plan. Sasaki had developed plans for the University of Virginia and the University of California at Berkeley, establishing the firm as national leaders in campus planning. Their publication "Iowa State University 1991 Campus Master Plan" has been the primary guide for development in the contemporary era. The report paid homage to the first designers of campus during the formative years in the late nineteenth and early twentieth century. It sought to reinforce the general form of campus with engineering disciplines to the west and agricultural disciplines to the east. At the center of campus, the disciplines of the College of Liberal Arts and Sciences were to remain dominant. The perimeter of campus, north of Pammel Drive and north of the Union Pacific Railroad tracks, was to be used for new research facilities. To the north of campus on Stange Road, Sasaki Associates identified opportunities for new residential developments on the east and new administrative facilities to the west. The twenty acres of the lawn area on central campus were to be maintained as open space being bounded by Beardshear Hall (west), MacKay Hall and Catt Hall (north), Curtiss Hall (east), and the Memorial Union (south).

Other goals that were set included the establishment of clear entries to campus. Reiman Gardens now provides the breathtaking views that Sasaki called for in the plan. Reinforcement of the pedestrian environment was also a concern. In response to the somewhat fragmented paths through campus caused by high-density development and small-scale urban courtyards, Sasaki suggested that specific main corridors be identified and developed as pedestrian thoroughfares. Further enhancing pedestrian circulation and comfort on campus, it was recommended to concentrate instruction and faculty offices at the core of campus within a ten-minute walking distance, and to site research and nonacademic offices outside of the core.

These rings would be further reinforced through the architectural character of new construction. Development on campus would be characterized by academic zones and settings. Academic zones would have their own design vocabulary and architectural style and be linked spatially through outdoor rooms and corridors. The primary concern was with the integrity of the central lawn area, continuing the identity of central campus with limestone structures in a classical style. Ringing the outer edge of central campus, buildings included stone trim, but the facade would primarily be finished with brick. Still farther from central campus, buildings would be faced with brick. Overall, the plan called for the enhancement of both Welch's vision and Olmsted's proposals. By integrating the formal geometric order of campus with the naturalistic spaces of the central lawn, Lake LaVerne, the Knoll, and Pammel Park, these legacies would be retained. The dominant landscape style of campus established by Welch as the informal, naturalistic park with the central lawn as its primary physical presence still establishes the primary image of campus.

The architectural character of campus would be maintained only through the preservation of identified landmarks. The most significant landmarks were determined to be Beardshear Hall, the Campanile, Alumni Hall, and Curtiss Hall, all surrounding central campus. Secondary landmarks that create the image of campus included the structures of Iowa State Center, including Jack Trice Stadium and Hilton Coliseum; Larch, Maple, and Willow dormitories; the power plant in northeast campus; Friley Hall; Marston water tower; the College of Design building; Lied Recreation/Athletic Facility; and the sculptures on top of Molecular Biology. These important campus structures evoke the image of the university that people carry with them for a lifetime.

Recent landscape development has retained the open character of the central mall. The density of campus increased while southern growth was planned. New construction to the west of campus in line with Town Engineering and the College of Design consumed what little remaining open space was left outside of central campus and the Parks Library quadrangle. Practice fields for athletics and the

*The constantly expanding and urbanizing campus of the twenty-first century still retains the pastoral, open core of central campus. (Used by permission of Iowa State University/Instructional Technology Center)*

marching band were occupied by Howe Hall (1999), which is linked to Hoover Hall (2003) by a skywalk across Bissell Road. Urban-scale courtyards were developed surrounding these new buildings. Smaller buildings located near central campus were razed in favor of larger structures, including the construction of a new College of Business (2004) building to the east of central campus.

The demolition of the Towers residential halls in 2005 signified a shift from the grand scale of the high-rise to the less dense, more apartment-style development of Hawthorne Court (2000). Student life is continually being enhanced with new developments, including the Thielen Student Health Center (1997), the new Ames/ISU Ice Arena (2000), the Jischke Honors Building (2002), and the Union Drive Residence Complex (2003). Keeping step with new technologies has led campus to develop a relatively invisible network of telecommunications and wireless installations and the only six-sided virtual reality theatre in the country. Classrooms have been rehabilitated and auditoriums added to many campus buildings. Students are more connected to Ames with the Cy-Ride bus service, networks of trail systems, and a potential revival of the old Dinkey train line from downtown to central campus. The architectural legacy of campus has undergone major rehabilitation work. Beardshear Hall, Curtiss Hall, Catt Hall, MacKay, the Memorial Union, Parks Library, and Morrill Hall have all been improved and restored recently.

Connections to the city of Ames are now strong. While the first sidewalk between town and campus was constructed in 1959 and the extension of Thirteenth

Street to campus was approved in 1972, the university's relationship to Ames was not as developed as needed. Today, the links encompass a recreational network connecting previously fragmented areas. Green space amenities including Brookside Park, which is owned by the university, Stuart Smith Park, Pammel Woods, the YMCA lands north and west of Veenker golf course and Reiman Gardens provide the fabric that knits together town and college and creates opportunities for intermingling student life with the life of the city. Redevelopment strategies for Campustown seek to enhance the relationship between student-dominated apartments and family-oriented housing.

Contemporary campus identities, established over the first 150 years of its physical development, reinforce the traditions, rituals, and values of its creators. The foresight of planners in collecting an extraordinarily diverse plant palette has maintained the campus as a world-class outdoor learning environment for students of horticulture, botany, landscape architecture, forestry, and other related disciplines. The quadrangle south of the library is a place of performance, protest, and free speech. New artwork surfaces on campus in the form of dance, sculpture, and murals continuing the tradition of Christian Petersen and Grant Wood. Pickup football, ultimate Frisbee, and soccer games erupt on the central lawn. The campus is alive with impassioned speech, dynamic play, and powerful works of creativity. Within the urban density of the campus grid, there lies the openness necessary for expression and the space to free the soul, join together with neighbors, and celebrate the power of life. Facilitating the changing needs of students and faculty, campus designers have created space for everyone to find oneself through education and expression. The wide open space of central campus becomes an oasis within the necessarily hardened urban spaces of contemporary campus; it is a place to reflect on the ideals of those who came before and who left a campus full of history and opportunity.

# Vignettes

## Pete Taylor: "The Most Loved"

For thirty-three years, Pete Taylor's voice defined Iowa State athletics. The highs, the lows, the triumphs, the defeats. To many, Pete Taylor WAS Iowa State athletics. An Iowa graduate, who ironically became synonymous with Cyclone athletics, Taylor was the radio play-by-play voice of Iowa State football and men's basketball from 1970 to 2003. A Des Moines native, he played baseball briefly at Iowa, where he graduated in 1967. Almost immediately, he started as a news-/sportscaster at KCCI-TV, the CBS affiliate in Des Moines. He was sports director at KCCI for twenty years, during which time he doubled as the voice of the Cyclones.

Through several different stations on the dial, seven football coaches and basketball coaches, and four athletics directors, Taylor was the one constant. In all, he called more than 1,300 Iowa State contests through more than three decades. In 1990, Taylor left television to join the Iowa State athletics department full-time as director of athletic fund-raising. He continued his radio play-by-play role for thirteen more years and held the title of associate athletics director for external affairs.

Taylor's play-by-play included no signature phrase, except for an occasional "oh brother" if things weren't going well. It took only a few seconds to get an idea of how a game was going just by listening to the tenor of his voice. Still, for Taylor, describing the action was more important than developing a signature phrase. After his death, *Sports Illustrated* columnist Steve Rushin summed it up best when he said, "Strange isn't it? The more he tried to shrink, the larger Taylor grew. In wanting to make stars of the Cyclones, he became the star."

Longtime KCCI-TV anchor Kevin Cooney told Rushin, "It's funny. The guy without the catch phrase lasted the longest here, and became the best loved."

Tom Kroeschell

# Gary Thompson: The Roland Rocket

Gary Thompson, "The Roland Rocket," was ISU's first one-thousand-point career scorer and the first Cyclone basketball player selected as a first-team All-American, following the 1957 season. He concluded his three-year career with 1,253 points, which still ranks fifteenth on ISU's all-time scoring list. His greatest legacy may be as Iowa State's first multisport All-American. Later, through television, Thompson built on his Iowa State legend as a nationally respected broadcaster whose name became as familiar with young Cyclone fans as with their grandparents, who had watched him star in the ISU Armory. Over five decades, on the court and off, Iowa State may not have had a greater ambassador than the man from Roland.

Thompson played on the 1956–1957 basketball squad that set an ISU record with eighteen victories in a season, including a stunning upset of No. 1 Kansas and Wilt Chamberlain. The Cyclone earned first-team all–Big Seven Conference honors as a senior, averaging 20.1 points per contest. In 1957, Thompson became the first Cyclone to be named Iowa State Athlete of the Year twice. United Press named Thompson Big Seven Conference Player of the Year in 1957, ahead of Chamberlain. The All-American was featured on Ed Sullivan's *Toast of the Town*.

As a junior, Thompson tallied 40 points against Vanderbilt to become the first Cyclone to score 40 points in a game. He averaged 19.1 points as a junior for ISU, earning first-team all-conference honors. Iowa State named him Athlete of the Year for 1955–1956, marking the first time the award was ever presented to a junior. The great Kansas coach Forrest "Phog" Allen paid Thompson the ultimate tribute: "Inch for inch, Gary Thompson is probably as good a player as the Big Seven has ever seen—and it's seen some fine ones."

A fifth-round draft choice of the Minnesota Lakers professional basketball team, Thompson became a successful convenience store and petroleum marketer in Ames and worked as a color commentator on NBC, ABC, ESPN, and Big Eight and Big 12 basketball telecasts.

In addition to his exploits on the basketball court, Thompson was an All-American shortstop for the Cyclone baseball team and helped the 1957 team to a berth in the NCAA College World Series. He hit .311 with four home runs and eighteen RBIs in twenty-seven games to help ISU capture the 1957 Big Seven crown. Thompson was the Cyclones' regular shortstop his entire three-year career.

Tom Kroeschell

# L. C. "Cap" Timm: A People Person

L. C. "Cap" Timm headed the Cyclone baseball program from 1938 to 1974, with the exception of the four years he served in the military. Timm tallied 340 career wins, leading the Cyclones to three conference titles. During his tenure at Iowa State, Timm coached varsity baseball for thirty-four years and junior varsity baseball for four seasons, and served as a football assistant for twenty-one years and basketball assistant for twelve years. He was a professor of education in the Physical Education Department.

Timm's 1957 team captured the Big Seven title and advanced to the College World Series for the first time in Iowa State history. Two of Timm's players from the 1957 team, Dick Bertell and Jerry McNertney, would later play in the major leagues. Timm led his team back to the World Series in 1970. That squad featured All-American catcher Larry Corrigan. The 1970 Cyclones captured the conference title with a 13-5 league mark. Timm's Cyclones repeated with another Big Seven crown in 1971.

The Cyclone mentor served as the head coach for the 1967 Pan American team and was a member of the U.S. Olympic Committee. He was instrumental in developing the structure of the College World Series.

"My joy, my satisfaction was working with these young men [at Iowa State]," Timm told the *Des Moines Register* in 1986. "I had no inclination to work with guys who worry about how much money they're going to make. I wanted to help shape young men. They've got to be coachable not only with you as coach but with themselves."

Timm was nationally recognized for his coaching prowess. He was awarded the Lefty Gomez award, honoring him for his outstanding and distinguished service to college baseball. Timm also served as the president of the American Association of College Baseball Coaches from 1963 to 1969.

Timm was honored with his induction into the National Baseball Coaches Association Hall of Fame in 1974. Iowa State named its baseball field in his honor. Timm and his wife, "Tippy" Timm, were both campus fixtures while living in a house on Ash Avenue in the midst of Iowa State's fraternities and sororities.

"The more you know Cap Timm, the more you have to love this man," said Clair Rierson, Timm's assistant coach, who took over as head coach after his mentor retired in 1974. "Cap Timm is a people person. He coaches people, teaches people, works with and for people. His intelligence, honesty, and integrity, unselfishness and love for Iowa State, for baseball and for people have made him a giant in college baseball. I am very thankful that I have had the opportunity to walk beside this man down the path of life."

Tom Kroeschell

*Chapter 10*

# Impacts of Iowa State University: Its National and International Presence and Its Enduring Legacies

John R. Anderson

If ever a seed was planted that would grow into a tall, far-reaching educational institution, it was the Iowa State Agricultural College and Farm, which was chartered on March 22, 1858, by the Iowa General Assembly.

Becoming a major international university was probably the farthest thing on the minds of the couple of hundred people who gathered on July 4, 1859, on the open prairie between Ames and Boone to celebrate the fact that their bid—a land and monetary commitment totaling $21,355—had been chosen by the governing board of the new college as its site, winning out over several other counties. It was quite a victory for Story County, "just entering its fifth year of organized existence, sparsely settled and reputed to be unusually swampy."[1]

The college first began to take shape in 1860 with the construction of the model farm and farm superintendent's home, what is today the Farm House Museum, and when it was designated one of the nation's first land-grant institutions on March 29, 1864. The college opened on October 21, 1868, for a special preparatory session for students, and on March 17, 1869, for its first actual class of ninety-three students. Its beginnings were indeed humble, but the vision and dreams of those who founded it and those who engineered its growth and development over the next century and a half have almost always been huge.

The land-grant movement—launched with the passage of the Morrill Act in 1862—was a totally new—many would say revolutionary—approach to higher education, not just in the United States but in the world. The Morrill Act would forever change the character of most, if not all, higher education institutions in the nation, with its focuses on open access, applied research, and extending the knowledge resources of the institution to the public, and Iowa State would have a profound impact on the land-grant mission.

Iowa State University played a key role in the development of the land-grant mission and ideals, which is a credit to the visionary people who were the institution's first leaders, as well as the leaders of Iowa, which, on September 11, 1862, became the first state in the nation to accept the terms of the Morrill Act.[2] Among Iowa State's most notable early contributions to the development of the land-grant institution's mission were the following:

*Equal access.* Iowa State's first class of students in the fall of 1869 included sixteen women, which made Iowa State the first land-grant institution to be co-

*Iowa State's Centennial Alumni, for the National Association of State Universities and Land-Grant Colleges' one-hundredth anniversary, were (from left) George Washington Carver, Carrie Chapman Catt, and John V. Atanasoff. (Used by permission of Iowa State University Library/Special Collections Department)*

educational from the day it opened. One member of Iowa State's class of 1880 was Carrie Chapman Catt, who went on to become president of the National American Woman Suffrage Association, president of the International Women Suffrage Alliance, and one of the founders of the League of Women Voters. Iowa State also admitted the first African American student who applied—George Washington Carver. Carver enrolled in 1891, received a bachelor of science degree in 1894, master of science degree in 1896, and was Iowa State's first African American faculty member, serving as an instructor and superintendent of the botany greenhouse from 1895 to 1896. In 1896, he was recruited to Tuskegee Institute by Booker T. Washington, where he launched a career that would make him one of the greatest educators and scientists of the twentieth century.

*Extension.* Adonijah Welch, the first president of the college, and agriculture faculty member Isaac Roberts presented the nation's first off-campus Extension programs, called farmers' institutes, during the winter of 1870–1871. In 1903, faculty member Perry Holden worked with farmers in Sioux County to create the nation's first county Extension program, and in 1904, Holden earned his reputation as the "Seed Corn Evangelist" when he organized a statewide program to address a critical shortage of seed corn. He delivered the programming by train, which became known as the "Corn Gospel Train." In 1906, the nation's first statewide Extension Service was established at Iowa State, with Holden as its director.

*Agricultural Experiment Station.* Iowa State faculty members Seaman A. Knapp, who would later serve as president of the college, and Charles Bessey drafted the legislation that would become the Hatch Act of 1887, which established the nation's system of agricultural research experiment stations. Iowa State's Agricultural Experiment Station was established in 1888.

*Iowa State's first members of the National Academy of Sciences were (from left) Henry Gilman, Jay Lush, and Frank Spedding. (Used by permission of Iowa State University Library/Special Collections Department)*

*Home Economics.* In 1871, Iowa State established the nation's first program in domestic science, later to become Home Economics, Family and Consumer Sciences, and now a part of the College of Human Sciences. Mary Welch, wife of President Welch, conducted the nation's first Extension program in home economics.

*Veterinary Medicine.* The first veterinary medicine program at a land-grant institution was established at Iowa State in 1870.

*Engineering research.* The nation's first Engineering Experiment Station was established at Iowa State in 1904.

*Incorporating the arts.* One of the little-known, but very significant, contributions of Iowa State University to the character of the land-grant institution's educational mission was in acknowledging the importance of the fine arts in its educational programs and educational environment. In 1934, this college of agriculture and mechanic arts, whose motto since 1898 had been "Science with Practice," became the first institution of higher education in the nation to have an artist-in-residence on staff. Danish sculptor Christian Petersen, who, three years earlier, had worked at Iowa State as part of Grant Wood's federally funded Public Works of Art Project to create the murals in the Iowa State Library, was hired by President Raymond Hughes as artist-in-residence, the first at any college or university in the nation.[3]

Over its first one hundred years, Iowa State also made significant contributions in the land-grant institution's mission to harness science and technology to benefit society, solve problems, create economic opportunity, and improve quality of life. Key advances include the following:

- Henry Gilman, professor of chemistry, who came to Iowa State in 1919 and who was the first Iowa State faculty member elected to the National Academy of Sciences, laid the foundation for the development of the plastic and polyethylene industries, and is considered by some as the "greatest pioneer in organometallic research."[4]
- Beginning in 1922, Iowa State Agriculture faculty and collaborators, led by M. T. Jenkins, developed nine of the earliest inbred lines of corn introduced in the maize industry, including one line that is the parent of nearly half of the corn that is produced in temperate regions of the world. In 1930, an undergraduate student in that project, Raymond Baker, left the institution to join Iowa State graduates Henry A. Wallace and Jay Newlin in the first successful large-scale private commercialization of the hybrid corn seed, forming a company that would become Pioneer Hi-Bred International, Inc.
- In the late 1920s and early 1930s, Orland R. Sweeney, professor of chemical engineering, led the development of a process to extract soybean oil, which significantly increased the economic value of soybeans and led to it becoming a major crop in the Midwest. Sweeney also pioneered the development of gasohol, a mixture of gasoline and corn-based ethanol. The first commercial sale of gasohol was at a gas station on Highway 30 in Ames as part of a demonstration project.
- John Vincent Atanasoff, professor of mathematics and physics, invented the electronic digital computer, with assistance from graduate student Clifford Berry, in a project that lasted from 1936 to 1942.
- Frank Spedding, professor of chemistry, materials science and engineering, and physics, directed Iowa State's part in the Manhattan Project during World War II, which led to the world's first controlled nuclear reaction. Under Spedding's direction, the Iowa State group led by Harley Wilhelm developed the process that is still used today to purify uranium and other rare earth materials, ultimately contributing one-third of the several tons of enriched uranium needed for the reaction.
- Jay L. Lush, professor of animal science, considered the "founder of scientific animal breeding,"[5] laid the foundation for modern genetic and biometric approaches to livestock breeding in a career that spanned several decades (1930–1966).

- In 1966, Wesley Buchele, professor of agricultural engineering, invented the round hay baler, which revolutionized the way hay was cut and stored as livestock feed.
- In 1971, David Nicholas, a graduate student in electrical engineering, invented the encoding process that led to widespread use of the fax machine.

For ninety years after the first students enrolled, the Iowa Agricultural College was pretty much that—a college, despite the fact that it had met one of the primary modern criteria for classification as a university (the awarding of graduate degrees) since 1877. In 1898, the name was changed to the Iowa State College of Agriculture and Mechanic Arts, to reflect the engineering curricula, which had been part of the institution from the beginning, and the motto "Science with Practice" was adopted. On July 4, 1959, exactly one hundred years after the Independence Day picnic celebrating the selection of the college site and following many years of struggle against interests in the state that opposed the college's elevation to the same status as the University of Iowa, the Iowa Board of Regents approved the new name "Iowa State University of Science and Technology."

Iowa State officially became a university on July 4, 1959, one year after the institution celebrated the centennial of its founding. However, Iowa State was, in many ways, a university in name only. It was still largely dominated academically by the curricula upon which it was founded or that it helped pioneer—agriculture, engineering, home economics, and veterinary medicine. The biological sciences were strong because of their importance to agriculture and veterinary medicine, and physical sciences were strong because of their importance to engineering.

Not until the 1960s did Iowa State University start coming into its own as a broad-based, multifaceted university—in its academic programs, research, outreach programs, and national and international presence.

Much of that growth and development occurred under the leadership of W. Robert Parks, Iowa State's longest-serving president, in office from 1965 to 1986. Under Parks, the university established three new colleges—Education in 1968, Design in 1978, and Business in 1985—and significantly expanded programs in the humanities. Parks's primary goal, as put forth in his 1965 inauguration address, was achieving a "new humanism," or a blend of sciences and the humanities. His administration oversaw the largest growth of the institution in enrollment, employment, physical facilities, and academic programs.

In addition to the academic, enrollment, and physical growth, Iowa State's emergence as a true university, and one with a national and international presence, can be marked by several milestone events, achievements, or developments. The purpose of this chapter is to highlight some of the more significant ones. They follow in no particular order.

Perhaps Iowa State University's most visible and dramatic statement that it was indeed a university came in the construction of the four buildings that were not core academic facilities but facilities that fulfilled much more peripheral and pub-

*Construction of the Iowa State Center, including C. Y. Stephens Auditorium, in the 1960s and 1970s propelled Iowa State into prominence in the performing arts. The New York Philharmonic opened Stephens Auditorium with a concert on September 13, 1969, with Iowa State's Oratorio Chorus. (Used by permission of Iowa State University Library/Special Collections Department)*

lic functions. They were the C. Y. Stephens Auditorium, completed in 1969; the James H. Hilton Coliseum, completed in 1971; the J. W. Fisher Theater, completed in 1974; and the Carl H. Scheman Continuing Education Building, completed in 1975. Together they are known as the Iowa State Center.

The Iowa State Center was the dream of Iowa State's tenth president, James H. Hilton, who proposed it shortly after becoming president in 1953. The 2,700-seat auditorium would attract major national and international orchestras to Ames; the 14,000-seat coliseum would be the venue for Iowa State's athletic teams as well as host to large concerts and other entertainment events; the 424-seat theater would house student theater productions and lectures; and the continuing education building would be a center for the university's growing continuing education and conference activities. And it would be financed entirely without state tax dollars.

Hilton organized what would become the Iowa State University Foundation to coordinate the private fund-raising, which eventually raised $13.8 million of the $20 million total cost. The remainder came from bonds backed by student fees because of the importance of the facilities to student programs and activities, including intercollegiate athletics.

The Iowa State Center—in particular, Stephens Auditorium and Hilton Coliseum—has had an impact on elevating Iowa State University's national and international image unlike any other building or set of buildings in its history. Their construction sparked the development of what would become known as Iowa State's "South Campus," which now also includes Jack Trice Stadium, Jacobson Athletic Building, Olson Building, and Bergstrom Indoor Practice Facility of Iowa State's Athletic Department; the Reiman Gardens; the College of Veterinary Medicine; and the ISU Research Park, as well as the Green Hills retirement community, which, while privately owned and operated, began as a retirement community populated largely by Iowa State retirees and their spouses.

Since its inaugural concert on September 13, 1969, by the New York Philharmonic, Stephens Auditorium has played host to virtually every major international orchestra, consistently receiving rave reviews for its excellent acoustics. The success of Iowa State's men's and women's basketball teams in Hilton Coliseum in the 1980s led to the coining of "Hilton Magic" for the capacity crowds and thunderous fan support, which have been instrumental in the rise to national prominence of those programs. And in 2005, Stephens Auditorium was named Iowa's "Building of the Century" by the Iowa Chapter of the American Institute of Architects. University commencements are held in Hilton Coliseum, and Stephens Auditorium plays host to several musical and performing groups each year in the "Season at Stephens" program.

Since 1988, the Iowa State Center, with the exception of the Brunnier Gallery and Museum, has been operated by a management firm under contract with the university. The first operating firm was Ogden Allied Facility Management, which held the contract until 2000. By contracting with a leading national firm in the entertainment industry, the center has been able to provide more nationally and internationally known entertainment events to patrons.

The electronic digital computer—possibly the single-most important technological advancement of the twentieth century—was invented at Iowa State in a project that spanned six years, from 1935 to 1942. Its inventor was John Vincent Atanasoff, professor of mathematics and physics, assisted by electrical engineering graduate student Clifford Berry.

The story of the invention and events that followed is well documented in several books, the most popular of which is *Atanasoff: Forgotten Father of the Computer,* by Clark R. Mollenhoff (1988). It is a story filled with inspiration, unselfish dedication, intrigue, deception, and even courtroom drama.

Atanasoff, working with Electrical Engineering graduate Clifford Berry, designed and built the world's first electronic digital computer at Iowa State between 1935 and 1942. Atanasoff undertook the project because he was tired of seeing his graduate students spend so much time using mechanical calculating machines to solve long linear equations. He wanted to invent something that would solve these equations much more quickly, thus freeing up students' time for more productive work and research. Atanasoff ultimately designed and built a machine that was the first to incorporate eight of the fundamental principals of electronic digital computing:

- a binary system of arithmetic
- separate memory and computing functions

- regenerative memory
- electronic amplifiers as on-off switches
- parallel processing
- circuits for logical addition and subtraction
- clocked control of electronic operations
- modular design construction

A prototype was completed and successfully demonstrated in October 1939, which resulted in Atanasoff receiving additional funding from Iowa State College to build his full-scale machine. The machine, later dubbed the Atanasoff-Berry Computer (ABC) by Atanasoff himself, was almost finished when Atanasoff was called away to Washington, D.C., in 1942 to join the World War II effort with the U.S. Navy. The ABC was never completed, and its concepts were never patented. It sat under a tarp in the basement of the Physics Building, where it had been assembled, for several years before finally being dismantled for parts in the early 1950s, save for several vacuum tubes and one of two cordite "memory drums."

The ABC may never have been known about or appreciated had it not been for a very brief entry in the little-known book *Electronic Digital Systems*, by R. K. Richards of Ames, published in 1962. The entry read, "The ancestry of all electronic digital systems appears to be traceable to a computer which will be called the 'Atanasoff-Berry Computer.' This computer was built during the period from about 1938 to 1942 under the direction of Dr. John V. Atanasoff, who was a professor of physics and mathematics at Iowa State University (then Iowa State College) at Ames, Iowa."[6]

This entry became extremely important in a federal district court battle between two of the computing giants of the 1960s. Sperry Rand, holder of the patent on the ENIAC, then considered the first electronic digital computer, was suing other companies for infringement of its ENIAC patents. One of the firms being sued was Honeywell Company of Minneapolis. In 1967, lawyers for Honeywell learned of Richards's book and decided to pursue this "John V. Atanasoff." What they discovered delighted them. Atanasoff still had all of his records, and his memories of that time in his life were still very clear. And what they learned from Atanasoff during one of their pretrial interviews absolutely astonished them: ENIAC coinventor John Mauchly had paid an extended visit to Atanasoff at Iowa State in 1941, and had spent many hours studying Atanasoff's machine, working on it and taking notes.

Armed with this information, and with Atanasoff as their prize witness, the lawyers argued that the ENIAC patents were invalid because they were based on a preexisting invention. After several years of trial, U.S. District Federal Court Judge Earl Larson agreed with Honeywell in his ruling, issued on October 19, 1971, stating, "(J. Presper) Eckert and Mauchly did not themselves first invent the electronic digital computer, but instead derived the subject matter from one Dr. John Vincent Atanasoff."[7] His decision was never appealed by Sperry.

The ruling should have sent shock waves through the academic and computing community, and caused historians to begin correcting textbooks, encyclopedias, and other references as to the inventor of the computer. But it did not. Despite the ruling, and despite many efforts by Iowa State faculty and staff to correct the historical record, Atanasoff, the ABC, and the ruling were largely dismissed by the computing industry, which was still dominated by Sperry and its successors, and the computing society, still dominated by the larger-than-life personae of the ENIAC inventors, Mauchly and Eckert. It must be remembered that the ENIAC was a monumental scientific and technological achievement, literally dwarfing the ABC in both size and capability. And the ENIAC was fully operational, including playing a role in World War II. It became the model for generations of computers to come.

The fact remained, however, that the ABC, despite its shortcomings, one of which was that it was never fully operational, was first. Over the next nearly fifteen years, Iowa State's efforts to earn Atanasoff his due achieved some measure of success, with a steadily increasing number of historians, authors, reference books, and computer scientists accepting Atanasoff as the inventor. Beginning in 1988, with the publication of Mollenhoff's book, public and scientific community acceptance of Atanasoff began to change significantly, culminating in what has been described as the "Big 3" recognitions in 1990 and 1991.

In 1990, Atanasoff received the National Medal of Technology from President George H. W. Bush, and the Institute of Electrical and Electronics Engineers presented Iowa State University with its Milestone Award, with the following inscription:

**Electrical Engineering Milestone**
**Atanasoff-Berry Computer**

*John Vincent Atanasoff conceived basic design principles for an electronic, digital computer in the winter of 1937 and, assisted by his graduate student, Clifford E. Berry, constructed a prototype here in October 1939. This was the first electronic calculating machine to use binary numbers, direct logic for calculation, and a regenerative memory. It embodied concepts that would be central to the future development of computers.*

April 1990
Institute of Electrical and Electronics Engineers

Finally, in 1991, the Information Age exhibition opened at the Smithsonian Institution's Museum of American History with Atanasoff's pioneering role in the invention of the computer documented and two of the few remaining components of the original ABC featured—a memory drum and an add/subtract array recreated from original ABC vacuum tubes, both on loan to the Smithsonian from Iowa State.

Despite the national recognitions, many ENIAC supporters and computer historians remained unconvinced, and one of their primary arguments against accepting Atanasoff and the ABC was the fact that the ABC was never fully operational. The limited prototype built by Atanasoff in 1939 and a "breadboard" built by technicians for the court trial both worked as designed but the computer itself never did. In 1994, a team of Iowa State scientists, staff, and graduate students set

*John V. Atanasoff invented the electronic digital computer while he was a faculty member at Iowa State in the 1930s. On the left is the original Atanasoff-Berry Computer. (Used by permission of Iowa State University Library/Special Collections Department) The original Atanasoff-Berry Computer was dismantled a few years after it was built, so one of the nagging questions had always been, "Did it work?" A team of ISU faculty, staff, and students answered that question when they built a working replica of the ABC and successfully ran it at a public unveiling in Washington, D.C., on October 8, 1997 (right). Shown with the replica are (from left) John Atanasoff II, son of the inventor; Arthur Oldehoeft, then chair of Computer Science; graduate student Charles Shorb; and John Gustafson, professor of Computer Science. (Used by permission of Ames Laboratory, U.S. Department of Energy)*

about to prove once and for all that the ABC was the first functioning electronic digital computer. They built a full-scale replica of the ABC, using Atanasoff's original designs, and as many original parts as could be found.

The project cost more than $350,000 and thousands of hours of work by the team members and others. On October 8, 1997, the completed replica—about the size of an office desk and weighing 750 pounds—was unveiled by Iowa State personnel at the National Press Club in Washington, D.C., before an international media audience. Atanasoff, who died in 1995, was represented by his son, John V. Atanasoff II, and Clifford Berry, who died in 1963, was represented by his son, David Berry, who turned on the ABC and had it solve a simple equation, $9 - (3 \times 2) = x$. That is a far cry from its design function of solving up to twenty-nine simultaneous equations with up to twenty-nine variables, but no one had the time to wait the several hours it would have taken to solve a more complex problem, working at 0.06 operations per second compared with the trillions of operations per second by modern computers. After about three minutes of operation, the counter on the ABC registered 3. (In other trials, the replica successfully solved much more complex equations.) The final obstacle to the Atanasoff-Berry Computer being accepted as the world's first electronic digital computer had been overcome.

Following an extensive national and state tour to museums and educational institutions, the ABC replica was put on permanent display in Hoover Hall of Iowa State University's Engineering Teaching and Research Complex. Another exhibit illustrating Atanasoff's landmark contributions to computing can be found in the foyer of ISU's Durham Center for Computation and Communication, and a recreation of Atanasoff's office, including many of his original artifacts and documents, is located on the third floor of the Durham Center.

One of Iowa State University's long-standing academic strengths has been in the physical sciences, with strong programs and faculty in engineering, chemistry, physics, and materials science. It was because of this strength, and, in particular, because of the presence of Frank Spedding, an Iowa State professor and renowned expert in the chemistry of rare earth materials, that Iowa State played a significant role in the Manhattan Project of World War II and the establishment of a permanent national research laboratory facility at Iowa State, the Ames Laboratory.

Under Spedding's direction, an Iowa State group led by Harley Wilhelm developed the process to produce and cast into metal ingots the large quantities of enriched uranium needed for a controlled nuclear reaction and at about one-twentieth the cost of previous production methods. Iowa State eventually produced more than two million pounds of enriched uranium for the Manhattan Project, and modifications of the process it developed are still used today for enriched uranium production.

After the war, Iowa State reorganized Spedding's group into the Institute for Atomic Research, and in 1947, the U.S. Atomic Energy Commission designated the institute as one of its major research installations. It was renamed the Energy and Mineral Resources Research Institute in 1974, and in 1975 it became a U.S. Department of Energy (DOE) national research laboratory with the creation of that department of the federal government.

Since then, the Ames Laboratory has been operated by Iowa State University under contract with the DOE. It is one of the smallest of the DOE's sixteen national research labs, but it is unique in that it is the only DOE research lab located entirely on a university campus. Major Ames Lab buildings connect with ISU's Physics Building and Gilman Hall, home of the Chemistry Department. Its proximity to and close connection with the campus allows for extensive interaction and joint faculty appointments for its more than 250 scientists and engineers with Iowa State's Chemistry, Physics, Materials Science, and several other academic departments. The Ames Lab is part of Iowa State's umbrella Institute for Physical Research and Technology, and its Materials Preparation Center is still known as the producer of the highest purity rare earth materials for academic and industrial use.

In the 1980s, the Ames Laboratory significantly expanded the scope of its research and technology transfer activities. Projects include design of synthetic molecules for solar energy conversion, magnetic refrigeration, hydrogen fuel cells, scalable computing, superconductors, quasicrystals, and the synthesis and study of nontraditional materials such as organic polymers and organometallic materials for superconductors, processable preceramics, and nonlinear optical systems.

Iowa State started out as a small college focused primarily on the educational needs of the students of its state and the needs of the state-based agricultural industry. It didn't take long, however, for Iowa State's expertise in agriculture to receive recognition from people outside the state of Iowa and the United States, thanks to the work of early faculty members like Charles Bessey, faculty member in botany from 1870 to 1884, and Charles Curtiss, who joined the faculty in 1891 and served as dean of agriculture from 1902 to 1932.

Iowa State records are unclear as to when the first international student enrolled, but it is believed to have been at around the turn of the century. By 1908, the number had grown to twenty-five students from twelve different countries, and that year, these students formed the institution's first international student organization—the Cosmopolitan Club.

International enrollment grew steadily through the twentieth century, topping 1,000 in 1976, 2,000 in 1984, and reaching a peak of 2,692 in 1993, when international students made up 10.7 percent of the total enrollment. It remained at approximately 2,500 until 2000. Upwards of 120 different nations were represented in ISU's student enrollments of 1984 and after.

Iowa State's first study-abroad program for students was the Agriculture Travel Course. Although this program was started in 1934, it did not have an actual foreign travel component until 1962. During the 1973-1974 academic year, seventy-seven Iowa State students participated in a study-abroad program, and in 2000, the number had grown to nearly one thousand students, with programs on every continent, including Antarctica.

Iowa State's earliest documented international development project began in 1945 with the creation of the Iowa State Center for Tropical Research in Guatemala. By the end of the twentieth century, Iowa State had 175 development, research, and educational agreements in place with institutions and government agencies in fifty-seven other nations. The university's oldest continuing international partner is Peru, dating back to 1962, through a U.S. Agency for International Development–funded project to develop economic and agricultural development strategies.

The creation in 1957 and development of the Center for Agricultural and Rural Development (CARD) served as a catalyst for Iowa State's entry into the world community in a major way. CARD, whose development was spearheaded by Earl O. Heady, professor of agricultural economics and Iowa State's first Charles F. Curtiss Distinguished Professor in Agriculture, did not start out as an international program, but rather as an effort to address the dire economic straits of farmers in Iowa and the Midwest.

In 1955, Heady chaired a new Agricultural Adjustment Research Committee at Iowa State to address these issues, and he was one of the leaders in a successful effort to obtain $100,000 in new state funding to support, according to House Resolution 15, which became the basis for the legislation, new research into "problems in the marketing, processing, and utilization of farm products; new uses for present production; and discovery of new crops and markets."[8] First named the Center for Agricultural Adjustment, it became the first research center in the nation with "agricultural adjustment" as its primary focus.

As Heady and CARD faculty increased their influence on national agricultural policy, such as through the development of a national econometric model in 1962, they began to set their sights on issues affecting U.S. agriculture beyond the na-

*Economist Earl Heady, shown with one of his many international honors, played a major role in expanding Iowa State's global focus. (Used by permission of Iowa State University Library/Special Collections Department)*

tion's borders. In 1962, CARD cosponsored the Conference on International Commodity Agreements, and in 1963, Heady began consulting with the Organization for Economic and Cooperative Development regarding agricultural adjustment centers in Europe. In 1967, he was appointed as an adviser to the U.S. State Department on world food production problems and foreign policy.

Heady's ingenious work in economic modeling attracted graduate students and postdoctoral researchers from many parts of the world, many of whom were sponsored by their governments so they would be able to implement Heady's models in their home nations after earning their graduate degrees. Under Heady's leadership CARD also led an expansion of the university's involvement in international agricultural and economic development projects, funded by such agencies as the U.S. Agency for International Development. Iowa State's global alumni network expanded significantly thanks to Heady, and many of his former students rose to become top government officials in their nations. It was said that Heady could land at any airport in the world and be greeted by one of his former graduate students. Heady retired in 1984 and died in 1987.

As Iowa State faculty became more involved in international projects and issues, new organizational structures were created to support their scholarly activities,

*Iowa State President Robert W. Parks opened the 1976 World Food Conference, hosted by Iowa State. (Used by permission of Iowa State University Library/ Special Collections Department)*

such as the World Food Institute, created in 1972, out of which grew Iowa State's largest single international event. The World Food Institute sponsored a World Food Conference at Iowa State in the summer of 1976, during the height of the nation's bicentennial activities. This conference was organized to address the growing issue of world hunger by bringing together leading international scholars in several of the disciplines involved in world food and hunger issues. The conference exceeded its planners' expectations by attracting scientists and scholars from 70 nations, 42 prominent international speakers, 660 registrants, and more than 1,600 attendees. The World Food Conference was one of seven international meetings or conferences hosted by Iowa State during the summer of 1976.

Iowa State was also in the international spotlight for more than six years in the 1980s and 1990s, but for a much different and unpleasant reason. Two Iowa State alumni—Terry Anderson and Thomas Sutherland—were kidnapped in 1985 by the Islamic Jihad in the Middle East and held captive until 1991. They were among several westerners kidnapped and held captive during that time, but their ordeal was the longest, and Sutherland's the longest of them all.

During their captivity, Iowa State organized public programs of support and remembrance on several of the annual anniversaries of their kidnapping and tolled the bells of the Campanile once for each month of captivity. The ceremonies and tolling received considerable news media attention from the local, national, and international news media. Upon his release on November 18, 1991, Sutherland told of being allowed to listen to the Voice of America radio broadcast on occa-

*ISU alumni Thomas Sutherland (left) and Terry Anderson, the longest-held U.S. hostages in Lebanon during the strife-torn period of the 1980s and 1990s, were reunited on the Iowa State campus after their release in November 1993. (Used by permission of Iowa State University Library/Special Collections Department)*

sion, and he actually heard the bells of the Iowa State University Campanile being tolled for him. "I was very, very moved when I heard . . . the Bells of Iowa State . . . I was extremely happy!" he said at a press conference following his release, adding that knowing people back in the United States were thinking about him helped keep him going during his difficult ordeal.

Sutherland and Anderson both returned to the Iowa State campus on several occasions after their release. Sutherland first returned in May 1992 when he and his wife, Jean, were marshals of the 1992 VEISHEA parade, and Anderson first returned when he was honored by the Greenlee School of Journalism and Mass Communication in November 1993.

The national spotlight shone brightly on Iowa State in 1995 when the Iowa State campus was turned into a "midwestern White House" as the university hosted the National Rural Conference on April 25, 1995, attended by President William Clinton, Vice President Al Gore, and Secretary of Agriculture Dan Glickman. This was one of the few times in U.S. history that those three top U.S. officials have been in the same place for an event outside of Washington, D.C. Glickman chose the Iowa State campus to host the culmination of a series of regional meetings on issues facing rural America, and Iowa State had about ten days to prepare for the onslaught of politicians, news media, and interested persons.

Carol Bradley, an assistant to President Martin Jischke, was given the assignment to coordinate everything involving Iowa State. The conference was held in

*The nation's eyes turned to Iowa State on April 25, 1995, when ISU hosted President William Clinton, Vice President Al Gore, and U.S. Secretary of Agriculture Dan Glickman for the National Rural Conference. The Great Hall of the Memorial Union was transformed into a U.S. Capitol-like hearing chamber for the conference. (Used by permission of Iowa State University Information Technology Services)*

the Great Hall of the Memorial Union, which was completely redecorated so that to television audiences it would look like a congressional hearing room in Washington, D.C., complete with red, white, and blue bunting hung from the balcony windows. A semicircular desk large enough to seat all of the dignitaries and panel members was constructed, as were several bookcases that would form the backdrop. The bookcases were even filled with books from the ISU Library having to do with rural issues.

The U.S. Secret Service literally took over the Union and much of the campus around it for security purposes. All classes were cancelled for the day and many students were encouraged to attend the conference. The conference lasted six and a half hours and involved thirty panelists. More than one hundred members of the national news media attended. Following the conference, President Clinton and Vice President Gore addressed more than eleven thousand people in the Hilton Coliseum before boarding their motorcade for the return to D.C.

It only took about ten hours from the time President Clinton and the other dignitaries arrived at the Memorial Union until they departed, but for those ten hours, the national spotlight was definitely on Iowa State University.

In 1991, the Iowa State University campus was listed as one of the twenty-five most beautiful in the nation in the book *The Campus as a Work of Art*. It wasn't always that way, however.

For its first sixty years, the institution had an art collection consisting mostly of a few portraits of college officials. That was to begin to change dramatically in 1928 when President Raymond Hughes organized the first institution-wide art collection committee to oversee the acquisition of objects of art. Over the next nine years, it would take advantage of everything from the Great Depression to a struggling sculptor needing a job to lay the foundation for this campus as a "work of art."

During the Depression, Hughes was able to use the Public Works of Art Project and the Works Progress Administration to commission the two murals in what is now the Parks Library, *When Tillage Begins, Other Arts Follow* and *Breaking the Prairie Sod,* both directed by Grant Wood and notable because they are the largest murals by Wood in the nation. One of the artists who worked with Wood on that project was a gifted young sculptor named Christian Petersen, and when Hughes discovered that Petersen was in desperate need of a job, he found one for him at Iowa State. Because Petersen did not have a college degree, Hughes could not appoint him to the faculty, so he appointed him "artist-in-residence." For the next twenty-one years, Petersen would create hundreds of art objects in his studio in the Veterinary Medicine Quadrangle, many of which still grace the Iowa State campus and have become some of the most enduring symbols of the institution, including the *Fountain of the Four Seasons* and the *Gentle Doctor.*

The project to build the Iowa State Center in the 1950s and 1960s would be the next significant artistic catalyst for Iowa State. Alumni Henry and Ann Brunnier were major contributors to the project, and in addition to their financial contribution, Ann donated her entire collection of dolls and decorative arts she had collected over many years of international travel. The more than four thousand objects filled two semitrailers and took months to catalog, and when the Carl J. Scheman Continuing Education Building opened on September 19, 1975, the Henry J. Brunnier Gallery, later named the Brunnier Art Museum, was located on the top floor to display objects from Ann's collection and to host other exhibitions from around the nation and the world.

In 1982, the university reorganized its three noncurricular arts divisions in order, in part, to gain accreditation from the American Association of Museums. University Museums was organized to encompass the Brunnier Art Museum, the Farm House Museum (the first building constructed on the Iowa State campus, restored as a museum to late nineteenth-century rural Iowa life, and designated a National Historic Landmark in 1965), and the Art on Campus Collection and Program.

Still, Iowa State's campus art collection was not very diversified, dominated primarily by Petersen's sculptures and Ann Brunnier's dolls and ceramics. What has been described as a modern arts "renaissance"[9] for the campus began in 1978 with the passage of the Art in State Buildings Program by the State of Iowa. This legislation directed that one-half of 1 percent of the total construction cost for public buildings be used for the commissioning or acquisition of art for that building. In the first twenty years after its enactment, Iowa State added 190 new art objects through this program.

In 1986, University Museums began a comprehensive conservation survey of its collection, and eventually determined that sixteen major objects of art were in

*Iowa State's Christian Petersen was the nation's first artist-in-residence at any college or university. His sculptures have gained increasing national attention, and in 2001, Iowa State presented his Cornhusker to the Smithsonian American Art Museum. Shown at the presentation are (from left) Elizabeth Broun, director of the museum; then–Iowa State President-elect Gregory L. Geoffroy; and ISU Interim President Richard Seagrave. (Used by permission of Iowa State University Museums)*

need of major conservation, including eight of Petersen's sculptures. Approximately $1 million—much of it raised privately—was spent over the next fourteen years and all sixteen objects were conserved. They are among the more than four hundred major works currently in the Art on Campus Collection.

In the years since his death in 1961, Petersen's reputation as one of this nation's most important regional artists has gradually increased, thanks largely to the persistent efforts of Lynette Pohlman, director of University Museums at Iowa State since 1975. Pohlman's efforts were rewarded in 2001 when the Smithsonian American Art Museum agreed to accept into its collection a bronze casting of Petersen's *Cornhusker* sculpture, gifted from Iowa State University. Two other castings of *Cornhusker* were made—one to be kept in the university's permanent collection and the other gifted to the Nelson-Atkins Museum of Modern Art in Kansas City, Missouri.

As noted earlier, Iowa State was very involved in the evolution of the land-grant movement and institutional mission of "teaching, research, and service" and strengthening the original ideals upon which land-grant institutions were founded—open access to its educational programs and practical research, or using the knowledge resources to benefit the public. In the second half of the twentieth century, Iowa State played a leadership role in what has been described as a modernization and revitalization of the land-grant mission and ideals, particularly in three areas: economic development, access to more students, and engagement with the broader society.

*Economic development.* Direct economic development is an outgrowth of outreach and Extension. Even before Iowa State opened as an educational institution for students, it was involved in supporting the economic development of Iowa. The Model Farm part of Iowa Agricultural College and Model Farm opened in 1860 and was a place where practical research on crop production and animal agriculture was conducted. It was the forerunner to the Agricultural Experiment Station system, established nationally by the Hatch Act in 1887, thanks to Iowa State's leadership.

This emphasis on practical research in agriculture spread to other parts of the institution, following the "experiment station" model. Under Dean of Engineering Anson Marston, Iowa State established the first Engineering Experiment Station in the nation in 1904, which included the Iowa Highway Commission because of Iowa State's expertise in roads and transportation. (The Iowa Highway Commission was separated from the experiment station in 1913 and became an agency of state government.)

Examples of practical research permeate the first fifty years of the twentieth century at Iowa State—invention of the computer, development of hybrid corn, livestock genetics, gasohol, rare earth purification, and animal vaccines and supplements. Extension was really the only formal organizational structure at Iowa State through which information was "transferred" from the campus to the people of Iowa, and that information was almost entirely focused on meeting the needs of production agriculture and rural families.

In 1963, in response to the rapid growth of manufacturing in Iowa, Iowa State created a new organization—the Center for Industrial Research and Service (CIRAS)—whose specific mission was to help Iowa manufacturers and businesses. It was a somewhat radical departure from a previously held "arm's length" policy toward the private sector (outside of agriculture), and it marked the beginning of what would become a major new emphasis in Iowa State's land-grant outreach mission and one of the first such efforts nationally. CIRAS was in the College of Engineering, but it became part of University Extension when that umbrella organization of outreach services was created in 1966.

For more than twenty years, CIRAS was Iowa State's primary contact with the manufacturing sector. An economic downturn in the 1980s, fueled by a severe recession in the agricultural sector, led to a rapid expansion of this part of the university's outreach mission and made the phrase "economic development" a key part of that mission.

The farm economy recession had a devastating effect in Iowa because Iowa's economy is so dominated by agriculture. As the recession worsened, state leaders looked for ways to help bring Iowa out of it and for ways to strengthen and diversify the state's economy so that it would not be so susceptible to agricultural recessions. They saw, in Iowa's two research universities—Iowa State University and the University of Iowa—vast untapped potential for economic development, and they decided to put it to use as "engines for economic development."

The effort was led by Governor Terry Branstad and Des Moines businessman Marvin Pomerantz, whom Branstad appointed to the Board of Regents, State of Iowa, which governs Iowa's three public universities (ISU, Iowa, and the University of Northern Iowa). Pomerantz's strong and sometimes controversial leadership as president of the regents is documented in other chapters of this book, but clearly he and Branstad, more than anyone else, ushered in the "economic development" era for Iowa's research universities.

Iowa State also decided to leverage its research strengths—particularly in the agricultural and physical sciences—and the state's political clout—with Iowa Third District Representative Neal Smith as ranking Democrat on the House Appropriations Committee—to increase federal government support for Iowa State's research and development efforts and to help Iowa's economy recover and diversify. With the support of Smith and several other members of the Iowa congressional delegation, including Senators Charles Grassley and Tom Harkin, Iowa State became one of the leading universities in the nation in securing direct congressional appropriations for research and technology development and technology transfer programs. Two of the largest, most important, and most durable programs established during this era were

- The Institute for Physical Research and Technology (IPRT), created in 1985 as an umbrella organization to secure federal funding to expand research in the physical sciences, with the specific goal of capitalizing on this research to create new economic opportunities for Iowans. New centers created under the IPRT umbrella, such as the Center for Nondestructive Evaluation, the Microelectronics Research Center, and the Center for Advanced Technology Development, tapped into the research programs of the Ames Laboratory and other physical science programs at Iowa State, including Engineering, to generate new economic opportunities by commercializing Iowa State–developed technologies. IPRT programs were so successful in technology transfer and starting new commercial ventures that U.S. Secretary of Commerce Ron Brown visited Iowa State programs on April 5, 1994, and stated, "I couldn't be more pleased, and more inspired, and more energized than I am by what I have seen here. It's apparent . . . that the future is now at Iowa State."[10]
- ISU Research Park and Iowa State Innovation System (ISIS) high-technology business incubator. One of the most important and most visible developments was the creation, in 1986, of the ISU Research Park and ISIS, a small business incubator, which for the first time provided a direct link between the university's research enterprise and the private business sector.

*Access.* One of the founding ideals of the land-grant movement was open access to higher education for all people in society. At the time the legislation was written by Justin Morrill in the 1850s, he was referring primarily to the children of the working classes and farmers. Significant expansions of the land-grant ideal of access occurred with the granting of land-grant charters to traditionally black colleges and universities in 1890 and to Native American institutions in 1920. However, there has been little change in terms of expanding access to land-grant institutions, on a grand scale, since.

In 1995, Iowa State University announced the largest single expansion of access to its educational programs in its history and the first major statewide need-based scholarship program in the nation by a land-grant institution. Christina Hixson, native Iowan and longtime assistant to Omaha and Las Vegas businessman and real estate developer Ernst Lied and sole trustee of the Lied Foundation Trust, created the Christina Hixson Opportunity Awards Program, through which one student from each county in Iowa, each year, receives a full tuition scholarship to attend Iowa State, renewable for up to four years.

As a high school graduate, Hixson could not afford to go to college, so she wanted to create an endowment that would help others in similar circumstances overcome this obstacle. Selection of Hixson award recipients is based partly on financial or other family hardship, two factors that often mark a student as "at risk" for college.

Beginning in 1995, approximately one hundred new Hixson students have enrolled at Iowa State. They receive special counseling and support from a staff member at Iowa State, and their success rate—as measured by retention and graduation rates—has consistently exceeded the university average by more than 10 percent. Hixson travels to Iowa State each year to meet with the new group of students.

*Engagement.* Before the Kellogg Commission on the Future of State and Land-Grant Universities started its work in 1996, the term "outreach" was generally used to describe the part of the land-grant mission that extended the resources of the institutions to help people in the states they served. The Kellogg Commission embraced the term "engagement" as a larger umbrella to encompass traditional outreach activities, such as Extension, as well as practical research and service and experiential learning for students. Iowa State President Martin Jischke was a member of the Kellogg Commission and he chaired the Engagement Committee, whose report called on the nation's state and land-grant universities to become more engaged with the larger society they serve.

Two significant expansions of Iowa State's engagement with the broader Iowa society began in the mid-1980s and continue today. In 1986, Iowa State agreed to host, with the City of Ames, the Iowa Special Olympics Summer Games. Each year, between 2,500 and 3,000 Special Olympians and their parents, teachers, and coaches stay in university residence halls and the university provides its athletic facilities for the competitions at no cost. In 1987, the State of Iowa launched the Iowa Games, a statewide amateur athletic competition, and chose Ames and ISU as the site for the annual summer games. These games involve upward of 15,000 Iowans competing in a wide variety of athletic events. Both events continue at ISU and Ames.

*There is probably no greater symbol of our tradition, our transformation, and our future than Morrill Hall, recently reopened after a remarkable renovation and upgrading. Morrill Hall is a beloved symbol of our land-grant heritage, . . .*

*"Afterword", Gregory L. Geoffroy*

# Afterword: Poised for the Future

Gregory L. Geoffroy

This history was commissioned to celebrate the sesquicentennial of Iowa State University's founding in 1858. From its early beginnings as the nation's first land-grant institution, ISU has become known nationally and internationally for the excellence of its programs—both teaching and research. This book records the facts of Iowa State's history as well as its rich legacy and proud traditions. In addition to being one of the world's leading research institutions, ISU is the place where thousands of students have experienced a first-rate education, developed as adults and citizens, prepared for meaningful careers, and met lifelong partners and friends.

As a member of the greater Iowa State family, you may have recalled pleasant memories as you read: old friends, fun times, great instructors, and special events from your Iowa State past. Perhaps you remember your nervousness and excitement moving into a residence hall and meeting your roommates. There were first classes—your first experience with professors and the lecture approach to instruction. As you recall your initiation into the campus life of your era, your selection of a major, late-night study sessions alone or with new friends, your extracurricular activities, sports, and eventually commencement, you may wish to return to campus, see the changes, see familiar places, rekindle old memories, and recall this important time in your life. We welcome your return, especially in connection with our sesquicentennial celebration.

A common theme throughout this book is our commitment to excellence. Over the years, many excellent faculty members have researched, mentored, and taught at Iowa State. These dedicated people have produced some of the most important scientific advancements of the last century. They exemplified the land-grant ideal of applying scientific knowledge to real-life issues, real-life problems, and real-life challenges—from Iowa's leadership role in the development of hybrid seed corn, to the pioneering work of Henry Gilman in organometallics and plastics, O. R. Sweeney in ethanol fuels, Jay Lush in scientific animal breeding, Frank Spedding and Harley Wilhelm in purifying rare earth metals, John Atanasoff in digital computing, and many, many others.

Today's faculty members uphold the standards of excellence from the past. One need only review the accomplishments of those who have earned the title of "Distinguished Professor," for example, to see that research excellence and the transfer of expertise to benefit Iowa's economy continues into the twenty-first century. ISU's national rankings demonstrate our success in making use of scientific knowledge: we're number one among all universities in the United States in licenses and options executed on our intellectual property, number two in licenses and options yielding income, among the top three in new patentable biotechnology, and number two in new and significant technological discoveries receiving R&D 100 Awards from *R&D Magazine*. Iowa State faculty members have turned their discoveries into dozens of companies that employ Iowans and enrich our state's economy, and the pace of such developments is accelerating.

Our faculty members have always received national and international recognition: peer election to the National Academy of Sciences and the National Academy of Engineering (the most prestigious societies recognizing research excellence in our country), honorary degrees from universities across the globe, and election as fellows of their respective academic societies. They have received awards for lifelong achievement and awards for early promise in their careers. An ISU faculty member discovered the world's second-hardest substance and a graduate student invented the encoding process that made fax machines commonplace. They developed plants with new properties that would enhance nutrition and health worldwide as well as produce better raw materials for industry. They developed C6, one of the world's only six-sided virtual reality labs, and the Wind Simulation and Testing Laboratory, which has drawn international attention for its ability to recreate tornadic conditions in order to research these and other deadly storms. They started the Information Assurance Center, which is at the forefront of computer security efforts in our nation, and the Center for Nondestructive Evaluation, a National Science Foundation Industry/University Cooperative Research Center. Transportation and Logistics faculty members are among the three most productive such groups in the country, while the Pappajohn Center for Entrepreneurship is in the first tier of such programs as reported in *Entrepreneur Magazine*.

Our achievements also reflect the outstanding students who have come to ISU. A key part of the land-grant tradition is that of access and opportunity. Iowa State has opened its doors to tens of thousands of students over the years: from Iowa, the nation, and more than one hundred countries across the globe. Students have changed in many ways over the years, but the desire to learn remains strong. We are proud of M. J. Riggs, George Washington Carver, Carrie Chapman Catt, Henry A. Wallace, and other outstanding students from Iowa State's early years. We are equally proud of alumni from the more recent past who have achieved life success and who still value their relationship with the university. The list is longer than there is space here to share, especially when you include today's young alumni who are just starting to make their mark in the world. Our current students share the same commitment to excellence in their life work as their predecessors did.

Finally, our achievements are supported by a hardworking and caring staff, people who extend themselves to meet the needs of our students, to maintain our beautiful campus, and to address the needs of Iowans as well as people throughout the world in our outreach programs and activities. On the worst day of winter, there is hot food in our dining halls, the power plant delivers heat to our buildings, the parking lots are plowed, and the sidewalks and steps are cleared.

Our excellence also reflects the men who assumed the burden of leadership as presidents of the university. W. Robert Parks, for example, presided over a two-decade-long period of great change. He emphasized the "new humanism," recognizing the key role the arts and humanities play in a well-rounded undergraduate education and in the life of a campus. He was president during the very difficult era that included the Vietnam War and the movements for civil rights and women's rights, providing outstanding leadership during those struggles. Gordon Eaton rejected the false sense of complacency that he feared was hindering the ongoing fulfillment of ISU's mission, and he insisted on a strengthened commitment to excellence, scholarship, and accountability. He understood the importance of research outside the boundaries of traditional disciplines, and we owe many of our important centers and institutes to his vision and leadership. Martin Jischke had a deep respect for the transforming power of the land-grant mission, especially the ideal of access and opportunity for all. He led a scholarship campaign, later expanded into a general capital campaign, that provided scholarship funds for some eight thousand students each year, and he had the vision to establish our great Plant Sciences Institute. I have been fortunate to carry on where they left off, and I am deeply committed to continuing the great tradition of achievement that is the hallmark of Iowa State University.

Iowa State University has faced difficult challenges amidst its many successes. These include major national crises—the great economic depressions of the 1890s and the 1930s, the world wars, and the Korean and Vietnam conflicts. They include the serious and potentially damaging budget challenges of the past several years and a recently turbulent VEISHEA. In the final analysis Iowa State is greater than any challenge, thanks to the dedication and determination of its people.

The histories of Iowa State University and the state of Iowa are inexorably and deeply intertwined. Iowa is an exceptional state, with its rich, dark soil of remarkable productivity and weather that, while well suited for agriculture, tests and strengthens individuals as they meet its annual challenges. Iowa is a state of strong communities where people truly care about their fellow citizens. Iowans have a strong tradition of placing quality-of-life issues—foremost among them, education—as their highest priorities. This has been true since the state was first settled: after the first homes and buildings were constructed, Iowans built schools. Most important of all, Iowa was the first state in the nation to adopt the Morrill Act, establishing the land-grant system of colleges and universities.

In many ways, the state of Iowa and Iowa State University are at an important crossroads. Iowa has to manage a slow-growth environment, find ways to add value to its agricultural production, maintain the quality of life in its communities, and attract businesses and young people to the state. Government and business leaders are working diligently on a variety of solutions, and I am confident they will succeed. A key part of any solution is Iowa State University—discovery by our faculty, learning by our students, and outreach by the institution as a whole. The university stands ready to contribute and to lead as it has done for a century and a half.

Similarly, Iowa State must adapt to a changing world, and we are doing so. We must be accountable stewards of the valuable resources the people of Iowa provide to us, through their elected representatives; we must demonstrate that our education meets the needs of the larger—now global—society that our graduates will enter; and we must continually prove our excellence and our worth through research, scholarship, and artistic endeavor.

Fortunately, we have an excellent guide to direct our efforts—our strategic plan. In 1990 the University unveiled its first five-year strategic plan, and by 2005 we had implemented our fourth. Our new plan—"Forward Thinking"— builds on the preceding plans. We embrace a mission of creating, sharing, and applying knowledge to make Iowa and the world a better place, doing so through innovation, collaboration, and continuous improvement; with honesty, integrity, and professional ethics; and with sensitivity and responsiveness to the needs of our state, nation, and the world. We value the ideals of higher education: a diversity of ideas, peoples, and cultures; intellectual freedom; leadership; and excellence in all that we do.

We have five priority goals: strengthening the education we provide students; increasing our research excellence, especially in the key areas of engineering, the physical sciences, the plant sciences, and the animal sciences; transferring our discoveries to improve the economy; helping to improve quality of life in Iowa; and ensuring that the university is a conducive environment for learning and working. In one respect, these goals reflect our beginnings as the nation's first land-grant institution—access and opportunity, practical education, useful research, and technology transfer. In another, they reflect the world of the twenty-first century, the needs of our state and our nation, and the challenges we all face.

Studies of economically successful regions across this nation have shown that at the core of every one is a nucleus of one or more strong research universities. Research universities are essential drivers for that economic success. They gather and nurture the talented workforce that modern industries need, and they conduct the cutting-edge research that fuels economic development. The future of Iowa as a state is closely linked to the success of its two complementary research universities—Iowa State University and the University of Iowa—and we embrace those responsibilities.

We know that organizations that meet the challenges before them are ones that are constantly "transforming." They transform themselves to meet the exigencies of the time, and they transform others to do the same, much as we help our students make the transition from adolescence to adulthood.

Iowa State University is a transformational institution. We seek to transform, in part, by energizing big ideas and research initiatives. Our faculty work across disciplines, generating intellectual excitement on campus. At times one can almost see the sparks from such conversations and collaborations.

Six key academic initiatives begun in 2002 demonstrate that our continuing commitment to research excellence, transferable technology, and strategic focus are evidence of our commitment to transform ourselves and to research that transforms the world about us. These initiatives are Combinatorial Discovery, Food Safety and Food Security, Human Computer Interaction, Bioeconomy, Information Infrastructure, and the Center for Integrated Animal Genomics.

To generate these initiatives faculty members across campus came together to discuss their research, potential areas for collaboration, and the combinations that might yield the best results, especially to benefit Iowa. A committee of dedicated faculty members winnowed the thirty resulting proposals into the final six. They are all "big idea" proposals. They are exciting. They bring researchers together across traditional fields of study. Most of all they are transformational in the same way that the Institute for Physical Research and Technology has been for work in engineering and the physical sciences and the Plant Sciences Institute is for work, drawn from many departments, in genomics and bioinformatics.

The Combinatorial Discovery Initiative is focused on discovering and testing new materials for a wide range of uses, particularly nano or high-performance materials, biomaterials and catalysts, using the combinatorial method. This relatively new chemistry method, used primarily in the pharmaceutical industry, randomly assembles molecules into thousands of combinations of compounds for testing over hours or days, far faster than the weeks or years in the traditional "one-at-a-time" approach, thus speeding greatly the pace of discovery.

The Food Safety and Food Security Initiative has strengthened existing programs and is developing strategic research and training programs that address human health risks associated with food processing, global warming and other environmental changes, globalization, and agroterrorism. It serves farmers, producers, processors, and consumers by focusing on such areas as foodborne infectious diseases, food production, food service and retail, international food security, public policy and communication, and foodborne disease models and risk analysis.

The Human Computer Interaction Initiative is built upon on our expertise and facilities in virtual reality that enable us to stay in the forefront of technological trends in computers and computing to advance the study of the relationship between people and increasingly powerful, yet portable, computers.

The Bioeconomy Initiative investigates the use of plants and agricultural crops to produce chemicals, fuels, materials, and energy, reducing the United States' risky reliance on imported petroleum, reducing air pollution associated with fossil fuels, and creating new opportunities for Iowa agriculture.

The Information Infrastructure Initiative brings together the numerous but scattered information technology research activities on campus, creating multidisciplinary teams in such areas as agricultural engineering, "smart" transportation systems, earthquake engineering simulations, air traffic control, genetic engineering and bioinformatics, and financial systems. It encompasses high-performance computing, new processor and memory designs, security, software engineering, and distributed computing.

The Center for Integrated Animal Genomics employs integrated systemwide genomics approaches to address current and future challenges and opportunities in animal agriculture and human health. Researchers are working to identify, map, and understand the function and control of genes to improve animal and human health, building on current strengths at Iowa State in areas predicted to be of particular importance in agricultural research in the next five to ten years.

These initiatives illustrate Iowa State University's commitment to excellence, to transformational activities, and to the land-grant tradition. There is probably no greater symbol of our tradition, our transformation, and our future than Morrill

Hall, recently reopened after a remarkable renovation and upgrading. Morrill Hall is a beloved symbol of our land-grant heritage, named for Senator Justin Morrill of Vermont, who authored the legislation that established the land-grant system. Iowa State alumni, friends, faculty, staff, and students responded enthusiastically and generously to our call for funds to restore this important landmark, symbol of Iowa and Iowa State's leadership in the land-grant movement. It has been completely renovated and restored, and now houses the Center for Excellence in Learning and Teaching, the Christian Petersen Art Museum, and the Center for Visual Learning in Textiles and Clothing. It is a beautiful and magnificent facility, and I urge you to visit it.

In its early years Morrill Hall served as Iowa State's library. From those humble beginnings, the Parks Library took over as library and became a vital campus resource. It too has been transformational—making the transition to the information age with the Electronic (or e-) Library, a service that is highly valued by Iowa State faculty and students. The resources available online to our community are amazing. At the same time our library houses our University Archives, our "institutional memory," it serves as a resource to move the university into the twenty-first century.

Another example of the tradition and transformation that characterize our university are the services we provide to students. The needs of Iowa State students have changed significantly over the years, yet we continue to meet those needs. Look around campus at the many computer laboratories, the renovated Student Services Building, the Student Health Center, the Lied Recreation/Athletic Facility, the new Hixson-Lied Student Success Center, the massive renovation of the residence department, and the Memorial Union. We hope the children and grandchildren of our former students will continue their Cyclone family tradition, so we can provide them with the same great experience that their parents and grandparents enjoyed.

Iowa State University will continue to be a meeting place for Iowans, especially because of our crown jewel, the Iowa State Center. Whether coming to enjoy sports competition, view an art exhibit, listen to a concert or a lecture, participate in a conference, or take a continuing education course, Iowans can benefit from some aspect of the Iowa State Center. The vision of President James H. Hilton for this magnificent and transformational center on what was once horse pasture serves us all.

Much as our campus continues to change, our outreach is transforming to meet the needs of Iowa in the twenty-first century. In 1998, the Iowa General Assembly supported our "Extension 21" initiative to enable our Cooperative Extension Service to better help Iowans add value to our agricultural bounty, through the Iowa Beef Center, the Iowa Grain Quality Initiative, the Iowa Pork Industry Center, and other field projects. Extension continues to evolve as it supports industry, with its leadership in the Iowa Manufacturing Extension Partnership, for example, and new programs for families at risk, rural and urban youth, and many others. Complementing Extension's work, Iowa State is offering an increasing number of courses and programs of study that take advantage of the Internet and information technology.

Iowa State University has made a significant and positive difference in our state, in our nation, and across the globe for the past 150 years. Now the university is positioned to make such contributions throughout another century. We will continue to provide a great education, and we will continue to create new knowledge and apply it for practical use. Service is our hallmark; excellence is our aspiration; our strategic plan is our guide. We are continually inspired by the words of alumnus George Washington Carver: "It is simply service that measures success."

Gregory L. Geoffroy is the fourteenth president of Iowa State University. He became president on July 1, 2001.

# Notes

## 1. FOUNDATIONS OF THE PEOPLE'S COLLEGE

1. Dorothy Schwieder, *Iowa: The Middle Land* (Ames: Iowa State University Press, 1996), 129–130.

2. Schwieder, 129–130; Earle Ross, *A History of Iowa State College of Agriculture and Mechanic Arts* (Ames: Iowa State College Press, 1942), 35, 39.

3. The preparatory course for poorly prepared entrants was discontinued in 1887, reinstated the next year, and lasted until roughly the 1899–1900 school year. The course was largely intended for farm-raised students who may not have had access to high schools in their communities. Board of Trustees, Iowa State College, Thirteenth Biennial Report of the Board of Trustees of the Iowa State Agricultural College and Farm, 1888–1889 (Des Moines: G. H. Ragsdale, State Printer, 1889), 18–19.

4. Ross, 69, 185; Board of Trustees, Iowa State Agricultural College, Fourth Biennial Report of the Board of Trustees of the Iowa State Agricultural College and Farm to the Governor of Iowa (Des Moines: G. W. Edwards, State Printer, 1872), 16–19.

5. Ross, 28–29, 51, 65, 174–175, 371–376.

6. Ross, 174.

7. Ross, 66, 329; Henry C. Taylor, *Tarpleywick: A Century of Iowa Farming* (Ames: Iowa State University Press, 1970), 98–100.

8. Ross, 58–59, 66–67, 154, 189; Andrea G. Radke, "'Can she not see and hear, and smell and taste?': Women Students at Coeducational Land-Grant Universities in the American West, 1868–1917," Ph.D. dissertation, University of Nebraska, 2002, 26, 200–202, 208; Adonijah Welch, "Inaugural Address," Addresses Delivered at the Opening of the Iowa State Agricultural College, March 17, 1869 (Davenport, IA: Gazette Premium Book and Job Printing, 1869), 22–40, Adonijah Welch Papers, RS 2/1, Special Collections, Iowa State University Library.

9. Radke, 200–208, 216–217, 237–238.

10. Faculty and Rules Committee, Official Rules Governing Student Conduct (Ames: Iowa State College, 1930), 16–17.

11. Radke, 238–239.

12. Radke, 306–322.

13. Adonijah S. Welch, "Plan of Organization, 1868," 10–11, Adonijah S. Welch Papers, Special Collections, Iowa State University Library.

14. Linda O. McMurry, *George Washington Carver: Scientist and Symbol* (New York: Oxford University Press, 1981), 32–51.

15. Karol Crosbie, "The Martin House: Honoring Kindness," *VISIONS* magazine, vol. 15, no. 2, Summer 2002, 36–37.

16. Schwieder, 129–130, 147–148; Deborah Fitzgerald, *Every Farm a Factory: The Industrial Ideal in American Agriculture* (New Haven: Yale University Press, 2003), 86.

17. Ross, 121–143, 327–329; William Wynn, as quoted by Ross, 145.

18. Board of Trustees, Iowa State College, Eighteenth Biennial Report of the Board of Trustees of the Iowa State Agricultural College and Farm, 1898–1899 (Des Moines: F. R. Conway, State Printer, 1899), 37–38.

19. Ross, 99–113, 123–124, 302.

20. William H. Thompson, *Transportation in Iowa: A Historical Summary* (Ames: Iowa Department of Transportation, 1989), 76–77.

21. Ross, 167–169, 176–181, 220.

22. Ross, 214–220.

23. Ross, 183–184, 199–203, 224–234, 247, 347.

24. Ross, 275–294, 304–306, 323, 330–334.

25. Ross, 307–310, 312.

26. Ross, 310.

27. Ross, 318–320.

28. Ross, 316–317, 326–330, 355–356, 422.

29. Ross, 339–342.

30. Ross, 322–323; *Green Gander,* vol. 8, no. 1, November 1921, 1; "Within the Inner Sanctum," *Green Gander,* vol. 8, no. 2, February 1922, 6–7; Faculty and Rules Committee, 22.

31. Chris Bertelson, "VEISHEA: The First Sixty Years," May 1982, 7–10; Faculty and Rules Committee, 26.

32. Megan E. Birk, "Playing House: The Role of Home Management Houses in the Training of Scientific Homemakers at Iowa State College, 1925–1958," master's thesis, Iowa State University, 2004, 2–3, 16–21, 75–79.

33. Iowa State College of Agriculture and Mechanic Arts, General Catalogue, 1920–1921 (Ames: Iowa State College, 1920), 155–161.

34. Robert Parks, "Foreword," in T. A. Bancroft, ed., *Statistical Papers in Honor of George W. Snedecor* (Ames: Iowa State University Press, 1970), ix–xvii.

35. Schwieder, 255–257; Ross, 363–364.

36. Ross, 364.

37. Ross, 364–366.

38. Lea Rosson DeLong, *A Catalog of New Deal Mural Projects in Iowa* (Des Moines: L. R. DeLong, 1982), 10, 22–23; Lea Rosson DeLong, *Christian Petersen, Sculptor* (Ames: Iowa State University Press, 2000), 26, 42, 46–47.

39. Schwieder, 257–259.

40. Ross, 422.

## 2. IOWA STATE AT MID-CENTURY

1. Charles E. Friley Papers, RS 2/9/1/1, Special Collections, Iowa State University Library.

2. Ibid.

3. Earle D. Ross, *A History of Iowa State College of Agriculture and Mechanic Arts* (Ames: Iowa State College Press, 1942), 367; Louis M. Thompson interview, Ames, IA, November 17, 2005; *Des Moines Tribune,* May 28, 1958.

4. 1935 *Bomb,* 25; 1936 *Bomb,* 34; 1937 *Bomb,* 28; 1939 *Bomb,* 15; 1940 *Bomb,* 10.

5. Report of the Iowa State Board of Education for the Biennial Period Ending July 30, 1942. Seventeenth Biennial Report (Des Moines: State of Iowa, 1942), 276. The report

listed students' majors but did not include the number of males and females enrolled; Ross, 422.

6. Dorothy Kehlenbeck, compiler, *The Iowa State College Chronology of Important Events of the First 100 Years* (Ames: ISC Library, 1948), 17. Chronology published for Iowa State's centennial.

7. Iowa State College Information Service release, March 17, 1951.

8. Charles E. Friley, "The Iowa State College and National Defense," Seventy-fourth Annual Session, September 17, 1941, *Iowa State College Bulletin,* vol. 60, no. 16, September 17, 1941, 1–10.

9. 1943 *Bomb.*

10. Ibid.

11. Don Muhm and Virginia Wadsley, *Iowans Who Made a Difference: 150 Years of Agricultural Progress* (West Des Moines: Iowa Farm Bureau Federation, 1996), 232–233.

12. Ibid., 144, 149. In 1943, Commander A. F. Duernberger replaced Lt. George C. Ray as head of the ISC Naval Training School. At the time, there were 1,500 naval trainees. See 1943 *Bomb,* 146.

13. 1943 *Bomb,* 14, 15, 147, 150; Kehlenbeck, 18.

14. *Bureau of Naval Personnel Training Bulletin,* August 15, 1944, issue no. NavPers 14921, 1, WWII, series no. 13/16/1, box 6, Special Collections, Iowa State University Library.

15. 1943 *Bomb,* 75, 76, 78; letter from Dean of Engineering Division T. R. Agg to Lt. R. H. Light, November 23, 1943, WWII, series no. 13/16/1, box 6, Special Collections, Iowa State University Library.

16. 1943 *Bomb,* 9, 374; Bonnie Calderwood interview, Ames, IA, March 2005.

17. 1943 *Bomb,* 46.

18. War Training Programs—World War II, Curtiss-Wright Engineering Cadette Training Program, Vol. A1, April 1, 1945 (Ames: Iowa State College), 1, Special Collections, Iowa State University Library.

19. Marjorie Allen, "Engineering Cadettes," *Iowa Engineer,* April 1943, 183; Bryan Arnold, "The Pioneering P-40s: Female 'Cadettes' Break New Ground in Aeronautical Engineering," *Iowa Engineering,* 94, Winter 1993, 9, 11.

20. Arnold, 9; Allen, 181.

21. 1943 *Bomb,* 37, 61.

22. Ibid., 56

23. Ibid., 30.

24. Ibid., 143.

25. 1945 *Bomb,* 86.

26. 1943 *Bomb,* 212–213.

27. *Des Moines Register,* August 14, 1985; September 13, 1992.

28. Dr. Frank H. Spedding interview, July 5, 1961, Oral Histories, RS 00/17, Special Collections, Iowa State University Library. There are different estimates as to the amount of uranium produced at Iowa State. In 2005, the public affairs manager of the Ames Laboratory stated that the lab produced two million pounds of uranium for the war effort between 1942 and 1946. See "Activists Want Aid for Nuclear Scientists," *Des Moines Register,* June 17, 2005.

29. Spedding interview, 5, 6.

30. Transcript of speeches made at the Army-Navy "E" Award, October 12, 1945, 3, WWII, series no. 13/16/2, box 6, Special Collections, Iowa State University Library.

31. Friley Convocation, September 1945, Friley Papers, RS 2/9/1/19, Special Collections, Iowa State University Library.

32. "In Loving Memory," May 27, 1945, World War II file; YMCA records, Special Collections, Iowa State University Library.

33. Friley Convocation, September 1945, Friley Papers, RS 2/9/1/19, Special Collections, Iowa State University Library.

34. Wayne Moore interview, March 21, 2006, Ames, IA.

35. *Iowa State Daily,* October 22, 1965.

36. Diane Ravitch, *The Troubled Crusade: American Education, 1945–1980* (New York: Basic Books, Inc., 1983), 13–14.

37. *Iowa State Daily,* October 22, 1965.

38. *Iowa State Daily,* May 16, 1946; *News of Iowa State,* September–October 1969; *Iowa State Daily,* October 22, 1965.

39. *Iowa State Daily,* October 3, 1974.

40. *Des Moines Register,* March 14, 1947.

41. Cedar Rapids *Gazette,* March 21, 1947.

42. Robert Underhill, *Alone Among Friends: A Biography of W. Robert Parks* (Ames: Iowa State University Press, 1999), 234; Moore interview.

43. *News of Iowa State,* vol. 3, no. 6, March 1951. New construction included the Metallurgy Building, built for the U.S. Atomic Energy Commission in 1949, and the Office and Laboratory Building of the Institute for Atomic Research (the Link), which connected the Chemistry and Physics buildings. In 1948, eight bowling lanes had been installed in the Memorial Union. See Kehlenbeck, 20.

44. Charles E. Friley died July 11, 1958, at his home in rural Ames.

45. *Des Moines Tribune,* May 28, 1958.

46. "Biographical Note," James H. Hilton Papers, RS 2/10/1/2, Special Collections, Iowa State University Library.

47. Rex Conn, "Jim Is Coming Back," *Alumnus Magazine,* January 1953, 6–7; Iowa State College Information Service release, November 6, 1953, 2.

48. Vincent B. Hamilton interview, June 5, 1971, Oral Histories, RS 00/17, Special Collections, Iowa State University Library. Hamilton later received the Alumni Recognition Medal from ISU.

49. Dorothy Schwieder, *Iowa: The Middle Land* (Ames: Iowa State University Press, 1996), 286–287.

50. "Address to Staff," September 16, 1953, Hilton Papers, RS 2/10/1/42, Special Collections, Iowa State University Library.

51. Staff Convocation, September 15, 1954, Hilton Papers, RS 2/10/1/42, Special Collections, Iowa State University Library.

52. See Dorothy Schwieder, "Cooperative Extension and Rural Iowa: Agricultural Adjustment in the 1950s," *Annals of Iowa,* 51, Fall 1992, 609–619.

53. Hamilton interview, 3.

54. Staff Convocation, September 15, 1954, Hilton Papers, RS 2/10/1/42, Special Collections, Iowa State University Library.

55. This fund-raising effort led to the creation of the ISU Foundation, which continues today.

56. Fall Convocation, September 1955, Hilton Papers, RS 2/10/1/42, Special Collections, Iowa State University Library.

57. Kehlenbeck, 22, 23.

58. Staff Convocations, September 3, 1959, and September 18, 1957, Hilton Papers, RS 2/10/1/42, Special Collections, Iowa State University Library; Underhill, 10–11.

59. James Hilton, "To Change the Name of the Institution," Hilton Papers, RS 2/10/1/42, Special Collections, Iowa State University Library.

60. Cedar Rapids *Gazette,* February 2, 1964; "Some Reactions to President Hancher's Memorandum of March 5, 1959, Entitled, 'Observations on Problems of Growth in the Three State-Supported Institutions of High Education,'" Hilton Papers, RS 2/10/10/25, Special Collections, Iowa State University Library.

61. "Some Reactions to President Hancher's Memorandum."

62. Staff Convocation, September 3, 1959, Hilton Papers, RS 2/10/1/42, Special Collections, Iowa State University Library.

63. Jim Wiggins, Chapel Hill, NC, telephone call with author, March 2004; Mason City *Globe Gazette,* May 25, 1956.

64. Cedar Rapids *Gazette,* June 6, 1956.

65. Marshalltown *Times-Republican,* May 29, 1956.

66. Underhill, 67.

67. Ibid., 67–69.

68. Convocation Address, September 4, 1962, Hilton Papers, RS 2/10/1/42, Special Collections, Iowa State University Library; letter to Dr. T. M. Mehta, the Maharaja Sayajirao University of Baroda, no signature or date; Report of Helen R. LeBaron to Dr. Douglas Ensminger, February 17, 1960, Hilton Papers, RS 2/10/10/76, Special Collections, Iowa State University Library.

69. Ravitch, 229; Convocation Speech, September 6, 1960, Hilton Papers, RS 2/10/1/42, Special Collections, Iowa State University Library; James Kirby Martin, et al., *America and Its Peoples* (New York: Longman, 1997), 943.

70. Underhill, 57, 71.

71. Convocation Address, September 5, 1961, Hilton Papers, RS 2/10/1/42, Special Collections, Iowa State University Library.

72. Convocation Address, September 3, 1963, Hilton Papers, RS 2/10/1/42, Special Collections, Iowa State University Library; following his retirement, Hilton served for two years as the university's director of development. He died on January 14, 1982. *Des Moines Register,* January 15, 1982.

73. Thompson interview.

74. Staff Convocations, September 3, 1959, and September 6, 1960, Hilton Papers, RS 2/10/1/42, Special Collections, Iowa State University Library.

75. Staff Convocations, September 4, 1962, September 3, 1963, and September 8, 1964, Hilton Papers, RS 2/10/1/42, Special Collections, Iowa State University Library. The $17.5 million also covered the cost of the Stange Road underpass and some utility improvements.

76. Associated Press release, January, 23, 1964, Hilton Papers, RS 2/10/13/71, Special Collections, Iowa State University Library; United Press release, Iowa City, January 29, 1964.

77. Cedar Rapids *Gazette,* February 2, 1964; United Press release, Iowa City, January 29, 1964.

78. Convocation Address, September 8, 1964, Hilton Papers, RS 2/10/1/42, Special Collections, Iowa State University Library.

79. Ibid.

80. Underhill, 12.

81. *Des Moines Register,* January 15, 1982; January 18, 1982.

## 3. SCIENCE WITH HUMANITY

1. An essential source for understanding Iowa State and the presidency of W. Robert Parks is Robert Underhill, *Alone Among Friends: A Biography of W. Robert Parks* (Ames: Iowa State University Press, 1999). In addition to Underhill's biography, this chapter also relies heavily on my own conversations with Robert Parks.

2. *Iowa State Daily,* September 10, 1965.

3. Chris Bertelson, "VEISHEA: The First Sixty Years," May 1982.

4. Godfrey Hodgson, *America in Our Time* (New York: Random House, 1976); David Burner, *Making Peace with the 60s* (Princeton, NJ: Princeton University Press, 1996); Allen J. Matusow, *The Unraveling of America: American Liberalism during the 1960s* (New York: Harper & Row, 1984).

5. Clark Kerr, *The Uses of the University* (Cambridge: Harvard University Press, 1963); John Thelin, *A History of Higher Education* (Baltimore: Johns Hopkins University Press, 2004).

6. Underhill, 15–74.

7. *Ames Daily Tribune,* August 1, 1985.

8. W. Robert Parks, Staff Convocation, September 7, 1965; Parks, "The Role of Iowa State University in the Scientific Age: Toward a New Humanism," March 22, 1966; Parks, "Our Usable Past," *Iowa State Alumnus,* October 1963, 4–6; Parks, "The Land-Grant Idea as a Working Process: The Search for the Relevant Education," October 27, 1968.

9. Underhill, 92–96.

10. Ibid., 10–12, 62–63, 212.

11. *Ames Daily Tribune,* August 1, 1985.

12. Ibid.

13. A brief overview of capital improvements may be found in the *Iowa Stater,* 12, May 1986.

14. *Iowa State Daily,* May 5, 1986.

15. Underhill, 210–211, 275, 276.

16. ISU Office of Information and Development, *ISU Center News,* vol. 1.

17. W. Robert Parks, Staff Convocation, September 5, 1978.

18. *Iowa State Daily,* September 10, 1965; *Ames Daily Tribune,* August 1, 1985.

19. *Ames Daily Tribune,* December 12, 1964.

20. Hodgson, 288–364; Matusow; W. J. Rorabaugh, *Berkeley at War: The 1960s* (New York: Oxford University Press, 1989).

21. *Ames Daily Tribune,* clipping, files of Cynthia Parks Hamilton.

22. *Ames Daily Tribune,* April 22, 1967. On the origins of Gentle Thursday, see Doug Rossinow, *The Politics of Authenticity* (New York: Columbia University Press, 1998), 261–263.

23. William Cotter Murray, "The Bearded, Sockless Radical of Moo U.," *New York Times,* April 9, 1967; *New York Times,* February 23, 1967.

24. Murray; "The Cow College and Smith," Council Bluffs *Daily Nonpareil,* April 11, 1967.

25. *Des Moines Tribune,* author's clipping file [1967].

26. *Iowa State Daily,* January 7, 1969; *Des Moines Register,* December 31, 1968.

27. *Des Moines Register,* December 31, 1968; January 8, 1969; *Ames Daily Tribune,* January 8, 1969; *Iowa State Daily,* January 7, 1969; January 8, 1969.

28. *Ames Daily Tribune,* January 13, 1968.

29. *Iowa State Daily,* May 5, 1986; May 10, 1972.

30. *Ames Daily Tribune,* May 11, 1970; *Iowa State Daily,* May 12, 1970; Bertelson, 119.

31. *Ames Daily Tribune,* August 1, 1985.

32. Underhill, 229–249.

33. One view of the WOI debate is Neil Harl, *Arrogance and Power: The Saga of WOI-TV* (Ames, IA: N. E. Harl and Heuss Printing, 2001).

34. Thelin, 271–274, 277–280.

35. *Des Moines Register,* September 29, 1977.

36. *Proceedings: The World Food Conference of 1976* (Ames: Iowa State University Press, 1977).

37. James Langley, Gary Vocke, and Larry Whiting, *Earl O. Heady: His Impact on Agricultural Economics* (Ames: Iowa State University Press, 1994).

38. A helpful appraisal of athletics during Parks's presidency may be found in Underhill, 199–227.

39. On college sports, see John Thelin, *Games Colleges Play: Scandal and Reform in Intercollegiate Athletics* (Baltimore: Johns Hopkins University Press, 1994); John Sayle Watterson, *College Football: History, Spectacle, Controversy* (Baltimore: Johns Hopkins University Press, 2000); and Murray Sperber, *Onward to Victory: The Crises That Shaped College Sports* (New York: H. Holt, 1998).

40. Underhill, 214–218.

41. The "death penalty" empowered the NCAA to prohibit a team guilty of serious rules violations from playing any games for one or more seasons. *Des Moines Register,* September 13, 1981; *Iowa State Daily,* September 10, 1981.

42. Gene McGivern, *Here's Johnny Orr* (Ames: Iowa State University Press, 1992).

43. W. Robert Parks, "A 'New Humanism" Revisited," May 17, 1986; *Des Moines Register,* July 6, 1986.

## 4. STRATEGIC FOCUS AND ACCOUNTABILITY

1. *Ames Daily Tribune,* October 30, 1985, 1; November 20, 1985, 1; November 21, 1985; Eaton e-mail to author, April 30, 2005.

2. See the "Presidents of ISU" page on the ISU Web site: http://www.iastate.edu/about/presidents.shtml.

3. See http://recenter.tamu.edu/data/popsd/pops19.htm for population figures by decade.

4. Eaton e-mail to author, April 30, 2005. As Eaton noted, ISU was the only public university in AAU not a Carnegie I institution.

5. Eaton e-mail to author, April 30, 2005; *VISIONS* magazine, Fall 1988, 15–23.

6. See Gordon Eaton, Inaugural Address, 1987, Special Collections, Iowa State University Library.

7. *Ames Daily Tribune,* August 20, 1988, W9. On biotechnology, see *VISIONS* magazine, Fall 1999, 23–25.

8. *Ames Daily Tribune,* December 10, 1986, 1.

9. *Ames Daily Tribune,* February 7, 1987, 1; Crow letter to author, April 14, 2005. This debate over the role of centers and departments and their purposes would continue for years; see the "Task Force on Centers and Institutes," April 1, 2004, http://www.provost.iastate.edu/documents/04.doc. Nearly 80 percent of centers and institutes came about during the Eaton-Jischke years. *Ames Daily Tribune,* March 19, 1987, 1.

10. *Ames Daily Tribune,* May 31, 1991; the *Ames Daily Tribune,* May 20, 1989, A1; *VISIONS* magazine, Fall 1988, 17. Eaton: "So we may reduce the number of departments. We are certainly going to reduce the number of degree programs," 17.

11. *Ames Daily Tribune,* December 5, 1988, A1; February 3, 1989, A4; *VISIONS* magazine, Fall 1988, 18; the *Ames Daily Tribune,* November 25, 1987, 1.

12. *Ames Daily Tribune,* February 6, 1989, A1.

13. *Ames Daily Tribune,* January 20, 1989, A1; January 25, 1989, A1; January 26, 1989, A1; December 12, 1988, 1.

14. *Ames Daily Tribune,* February 3, 1989, A1; February 4, 1989, A1.

15. *Ames Daily Tribune,* February 3, 1989, A4; March 2, 1989, A1; March 13, 1989, A1; May 4, 1990, A3; May 3, 1989, A11; March 29, 1989, A1.

16. *Ames Daily Tribune,* May 18, 1989, A1.

17. *Ames Daily Tribune,* June 21, 1989, A1; June 28, 1989, A1; September 9, 1989, A1; December 3, 1989, A1.

18. *Ames Daily Tribune,* November 6, 1989, A1; March 21, 1990, A8; April 13, 1990, A1; April 19, 1990, A1. For a good summary of the planning process and the regents duplication review, see *VISIONS* magazine, Winter 1990, 13–17.

19. *Ames Daily Tribune,* February 22, 1989; February 2, 1990; April 20, 1990, A1.

20. Pickett e-mail to author, March 25, 2005; Watson interview, March 26, 2005; Custer interview, May 13, 2005.

21. *Ames Daily Tribune,* November 25, 1987, 1.

22. *Des Moines Register,* November 18, 1989, 1A; *VISIONS* magazine, Spring 1988; *Ames Daily Tribune,* February 4, 1989, 1.

23. Pickett e-mail to author, March 25, 2005; Anderson e-mail to author, April 15, 2005; Custer interview, May 13, 2005.

24. *VISIONS* magazine, Summer 1988, 6–7; *Ames Daily Tribune,* May 9, 1988, A1.

25. *Iowa State Daily,* June 18, 1986; *Ames Daily Tribune,* July 24, 1986; July 25, 1986; September 11, 1986; *Iowa State Daily,* September 25, 1986; October 3, 1986; November 13, 1986; November 14, 1986; April 20, 1987; Eaton e-mail to author.

26. *Ames Daily Tribune,* July 7, 1990, A3.

27. *Ames Daily Tribune,* July 18, 1990, A1.

28. Cedar Rapids *Gazette,* July 19, 1990, A8; *Des Moines Register,* July 19, 1990, 1A; "Eaton Fit the Short-term Role," *Des Moines Register,* July 26, 1990. See also the *Des Moines Register,* July 23, 1990, and the Cedar Rapids *Gazette,* July 22, 1990: "Eaton was charged with charting a new course for the institution . . . Eaton has ruffled feathers . . . on balance, it must be said that Gordon Eaton acquitted himself well. . . . When the reformation is complete, Iowa State should be able to compete with the best in the world for money and talent." *Ames Daily Tribune,* February 6, 1989, A6; May 24, 1989, A10; July 11, 1990, A10; October 3, 1990.

29. *Des Moines Register,* July 23, 1990; August 12, 1990; August 20, 1990.

30. *Ames Daily Tribune,* June 21, 1991, editorial.

31. *Ames Daily Tribune,* February 22, 1991, A1.

32. See www.iastate.edu/about/presidents.shtml. See also *VISIONS* magazine, Spring 1991, 6, and Summer 1991, 14–19, about the new president and the campus reaction to his appointment.

33. See "Celebrating the Land-Grant University: Pursuing Excellence for Iowa," in RS 2/13, Martin C. Jischke, Special Collections, Iowa State University Library. See also *VISIONS* magazine, Summer 1996, 11–16, for a recap of his address and for Jischke's summary of progress over five years.

34. See the *Des Moines Register,* July 20, 2000, 1B; "ISU Class Master Excuses Himself," August 5, 2000, 1B—how many people would have an article in the newspaper decrying their leaving town? See also the *Ames Daily Tribune,* August 8, 1994, C1; May 5, 1997, A4.

35. *Ames Daily Tribune,* October 25, 1994, A2; November 9, 1994, A8; May 19, 2000, B3.

36. On downplaying the importance of teaching, see the *Des Moines Register,* April 5, 1993; February 8, 2000; February 10, 2000; and the Cedar Rapids *Gazette,* February 24, 2000; on overvaluing corporate funding, see "ISU: Model University or University for Profit," "Can Research Make ISU the Best?" *Des Moines Register,* November 27, 1998; also April 7, 1999; April 13, 1999; May 24, 1999; March 20, 2000.

37. See Jischke archives in RS 2/13, Special Collections, Iowa State University Library, for background on these all-day community visits.

38. See the Cedar Rapids *Gazette,* September 28, 1995, and *Inside Iowa State,* April 3, 1998, and September 24, 1999, for examples of itineraries for these Roads Scholar tours: http://www.iastate.edu/Inside/98index.html#apr3 and http://www.iastate.edu/Inside/99index.html#sep24.

39. *Ames Daily Tribune,* July 20, 1991; *Des Moines Register,* November 24, 1991, 1B; July 12, 1992, 1B.

40. *ISU Fact Book, 2004–2005,* 96.

41. *Ames Daily Tribune,* December 17, 1985, 1; December 19, 1985, 1.

42. *Des Moines Register,* February 7, 1992; February 15, 1992; March 12, 1992; April 11, 1992; May 12, 1992; May 21, 1992.

43. *Des Moines Register,* June 25, 1992; Cedar Rapids *Gazette,* July 17, 1992; *Des Moines Register,* October 25, 1992; November 11, 1992; December 15, 1992; March 11, 1993; November 25, 1993; Cedar Rapids *Gazette,* December 16, 1993; *Des Moines Register,* February 16, 1994; February 17, 1994; March 1, 1994. For a good summary as the case went to court, see "Who'll Win It?" *VISIONS* magazine, Summer 1993, 17–23.

44. *Des Moines Sunday Register,* March 22, 1992; Blackwelder e-mail to author, March 29, 2005; *VISIONS* magazine, Summer 1988, 42; *Ames Daily Tribune,* August 21, 1990; September 8, 1990, A1.

45. *Ames Daily Tribune,* July 7, 1993, noted it was the twelfth largest campaign in the history of public higher education in America. See "Campaign for Iowa State University: Capital Campaign Summary Report, October 1993," ISU Foundation.

46. *Des Moines Register,* February 18, 1995; *Iowa Stater,* www.iastate.edu/IaStater/1995/.

47. *Iowa Stater,* September 1996, www.iastate.edu/Iastater/1996; *VISIONS* magazine, Fall 1996, 13–15 for campaign kickoff; www.iastate.edu/IaStater/1997/Feb; www.iastate.edu/IaStater/1998/0298; www.iastate.edu/IaStater/1998/1198; www.iastate.edu/IaStater/2000/nov.

48. *Des Moines Register,* September 21, 1996; August 26, 1999; September 10, 1999; Carroll *Daily Times Herald,* September 25, 1995.

49. See Office of the President, "To Become the Best: Benchmarking Progress on Strategic Plan," 1995–1996; 1996–1997; 1997–1998; 1998–1999; 1999–2000; *Des Moines Register,* February 5, 1999; June 19, 1999; September 17, 1999; Cedar Rapids *Gazette,* October 31, 1999; September 13, 1999; *Omaha World-Herald,* January 29, 2000. Initially, the legislature had good intentions; see "$2 Million Tagged for ISU Research Center," Cedar Rapids *Gazette,* April 6, 1999. See the Plant Sciences Institute Web page, http://www.plantsciences.iastate.edu/, for a discussion of its organization and the research centers.

50. *Des Moines Register,* October 3, 1998; February 3, 1999; February 23, 1999; April 30, 1999; October 31, 1999; Cedar Rapids *Gazette,* May 1, 1999; *Ames Daily Tribune,* June 12, 1994, A3; February 23, 1995, A1; May 12, 1995, A1; July 17, 1995, A1; July 22, 1995, A1; August 20, 1996, A1; June 23, 1997, A4; June 20, 1997, A8; April 29, 1999, B3; Wintersteen e-mail to author, May 4, 2005. See *Des Moines Sunday Register,* January 8, 1995, for a criticism of the swine farm proposal, and *VISIONS* magazine, Spring 1995, 16–19, for an informative discussion of the hog confinement odor and spillage issues.

51. Lynn Seiler, FP&M "Visitor's Guide to ISU Facilities," revised November 2004.

52. *Des Moines Register,* July 10, 1993; July 11, 1993; July 13, 1993; July 20, 1993.

53. *Des Moines Register,* December 6, 1995; December 15, 1995; July 18, 1995; February 17, 1996; March 5, 1997; February 4, 1999; *Iowa State Daily,* February 8, 1999; December 17, 1997; July 1, 1997; March 24, 1997; November 28, 1995; July 6, 1996; October 2, 1996; December 12, 1996; December 15, 1997; April 7, 1998; June 16, 1998; August 24, 1998.

54. See Big 12 Conference Web site, http://big12sports.collegesports.com/; *Quad-City Times,* March 1, 1993; *Kansas City Star,* February 26, 1994, A15; *Des Moines Register,* February 9, 1995.

55. *Des Moines Sunday Register,* August 15, 1993; October 10, 1993; *Des Moines Register,* August 12, 1994; September 22, 1994; November 4, 1994; November 24, 1994. See also "ISU Won't Renew Athletic Director's Pact," *Des Moines Register,* February 6, 1993; also February 6, 1993, Mark Hansen's editorial column, "If Max Urick Is Being Ushered Out the Door at Iowa State, Can Jim Walden Be Far Behind?"

56. *Des Moines Register,* April 28, 1993; April 29, 1993; (hiring of Gene Smith as athletics director: *Des Moines Register,* May 22, 1993); April 15, 1994; May 6, 1994; July 29, 1998; April 29, 2003; *Ames Daily Tribune,* May 6, 2003, A1; April 29, 2003, A1.

57. Cedar Rapids *Gazette,* March 3, 1994; *Des Moines Register,* June 25, 1994; November 24, 1994; December 14, 1994; December 24, 1994; January 18, 1995; January 21, 1995; February 8, 1995; February 9, 1995; "Football Downturn Clips ISU," Cedar Rapids *Gazette,* May 10, 1995; also May 16, 1999; "Football a Cloud on ISU Sports Horizon," *Des Moines Register,* June 1, 1999; *Ames Daily Tribune,* April 3, 2001, C1; *Des Moines Register,* April 3, 2001, 1A; "Arizona State Hires Smith," July 27, 2000.

58. *Des Moines Register,* August 30, 1994; *Ames Daily Tribune,* September 16, 1994, A3; September 11, 1995, A1; September 13, 1996, A1; September 11, 1997, A3; September 11, 1998, B1; November 13, 1999, B1; September 6, 2000, A1. See also *ISU Fact Book,* 2004–2005, 31.

59. *Iowa State Daily,* June 18, 1998; *Des Moines Register,* August 23, 1999; *Iowa State Daily,* February 28–March 3, 2000; November 9, 2000; August 28, 2001. See "ISU to Bulldoze Its Crumbling Towers," *Des Moines Register,* October 31, 1998.

60. *Des Moines Register,* May 2, 1992, 1A; May 5, 1992; May 8, 1992. See "Can We Put VEISHEA Back Together Again?" *VISIONS* magazine, Spring 1993, 14–20.

61. *Ames Daily Tribune,* April 23, 1994, A1; April 25, 1994, A1; "Editorial: Don't Deny the Fact: That Was a Riot," April 25, 1994, A6.

62. *Des Moines Register,* April 21, 1997; April 25, 1997. In the aftermath of the 2004 VEISHEA riot, Iowa State compiled all of the previous VEISHEA reports into one notebook for easier review. See Task Force on Assuring Successful VEISHEA and Other Student Community Celebrations, RS 8/6/179, Special Collections, Iowa State University Library.

63. *Ames Daily Tribune,* August 28, 1997, A1; September 4, 1997, A1; September 5, 1997, A1; *Omaha World-Herald,* September 6, 2000; *Des Moines Sunday Register,* September 14, 1997; *Ames Daily Tribune,* September 27, 1997, A1; *Des Moines Register,* October 23, 1997. Thereafter, until he left Iowa State, Jischke continued to insist that the student organizations reaffirm the no-alcohol pledge for VEISHEA to continue that coming spring.

64. *Des Moines Register,* October 12, 1993; October 13, 1993; August 23, 1994; *Des Moines Register,* April 5, 1994; "Carrie Chapman Catt, a Bigot?" *Des Moines Sunday Register,* July 11, 1993, an editorial by Louise Noun; November 3, 1995; March 28, 1996; *Iowa State Daily,* October 24, 1996; November 8, 1996. See "ISU Panel: Action of Professor in Bounds," *Des Moines Register,* December 1, 1993, for a summary of a faculty panel investigation of student complaints of Pope's class.

65. See Carrie Chapman Catt, *Women Suffrage by Federal Constitutional Amendment* (New York: National Women Suffrage Publishing Co., 1917). The students misused Catt's argument to southern whites as her support for white supremacy. For examples of the coverage, see the *Iowa State Daily,* October 17, 1997; October 22, 1997; November 4, 1997; December 5, 1997; December 8, 1997; December 9, 1997; January 21, 1998; January 29, 1998; February 6, 1998; February 17, 1998; February 23, 1998; March 4, 1998; March 24, 1998; April 7, 1998; April 22, 1998; April 30, 1998; June 18, 1998; September 29, 1999; October 4, 1999; October 26, 1999. See also the *Ames Daily Tribune,* October 12, 1996; March 4, 1997; September 30, 1997; December 4, 1997; April 7, 1998; April 23, 1998; June 18, 1998. See also the *Des Moines Sunday Register,* March 28, 1996; *Des Moines Register,*

March 31, 1996; September 4, 1996; November 24, 1996; *Omaha World-Herald,* February 21, 1997; *Des Moines Register,* September 30, 1997; December 4, 1997; *Iowa State Daily,* September 29, 1999.

66. Thomas Hill, comment to author, April 21, 2005; Charles M. Dobbs, personal recollection.

67. Cedar Rapids *Gazette,* February 29, 2000; *Des Moines Register,* May 7, 2000.

68. Beverly Crabtree and Peter Rabideau, recollection to author; Hamilton Cravens, recollection to author.

69. *Des Moines Register,* March 10, 1999, 1M; April 27, 2000, 2B; March 18, 2001, 16A.

70. *Des Moines Register,* October 9, 2001, 13A.

71. *Ames Daily Tribune,* April 14, 2000, B1; April 21, 2000, B1; May 9, 2000, B3; *Des Moines Register,* May 19, 2000; May 23, 2000; *Ames Daily Tribune,* May 23, 2000, A1; *Des Moines Register,* May 24, 2000 (both Hansen's and the editorial page's editorials); *Omaha World-Herald,* May 24, 2000; Cedar Rapids *Gazette,* May 25, 2000; *North Scott Press,* June 21, 2000.

72. *VISIONS* magazine, vol. 13, no. 3, September/October 2000, 30. There were many positive views of Jischke's achievements; see the *Des Moines Register,* May 23, 2000; May 24, 2000. There were also many positive views of the achievements of Patty Jischke. See *VISIONS* magazine, September/October 2000, 31–33, which notes among other achievements past president of the Reiman Gardens Co-Horts, chair of the ISU Library Development Council, cochair of the Steering Committee of the Iowa Summit '98, and founding member, Iowa Asset Building Coalition. On regaining Carnegie I status, see the *Des Moines Register,* April 7, 1994; *Ames Daily Tribune,* April 7, 1994. On the Atanasoff-Berry Computer replica project, see *Exponent,* Fall 1997; *Des Moines Register,* October 9, 1997; *Canberra Times,* October 8, 1997; *Des Moines Register,* October 8, 1997; *Ames Daily Tribune,* October 9, 1997. On the century medallion from the American Society of Landscape Architects, see the *Ames Daily Tribune,* August 6, 1999; September 10, 1999; *Iowa State Daily,* September 2, 1999. Finally, on the sale of ISU Press, see the Cedar Rapids *Gazette,* February 15, 2000; *Des Moines Register,* February 15, 2000; *Omaha World-Herald,* July 18, 2000; *Des Moines Register,* July 18, 2000; *Iowa State Daily,* July 18, 2000; August 22, 2000; September 11, 2000.

## 5. LOYAL AND FOREVER TRUE

1. Reminisces of Winifred Dudley Shaw in *History and Reminisces of Iowa Agricultural College* (Des Moines: George A. Miller Printing and Publishing Company, 1897), 114–115.

2. "Report of the President," in the Fifth Biennial Report of the Board of Trustees of the Iowa State Agricultural College and Farm to the Governor of Iowa (Des Moines: G. W. Edwards, State Printer, 1874), 46–51.

3. Ibid.; John Boyd Hungerford, "Sketches of Iowa State College," published as "Appendix One: Student Life and Interests in the 1870s," in Earle D. Ross, *A History of Iowa State College of Agriculture and Mechanic Arts* (Ames: Iowa State College Press, 1942), 372.

4. J. C. Schilletter, *The First 100 Years of Residential Housing at Iowa State University, 1868–1968* (Ames: J. C. Schilletter, 1970), 22, 29–31.

5. Schilletter, 36–37; "Report of the President," in the Fourth Biennial Report of the Board of Trustees of the Iowa State Agricultural College and Farm to the Governor of Iowa (Des Moines: G. W. Edwards, State Printer, 1872), 20–21.

6. Ross, 177–180; "The Rise and Development of Literary Societies at ISC," *Alumnus,* March 1909, 7–10; Program, "Annual Dramatic Exercises of the Literary Societies," Iowa State Agricultural College (November 13, 1871), Student Organizations Records, RS 22/7/0/1, Special Collections, Iowa State University Library.

7. Walter James Miller, *Fraternities and Sororities at Iowa State College* (Ames: Iowa State College Interfraternity Council, 1949), 17.

8. Ibid., 21–27, 37–39.

9. Ibid., 35; Schilletter, 49, 59.

10. Jenny Barker Devine, *A Century of Brotherhood: Sigma Alpha Epsilon at Iowa State University* (Ames: Sigma Alpha Epsilon Fraternity, 2005), 4–9.

11. "Pre-VEISHEA Celebrations," in "VEISHEA: Iowa State's Rite of Spring," an online exhibit by the University Archives, Special Collections, Iowa State University Library (accessed 24 July 2005), http://www.lib.iastate.edu/spcl/exhibits/VEISHEA/index.htm.

12. Ross, 304–305.

13. "Assignments Made for Women's Work," *Iowa State Student,* April 19, 1917; "Tractor School for Girls Now Possible," *Iowa State Student,* May 10, 1917; Ross, 304–305; *Iowa State Student,* May 17, 1918.

14. D. P. Gibson to the faculty at the Iowa State College of Agriculture and Mechanical Arts, December 30, 1917, in Department of Military Science Records, RS 13/16/1, Special Collections, Iowa State University Library; C. E. Beer to Maria Roberts, January 8, 1918; Paul A. Tierney to Bernard Fridholm, September 28, 1966; "Clyde Beer Makes Supreme Sacrifice," *Alumnus,* November 1918, in Department of Military Science Records, RS 13/16/1, Special Collections, Iowa State University Library.

15. Becky Jordan, "1919: A Glimpse of Campus Life Seventy Years Ago," Exhibit Catalog no. 43, Special Collections, Iowa State University Library, 2–3; Ross, 310.

16. Jordan, 4–7; "A Message from the President," *Iowa State Student,* April 15, 1919.

17. Harold E. Pride, *The First Fifty Years: Iowa State Memorial Union* (Crystal Lake, IL: P. P. & J. A. Sheehan, 1972), 80.

18. Miller, 108.

19. "Constitution of the Senior Honor Society of Cardinal Key, Iowa State College, Ames, Iowa" no date, in Cardinal Key Records, RS 22/2/1, Special Collections, Iowa State University Library; "Traditions and Accomplishments," in Mary Kelly Shearer, History of Local Mortar Board of Iowa State College (January 1969), 12–13, in Mortar Board Records, RS 22/2/3, Special Collections, Iowa State University Library.

20. Ross, 363–364.

21. Schilletter, 73, 91–92.

22. Julia Faltinson Anderson interview by Mary Ann Evans, April 30, 2003, Special Collections, Iowa State University Library.

23. Schilletter, 92–93.

24. "Fifty Years Ago Their Pants Were Narrow, So Were Their Liberties," *Iowa State Student,* April 7, 1936.

25. "The President of Iowa State College Places Iowa State on War Footing," 1942 *Bomb,* 21.

26. 1942 *Bomb,* 36.

27. John Rigg, "No Students Trained on Campus during War, Officials Claim," *Iowa State Daily Student,* December 9, 1945.

28. Lyle Abbot, "Plan Draft Meetings: Question, Answer Session Scheduled in Memorial Union," *Iowa State Daily Student,* December 11, 1942; "Defense Stamp Innovation at Formal," *Iowa State Daily Student,* January 21, 1942; "Students to Make Candy for Men in Armed Forces," *Iowa State Daily Student,* February 17, 1942; "2,000 Pull Taffy," *Iowa State Daily Student,* February 21, 1942; 1943 *Bomb,* 162.

29. 1942 *Bomb,* 26, 30.

30. 1944 *Bomb,* 78–79.

31. 1942 *Bomb,* 75, 61, 26, 36; 1943 *Bomb,* 56.

32. Madge McGlade to Dr. Robert Foster, in Lorris Foster Scrapbook, RS 21/7/147, Special Collections, Iowa State University Library.

33. Schilletter, 105–108; 1943 *Bomb*, 52; "Five Women Are Now Enrolled in Iowa State's Engineering Division," *Iowa State Daily Student*, October 17, 1941; 1945 *Bomb*, 161.

34. Bob Parker, "College Does Secret Atomic Power Work," *Iowa State Daily Student*, August 8, 1945; "News of Atomic Bomb Causes Mixed Emotion," *Iowa State Daily Student*, August 10, 1945.

35. "World War 2 Ends!!" and "Victory News Gets Jubilant Reception," *Iowa State Daily Student*, August 15, 1945; "Iowa State Observes Victory Over Japan by 2-Day Holiday, Convocation, Parties," *Iowa State Daily Student*, August 17, 1945.

36. "Alumni Days 2002: The Iowa State Class of 1952" (Ames: Iowa State University Alumni Association, 2002), 104.

37. "Alumni Days 1999: The Iowa State Class of 1949" (Ames: Iowa State University Alumni Association, 1999), 161.

38. "Alumni Days 1999: The Iowa State Class of 1949," 133; "Alumni Days 2002: The Iowa State Class of 1952," 87.

39. Karol Crosbie, "The Long Good-Bye," *VISIONS* magazine, vol. 10, no. 2, Summer 1997, 10.

40. "Alumni Days 1998: The Iowa State Class of 1948" (Ames: Iowa State University Alumni Association, 1998), 68; "Alumni Days 1999: The Iowa State Class of 1949," 5.

41. "President's Book, 1948–1953," American Society of Agricultural Engineers Student Wives' Club Records, RS 22/5/0/14, Special Collections, Iowa State University Library.

42. Harold Pride, director of the Memorial Union, interview by Dorothy Kehlenbeck, January 14, 1959, Oral Histories, Transcripts, RS 00/17/03, Special Collections, Iowa State University Library.

43. "Student Government Proves Its Worth," *Iowa State Daily*, February 17, 1962; "Candidates Should Realize Powers of Government," *Iowa State Daily*, March 9, 1961; Allen Ambrose, "Candidates for Senator-at-Large State Platforms," *Iowa State Daily*, March 9, 1962.

44. "Student Government Proves Its Worth"; "OK Elective ROTC: Three Year Trial to Start Sept. 1," *Iowa State Daily*, March 10, 1962; "College Nominees Explain Student Government Ideas," *Iowa State Daily*, March 9, 1962.

45. "Guild Votes Extension of Women's Hours," *Iowa State Daily*, March 17, 1960; Schilletter, 149–150.

46. "Rioters Damage Sororities, Dorm," *Iowa State Daily*, May 20, 1964; Donald B. Siano, "Some Notes on Early Anti-War Activity at ISU" (June 1995), in University General, Political Demonstrations Records, RS 0/12, Special Collections, Iowa State University Library.

47. "Election Reaction in Iowa Topic at Last News Forum," *Iowa State Daily*, February 18, 1967; "Election Reaction Not Product of Students' Apathy as *Register* Reported Sunday," *Iowa State Daily*, February 18, 1967; "State of the Campus Address," *Iowa State Daily*, March 16, 1967; David Schworm and Bob Arceri, "Ask Students to Sign Impeachment Petition," *Iowa State Daily*, April 7, 1967.

48. Resignation speech by Don Smith (April 1973), Government of the Student Body Records, RS 22/1/2, Special Collections, Iowa State University Library.

49. Jerry Parkin interview by Stanley Yates, May 27, 1970, Political Demonstrations, Vietnam War Records, RS 0/12/0/0, Special Collections, Iowa State University Library.

50. Carole Zike, "CSA Finds No Answer for Campus Obscenity," *Iowa State Daily*, September 26, 1968; Jerry Knight, "Epidemic of Dirty Words Poses Problem at ISU," *Des Moines Register* (no date) in Government of the Student Body Records, RS 22/1/2, Special

Collections, Iowa State University Library; "The Times They Are A-Changin': Political Protests—Iowa State University—May 1970," an online exhibit by the University Archives, Special Collections, Iowa State University Library (accessed 2 August 2005), http://www.lib.iastate.edu/spcl/exhibits/timesachangin/revised_summer_2005/protests_index.html.

51. Clyde Brown interview by Stanley Yates, [no date], Political Demonstrations, Vietnam War Records, RS 0/12/0/0, Special Collections, Iowa State University Library.

52. Thomas G. Goodale interview by Stanley Yates, June 2, 1970, Political Demonstrations, Vietnam War Records, RS 0/12/0/0, Special Collections, Iowa State University Library; "The Times They Are A-Changin': Political Protests."

53. Jeanne Gustkowski, "Dorms Reorganized for Coed Housing in 1969," *Iowa State Daily,* November 12, 1968; "Co-Ed Housing Begins as Women Move into Helser," *Iowa State Daily,* November 5, 1969.

54. Lyn Jones, "Residence Department Experiment," *Iowa State Daily,* November 10, 1967; "Dorms Hire Grad Advisors," *Iowa State Daily,* September 17, 1969.

55. "17-Month-Old Girl Moves into Home and Hearts," *Iowa State Daily,* November 11, 1978.

56. Nancy Anderson, "Feelings, Policies Revealed on Discrimination," *Iowa State Daily,* March 28, 1961.

57. *Black Cultural Center,* pamphlet published by the Black Cultural Center, Inc., no date, Multicultural Student Affairs Records, RS 7/5, Special Collections, Iowa State University Library; report, "Iowa State University Black Cultural Center, Inc.," no date, Multicultural Student Affairs Records, RS 7/5, Special Collections, Iowa State University Library

58. David Dawson, "The BCC: Student Adjustment Is What It's About," *Ames Daily Tribune,* November 11, 1976.

59. Patty Morgan, "Title IX Affects Honorary: Cardinal Key Open to Women," *Iowa State Daily,* December 18, 1975; "Honoraries Open to Men, Women," *Iowa State Daily,* April 1, 1976.

60. Susan Caslin, "Space Given for Women's Center," *Iowa State Daily,* January 15, 1981; "Women's Center on Display," *Iowa State Daily,* November 10, 1981.

61. "Streaking Fad Hits Iowa State," *Iowa State Daily,* March 7, 1974; "Daily Bares All to Cover the Streakers of 1974," *Iowa State Daily,* April 15, 1983.

62. Angela Reilly, "Life in the 'Me' Decade," *Iowa State Daily,* December 18, 1979.

63. "ISU's 54 International Agreements Involve 30 Countries," Iowa State University Information Service (April 23, 1987), International Programs Records, RS 3/4/3/0/0, Special Collections, Iowa State University Library; Wendy Weissenburger, "ISU Has 61 Foreign Agreements," *Iowa State Daily,* February 6, 1991; "Ready for a New Adventure?" *Iowa State Daily,* August 28, 1989; Tori Rosin, "Study Abroad Celebrates 'Success Story,'" *Iowa State Daily,* October 18, 1999.

64. Matt Kuhns, "Reverse Culture Shock Strikes," *Iowa State Daily,* March 10, 1999.

65. Susan Whitaker, "Speaker to Explore Science, Math Fields," *Spencer Daily Reporter,* October 14, 1990; Julie Anderson, "Program Shows Women Road Less Traveled," *Iowa State Daily,* January 22, 1988; "ISU Grant Will Promote Women in Science, Engineering," Iowa State University Information Service (March 17, 1988).

66. "Women Interns Prepare for Technological Futures at ISU," Iowa State University Information Service (June 3, 1988); Mike Krapel, "Getting Girls into Scientific Careers," *Ames Daily Tribune,* July 1, 1991, in Program for Women in Science and Engineering Records, RS 3/10/0/0; "Interns Making Their Mark," *Iowa Stater,* August 1990; Liz Allen, "ISU Program Provided Women with Internships," *Ames Daily Tribune,* August 8, 2000.

67. Julie Janssen, "Learning Communities Get Permanent Funding," *Iowa State Daily,* September 20, 2001; Samantha Beres, "Bonuses Abound in Learning Communities," *Iowa State Daily,* January 28, 2005; Samuel Berbano, "Learning Groups Continue Growth as DOR Shrinks," *Iowa State Daily,* March 22, 2005.

68. Emily Sickelka, "Learning Communities Offer Resources," *Iowa State Daily,* September 16, 2002; William Dillon, "Entrepreneurial Community to Have Twice the Students," *Iowa State Daily,* January 15, 2005; Beres, "Bonuses Abound in Learning Communities," in Department of Residence Records, RS 7/4/0/0, Special Collections, Iowa State University Library.

69. Jessica Anderson, "New Fraternity Focuses on Brotherhood, Gay Issues," *Iowa State Daily,* December 13, 2004; Eric Lund, "LGBT Community Honored at Small Victories Celebration," *Iowa State Daily,* January 21, 2005.

70. Tracy Call, "Looking Forward to National Coming Out Week," *Iowa State Daily,* October 7, 1996; Keeisa Wirt, "Learning About LGBT Diversity," *Iowa State Daily,* March 25, 1998; "The Right to Campanile," *Iowa State Daily,* April 3, 1998.

71. Sinenahita and W. Houston Dougharty, "Safe Zone Success," *Iowa State Daily,* December 3, 1997; Kate Kompas, "LGBT Awareness Week Increases Visibility," *Iowa State Daily,* March 30, 1999.

72. Reminisces of W. A. Murphy in *History and Reminisces of Iowa Agricultural College,* 146; Chris Lursen interview by Michele Christian, November 21, 2002.

## 6. ATHLETICS AT IOWA STATE UNIVERSITY

1. 1895 *Bomb,* 105.
2. "Andy Woolfries Gets Degree," *Des Moines Tribune,* October 1947; and *Des Moines Register,* December 14, 1975.
3. ISU Athletic Department receipts, 1933, ISU Athletic Department.
4. Dick Cole interview by Thad Dohrn, October 8, 1996.
5. Waldo Wegner interview by Thad Dohrn, February 21, 1997.
6. Iowa State 2004–05 Men's Basketball Media Guide (Ames: ISU Athletic Department), 104–105.
7. 1895 *Bomb,* 105.

## 7. IOWA STATE FACULTY

1. Olivia Madison, Wayne Osborn, and Rae Haws, "Iowa State University Faculty Council, 1954–1988: A History," April 1988.
2. "The Faculty Council of the Iowa State College Basic Document, January 1954," RS 8/4/3, ISU Faculty Council records 1953–1988, box 1, folder 1, Special Collections, Iowa State University Library.
3. "Division of Home Economics Policies Concerning Selection and Promotion of Teaching Staff—Sept. 1957," RS 8/4/3, box 2, folder 5, Special Collections, Iowa State University Library.
4. "Statement on Academic Freedom as Prepared by a Committee of the Faculty Council," [no date, ca. May 1957], RS 8/4/3, box 2, folder 2, Special Collections, Iowa State University Library.
5. Report to Faculty Council from Conditions of Employment Committee, April 9, 1963, RS 8/4/3, box 3, folder 1, Special Collections, Iowa State University Library.
6. Faculty Council minutes, December 10, 1963, RS 8/4/3, box 3, folder 1, Special Collections, Iowa State University Library.
7. "Support for Scholarly Endeavors at ISU: A Proposal Submitted to the Faculty Council," October 2, 1964, RS 8/4/3, box 3, folder 1, Special Collections, Iowa State University Library.

8. John Schlebecker to William Switzer, November 29, 1960, RS 8/4/3, box 2, folder 12, Special Collections, Iowa State University Library.

9. "Faculty Council: Faculty and Student Relations Committee Report on Survey of Student Opinion," May 24, 1966, RS 8/4/3, box 4, folder 12, Special Collections, Iowa State University Library.

10. "Involvement of Students in Affairs of the University," [no author], April 24, 1968, RS 8/4/3, box 6, folder 4, Special Collections, Iowa State University Library.

11. Faculty Council minutes, October 8, 1968, RS 8/4/3, box 5, folder 6, Special Collections, Iowa State University Library.

12. William Larsen to A. C. MacKinney, December 20, 1967, RS 8/4/3, box 6, folder 4, Special Collections, Iowa State University Library.

13. Dan Griffen, comments on long-range planning committee resolution, March 10, 1967, RS 8/4/3, box 5, folder 6, Special Collections, Iowa State University Library.

14. Faculty Council minutes, January 11, 1972, RS 8/4/3, box 7, folder 9, Special Collections, Iowa State University Library.

15. Faculty Council minutes, October 9, 1969, and January 13, 1970, RS 8/4/3, box 6, folder 9, Special Collections, Iowa State University Library.

16. Faculty Council minutes, May 11, 1970, RS 8/4/3, box 6, folder 9, Special Collections, Iowa State University Library.

17. Faculty Council document, [no title, no author], July 8, 1970, RS 8/4/3, box 6, folder 9, Special Collections, Iowa State University Library.

18. Ibid.; and Faculty Council minutes, October 12, 1971, RS 8/4/3, box 7, folder 8, Special Collections, Iowa State University Library.

19. Faculty Council minutes, September 8, 1970, RS 8/4/3, box 7, folder 8, Special Collections, Iowa State University Library.

20. Faculty Council document, [no title, no author], July 8, 1970, RS 8/4/3, box 6, folder 9, Special Collections, Iowa State University Library.

21. Faculty Council minutes, January 11, 1972, RS 8/4/3, box 7, folder 9, Special Collections, Iowa State University Library.

22. Congressional Record—Senate, June 30, 1972, S10963, "The War Still Tears Americans' Consciences."

23. "Appendix C of the Faculty Handbook: Guidelines Concerning Promotions: Faculty and Administration Relations Committee Report, 1972–73," [no author, no date, ca. spring 1973], RS 8/4/3, box 8, folder 16, Special Collections, Iowa State University Library.

24. "Faculty-Administration Relations Committee, Report to Faculty Council," February 12, 1974; and "Faculty and Administration Relations Committee, Report to Faculty Council—Open Promotion, Tenure and Salary Policy," May 14, 1974, RS 8/4/3, box 9, folder 16, Special Collections, Iowa State University Library.

25. Letter from the Status of Women Subcommittee of Faculty Development and Welfare Committee, January 10, 1974; and "Report of Faculty Development and Welfare Committee on Status of Women," March 12, 1974, RS 8/4/3, box 10, folder 13, Special Collections, Iowa State University Library.

26. "Salaries, Retirement and Enrollment at ISU in the 1980s: Issues and Options," prepared by Faculty Council, May 1980, RS 8/4/3, box 16, folder 4, Special Collections, Iowa State University Library.

27. "Some Pertinent Facts About Faculty Workload, Prepared for Members of the General Assembly by the State Board of Regents", v. 1 no. 4, February 23, 1970, RS 8/4/3, box 6, folder 9, Special Collections, Iowa State University Library.

28. "Salaries, Retirement and Enrollment at ISU in the 1980s: Issues and Options."

29. "Faculty Resignation Survey," by the Faculty Budgetary Advisory Committee, [no date, ca. spring 1978]; and ISU Faculty salary situation and its implications: 1969–1982: executive summary, [no author, no date, ca. 1983], RS 8/4/3, box 16, folder 4, Special Collections, Iowa State University Library.

30. "Faculty Council Salary Study, 1967–1988," by the Faculty-Administration Relations Committee, January 1988, RS 8/4/3, box 20, folder 19, Special Collections, Iowa State University Library.

31. "Faculty Governance," document prepared by the Faculty and Administration Relations Committee of Faculty Council, May 7, 1985, RS 8/4/3, box 18, folder 8, Special Collections, Iowa State University Library.

32. "Faculty Senate Basic Document, Amended by the General Faculty, April 6, 1988," RS 8/4/4, box 1, folder 1, Special Collections, Iowa State University Library.

33. Joan Hugen, "Senate Debates LRSPC Issue," *Iowa State Daily*, March 1, 1989, 1.

34. "Ad Hoc Committee Report I: Observations on the Presidency of ISU, Oct. 30, 1990," [no author], RS 8/4/4, box 6, folder 4, Special Collections, Iowa State University Library.

35. Linda Charles, "Faculty Survey: Mixed Review for ISU," *Inside Iowa State,* May 22, 1922, 2.

36. ISU General Docket, July 1992, [no author], RS 8/4/4, box 7, folder 14, Special Collections, Iowa State University Library.

37. Bob Dart, "Report Says College Profs Paid More to Teach Less," September 15, 1992, Cox News Service report.

38. "Faculty Workload Study, ISU," Iowa Board of Regents, May 12, 1989, RS 8/4/4, box 3, folder 9, Special Collections, Iowa State University Library.

39. Faculty Senate minutes, October 12, 1993, RS 8/4/4, box 11, folder 6, Special Collections, Iowa State University Library.

40. Charles, 2.

## 8. THE PEOPLE'S UNIVERSITY

1. For more on the efforts to reform rural America and the reaction of rural people to those reforms, see David B. Danbom, *Born in the Country: A History of Rural America* (Baltimore: Johns Hopkins University Press, 1995), 167–175.

2. Earle D. Ross, *A History of Iowa State College of Agriculture and Mechanic Arts* (Ames: Iowa State College Press, 1942), 164–165. Although the college's name had not been formally changed, by 1870, officials referred to the school as Iowa Agricultural College.

3. Dennis S. Nordin and Roy V. Scott, *From Prairie Farmer to Entrepreneur: A History of Midwestern Agriculture* (Bloomington and Indianapolis: Indiana University Press, 2005), 33–34; Dorothy Schwieder, *75 Years of Service: Cooperative Extension in Iowa* (Ames: Iowa State University Press, 1993), 16–18.

4. Wayne D. Rasmussen, *Taking the University to the People: Seventy-five Years of Cooperative Extension* (Ames: Iowa State University Press, 1989), 34–36; Schwieder, 18–20.

5. Schwieder, 20–22.

6. "Courses of Work for the Iowa Boys and Girls Club, 1912," Circular No. 16, Paul Taff Papers, box 9, folder 16, Special Collections, Iowa State University Library.

7. Rasmussen, 46–52.

8. Schwieder, 24.

9. University Extension, Office of Continuing Education, box 1, folder 1, Special Collections, Iowa State University Library.

10. Schwieder, 48–55.

11. Clifford Johnson interview by author, Council Bluffs, IA, December, 14, 2002.

12. R. Douglas Hurt, *Problems of Plenty: The American Farmer in the Twentieth Century* (Chicago: Ivan R. Dee, 2002), 96–101.

13. Schwieder, 101–108.

14. Memorandum No. 1, September 14, 1942; Sarah Porter Ellis to R. K. Bliss, September 15, 1942, Taff Papers, box 2, file 17, Special Collections, Iowa State University Library.

15. Annual Attendance Report, Short Courses, Conferences, Off-Campus Credit Courses & Field Days, July 1, 1968–June 30, 1969, University Extension, Extension Courses and Conferences, Iowa State University, Ames; University Extension, Office of Continuing Education, box 1, file 1, Special Collections, Iowa State University Library.

16. Neil Harl, *Arrogance and Power: The Saga of WOI-TV* (Ames, IA: N. E. Harl and Heuss Printing, 2001), 1–3, 22–23.

17. Radio and Television at Iowa State, 1969, WOI Advisory Committee Records, Special Collections, Iowa State University Library; Robert W. Parks, Policy Memorandum Regarding WOI-TV, December 20, 1965, ISU WOI Radio and Television, *Arrogance and Power* Appendices, box 1, file 1; WOI Advisory Committee, May 12, 1977, WOI Advisory Committee Records.

18. *Wallaces' Farmer and Iowa Homestead,* "More Management Help for Farmers," February 5, 1955; Schwieder, 139–146.

19. "Cutting Costs in Today's Farming," Agricultural Extension Service, Iowa State College, Ames, Pamphlet 222, February 1956.

20. "A Growing Concern About Economic and Social Change in Iowa," *Iowa Farm Science,* June 1959; *Iowa Book of Agriculture, 1960–1961* (Des Moines: State of Iowa, 1962), 289–290.

21. Schwieder, 165.

22. *Iowa Book of Agriculture, 1968–1969,* 296–297; Jim Johnson interview by author, Eldora, IA, June 21, 2004; Schwieder, 176–179; *Iowa Book of Agriculture, 1964–1965,* 264.

23. Schwieder, 167–168; *Iowa Book of Agriculture, 1968–1969,* 300.

24. Schwieder, 170.

25. Schwieder, 176–177.

26. Paul J. Horick, editor, *Water Resources of Iowa* (Iowa City: Iowa Academy of Science, 1969).

27. Schwieder, 191–197.

28. *Iowa Book of Agriculture, 1979–1981,* 110; Schwieder, 196–197.

29. *Iowa Book of Agriculture, 1975–1977,* 233.

30. Lynn Henderson, "C. J. Gauger: The Man Who Is 4-H in Iowa," *Iowa Agriculturist,* Fall 1971.

31. Al Bull, "How Farm People View Their Extension Service," *Wallaces' Farmer,* February 12, 1972.

32. Neil Harl, *The Farm Debt Crisis of the 1980s* (Ames: Iowa State University Press, 1990), chapter 2.

33. Schwieder, 202–208; *Iowa Book of Agriculture, 1983–1985,* 86.

34. Schwieder, 206–208.

35. Schwieder, 209–210.

36. *Iowa Book of Agriculture, 1981–1983,* 124; *Iowa Book of Agriculture, 1983–1985,* 86; Soybean Workshop program, University Extension Office of Continuing Education, box 2, folder 29.

37. *Iowa Book of Agriculture, 1983–1985,* 86.

38. *Iowa Book of Agriculture, 1979–1981,* 110; *Iowa Book of Agriculture, 1981–1983,* 124; *Iowa Book of Agriculture, 1983–1985,* 86.

39. To Dean Elizabeth Elliott from Eleanor Kniker, July 14, 1989, and attachment "FY89 Telebridge Activity," Vice Provost for Extension, Office of Continuing Education; to Kathleen Stinehart from Eleanor Kniker, February 29, 1988, Vice Provost for Extension, Office of Continuing Education.

40. University Extension, Annual Report, 2000, 15.

41. Iowa State University, University Extension Annual Report, 1996, 3; "After the Flood: Assessing, Repairing, and Rebuilding Basements," Iowa State University Extension, March 30, 1994, University Extension, Office of Continuing Education, box 7, folder 7.

42. University Extension, Annual Report, 1997, 14–15.

43. University Extension, Annual Report, 1996, 21.

44. University Extension, Annual Report, 1996, 12–13; University Extension, Annual Report, 1998, 13, 20–21; University Extension, Annual Report, 2002, 14; University Extension, "Extension at 100 Years," *Extension Connection,* Annual Report Edition, 2003, 14.

45. University Extension, Annual Report, 1998, 3.

46. Jerry Perkins, "New Outreach at ISU," *Des Moines Sunday Register,* January 1, 2005. Johnson resigned his position in 2005.

47. Leadership Partners, *Iowa State University Extension to Communities Newsletter,* vol. 1, Fall 2001; *Community Vitality Update,* August 2005, Issue No. 20.

48. University Extension, Annual Report, 1997, 16–17.

49. University Extension, "Extension at 100 Years," 10.

## 9. THE PRACTICAL AND THE PICTURESQUE

1. Professor Emeritus of Landscape Architecture Robert R. Harvey provided the author extensive guidance in the development of this chapter. His more than forty years of experience and knowledge gained through teaching landscape architecture history and working on campus was indispensable to the project.

2. Robert William Werle, "A Historical Review and Analysis of the Iowa State University Landscape from 1858–1966," master's thesis, Iowa State University, 1966, 36–37.

3. Earle D. Ross, *A History of Iowa State College of Agriculture and Mechanic Arts* (Ames: Iowa State College Press, 1942), 172.

4. Ibid., 170.

5. H. Summerfield Day, *The Iowa State University Campus and Its Buildings, 1859–1979* (Ames: Iowa State University, 1980), 147.

6. Ibid., 149.

7. Ibid., 307.

8. Ibid., 307.

9. John D. Corbett, *Frank Harold Spedding, 1902–1984. Biographical Memoirs, Volume 80* (Washington, D.C.: National Academy Press), 13.

## 10. IMPACTS OF IOWA STATE UNIVERSITY

1. Earle D. Ross, *A History of Iowa State College of Agriculture and Mechanic Arts* (Ames: Iowa State College Press, 1942), 25–27.

2. Ibid., 39–40.

3. Mary Atherly, Lynette Pohlman, and Renee Thomason Senter, *University Museums Collections Handbook* (Ames: Sigler Printing and Publishing, Inc., 2000), 11.

4. *Profiles of Iowa State University History* (Ames: Iowa State University, 1977), 76–77.

5. Ibid., 82.

6. R. K. Richards, *Electronic Digital Systems* (New York: Wiley, 1966), 3.

7. Earl R. Larson, U.S. District Court Judge, Findings of Fact, Conclusions of Law and Order for Judgment, Honeywell Inc. vs. Sperry Rand Corporation and Illinois Scientific Developments, Inc., No. 4-57 CIV 138 (U.S. District Court District of Minnesota Fourth Division, 1973), 49.

8. Center for Agricultural and Rural Development, *CARD Report*, vol. 11, no. 2, Summer 1998, 3.

9. Atherly, Pohlman, and Senter, 10.

10. Institute for Physical Research and Technology, *IPRT Link,* vol. 2, no. 5, 1994, 1.

# Index